MW01196084

The Western
Esoteric Traditions

The Western
Esoteric Traditions

A Historical Introduction

NICHOLAS GOODRICK-CLARKE

OXFORD
UNIVERSITY PRESS

2008

OXFORD
UNIVERSITY PRESS

Oxford University Press, Inc., publishes works that further
Oxford University's objective of excellence
in research, scholarship, and education.

Oxford   New York
Auckland   Cape Town   Dar es Salaam   Hong Kong   Karachi
Kuala Lumpur   Madrid   Melbourne   Mexico City   Nairobi
New Delhi   Shanghai   Taipei   Toronto

With offices in
Argentina   Austria   Brazil   Chile   Czech Republic   France   Greece
Guatemala   Hungary   Italy   Japan   Poland   Portugal   Singapore
South Korea   Switzerland   Thailand   Turkey   Ukraine   Vietnam

Copyright © 2008 by Nicholas Goodrick-Clarke

Published by Oxford University Press, Inc.
198 Madison Avenue, New York, New York 10016

www.oup.com

Oxford is a registered trademark of Oxford University Press

Library of Congress Cataloging-in-Publication Data
Goodrick-Clarke, Nicholas.
The western esoteric traditions: a historical introduction /
Nicholas Goodrick-Clarke.
   p. cm.
Includes bibliographical references and index.
ISBN 978-0-19-532099-2
1. Occultism. I. Title.
BF1411.G66 2008
135—dc22   2008009795

9 8 7 6 5 4 3 2 1

Printed in the United States of America
on acid-free paper

To Clare, who has always shared the journey

Acknowledgments

My introductory history of the Western esoteric traditions is both the digest and fruit of many years' work in this fascinating and now rapidly expanding field. While I have worked this terrain since the mid-1970s, I owe a special debt of gratitude to friends and colleagues who have encouraged my interest in new directions. Here I should like to mention Ralph White, director of the New York Open Center, whose international conferences devoted to the Western esoteric traditions at Cesky Krumlov (1995), Prague (1997), Bardsey (1999), Florence (2000), Kutna Hora and Weimar (2006), and Granada (2007) have been an inspiration.

Another dimension in my exploration of the field began in 2000, when I was invited to join the annual June conferences of the Palladian Academy, where I have enjoyed many interesting discussions with participants, including Jean-Pierre Brach, Antoine Faivre, Joscelyn Godwin, Claire Fanger, Deborah Belle Forman, Clare Goodrick-Clarke, Hans Thomas Hakl, Wouter Hanegraaff, Jean-Pierre Laurant, Christopher McIntosh, Marco Pasi, Kocku von Stuckrad, and Arthur Versluis. Their specialist studies and general perspectives on the field have, in their individual ways, been a constant source of intellectual stimulation and spiritual insight.

These same years witnessed the gestation of the *Dictionary of Gnosis and Western Esotericism,* edited by Wouter Hanegraaff in collaboration with Antoine Faivre, Roelof van den Broek, and Jean-Pierre Brach. Again, their work and that of the many contributors, among whom I was privileged to work, have found its echo in this volume, and I must pay tribute to the indefatigable industry and expertise of the editors.

I should also like to express my gratitude to the trustees of the Blavatsky Trust for the far-sighted encouragement and financial support of the Exeter Centre for the Study of Esotericism (EXESESO), of which I am director, at the University of Exeter since 2005. I am also grateful to Jonathan Barry, head of the School of Humanities and Social Sciences in the University, for encouraging the establishment of EXESESO.

I owe thanks to the librarians at the British Library, the Bodleian Library at Oxford, and the Warburg Institute, University of London, for their helpful and efficient services. I should also like to thank Barry Thompson, librarian of the Theosophical Society in England at London, for advice and publication lending.

Again, I wish to thank my wife, Clare, for conversation, collaboration, and shared interests bearing on our mutual exploration of this field throughout our marriage.

Contents

The Western
Esoteric Traditions

Introduction

The Western esoteric traditions have their roots in a religious way
of thinking, which reaches back to Gnosticism, Hermeticism, and
Neoplatonism in the Hellenistic world during the first centuries A.D.
In the Renaissance, the rediscovery of ancient texts led to the scholarly revival of magic, astrology, alchemy, and Kabbalah. Following the
Reformation, this spiritual current gave rise to theosophy, Rosicrucianism, and Freemasonry, and the modern occult revival extends
from nineteenth-century spiritualism, H. P. Blavatsky's Theosophy,
and ceremonial magical orders to twentieth-century esotericists such
as Rudolf Steiner, Alice A. Bailey, and George Ivanovitch Gurdjieff,
and the analytical psychology of Carl Gustav Jung.

The scholarly study of Western esotericism is a comparatively recent phenomenon. There are three dedicated university chairs in the
subject at the Sorbonne, Amsterdam, and Exeter, and master's pro-
grams in the subject are offered at the latter two universities. Faculty
at a growing number of other universities in Europe and the United
States offer courses involving Hermetic philosophy, mystical traditions, and the history of esotericism in the medieval, Renaissance,
and modern periods. This volume is intended to serve as an introduction to this growing field of study, offering a concise historical survey
of its major movements and figures, and a guide to further reading.

What is esotericism? From the Enlightenment until the middle
of the last century, magic, astrology, and occultism, to take a few of the

subjects now considered under the rubric of esotericism, were generally perceived as survivals of superstition and irrationalism. The intellectual status of such topics was denigrated, and they were kept in epistemological quarantine lest they cause a relapse from progressive rationalism. Just as the established churches had once excluded heterodox doctrine as heresy, the modern post-Enlightenment world rejected magic and occultism as a violation of reason, its dominant criterion of acceptable discourse. These disqualifications are perhaps best illustrated in the sociology of occultism, which still tends to focus on marginality and deviance.

Far from treating esotericism as a "rejected form of knowledge," specialist scholars of the subject seek instead to distinguish the intrinsic philosophical and religious characteristics of esoteric spirituality. They are also concerned to document the history of esotericism as a particular form of spirituality that has characterized and illumined Western thought in various schools and movements from late antiquity to the present. Through such a historical approach, it is possible to examine the cultural and social circumstances that favor the emergence of esotericism as a worldview and to document its significant influence on philosophical, scientific, and religious change. In this project, esotericism is restored to a position of historical importance rather than relegated to a casualty of positivist and materialist perspectives during the nineteenth century.

Historians of the ancient world and the European Renaissance were among the first to reconsider this evaluation. Studies of ancient religion, mythology, symbols, and iconography required a sympathetic engagement with pagan and nonrational modes of thought and imagination. Even before the Second World War, scholars were discovering a rich heritage of Neoplatonic and Hermetic thought and practice in the West. A few examples will suffice to demonstrate the vigor and breadth of this enterprise, which emerged from the margins of academic and cultural discourse in order to illuminate pivotal linkages in European cultural history. Just as the Latin West had once assimilated Arab science, Jewish mysticism, and Greek philosophy in response to geopolitical changes in the medieval and Renaissance periods, so the renewed persecution of the Jews in Central Europe in the 1930s led to the relocation of Aby Warburg's famous library from Hamburg to the University of London. A succession of brilliant scholars at the Warburg Institute, first German-Jewish and then British, including Edgar Wind, Ernst Cassirer, Frances Yates, and D. P. Walker, pioneered a history of ideas that bridged the Classical and European worlds while embracing astrology, alchemy, magic, and their influence in the sixteenth and seventeenth centuries.

The cultural and intellectual history practiced at the Warburg Institute achieved a major revaluation of overlooked and neglected topics in the Western heritage. D. P. Walker (1914–1985), an Oxford-trained scholar who spent most of his career at the institute, published *Spiritual and Demonic Magic from Ficino to*

Campanella in 1958. It was a landmark study in Renaissance culture showing that magic was part of the mainstream in the late fifteenth and sixteenth centuries, closely connected with religion, music, mathematics, and medicine. Walker introduced his readers to the role of magic in the thought of major Renaissance figures ranging from Marsilio Ficino, Giovanni Pico della Mirandola, and Jacques Lefevre d'Etaples to Jean Bodin, Francis Bacon, and Tommaso Campanella. A few years later, Frances A. Yates (1899–1981) published her seminal book, *Giordano Bruno and the Hermetic Tradition* (1964). Previous Renaissance historians such as Paul Kristeller, Ernst Cassirer, and Eugenio Garin had argued that Hermetic ideas in the Renaissance had contributed to the development of modern science. However, Yates restored Hermeticism to a place of vital philosophical and theological significance in the Western intellectual tradition. She went far further by asserting that the Hermetic themes of human spiritual sovereignty and man's potential for achieving parity with God in creative thought and action had empowered Western man to achieve mastery of knowledge over all nature. To this extent, Renaissance Hermeticism was a precondition for the scientific revolution a century later. The Warburg Institute's role in the recovery of Neoplatonism and Hermeticism as important influences in the development of early modern thought is crucial to any account of the emergence of the study of esotericism.[1]

Meanwhile, other scholars also traveled across cultural borders. Just as the nineteenth-century esotericists Helena Blavatsky and George Ivanovitch Gurdjieff sought an ancient wisdom in the East, so scholars of spiritual traditions returned with unexpected riches throwing light on forgotten East-West exchanges and shared traditions. A notable example is Henry Corbin (1903–1978) who, after initial training at the Sorbonne, spent many years in Turkey and Iran assimilating the esoteric imaginaries of Sufi and Persian spirituality. His findings inspired another generation of Arabic scholars, whose work on Islamic mysticism has entered Western academic discourse.

François Secret (1911–2003), the holder of the Sorbonne chair in mystical currents, unveiled the intricacies of Christian Cabala from the fifteenth century onward. His successor, Antoine Faivre (b. 1934), developed the parameters of a formalized discipline following his pioneering works on theosophy, illuminism, and the philosophy of nature in the eighteenth and nineteenth centuries. Corbin and Faivre elaborated analytical approaches that have provided a firm philosophical basis for scholarship in esotericism. Corbin emphasized a cross-cultural approach to spiritual hermeneutics by comparing Swedenborgian theosophy with Ismaelian gnosis. Corbin did not see himself only as a historian of ideas, but as an active explorer of the spiritual realms revealed by this kind of hermeneutics. Behind the historical record of illumination that gave rise to Scripture lay a spiritual experience.

Corbin also worked extensively on the Arab philosopher Avicenna (ca. 980–1037) and on his own theory of the imagination. His book *Avicenna and the Visionary Recital* (1960; first published in French in 1952) examined the Islamic interpretation of the esoteric mystery of God's presence to the human being. A seminal aspect of Corbin's work was his notion of the imagination as both cognitive and creative. Following Persian philosophers, Corbin identified the imagination as an autonomous world of intermediaries, the *mundus imaginalis*, where visions, apparitions, angels, and hierarchies occurred independently of any perceiving subject. Corbin wrote:

> This world is as real and objective, as consistent and subsistent as the intelligible and sensible worlds; it is an intermediate universe "where the spiritual takes body and the body becomes spiritual," a world consisting of real matter and real extension, though by comparison with sensible, corruptible matter these are subtle and immaterial. The organ of this universe is the active Imagination; it is the *place* of theophanic visions, the scene on which visionary events and symbolic histories *appear* in their true reality.[2]

Corbin's profound speculations on creative imagination in Sufism and in the theosophical ideas of Marsilio Ficino, Giordano Bruno, Jacob Boehme, and Emanuel Swedenborg led him to formulate the twofold dimension of all creatures: "The Creative Imagination is theophanic Imagination, and the Creator is one with the imagining Creature because each Creative Imagination is a theophany, a recurrence of the Creation."[3]

Corbin's attempts to define a phenomenology of spirituality and mystical states, drawing comparisons between Christian, Jewish, and Islamic theosophies, indicated a theological and philosophical engagement with esoteric thought which has had a powerful influence in the defining of esotericism in terms of its own characteristics, rather than by reference to its historical or epistemological exclusion from dominant modes of secular or rational thought.

Antoine Faivre, now emeritus professor of the history of esoteric and mystical currents at the École Pratique des Hautes Études in the Sorbonne, assimilated Corbin's concept of creative imagination into his own work on esotericism as a form of spirituality. A Germanist by training, Faivre had a specific interest in the theosophers and illuminists of the eighteenth century and the Romantic period, and his doctoral dissertation on Karl von Eckartshausen (1752–1803) and Christian theosophy was published in 1969. This study and his earlier book on Baron Kirchberger, the correspondent of the French theosopher Louis Claude de Saint-Martin (1743–1803), paved the way for his comprehensive survey *L'Esoterisme au XVIIIe siècle en France et en Allemagne* (1973). Appointed to a unique chair at the Sorbonne in 1979, Faivre continued his work on the religious history of the Renaissance and early modern period and went on to offer a philosophical definition of esotericism as a "pattern of thought" (*forme de pensée*). It has been so influential as a touchstone for the academic study of esotericism that it is worth reviewing it briefly here.

Faivre surveyed the West as an extensive Greco-Roman philosophical heritage, with which the Jewish and Christian religions, together with Islam as an external factor, have interacted to produce the "Western esoteric traditions." Their origins lie in various forms of Hellenistic philosophy, notably Gnosticism, Alexandrian Hermetism, and pagan Neoplatonism, which have in turn left vital traces in the three Abrahamic religions. The traditional Hermetic sciences of alchemy, astrology, and magic had their rationale in this spiritual worldview and offered a continuity of practice and speculation from the late ancient world through Byzantine and Islamic culture into the medieval Latin West. However, it was in the European Renaissance that these originally Hellenistic traditions and sciences first came to be combined with new additions from Jewish Kabbalah (following the expulsion of Jews from Spain in 1492) to create a reformulated "perennial philosophy" (*philosophia perennis*) in which Renaissance scholars discerned multiple concordances.[4]

During the medieval period, Neoplatonic and Hermetic impulses had survived in both Christianity and Islam, notably in the celestial hierarchies of Pseudo-Dionysius (fl. 500), who had probably studied in the pagan schools of Athens, and later in the visionary world of Avicenna. However, influenced by Averroes (1126–1198), Western medieval thought tended toward Aristotelian ideas, separating revealed theology and a philosophy that proclaimed its independence through rational thought. Avicenna's perspective of creative imagination, angels, and hierarchies was relegated to marginal status in scholastic theology. Henceforth, Neoplatonism and Hermeticism would occupy a space outside theology, where they maintained a delicate relationship with the established church and ultimately forged links with empirical forms of natural philosophy, finding expression in astrology, alchemy, and medicine. Their basis lay in a cosmology and metaphysics that related the manifested world to divine forms through intermediary hierarchies of beings. This referential corpus of Renaissance esotericism laid particular emphasis on the notion of an ancient theology (*prisca theologia*) deriving from such founder-figures and representatives as Moses, Zoroaster, Hermes Trismegistus, Plato, and Orpheus, who had supposedly bequeathed this unitary wisdom tradition to humankind in times immemorial.

Taking the Renaissance concordance of Neoplatonism, Hermeticism, and Kabbalah, along with astrology, alchemy, and magic, Faivre deduced six fundamental characteristics of esoteric spirituality. The first four of these he described as *intrinsic* in the sense of all being necessary for a spirituality to be defined as esoteric. To these he added two more characteristics, which although not necessary, are frequently found together with the others in esoteric traditions.[5] The six characteristics are as follows:

1. *Correspondences.* The entire realm of nature in all its constituent levels of being (stars, planets, humans, animals, plants, minerals, humors, states of mind, health and disease) are considered to be linked through a series of correspondences or analogies. This connection is not understood causally, but rather symbolically through the ancient idea of the macrocosm (the universe or heavens) being reflected in the microcosm (the constitution of the human being) and expressed in the Hermetic axiom "As above, so below." These correspondences, essentially expressing the divine origin of all manifestation and its underlying "cousinhood" in a taxonomy of creation, are often veiled but are intended to be deciphered by humans as the seals or signatures of the divine. Thus links, seen and unseen, exist between the seven planets and the seven metals, between the planets and plants and between plants and parts of the human body. Such correspondences between the natural, celestial, and supercelestial worlds provide the theoretical basis of astrology, alchemy and magic and played an important role in Paracelsian medicine. Correspondences also exist between the cosmos, history, and revealed texts, giving rise to Jewish and Christian Kabbalah, esoteric biblical exposition, and eighteenth-century forms of "sacred physics." The universe is conceived as a cosmic hall of mirrors, in which everything finds an analogy or reflection in something else.

2. *Living nature.* This idea comprehends the cosmos as a complex, plural, hierarchical entity that is continuously animated throughout by a living energy or soul. The idea that nature is alive in all its parts underlies the esoteric conception of the correspondences possessing a vital, responsive connection with one another. In the practice of natural magic (*magia naturalis*), the magician knows how to exploit the sympathies or antipathies that link herbs, stones, and substances, and how to invest talismans with their powers. The idea of living nature is a defining characteristic of Paracelsianism and continues in modern expressions such as German Romantic *Naturphilosophie* and the vital fluid of Mesmerism.

3. *Imagination and mediations.* Faivre's third intrinsic characteristic of esoteric spirituality rehearsed Henry Corbin's idea of Creative Imagination. Faivre speaks of a "kind of organ of the soul" which can establish a

cognitive and visionary relationship with a mesocosm, an independent world of hierarchies and spiritual intermediaries which link the macrocosm and microcosm. This mesocosm is identical with Corbin's *mundus imaginalis,* which although drawn from the latter's study of Islamic spirituality, finds a strong parallel in such Western esoteric figures as Paracelsus, Boehme, and Swedenborg. Faivre notes that that this idea of mediation also represents a functional difference between mystical and esoteric spirituality. Whereas the mystic typically seeks a direct and immediate *unio mystica* with God without any intervening images or intermediaries, the esotericist tends to focus on the intermediaries (angels, devas, *sephiroth,* hypostases) that extend up and down the ladder of spiritual ascent as a preferred form of contemplation. Imagination and mediations thus give rise to the rich iconographic imagery of alchemy, theosophy, cosmology, and spiritual anatomy that characterize esotericism from the seventeenth century onward.

4. *The experience of transmutation.* Faivre's final intrinsic characteristic concerns the inner experience of esoteric spirituality. Esotericism does not simply describe some intellectual or speculative knowledge of the cosmos but rather an understanding that fundamentally transmutes the speculative subject. Just as there is a change of state in alchemy, so there is a change of being as a result of the illuminated knowledge (gnosis) that the esotericist experiences through active imagination and engagement in the mediations between the microcosm and the macrocosm. Corresponding to alchemy's central metaphors of refinement and purification, illumination offers the experience of transmutation, a change of state and spiritual ascent. By virtue of this revealed knowledge, the human being experiences an inner metamorphosis or "second birth."

To these four essential and necessary characteristics of esotericism, Faivre added two secondary characteristics, often found in association with the preceding four:

5. *The practice of concordance.* From the end of the fifteenth century onward, an intellectual tendency to establish similarities between various esoteric traditions is marked. The Renaissance esotericists were excited to discover homologies between Neoplatonism, Hermeticism, and Kabbalah. Their motivation was not simply a matter of establishing intellectual harmonies, but rather the implication that these traditions sprang from a single, authentic, and divine source of inspiration, thus representing the branches of an ancient theology (*prisca theologia*). With the advent of

comparative religion and knowledge of Asian religions in the nineteenth century, modern Theosophy repeated this project positing an ancient wisdom tradition inspiring all religions and esoteric traditions.

6. *Transmission.* Many esoteric traditions imply that the full profundity of the teaching can only be passed from master to disciple through an established path of initiation. The validity of the teaching is attested by various forms of certification or authentication bearing on the tradition, lineage, and credentials of the group, order, or secret society (as in Rosicrucian orders or Freemasonry), and the process of individual initiation represents the ritualization of the reception of that tradition.

Such a taxonomy offers a means of systematically comparing traditions with one another.

Over the past decade, several other definitions have been proposed by scholars working in the field. Wouter Hanegraaff, currently the chair of the History of Hermetic Philosophy and Related Currents at the University of Amsterdam (established in 1999), has identified a variety of formulations. These range from the pro-esoteric universalist and religionist definitions of Gilles Quispel, Pierre Riffard, and Traditionalism to hostile definitions that typically regard esotericism as a "disease of reason." He notes that the sociology of the occult, in particular, has tended to pursue a reductionistic approach to esotericism, seeing it simply as deviance, with little understanding of the role and development of esotericism in the history of ideas.[6] Hanegraaff favors historical constructs on an empirical foundation and compares the typology of Faivre with the approaches of Gershom Scholem and Joseph Dan to Jewish mysticism and Kabbalah, as being theoretical generalizations about a collection of historically unique phenomena. Hanegraaff notes that Scholem and Dan construe mysticism or esotericism as a coherent tradition of commentary (i.e., texts) rather than as a series of mystical experiences. Citing the work of Dan Merkur, who regards gnosis as a tradition of visionary and unitive practice rooted in late antiquity and traceable in the three scriptural traditions, Hanegraaff concludes his comparison with a plea for an ongoing dialectical debate involving the practice of criticism and proposition of theoretical constructs at an etic level but with constant reference to the emic or believer's point of view.[7]

Arthur Versluis, professor of American Studies at Michigan State University, editor of the academic online journal *Esoterica,* and founding president of the (American) Association for the Study of Esotericism (ASE), has developed an alternative methodology for the study of Western esotericism.[8] Versluis comments that although Faivre's model takes full account of the cosmological domain (correspondences, living nature), it fails to emphasize *gnosis* as a central element of Western esotericism. Here Versluis understands "cosmological gnosis" as "knowledge or direct perception of hidden or esoteric aspects of the cosmos," which he contrasts with "metaphysical gnosis" in the sense of "direct spiritual insight into complete transcendence." The former is still a form of knowledge involving a subject-object dualism, and its correspondences form the basis of alchemy, astrology, and magic. The latter form of gnosis is nondualistic spiritual insight, as in the *via negativa* of Meister Eckhart or the *Ungrund* of Jacob Boehme. Taking the *Corpus Hermeticum* as an example, metaphysical gnosis reflects direct insight into the Supreme Mind or *Nous*.

Versluis continues his critique of methodology by questioning Hanegraaff's sharp division between a "religionist" (essentialist and emic) perspective and an "empiricist" approach. Versluis considers that the rejection of an emic approach implies an arrogant dismissal of the actual discourse in an alchemical, magical, or theosophical text as neither important nor true. An extreme etic approach often involves a reductionism that privileges present-day academic interpretative fashions or political preoccupations such as social equality, race, or gender.

Here Versluis recalls the view of Mircea Eliade that the reduction of culture to something lower (sexuality, economics, history) is a neurotic attitude, a failure to believe in higher meanings, and almost always reflects the imposition of some form of ideology upon the subject of one's study. Here Versluis asks for a sympathetic neutrality so that the scholar may enter imaginatively into the alternative worldview and communicate it faithfully to his or her readers.[9]

Other scholars have commented that Faivre's definition of esotericism is closely based on his own specialist studies in Renaissance Hermeticism, Christian theosophy and Romantic *Naturphilosophie,* thereby creating an "ideal" typology which reflects a particular cultural and historical field in the history of esotericism, that is specifically Western. Kocku von Stuckrad has argued that Faivre's model may not be sufficiently comprehensive to address Jewish and Islamic esotericism or the influence of Buddhism on twentieth-century esotericism. Stuckrad uses a model based on the plurality of discourses in the European history of religion to suggest that religious identities arise through communication, debate, modification, and assimilation. This approach, much indebted to the sociology of knowledge, is favored by the German professor of religious studies Hans Kippenberg, with whom Stuckrad has collaborated.[10] Stuckrad regards religious pluralism as a structural element of European cultural history, and accordingly sees esotericism as an element of discourse that can migrate from religion into science, philosophy, literature, and art.

Thus Stuckrad attempts to shed the idea that "esotericism" exists as an independent historical phenomenon, insisting that it exists only as a scholarly classification, as, for example, in Faivre's ideal typology. Stuckrad thinks that "esotericism" suggests a coherent doctrine or continuous body of tradition, whereas "the esoteric" is an element of cultural processes. In his view, these cultural processes involve sociological ideas of discourse and *discursive transfer* between fields of knowledge (science, philosophy, etc.). Dismissing the idea of an autonomous esoteric tradition, Stuckrad identifies "the esoteric" as an element of discourse that specifically makes *claims* to "real" or absolute knowledge and the *means* of making this knowledge available.[11] These means may involve ascent experiences as described in Hermetic or Neoplatonic texts, communication with spiritual beings (intermediaries), or even scientific discoveries. Stuckrad goes on to describe this discourse of absolute knowledge as a "dialectic of the hidden and revealed," involving the rhetoric of a hidden truth whose revelation requires special measures and is contrary to other interpretations of the cosmos and history, usually the dominant worldview.

Stuckrad's analysis essentially proposes a sociocultural explanation and definition of the esoteric in which all forms of knowledge are socially constructed. But this is a partial view, informed by the rise of social sciences which suggest that modern scientific research and its quest for definite factual knowledge concerning the natural world is a social construct. But science is itself defined as knowledge, and most scientists consider their findings to be real, their laws absolute. Stuckrad's real and absolute esoteric knowledge is further defined as being an alternative to the dominant worldview. To Galileo's contemporaries, his scientific revelations could be regarded as both an alternative to the dominant religious worldview and esoteric in their claim to "real" or absolute knowledge. However, in our era, such astronomical knowledge is generally accepted as true and absolute, and it forms an integral part of the dominant worldview of nature. Thus Galileo's ideas are no longer esoteric.

In Stuckrad's socio-cultural analysis, definitions of the esoteric also gravitate towards concepts of 'otherness' and 'deviance'.[12] The use of these categories in the evaluation of esotericism was marked in the 1970s when Marcello Truzzi elaborated a sociology of the occult on the basis of its ahistorical presentation as irrationalism and unscientific thinking.[13] At the same time, the British historian James Webb (1946–1980) wrote several well-documented histories of occultism in which "rejected knowledge" is viewed as a revolt against the Enlightenment and the rise of irrationalism in the nineteenth and twentieth centuries.[14] Stuckrad, however, sees this "otherness" or "deviance" not as a category of cultural failure or rejection but as a project in the construction of new religious, philosophical, and scientific ideas and identities.

My own perspective on this debate is that definitions of "the esoteric" in terms of discourse, social constructions, and legitimacy lack a hermeneutic interpretation of spirit and spirituality as an independent ontological reality.

By seeking to define the esoteric in terms of human behavior and culture, it becomes a reflective cultural category rather than a philosophical or spiritual insight, which remains the essential component of any claims to real or absolute knowledge. Precisely because esotericism addresses itself to a "higher" reality, above the concrete world of nature and second causes, it invokes ideas of correspondences, an ensouled nature, hierarchies and intermediaries in a mesocosm, and the transmutation of persons who are initiated into this higher reality. Stuckrad himself suggests that esoteric discourses continuously crystallize into new constellations in history but that these all tend to involve a holistic or monistic view of the material and nonmaterial aspects of the cosmos as a unity. The notion of correspondences makes connections between transcendence and immanence, body and soul, matter and spirit.[15] It is notable that these constellations reflect the continuing value of Faivre's categories. Moreover, these perennial characteristics of the esoteric worldview suggest to me that this is an enduring tradition which, though subject to some degree of social legitimacy and cultural coloration, actually reflects an autonomous and essential aspect of the relationship between the mind and the cosmos.

The historical incidence and efflorescence of esoteric ideas at times when the dominant worldview no longer commands general assent is suggestive of their social construction and selection, but it also begs the question of their function. It is notable that esoteric ideas often attend the breakdown of settled religious orthodoxies and socioeconomic orders. Hermetic, Neoplatonic, and Gnostic works of literature were produced in the first three centuries a.d. in the Hellenistic arena of the Roman Empire where globalization, urbanization, and multiculturalism confused older traditions and simpler faiths. Likewise, the European Renaissance was launched in Western cities where dynamism and economic and cultural progress collided with the waning of medieval assumptions in theology and philosophy. This was the period when Hermeticism, alchemy, astrology, magic, and Kabbalah were reformulated from their sources in late antiquity to form a new *philosophia perennis* embracing Christianity and ancient wisdom traditions. In the late nineteenth century, when Europe entered a period of sustained urban and industrial growth simultaneous with a decline of organized religion in the face of the challenges of secularism and science on the other, occultism and esoteric societies enjoyed a vogue, entering public discourse on a scale not seen since the sixteenth century.

It is also significant that exotic religions and philosophies play a crucial role in the historical stimulus of esotericism. Cosmopolitan Hellenistic culture was receptive to Egyptian, Jewish, Syrian, Babylonian and Persian currents, which combined with Greek thought to produce Neoplatonism, Hermeticism, and Gnosticism. The Italian Renaissance city-states, likewise crucibles of modernity and cultural experimentation in the fifteenth century, assimilated Greek (Byzantine) philosophy from the Ottoman East and Kabbalah from the Iberian West to produce a new concordance of Christianity, Neoplatonism, Hermeticism and Kabbalah. These esoteric Renaissance traditions continued to flourish amid the confessional challenges and turbulence of the Reformation in Germany, producing such movements as theosophy, Rosicrucianism, pietism, illuminist societies, and mystery lodges of high-grade Freemasonry in the seventeenth and eighteenth centuries. Where trade and imperial rule went, exotic religions were discovered. In the eighteenth and nineteenth centuries, the European world was preeminent in commerce and colonial expansion. Great Britain, France, and Germany embraced an orientalism that later seeded the combination of the Western esoteric traditions with Eastern religions such as Advaita Vedanta and Buddhism in Helena Blavatsky's Theosophy and its many successor movements.

These historical points of resurgence in esotericism represent an efflorescence of heterodox new perspectives and paradigms in response to the waning hold of orthodoxy. This estimate is intrinsic to understanding how Christian and Gnostic sects gained ascendancy in the late Roman Empire, how Renaissance Hermeticism was a pioneer of those ideas of human sovereignty that ultimately enabled the scientific worldview, and how modern occultism has offered fruitful insights in science, medicine, and art. Viewed in this light, esotericism appears as a diastole of renascent cultural and spiritual energy, after the systole of consolidated orthodoxy in ideas and institutions. These new energies are also attributable to the absorption of exotic religion and philosophy amid a quickening cosmopolitanism. While Stuckrad's concepts of discourse and discursive transfer for the construction of new religious identities have validity in this model, the historical evidence suggests that esotericism also involves a return to sources, to some archetypal forms of thought and energy which generate a fresh round of cultural and spiritual development. In this regard, esotericism is an essential element of renewal in the historical process.

My historical introduction to the study of Western esotericism is intended to offer a convenient overview of the main movements, currents, and figures of these traditions from late antiquity to the twentieth century. I hope to demonstrate not only their persistent vitality, but also their importance in the scientific and religious debates of the West.

I

Ancient Hellenistic Sources of Western Esotericism

Historical and Geographical Context

Following Faivre's typology, the Western esoteric traditions have their basis in certain distinct patterns of thinking about the divine, man, and the universe which stretch back into classical antiquity. These patterns concern correspondences between a higher divine reality, the universe, the earthly realm, and human beings; the idea of a living, ensouled, or animated universe; notions of spiritual intermediaries in the form of hierarchies, planes, and angels acting as a ladder of descent and ascent between the higher and lower worlds; and the idea of the human soul's transmutation through reawakening and returning to these higher worlds. These patterns of thought are found in such ancient teachings as Alexandrian Hermetism, Neoplatonism, theurgy, and to a limited extent in Gnosticism, which all originated in the eastern Mediterranean area during the first few centuries A.D.[1]

Ancient Egypt was the cradle of these religious doctrines, but this was not the Egypt of the pharaohs. Nectanebo II, the last pharaoh of the last dynasty, had already been defeated by the Persians when Alexander the Great founded a city in his own name in 332 B.C. west of the mouth of the Nile. Once Alexander the Great had conquered Syria, Egypt, Mesopotamia, and Persia, fighting his way into India, the backwash of empire had led to an awed reverence for the older civilizations of the East. When Alexander died in 305 B.C., Ptolemy, one of his generals, took control of Egypt, and twenty monarchs of his dynasty succeeded him until Mark Antony and Cleopatra were defeated by the Roman emperor Octavian in 31 B.C. Egypt was henceforth absorbed into the Roman Empire. An ancient culture of pyramids, temples, and exotic gods, along with penetration by Western influences and access to the oriental world made Hellenistic and later Roman Egypt the principal channel for the reception of oriental religion, magic, astrology, and alchemy in the Graeco-Roman world.[2]

With the rise of the Roman Empire, there was a notable change in people's religious needs. Greek rationalist philosophy had made the gods abstract and remote from human needs. While public worship of the Olympian gods and agricultural rites were maintained, the absorption of independent cities and states into the empire had created a climate of multiculturalism and religious relativism. At the same, time, urbanization removed people from the settled life, customs, and religious practices of the countryside. Increased social mobility, the breakdown of strong family units, and cosmopolitanism all fostered a need for a more direct and personal relationship with the divine than the official state cults could offer. New religions, mystery cults, sages, prophets, magicians, and healers arose in response to these new circumstances.

The cosmopolitan nature of Hellenistic Alexandrian culture chiefly expressed itself in religion through syncretism.[3] Given colonial contact with the oriental world of Egypt and Chaldea (Babylonia and Assyria), the rational mind of Greece combined with the enthusiastic cults and mysterious wisdom-traditions of other nations, to create new religious belief and practice. Alexandrian culture became adept at "philosophizing" and systematizing the exotic mythology, theosophy, and gnosis of the East and introducing their oracles, apocalypses, and initiatory lore to the Western mind.[4]

Alexandrian Hermetism

Foremost among the sources of Western esotericism are the *Hermetica*, a diverse collection of works on theosophy, astrology, and magic which have their origin in Alexandria, the primary metropolis of Hellenistic culture, which functioned as a clearing-house for Greek and Eastern ideas, myths and religious beliefs. The texts contain revelations attributed to various deities, but chiefly to Hermes Trismegistus, or Thrice-Great, an ancient sage identified with Thoth, the Egyptian god of wisdom and magic. This identification with Thoth is a vital key to understanding the exalted reputation of Hermes Trismegistus in both the ancient world and in Renaissance Europe.

From Thoth to Hermes Trismegistus

Western esotericism has been shaped by its major source, the *Hermetica*, a disparate collection of writings on cosmology, astrology, alchemy and magic, attributed to Hermes Trismegistus, the "Thrice-Great" Egyptian sage. Thoth, the Egyptian god of wisdom and magic, later became fused with the Greek Hermes, and this syncretic god was to become a powerful influence on the whole development of esoteric thought from its ancient roots right through to Renaissance Europe.

From earliest times, Thoth, one of the most popular Egyptian gods, was associated with the moon. As a moon god, he served the solar divinity Ra as both his secretary and counselor. This identification of Thoth with the moon was of immense practical importance to Egyptian culture for the moon's phases governed the great rhythms of flood and drought across the Nile delta. It was from these rhythms that the Egyptians measured time and seasons, and Thoth became associated with the governance of Time itself as well as the arbiter of individual destinies. As a psychopomp, Thoth conducted the souls of the dead to the kingdom of the gods, where he presided at the judgment of their souls.[5]

All of Egyptian national life fell under his jurisdiction, for he was the origin of order, both in the great world of the cosmos and in the little world of religious and civil institutions. He was lawgiver, divine scribe, and magus. From him the priesthood and temple cults derived their wisdom and sacred literature, including parts of the *Book of the Dead*. All magical and occult powers were attributed to Thoth.

The cult of Thoth continued to inspire allegiance throughout the Ptolemaic and Roman periods. At the beginning of the Christian era, Alexandria was the chief center of Hellenistic culture; here Greek philosophy encountered Eastern ideas, myths, and beliefs. Because of his power and influence, Greek settlers in Egypt quickly came to identify Thoth with their god Hermes, whose cultic center was at Hermoupolis.[6]

Hermes was also a psychopomp associated with the moon. In addition to their formidable attributes as arbiters of time and national life, both Thoth and Hermes had a lighter side which sealed their popularity; they were seen as trickster figures, inventive and playful, even as they functioned as messengers of the gods and interpreters of divine will.

Greek magical papyri present the new composite Hermes as a cosmic power, creator of the universe, presiding over night and day, life and death, fate and justice. In time the Hellenistic Hermes became identified among the Stoics with the *logos* and demiurge (*pantocrator, cosmocrator*).[7] To him is revealed "all that is hidden under the heavenly vault, and beneath the earth." Magical spells addressed to Hermes seek arcane knowledge or oracles, or they invite the god himself to appear in a dream and to bestow the blessings of a favored life (food, success, happiness). At the same time, he is one who can be known intimately in oneself. "I know you, Hermes, and you know me. I am you and you are me." This self-identification with Hermes may have derived, as Fowden and Faivre suggest, from an euhemerist tendency to see Thoth as a divinized human being. Once human and mortal in the long-distant past, Hermes-Thoth became, through his own efforts of spiritual advancement, an intermediary hovering between the divine and human worlds, rather like a *Bodhisattva* who has attained immortality but remains in the human world as a channel for the divine.[8]

The Corpus Hermeticum

The *Hermetica* consist of several small scattered works. These include both the technical *Hermetica* on magic and the philosophical collections. Brian Copenhaver has commented that both the technical and philosophical works of the *Hermetica* most probably derive from a common environment. The distinction between them owes something to the circumstances of their Byzantine transmission and edition. However, it is evident that the philosophical collections blend theology, cosmology, soteriology, and eschatology, with scant reference to magic and other occult sciences aside from traces of astrology. Forty Hermetic texts including the *Kore Kosmu* (The Virgin of the World) are gathered in the anthology of Stobaeus (early fifth century A.D.), some late second- or third-century fragments are preserved at Vienna, while the discovery of mainly Gnostic texts at Nag Hammadi in 1945 also included a number of philosophical *Hermetica*. However, in the history of Western esotericism, the most famous and influential philosophical text, discovered in 1460, is the *Corpus Hermeticum*, which brings together seventeen treatises written in Greek in the second and third centuries A.D.[9]

These treatises are variously addressed: some by Hermes to his son and disciple Tat; others by Hermes to his disciple Asclepius and others; others, including the famous first book *Poimandres* (The Divine Pymander), by the god Nous (Supreme Intellect) to Hermes. Throughout the treatises, Hermes Trismegistus plays the role of initiator into wisdom and mysteries. Man is summoned to make himself equal to God, in order to apprehend God. "See what power you have and what speed! You can do all these things and God cannot? Reflect on God in this way as having all within Himself as ideas: the cosmos, Himself, the whole. If you do not make yourself equal to God you cannot understand him. Like is understood by like."[10]

What are we looking for, or what do we *recognize*, in a text that makes it Hermetic? It is a certain philosophical perspective—set forth in the *Corpus Hermeticum*—based on the scenario of a fall into matter and a redemptive reintegration with the divine. Key themes are:

- "As above, so below." Nous instructs us to reflect the universe in our own mind and to grasp the divine essence in nature. This we are equipped and able to do because the human being possesses a divine intellect.
- There is an emphasis on will, both divine and human.
- The universe is a "book" to be "read." The Creator God is known by the contemplation of his creation.
- The universe is full of the manifestation of God, and with our divine intellect we can decipher the symbols it contains which point toward God. We should therefore be interested in everything that is in the world. The concrete and the particular are important, as incarnation and embodiment are the ways in which God makes himself manifest to our experience.
- There is an absence of dualism, since the world is recognized as being of divine origin. There is an acceptance of the world, even though there may be some pessimism or discouragement about the consequences of the Fall and the restraint of matter on spirit.
- The Hermetic project is one of transmutation of lower, baser, and more material into higher, finer, and more spiritual. There are clear parallels with alchemy, which also flourished alongside Hermetism in Alexandria in late antiquity.
- Humanity is called to a regenerative work of reascension and reintegration with the divine.
- Our intellect can connect to intermediary spiritual intelligences and use them as ladders of ascent. An astrological cosmos of an ascending hierarchy of planetary spheres exists and is part of the initiatory process and spiritual ascent. The earth is part of this cosmos and is susceptible to improvement.
- Because humanity is connected both to the divine and to the earthly realms, it is able to help the earth to recover its former glorious state.
- Hermetic treatises present a guide or mentor figure who helps to raise souls by reawakening them to their divine nature, assisting in their spiritual transmutation, and leading them toward their heavenly destiny.

The *Corpus Hermeticum* strongly implied a partnership between the human spirit and God. Whereas Judaism and Christianity tended to regard God as transcendent and thus beyond human comprehension, the *Corpus Hermeticum* attributed a divine intellect to humans, whereby they could reflect the whole universe in their minds. The theme of the divine intellect as a "mirror," on which "speculating" is a continuous exchange with higher spiritual entities, is a major theme of esotericism. Because God created the universe, it is saturated with his spiritual symbols. Once humans learn to read these symbols, they can know God directly. In this way, Hermetism negates any absolute ontological dualism between God and his Creation.[11]

Alexandrian Hermetism also emphasized the mythical themes of fall and reintegration. Notions of humanity's fall into matter through the attraction of the sensual were balanced by ideas of reascension to the godhead. This did not imply a contempt for nature, but rather a discovery of the intermediary spiritual intelligences or astral elements, which the human intellect can then ascend like a spiritual ladder to higher planes of being. These ideas hark back to the neo-Pythagoreans Nicomac of Gerase and Moderatus of Gades, who linked numbers to an ordered procession of souls after death and a whole series of mediating processes in which the planets and stars are the stages. Plutarch (A.D. 46–120?) gave a bold interpretation of Plato's *Timaeus* in which souls rise toward the moon after death. Only with this Hermetic model of spiritual hierarchies, whose ascent gives ever greater insights into God's will and the meaning of the cosmos, can one understand the Renaissance magic which runs from the astrology of Marsilio Ficino to the theurgic invocations and angelology of John Dee and Edward Kelley.[12]

With the exception of the *Asclepius*, the Hermetic treatises were unknown to the Middle Ages. However, their recovery from Byzantine Greece by Cosimo de' Medici of Florence and translation into Latin by Marsilio Ficino in 1463 marks the revival of Hermetic ideas and esotericism in the modern era (see chapter 2).

Neoplatonism

Closely related to Hermetism in its ancient context is pagan (i.e. pre-Christian) Neoplatonism. Plato had clearly separated the higher world of Ideas from the lower world, but he provided for a soul which was capable of being reminded of the higher world through its sensory experience of things in this lower world. The Neoplatonists gave new direction to Platonic philosophy between the third and the sixth centuries A.D. They conceived of reality as spiritual activity or states of consciousness and regarded the human soul as a voyager, fallen and encumbered by bodily existence but perfectible by a path of ascent to its divine origins. Neoplatonic philosophy held a particular appeal for the educated classes of the later Roman Empire, who were beset by a sense of material decline and religious anxiety.[13]

Neoplatonic thought is characterized by the idea that there exists a plurality of spheres of being, arranged in a descending hierarchy of degrees of being. The last and lowest sphere of being comprises the universe existing in time and space perceptible to the human senses. Each sphere of being derives from its superior by a process of "emanation," by which it reflects and expresses its previous degree. At the same time, these degrees of being are also degrees of unity, whereby each subsequent sphere generates more multiplicity, differentiation, and limitation, tending toward the minimal unity of our material world.

Plotinus

The leading figure of this movement was Plotinus (A.D. 205–270), who studied in Alexandria under Ammonius Saccas. As a young man, Plotinus sought acquaintance with the ideas of Persia and India by joining Emperor Gordian's disastrous military campaign against the Persians in A.D. 238–244 and then went to live in Rome from A.D. 245 until his death. Here he gathered various disciples, including Porphyry, who published Plotinus's works as the *Enneads*.[14]

Plotinus posited an absolute, transcendent One or Good, defined in Aristotle's phrase as "that to which all things aspire." Its existence was inferred from the necessity of unity in everything that exists. Below the One, Plotinus described a cosmology of continuous creative emanation, whereby the higher level of reality is imparted to the lower without being diminished. However, each new level of emanation is necessarily less perfect than its begetter, to which it longs to return. Plotinus posited three grades of higher being: Intellect; the higher Soul, whether World Soul or individual Soul, which transcends the physical and enjoys eternal contact with Intellect; and the lower Soul or Nature. Both Intellect and Soul are termed the *logos* of their previous higher state, meaning that they represent it as formative and regulative principles at the subsequent, lower level of creation. At the outset of creation, unformed Intellect begins to fill with intelligible forms, which are themselves perfect archetypes of everything that will exist in the world of sense. These ideal forms within Intellect contain not only generic forms or species, but also forms of individuals. Plotinus used Platonic arguments to establish the immortality of the incorporeal soul as the cause of life and movement. However, Plotinus differed from Plato by referring to the individual soul and the unique value of the personal self.[15]

Plotinus also insisted on the unplanned and spontaneous creation of the material world by the lower Soul, or Nature, a marked contrast with Plato's conception of creation as conscious design described in *Timaeus* and in Jewish

CHART OF THE ORPHIC THEOGONY.

Unaging Time.

The Primordial Triad	The One-Many-All	△	Universal Good Universal Soul Universal Mind

Super-sensible World.

Noëtic Triad
— Being [Vestibule of the Good]

- Bound (Hyparxis—Father) [One] { Æther, Chaos, Egg
- Infinity (Power—Mother) [Many] { Egg [Night] containing the Triple [The "Dragon God of Wisdom"]
- Mixed (Mind—Son) [All] [Beauty] [Truth] [Symmetry] { Phanes [Gt. Grandfather —Manifestor— Ericapæus Animal Itself] Metis

Noëtic-noëric Triad — Life

- Essence "The Abiding" Supercelestial Place [Plain of Truth ; Kingdom of Adrastia]
- Life
- Intellect
- Infinite Power
- Intelligible Life "The Proceeding" Celestial Arch Uranus [Heaven] [Grandfather]
- Intelligible Intellect "The Returning" Subcelestial Arch

Noëric Triad [Hebdomadic] — Intellect

- Cronus—Saturn [Father] [and a septenary hierarchy]
- Rhea [and a septenary hierarchy] Curetic or Unpolluted Triad [each a septenary hierarchy]
- Zeus—Jupiter (Demiurgus) [and a septenary hierarchy]
- The Seventh Monad [The Separative Deity] Oceanus

Sensible World.

Super-cosmic Order

- Demiurgic Triad { Jupiter—Celestial Jupiter (Ruler of Inerratic Sphere), Neptune—Marine Jupiter (Ruler of Planetary Spheres), Pluto—Subterranean Jupiter (Ruler of Sublunary Region)
- Zoogonic Triad { Coric Diana, Coric Proserpine, Coric Minerva The Corybantic Triad
- Apolliniacal Triad { Apollo, the Triple Sun Superessential Light, Intellectual Light, Sensible Light

Liberated Order [Dodecad]

- Jovian Monad
- Vestan Monad The Decad [completed by] { Apollo or the Prophetic Life, Mars or the Divisive Life, Venus or the Amatory Life

Cosmic Order [Dodecad]

Fabricative Triad—Jupiter	Neptune	Vulcan	
Defensive Triad—Vesta	Minerva	Mars	
Vivific Triad —Ceres	Juno	Diana	
Harmonic Triad —Mercury	Venus	Apollo	

FIGURE 1.1. Orphic Theogony, in G. R. S. Mead, "Orpheus," *Lucifer* 17 (1895–1896), 9–10.

and Christian scripture. Plotinus's emphasis on the creative emanation of the material universe from the thought of God was essentially cosmological. The idea was closely linked to the Ptolemaic view of the universe as a hierarchical system of nine concentric spheres, ranging from the outermost sphere of God as Prime Mover through the sequence of planetary spheres to the lowest sphere of earth. Plotinus saw the universe as "a single living being embracing all living beings within it." Possessed of a single Soul permeating all its parts, the material universe participates in this World Soul and is influenced by other parts to the extent of their integration and the correspondence of their constituent elements. Thus a sympathy pervades this universe, manifested as a system of correspondences existing among the stars, animals, plants, minerals, and human organs, giving rise to the idea of a mapping between the macrocosm of the universe and the microcosm of a human being. Plotinus wrote about astrological divination, prayer, and the votive cult of statues, in which the powers of a god were embodied in its sculptured form, to show the effectiveness of affinities, which connected different parts of the world to each other. Magical results were not the result of a god's direct action but rooted in the sympathy that linked different particular emanations of the World Soul—a direct result of the underlying "cousinhood" of all creation.

Though Plotinus believed in the efficacy of prayer, magic, and astrological divination, there is no evidence that he practiced them. A philosopher by nature, he regarded these phenomena primarily as evidence of spiritual harmony and the interdependence of the universe. By representing reality as ordered and harmonious, everywhere tending to the Good, Plotinus offered a powerful comfort in times of change and instability. The individual soul, discovering its identity with the World Soul, has perfection within its reach. Evil and suffering cannot touch the true self, and external events and physical circumstances are irrelevant to happiness. Plotinus is thus important as a systematic philosopher to refine concepts of macrocosm-microcosm correspondences, hierarchies, the equivalence of the World Soul and individual soul and its spiritual reintegration. In his case, Neoplatonism is primarily a philosophy for the purification and ascent of the soul.

Porphyry, Iamblichus, and Proclus

Born in Tyre, Porphyry (ca. A.D. 232–305) went to Athens in his early twenties to study under the philosopher Longinus. There he mastered literary, textual, and historical criticism and possibly became acquainted with Platonic and Pythagorean traditions. On learning of Plotinus's teachings around A.D. 263, Porphyry resolved to go to Rome and study under him. In his *Life of Plotinus*, Porphyry describes his master's spiritual life as a "continuous turning in contemplation to his intellect." Plotinus kept his soul pure and ever strove toward the divine. "He did everything to be delivered and escape from the bitter wave of blood-drinking life here." A strict asceticism, little food, abstinence from flesh-eating and from sexual relations all reflect a regime of purification intended to remove oneself from the sensible world. However, this asceticism extended neither to outright world-rejection nor to withdrawal from human affairs. Plotinus actively concerned himself with his disciples and with the education of the children of high-ranking Romans entrusted to him. Porphyry's account also recorded the Plotinian experience of union with God. In ascending through the hierarchical levels of reality, the human soul passed through distinct stages of spiritual progress. It became conscious of itself and discovered its dependence on the divine Intellect, which illuminates it and gives it the power of thought. The soul also realized that it ultimately emanated from the transcendent Good that is in turn superior to Intellect. The soul thereby separates from the body, leaping up above the sensible world to apprehend the eternal and all things in the intelligible world. This process here reflects the ascent to the Beautiful described by Diotima in Plato's *Symposium*, whereas the intelligible world is the world of Forms or Ideas.[16]

Porphyry wrote many works, including *The Life of Pythagoras*, *Life of Plotinus*, an *Epistle to Anebo the Egyptian* (on the topic of theurgy), a *Commentary on the Harmonics of Ptolemy*, *On the Abstinence from Animal Food*, the *Homeric Questions*, and his *Launching-Points to the Realm of Mind* (otherwise known as *Auxiliaries to the Perception of Intelligible Natures*). He also wrote two works relating to Christianity. *Against the Christians* contained a critique of the historical accuracy of the Book of Daniel and highlighted the inconsistencies of the gospel narratives. His commentary on the *Chaldean Oracles* noted that the gods of the oracles spoke highly of Jesus as a spiritual teacher, but he considered it erroneous that Jesus's followers identified Jesus with the supreme principle. Porphyry also insisted on the value and purifying effect of theurgy in assisting the soul's release from the sensible world and ascent through intermediaries to the intelligible realm. This concept of mystical ascent is given expressive formulation in his *Letter to His Wife Marcella concerning the Life of Philosophy and the Ascent to the Gods*.[17]

Iamblichus, a disciple of Porphyry, was born at Chalcis in Syria around A.D. 260 and died in A.D. 330. As a Neoplatonic philosopher, his reputation as a teacher and thinker was widespread, even earning the praise of Emperor Julian. Iamblichus went much further than Porphyry in asserting the claims of theurgy as a means of putting men in contact with the gods or constraining spirits. Iamblichus wrote his famous work *On the Mysteries of the Egyptians* as a response to Porphyry's *Letter to Anebo*. The philosophical defense of theurgy influenced the Christian theology of sacraments. Iamblichus subordinated philosophy to theurgy, claiming that the gods are responsive to us. Oracular inspiration was sought through the manipulation of symbolic objects and the use of occult linguistic formulas. In Iamblichus's account, the theurgist receiving divine inspiration behaves in a manner suggestive of modern mediumship (descent of a spiritual form into medium, enlargement or floating of body, changes in voice). This process of divine possession is viewed as an ascent and reversion to a higher spiritual plane. Such divination unites humans with the gods. It enables humans to share in the life of the gods and thereby attain to divinity.[18]

Proclus (A.D. 410–485), the last major pagan Neoplatonist teaching at Athens, also asserted the unitary principle of all things, which expressed itself in *henads*, or primal unities within the first plane of being. Proclus addressed the problem of how higher realities can be both transcendent and yet immanent at lower levels. He claimed that each form has a transcendent, unitary, or "unparticipated" aspect and an immanent, or "participated" aspect. The One is thereby unparticipated unity, while the *henads* are participated unity. As the influence of the gods reach down through all levels of creation, theology becomes for Proclus the study of the nature and powers of the *henads*. Proclus's thought thereby anticipates the overlap between theology and natural philosophy in modern esotericism. Proclus was also strongly sympathetic to the ideas and practices of theurgy based on the magical sympathy among all things.[19]

The later Neoplatonists' interest in theurgy indicates a shift from Plotinus's philosophical appraisal of the ensouled universe to acts of magical intervention based on a knowledge of its correspondences. The practical operation on the spiritual realities of a sympathetic universe clearly anticipate the concerns of Renaissance magic at the dawn of modern esotericism.

The Chaldean Oracles

Theurgy means "acting on the gods" through knowledge of the theory and practice of establishing contact with gods and spirits. This contact is achieved not only by raising or purifying our consciousness but also through rituals, ceremonies, invocations, and material objects that will set in motion divine influences or conjure angelic and demonic beings into our presence. The *Chaldean Oracles* were a cardinal statement of ancient theurgy. Produced by Julian the Theurgist during the second century A.D. in Syria, possibly through mediums' trances, this text elaborated a complex cosmology including an ensouled or animated universe replete with spiritual and demonic intermediaries.

Just as the *Hermetica* offered Hellenism an opportunity to philosophize the ancient wisdom of Egypt, the *Chaldean Oracles* represented a parallel project with the wisdom of Chaldea. (Chaldea is a transliteration of the Assyrian name Kaldu and was a Greek synonym for Babylonia.)

The cosmology of the *Chaldean Oracles* involves a hierarchy of planes, commencing with the First Paternal Intellect, absolutely transcendent, in the uppermost world of supramundane light. This plane contains the Intelligible Triad of Father, the Magna Mater or Hecate, and Intellect. Hecate acts as a channel for influences traveling between the intelligible and sensible realms. Beneath this world of the Intelligible Triad lie the three successive descending Empyrean, Ethereal, and Elemental Worlds. The *Oracles* identify a Second Demiurgic Intellect as representative of the divine power in the Empyrean World, a Third Intellect in the Ethereal World, while the fourth or Elemental World is governed by Hyperzokos or Flower of Fire. The oracles describe the physical world as a prison from which the higher human soul must escape by shedding the body that the lower soul has acquired on its descent through the stars and planets. Asceticism and theurgic ritual will free the soul from the astrological bonds of fate and protect it from the demons that fill the space between the gods and mortals. The oracles describe rites that call a god down into a statue or into a human medium, in order to help the human soul escape its bodily prison and rise up to divinity.[20]

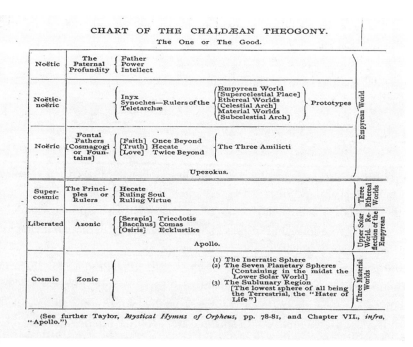

FIGURE 1.2. Chaldæan Theogony, in G. R. S. Mead, "Orpheus," *Lucifer* 17 (1895–1896), 102.

Porphyry and later pagan Neoplatonists esteemed the *Oracles*. Porphyry collected the oracles in a work, since lost, titled *On the Philosophy of the Oracles*. Iamblichus and Proclus also wrote elaborate treatises on the subject. Syrianus wrote a "symphony" of Orpheus, Pythagoras, and Plato with reference to the *Oracles*. In his treatise *On Providence*, Hierocles sought to harmonize the *Oracles* with the doctrines of the theurgists and the philosophy of Plato.

Gnosticism

As a major current of Christian thought in late antiquity, Gnosticism has some bearing on the ancient sources of esotericism. In the first place, Gnosticism is defined by its exaltation of a special spiritual *gnosis* (knowledge) of God and higher realities. The many Gnostic sects, which appeared in the first two centuries of the Christian era, subscribed to a radical form of ontological dualism between good and evil. The Gnostic sects traced the origin of all things to a first principle. This pure, perfect, and supreme power is eternal, infinite, and absolute. This God is a hidden deity, unknown and unknowable. However, once the godhead had manifested himself as God, he became an active principle. Gnostics saw subsequent creation as a series of cosmological emanations from the divine unity, personified by various mythological figures known as aeons. In the various Gnostic systems, Christ was often identified as one of the aeons and regarded as a redeemer and an agent of God, but not as wholly divine. The combined series of aeons was known as the *pleroma* (fullness), signifying the complex metaphysical structure of the cosmos beyond time and space. Beneath this metaphysical order lay the *hystereme* (the world of deficiency), which represented the fallen world of matter. This universe of ours, the Gnostics held, is produced not by God but by an inferior being known as the demiurge or by an evil being.

Gnostic cosmology always contrasts these two worlds. One is the eternal world of God and the heavenly hierarchy of the *pleroma*, which includes a variety of angelic beings such as archangels, cherubim, seraphim, amens, voices, virtues, guardians, and splendors, variously grouped into principalities, powers, thrones, dominions, and authorities. This is the world of reality and perfection, the noumenal world of things. The other is the world of illusion and imperfection, a phenomenal world of time and change. Here Man is trapped, separated from real God by the demiurge and its defective creation. However, *gnosis* can restore man to his divine birthright. The possession of *gnosis* enables the orphaned human soul to climb the heavenly hierarchy by an ascent through the angelic aeons, while overcoming the hostile opposition of a matching hierarchy of evil archons.[21]

The numerous Gnostic doctrines present many variations on these basic themes. Notable members of the heavenly hierarchy include Sophia, a female aeon of major importance in Gnosticism; and Satanel, a former chief of the angelic host who later became the demiurge or creator of the material world and known as Satan. In some accounts he was the elder brother of Jesuel (the heavenly Jesus). The idea of a fall is intrinsic to Gnostic doctrine, typically presented as a relegation of an aeon to lower planes. Satan fell through pride, Sophia through curiosity, and Adam through disobedience. The Gnostics also identified Jehovah, the god of the Old Testament, as the demiurge and hostile to the supreme God. The Gnostics decried the Hebrew deity as a merciless, angry, and jealous god who severely chastised his people for minor affronts and showed no mercy or love. In general, the Gnostics rejected the Old Testament as a Jewish bid for theological monopoly.

While intricately involved with Egyptian mythology, Chaldean magic, and Jewish mysticism, Gnosticism essentially reflected a myriad of heterodox Christian beliefs that stressed Christ's importance in human salvation. There are extensive Gnostic speculations on the divine and human aspects of Jesus, his ancestry and parentage, and the virgin birth. Apocryphal Gnostic gospels describe incidents in his childhood. Certain Gnostics denied the Incarnation, reasoning that Christ was a divine, eternal, and perfect being, he could not have become flesh, as matter was evil and impure. Others denied that Christ could assume any aspect of human nature, as this too would imply imperfection and deficiency. Other Gnostic writers suggested Jesus was a good man, in whom the Christ the Logos became incarnate at the moment of his baptism by John. Still others questioned the Crucifixion as an illusion or the fate of a substitute and rejected its theological importance.

Gnosticism attributes an important role to Man in the cosmic scheme. According to the Gnostics, man is a dual being. He possesses an immortal soul imprisoned in a physical body. Man's true home is the higher world of light in the *pleroma*, but as a result of the fall, he is enmeshed in the snares and impurity of matter. Man is thus a unique mixture of spirit and earth. In this respect, the special spiritual knowledge of *gnosis* is primarily concerned with redemption and the deliverance of man's pure, exiled soul from the evil material world. *Gnosis* is thus an ontological passport to the human soul through the boundary between the two worlds and thence back to the godhead.

Hermetism, Neoplatonism, and Gnosticism have many of the same elements, and their schools and texts exercised a mutual influence on one another. Both Hermetism and Neoplatonism emphasize continuity and correspondences between the hierarchical planes of being, the macrocosm and the microcosm, which reach down to the individual human soul. The soul is enjoined to become aware of its higher patrimony in the higher order, to cast off the dross of sensual restraint and to apprehend the intelligible world. For this purpose, intermediary spirits offer a ladder of descent and reascent between the higher spiritual world and the lower earthly world. Hermetism and Christianity also share a high regard for humanity's place in the cosmos and its development. Both regard incarnation of the soul as important, as humanity has talents and gifts to use in the development and transmutation of the created world in accordance with the higher world of the macrocosm.

Gnosticism's elaborate cosmologies, replete with aeons and archons, demonstrate a hierarchy of intermediaries typical of oriental religious mythology. These are also conceived as a ladder of spiritual descent into matter and a means of redemption for the soul. Gnosticism's chief legacy to the esoteric tradition consists in the rich variety of intermediaries which throng the *pleroma*. However, Gnosticism differs from both Hermetism and Neoplatonism in its strong ontological dualism. While the former are generally optimistic concerning creation, Gnosticism is pessimistic and world-rejecting. Gnosticism regards the soul as an alien exile in matter, exaggerates the huge gulf separating the soul from the true God, and thus paints a tragic and humiliating image of humanity on earth. The Gnostic negation of this world is essentially at odds with the esoteric principle of continuous correspondences between the macrocosm and microcosm and the fundamental goodness of God's creation.[22]

FURTHER READING

Hermetism

Patrick Boylan, *Thoth: The Hermes of Egypt* (1922; Oxford: Oxford University Press, 1999).

Brian P. Copenhaver, *Hermetica: The Greek* Corpus Hermeticum *and the Latin* Asclepius *in a New English Translation, with Notes and Introduction* (Cambridge: Cambridge University Press, 1992). The introduction (pp. xiii–lxi) is very useful for the historical and cultural background.

Florian Ebeling, *The Secret History of Hermes Trismegistus: Hermeticism from Ancient to Modern Times*, translated from the German by David Lorton (Ithaca: Cornell University Press, 2007).

Antoine Faivre, "Ancient and Medieval Sources of Modern Esoteric Movements," in *Modern Esoteric Spirituality*, edited by Antoine Faivre and Jacob Needleman (London: SCM, 1993), pp. 1–70 (especially pp. 1–29).

———, *The Eternal Hermes: From Greek God to Alchemical Magus* (Grand Rapids, Mich.: Phanes Press, 1995), especially the first three chapters.

Garth Fowden, *The Egyptian Hermes: A Historical Approach to the Late Pagan Mind* (Princeton, N.J.: Princeton University Press, 1986).

Erik Hornung, *The Secret Lore of Egypt: Its Impact on the West*, translated by David Lorton (Ithaca: Cornell University Press, 2001).

G. R. S. Mead, *Thrice-Greatest Hermes: Studies in Hellenistic Theosophy and Gnosis* (1906; York Beach, Maine: Weiser, 2001).

Walter Scott, *Hermetica: The Ancient Greek and Latin Writings Which Contain Religious or Philosophic Teachings ascribed to Hermes Trismegistus*, 4 vols (1924–36; London: Dawsons, 1968).

The Way of Hermes: The Corpus Hermeticum, translated by Clement Salaman, Dorine van Oyen, and William D. Warton (London: Duckworth, 1999), offers an accessible reading text.

Neoplatonism

Charles Bigg, *Neoplatonism* (London: SPCK, 1895).

H. J. Blumenthal, *Neoplatonism and Early Christian Thought* (London: Variorum, 1981).

Konrad Eisenbichler, *Ficino and Renaissance Neoplatonism* (Ottawa: Dovehouse, 1986).

John Gregory, *The Neoplatonists: A Reader*, 2nd ed. (London: Routledge, 1999).

Pierre Hadot and H. D. Saffrey, "Neoplatonist Spirituality," in *Classical Mediterranean Spirituality: Egyptian, Greek, Roman*, edited by A. H. Armstrong (London: Routledge & Kegan Paul, 1986), pp. 230–265.

Hans Lewy, *Chaldaean Oracles and Theurgy: Mysticism, Magic, and Platonism in the Later Roman Empire* (Paris: Etudes Augustiniennes, 1978).

A. C. Lloyd, *The Anatomy of Neoplatonism* (Oxford: Clarendon, 1990).

Philip Merlan, *From Platonism to Neoplatonism* (The Hague: Martinus Nijhoff, 1953).

———, *Monopsychism, Mysticism, Metaconsciousness: Problems of the Soul in the Neo-Aristotelian and Neo-Platonic Tradition* (The Hague: Martinus Nijhoff, 1969).

Parviz Morewedge, *Neoplatonism and Islamic Thought* (Albany: State University of New York Press, 1992).

Ian Richard Netton, *Muslim Neo-Platonists: An Introduction to the Thought of the Brethren of Unity (Ikhwān-al-Safā)* (London: Allen & Unwin, 1982).

Nesca Adeline Robb, *Neo-Platonism of the Italian Renaissance* (London: Allen & Unwin, 1935).

Gregory Shaw, *Theurgy and the Soul: The Neoplatonism of Iamblichus* (University Park: Pennsylvania State University Press, 1995).

D. P. Walker, *The Ancient Theology: Studies in Christian Platonism from the Fifteenth to the Eighteenth Century* (London: Duckworth, 1972).

Richard Tyrell Wallis, *Neoplatonism* (London: Duckworth, 1972).

Thomas Whittaker, *The Neo-Platonists: A Study in the History of Hellenism* (Cambridge: Cambridge University Press, 1918).

Plotinus

Arthur Hilary Armstrong, *The Architecture of the Intelligible Universe in the Philosophy of Plotinus: An Analytical and Historical Study* (Amsterdam: Adolf M. Halekert, 1967).

———, *Plotinus*, 6 vols. (Cambridge, Mass.: Harvard University Press, 1966–1988).

————, *Plotinian and Christian Studies* (London: Variorum, 1979).

H. J. Blumenthal, *Plotinus' Psychology: His Doctrines of the Embodied Soul* (The Hague: Martinus Nijhoff, 1971).

Mark Julian Edwards, *Culture and Philosophy in the Age of Plotinus* (London: Duckworth, 2006).

Eyjolfur Kjalar Emilson, *Plotinus on Intellect* (Oxford: Oxford University Press, 2007).

Lloyd Philip Gerson, *Plotinus* (London: Routledge, 1994).

Kenneth Sylvan Guthrie, *Plotinus: Complete Works* (London: Bell, 1918).

Pierre Hadot, *Plotinus, or, the Simplicity of Vision* (Chicago: Chicago University Press, 1993).

William Ralph Inge, *The Philosophy of Plotinus: The Gifford Lectures, 1917–1918,* 2nd ed. (London: Longman, Green & Co, 1923).

John Michael Rist, *Plotinus: The Road to Reality* (Cambridge: Cambridge University Press, 1967).

Paul E. Walker, *Early Philosophical Shiism: The Ismaili Neoplatonism of Abu Yaqub al-Sijistani* (Cambridge: Cambridge University Press, 1993).

Gnosticism

Ugo Bianchi, *The Origin of Gnosticism: Colloquium of Messina* (Leiden: Brill, 1966).

Roelof van den Broek, *Studies in Gnosticism and Alexandrian Christianity* (Leiden: Brill, 1996).

————, *Studies in Gnosticism and Hellenistic Religion (presented to Gilles Quispel on the occasion of his 65th Birthday)* (Leiden: Brill, 1981).

Francis T. Fallon, *The Enthronement of Sabaoth: Jewish Elements in Gnostic Creation Myths* (Leiden: Brill, 1978).

James K. Feibleman, *Religious Platonism: The Influence of Religion on Plato and the Influence of Plato on Religion* (1959; Westport, Conn.: Greenwood Press, 1971).

Giovanni Filoramo, *A History of Gnosticism* (Oxford: Basil Blackwell, 1990).

Werner Forester, *Gnosis: A Selection of Gnostic Texts.* Vol. 2: *Coptic and Mandean Sources,* edited by R. McL. Wilson (Oxford: Clarendon, 1974).

Clare Goodrick-Clarke and Nicholas Goodrick-Clarke, *G.R.S. Mead and the Gnostic Quest,* Western Esoteric Masters series (Berkeley, Calif.: North Atlantic Books, 2005).

Stephan A. Hoeller, *Gnosticism: New Light on the Ancient Tradition of Inner Knowing* (Wheaton, Ill.: Theosophical Publishing House, 2002).

Hans Jonas, *The Gnostic Religion: The Message of the Alien God and the Beginnings of Christianity* (Boston, Mass.: Beacon Press, 1958).

A. F. J. Klijn, *Seth in Jewish, Christian, and Gnostic Literature* (Leiden: Brill, 1977).

Martin Krause (ed.), *Gnosis and Gnosticism* (Seventh International Conference on Patristic Studies, Oxford, 8–13 September 1975) (Leiden: Brill, 1977).

Alistair H. B. Logan, *Gnostic Truth and Christian Heresy: A Study in the History of Gnosticism* (Edinburgh: T & T Clark, 1996).

————, *The Gnostics: Identifying an Early Christian Cult* (London: T & T Clark, 2006).

Christoph Markschies, *Gnosis: An Introduction* (London: T & T Clark, 2003).

Robert McLachlan, *The Gnostic Problem: A Study of the Relations between Hellenistic Judaism and the Gnostic Heresy* (London: Mowbray, 1958).

Svend Auge Pallis, *Mandaean Studies: A Comparative Inquiry into Mandaeism and Mandaean Writings and Babylonian and Persian Religions, Judaism and Gnosticism* (Amsterdam: Philo Press, 1974).

Birger A. Pearson, *Ancient Gnosticism: Traditions and Literature* (Minneapolis, Minn.: Fortress Press, 2007).

———, *Gnosticism and Christianity in Roman and Coptic Egypt* (London: T & T Clark, 2004).

———, *Gnosticism, Judaism, and Egyptian Christianity* (Minneapolis, Minn.: Fortress Press, 1980).

Carl B. Smith, *No Longer Jews: The Search for Gnostic Origins* (Peabody, Mass.: Hendrickson Publishers, 2004).

John Douglas Turner, *Sethian Gnosticism and the Platonic Tradition* (Quebec: Presses de l'Université Laval, 2001).

Benjamin Walker, *Gnosticism: Its History and Influence* (Wellingborough, Northants: Aquarian Press, 1983).

Michael Allen Williams, *Rethinking "Gnosticism": An Argument for Dismantling a Dubious Category* (Princeton: Princeton University Press, 1996).

2

Italian Renaissance Magic and Cabala

The Byzantine Legacy

The history of Western esotericism in the Middle Ages is largely one of exotic transmission. Following the sack of Rome in A.D. 410, the western part of the empire was engulfed by the mass migration of barbarian peoples, and the Eastern Roman Empire of Byzantium (Constantinople) became the principal channel of classical and Hellenistic civilization. Hellenism had not only assimilated Eastern ideas and religions, but also proved the most durable of all ancient cultures. By Arnold Toynbee's reckoning, the Hellenistic world passed through several eras including the Ptolemies, the Roman Empire, and the advent of Christianity.[1] While the Latin West entered the Dark Ages, Byzantium still basked in the sunny climes of the Greek East and inherited the mantle of the eternal city as the "second Rome." Its pagan schools in Athens remained loyal to the Neoplatonists until the sixth century. As the major regional power across the Balkans, the eastern Mediterranean, and the Near East, Byzantium carried the torch of Alexandrian world culture for a millennium until the final onslaught of the Ottoman Turks from Central Asia in 1453.[2]

However, by the sixth century, the Arabs were an ascendant power on Byzantium's eastern flank, where they settled the Middle East and Egypt. Confronted by the ancient and mysterious cultures of Egypt and Chaldea, Arabian culture swiftly assimilated the esoteric sciences of astrology, alchemy, and magic, all based on ideas of correspondences between the divine, celestial, and earthly spheres. The Arabs were also fascinated by the figure of Hermes Trismegistus, and they produced their own Hermetic literature with revelations of theosophy, astrology, and alchemy. The most famous example, the *Emerald Tablet* (sixth to eighth century A.D.), introduced the motto "As above, so below," which would become well known to the Western world after the fourteenth century.[3]

Michael Psellus, a Byzantine Platonist of the eleventh century, used the Hermetic and Orphic texts to explain the Scriptures. A notable number of medieval scholars including Theoderic of Chartres, Albertus Magnus, Alain of Lille, William of Auvergne, Roger Bacon, Bernard of Treviso, and Hugh of Saint Victor also mentioned Hermes Trismegistus or quoted the *Asclepius*, the only Hermetic treatise known to medieval Europe.[4] Although condemned by church authorities, astrology, alchemy, and ritual magic were all practiced in medieval Europe.[5] Meanwhile, scholastic theology was increasingly divorced from natural philosophy. The growing interest in nature and the sensible world, together with the foundation of the universities and secular study, created an intellectual space within which Platonism and the *Hermetica* could be received in the Latin West.

Geopolitical factors in the Mediterranean world and Near East played a vital part in this process of cultural transfer. As the ascendant Ottoman Turks succeeded the medieval Arab caliphates as the dominant regional power in the Middle East, they increasingly impinged on the old Byzantine or Eastern Roman Empire, which had been the major political and cultural force in southeastern Europe and Anatolia since the fall of Rome. As the Turks pressed on westward across the Greek islands and into the Balkans, the territory of Byzantium began to dwindle. The rich repository of Classical, Greek, and Arab learning, formerly the powerhouse of the Byzantine cultural sphere, also began to shift westward through the movement of refugee intellectuals, churchmen, libraries, manuscripts, and other treasures.[6]

This increased contact with the Greek world of the declining Byzantine Empire in the fifteenth century brought with it a significant philosophical shift in the Latin West, which in turn produced a revised outlook on nature and the heavens and, ultimately, a new vision of man, science, and medicine. This shift in philosophy favored Plato over Aristotle, whose works had formed the mainstay of medieval thought and science following their introduction to the Arab world in the eleventh and twelfth centuries.

The Importance of Florence

The center of this revival of Platonism was Florence, the flourishing Renaissance city which lay in the Tuscan plain. Coluccio Salutati, chancellor of the republic from 1375 until his death in 1406, had played a major role in establishing humanism as the new cultural fashion, thereby boosting Florence's importance throughout Italy. More especially, he recognized the importance of original Greek sources for a deeper understanding of Roman authors. In 1396, he persuaded the Florentine government to appoint Manuel Chrysoloras, the leading Byzantine classical scholar, to teach at the local university. The appointment created a nucleus of humanists who were able to pass on their skills to the next generation for the study and translation of ancient Greek literature.[7]

Thanks to Salutati's initiative, there were sufficient numbers of new Italian Hellenists to receive and articulate the next wave of Greek thought and letters that arrived in Florence from the Byzantine world. In 1438–1439, the Council of Ferrara—moved in midsession to Florence—was held to discuss the reunion of the Eastern Church with Rome. Leading figures in the Byzantine delegation were Georgios Gemistos Plethon (ca. 1355–1452) and John Bessarion of Trebizond (1395–1472), the young patriarch of Nicaea. The elderly Plethon espoused a pagan Platonic philosophy that understood the ancient Greek gods as allegories of divine powers. Bessarion, who later became a cardinal, composed a defense of Plethon and Platonism against the Aristotelian George of Trebizond, who had attacked Plethon's ideas. The ensuing wave of philosophical disputes, together with their translation and discussion among the humanists of Florence, prepared the ground for a major efflorescence of Platonism in the second half of the century.[8]

Wealth and patronage also played an important part in the Platonist revival at Florence. Cosimo de' Medici (1389–1464), the leading merchant-prince of the Florentine republic, played a vital part in the Platonist revival. Building on the power and prestige of his father, Giovanni de' Medici (1360–1429), who realized an immense fortune through banking and trade, Cosimo effectively became the absolute ruler of Florence, while remaining a private citizen of a republic jealous of its liberty. But Cosimo demonstrated royal generosity in his patronage of the arts and letters. In addition to his magnificent palace in the city, he built villas at Careggi, Fiesole, and elsewhere. His ecclesiastical foundations were numerous, including the basilica at Fiesole, the church of San Lorenzo in Florence, and a hospice in Jerusalem for pilgrims. In the world of fine art, he was the patron of Donatello, Brunelleschi, Ghiberti, and Luca della Robbia, whose paintings and sculptures gave full expression to the color and vibrancy of the Renaissance world.[9]

Greek philosophy and learning were especially dear to Cosimo's heart. During the Council of Florence, he frequently entertained Plethon and was deeply impressed by his exposition of Platonist philosophy. Later, after the final collapse of Byzantium to the Ottoman Turks in 1453, many learned Greek refugees from Constantinople found refuge in his palace. Thanks to Cosimo's interest in this Platonist stream of ideas from an exotic and waning world and his capacity for munificent patronage, both Platonism and the *Hermetica* were cultivated and promoted by a gifted circle of young idealists at Florence.[10]

Marsilio Ficino and the Hermetic Revival

Many Florentine thinkers had been attracted by Plethon's claims that all Greek philosophies could be harmonized and that a profound knowledge of Plato could become the basis of religious unity, the very subject under debate at the Council of Florence. But others were more receptive to ideas of a new spirituality. These seekers found in Platonism and the *Hermetica* an inspiration which promised far more than ecclesiastical concord. Prominent among these idealists was the young Florentine humanist called Marsilio Ficino (1433–1499) who, under Cosimo's auspices, became the chief exponent of this revived Platonism and the high priest of the Hermetic secrets within a new Platonic Academy.[11]

The son of a physician, Marsilio Ficino first studied philosophy as part of his own medical studies. The curriculum at the university was still dominated by scholasticism, and the young Ficino was repelled by the naturalism of Aristotle. Its dry statement of material facts could not slake his thirst for spiritual mystery, and its implicit denial of the immortality of the human soul struck at the very root of his search for divine inspiration. In Plato's idea of two coexisting worlds—a higher one of Being that is eternal, perfect, and incorruptible, a sharp contrast to the material world—Ficino found precisely what he had sought. The higher world of Ideas or Forms provided archetypal patterns of everything that existed on the lower mundane plane. The human soul originated in the higher world but is trapped in the body in the lower world, and Plato's writings sometimes describe the return or ascent of the soul to its true, perfect home.

The patron found the idealist. By 1456, Marsilio Ficino had begun to study Greek with a view to examining the original sources of Platonic philosophy, and he translated some texts into Latin. By 1462, Cosimo had given Ficino a villa in Careggi and commissioned him to translate a number of Greek manuscripts. But the new spirituality soon recruited Hermeticism alongside Platonism. Just as Ficino was preparing to translate numerous Platonic dialogues for his master, new Greek wonders arrived from the East. In 1460, a monk, Leonardo da Pistoia, arrived in Florence from Macedonia with a Greek manuscript. Cosimo employed many agents to collect exotic and rare manuscripts for him abroad, and this was one such delivery. However, this particular manuscript contained a copy of the *Corpus Hermeticum*. Gleaning something of its mystical cosmology, the elderly Cosimo was convinced that the *Hermetica* represented a very ancient source of divine revelation and wisdom. In 1463, Cosimo told Ficino to translate the *Hermetica* before continuing his translation of Plato. Within a few months, Ficino had made a translation that Cosimo was able to read.[12]

Until as late as 1610, the works collected as the *Hermetica* were believed to date far back beyond their actual composition in the first two centuries A.D. Ficino and his successors regarded Hermes Trismegistus as a contemporary of Moses, and his teachings were seen as a *philosophia perennis*, a perennial philosophy predating yet anticipating Christianity with its roots in pharaonic Egypt. The diffusion of these ideas can readily be illustrated, even in the Church. Pope Alexander VI (1492–1503) had the Borgia apartments in the Vatican adorned with a fresco full of hermetic symbols and astrological signs. In the entrance to Siena Cathedral, one can still see, in a work on the marble floor dating from 1488, the figure of Hermes Trismegistus as a bearded patriarch.[13] Renaissance writers also regarded the Hermetic treatises as unique memorials of a *prisca theologia* (ancient theology) in the sense of the divine revelation granted to the oldest sages of mankind and handed down through a great chain of initiates. It was generally agreed that Hermes Trismegistus was a principal among these ancient sages together with Moses, Orpheus, Zoroaster, Pythagoras, and others in varying orders of descent.

After translating the *Hermetica,* Ficino resumed work on Plato, and Cosimo was able to read ten of Plato's dialogues before his death in 1464. Ficino completed his translation of the collected works of Plato, the first into any Western language, in 1469, and in the same year he wrote his famous commentary on Plato's *Symposium.*[14] From 1469 to 1474, he worked on his own chief philosophical work, *Platonic Theology.*[15] In late 1473, he became a Catholic priest, and he later held a number of ecclesiastical benefices, eventually becoming a canon of Florence Cathedral. About the same time he began to collect his letters, which give valuable insights into his life and activities over the next twenty years and include some smaller works of philosophy.[16] After 1484, he devoted himself to his translation and commentary of Plotinus, the leading Neoplatonist of antiquity, which was published in 1492.

Although he lived a contemplative life as a scholar and priest, Ficino had a far-reaching influence on the world of Renaissance thought. Encouraged by Cosimo, he had already founded the new Platonic Academy at his villa in Careggi by 1463. Unlike a formal college, the Academy functioned chiefly as a loose circle of friends inspired by the spiritual ideas of Platonism and the *Hermetica*. Accounts of its activities indicate Ficino's desire to found a lay religious community with discussions, orations, and private readings of Plato and other texts with younger disciples. Plato's birthday was celebrated with a banquet at which each

FIGURE 2.1. Giovanni di Stephano, floor intarsia showing Hermes Trismegistus, Plato and Marsilio Ficino (1488), west entrance, Siena Cathedral.

participant made a philosophical speech. Public lectures on Plato and Plotinus were held in a nearby church. Humanists and other distinguished adherents from Italy and abroad frequented the Academy, and Ficino kept up an extensive correspondence with them.[17]

But what was Ficino actually teaching in the Academy? What was so novel and exciting about this newfound spirituality based on the new reception of Platonism and the *Hermetica*? The answers to these questions lie in Ficino's cosmology and the role in it that he assigned to the human soul. His model of the universe was derived from Neoplatonic and medieval sources, essentially a great hierarchy in which each being has its assigned place and degree of perfection. God was at the top of this hierarchy, which descended through the orders of angels, the planets, and the elements to the various species of animals, plants, and minerals.

This cosmology, itself the historical product of ancient and medieval speculation, had long remained essentially static. Within the hierarchy, each degree
was merely distinct from the next by some gradation of attributes. Through
his Platonic emphasis on the soul as the messenger between the two worlds,
Ficino introduced a new dynamic into the traditional cosmology. He revived the
Neoplatonic doctrine of the world soul to suggest that all the parts and degrees
of the hierarchy were linked and held together by the active forces and affinities of an all-pervading spirit. In his scheme, astrology was intrinsic to a natural
system of mutual influences between the planets and the human soul.[18]

But prime of place was granted to the human soul in Ficino's cosmology.
Ficino taught that thought had an influence upon its objects. In Plato's
Symposium, Socrates identifies love as an active force that holds all things
together. Ficino attributed the active influence of thought and love to the
human soul, which could reach out and embrace all things in the universe.
This magical equivalence between each human soul and the world soul thus
became the hallmark of Renaissance Neoplatonism. By placing the human
soul, like a droplet of divinity, at the center of the universe, Ficino initiated
a fundamental spiritual revolution in man's self-regard. Within his dynamic
cosmology, the soul thus combined in itself everything, knew everything,
and possessed the powers of everything in the universe.

This cosmology was not just a formal intellectual model but rather a map
for the travels and ascent of one's own soul. In his emphasis on the inner, contemplative life, Ficino gave a personal and practical slant to his theory of the
soul. Through meditation, Ficino believed, the soul exchanged its commerce
with the mundane and material things of this outer world for a new contact with
the spiritual aspects of the incorporeal and intelligible world of higher planes.
Such spiritual knowledge is unobtainable as long as one's soul is enmeshed
in ordinary experience and the noisy concerns of this troubled world. In these
lower states of consciousness, the soul is barely awakened. But once the attention is directed inward, the soul begins to ascend the spiritual hierarchy of the
cosmos, all the while learning and interacting with higher spiritual entities.

Ficino always presented these mystical exercises and ascent experiences as
journeys of the soul toward higher degrees of truth and being, culminating in
the direct knowledge and vision of God. This initiatory aspect of Ficino's philosophy certainly helps to explain the intense attraction his ideas held for the
Academy audiences. His listeners felt their souls were being invited to join in a
cosmic voyage of spiritual exploration, an ascent toward the godhead, and a vision of universal truth. Ficino never doubted that his thought was Christian. For
him, Jesus Christ was the exemplar of human spiritual fulfillment. His Christianity was, of course, a more esoteric, elite, spiritualized form of religion than

that proffered to the credulous masses by the friars. Ficino saw himself as a phy-sician of the soul, guiding his students on a path that could free them from the dross of this world and open their spirits to the dazzling radiance of divinity.[19]

Natural or Spiritual Magic

Ascent experiences implied wisdom, but the magic of the *Hermetica* offered power over nature. Ficino was deeply impressed by the Hermetic treatise known as *Asclepius*, in which ancient Egyptian priests described how, to make the common people believers in the gods, they invested their statues with di-vine properties. Ficino comments that he once, like Aquinas, had thought this something demonic. Now, following Hermes Trismegistus and Plotinus, he thinks of this process as a channeling of celestial powers or virtues inherent in herbs, trees, stones, or fragrances, which are themselves emanations of the divine. Thus the principle of magic is indivisible from Neoplatonic cosmology in which the power of the godhead is diffused from its point of origin through a hierarchy of planes, in which each piece of creation assimilates a virtue that defines it and is special to itself.[20]

Ficinian spirit-magic is preeminently astrological as the occult virtues in all things and creatures resonate primarily with the virtue of their governing star or planetary body. The successful magician who wishes to capture the power of Venus must therefore know what plants belonged to Venus, the appropriate stones, met-als, and other objects, and bring all these to bear in an invocation of the planet. The magician should know the signs of Venus and how these are to be marked on talismans made of Venus materials and at a suitable astrological time.[21]

Ficino made widespread use of this form of sympathetic magic. His major treatise on the subject, *De vita coelitus comparanda*, was recommended especially to scholars, whose book-learning and concentration render them susceptible to melancholy and the influence of Saturn, which is also the planet of the melancholy temperament and the star most opposed to the vital forces of youth. Ficino advises such melancholy subjects to avoid all contact with stones, herbs, plants, and ani-mals under the sign of Saturn. Instead, they should expose themselves to plants, animals, and herbs belonging to the more fortunate, cheerful, and life-giving plan-ets, the Sun, Jupiter, and Venus. Ficino praises gold as a metal abundant in Solar and Jovial spirit, whose astral influences can greatly relieve melancholy. The color green is also beneficial in this respect, and Ficino suggests walks in the country-side, where one may pluck roses or the crocus, the golden flower of Jupiter.[22]

Francesco da Diacetto, a close disciple of Ficino, describes a Ficinian rit-ual in which the magician seeks to direct a powerful channel of solar energies.

Robed in a mantle of solar color, such as gold, the subject should burn incense made from solar plants before an altar adorned with an image of the sun enthroned and crowned, wearing a saffron cloak. Anointed with unguents made from solar materials, he sings an Orphic hymn to the Sun. This concentration of solar properties and influences in the lower, mundane world serves as a kind of lens to focus the solar influences from the higher, astral world. The solar aspect of the various creatures, images, and artifacts attracts the downpouring of solar energy from the Sun and concentrates it around the figure of the magician.[23]

D. P. Walker has shown how Ficino was greatly concerned to distinguish his spiritual magic from the old-fashioned demonic magic of the medieval period. Ficino laid great emphasis on music in his theory of magic. He suggested that the physical medium of musical notes, air, resembled lightly embodied spiritual substances (like the lower soul). As the strings of a lyre could resonate with the cosmic tones of planets and stars, so the magus could communicate with these celestial powers through music.[24] In Ficino's view, this kind of spiritual magic was quite distinct from the demonic magic practiced by magicians through invocations to nonhuman agents. However, there remained a tension in Ficino's theory, as he sang Orphic hymns in accompaniment to his music. He also believed that demons, both good and bad, were associated with the planets and their constant influence on the human body, spirit, and soul.

Ficino's ideas of sympathetic magic indicated a new relationship between man and nature. Just as the Neoplatonic scheme of divine inspiration from God through the hierarchies of creation created a ladder of being, so man was a microcosm who combined within himself all the powers, virtues, and properties of the natural world, or macrocosm, around him. The intermediate position of the human soul in the ladder of being thus enabled man to interact with intention and design upon the world of nature.

Marsilio Ficino effected a major revival of Neoplatonism and Hermetism in his time. His doctrines of the soul and sympathetic magic opened up a new vista of the cosmos and man's ability to channel the powers of nature for his own benefit. As Ficino lectured and conducted magical rites at his Academy, his audiences eagerly embraced the promise of spiritual elevation and communion with astral powers.

Pico della Mirandola and the Cabala

Giovanni Pico della Mirandola (1463–1494), a young contemporary of Ficino, developed an even more powerful variety of Renaissance magic by introducing the Jewish Kabbalah into Western thought. Pico's wealth, nobility, personal charm, and handsome face have combined with his precocious brilliance and early death to make him one of the famous figures of the Renaissance. Unlike Ficino, the retiring cleric and scholar, Pico led a varied life within the few years granted to him. His ambitious claims for Renaissance magic initially brought him into conflict with various theologians, and his work was condemned by Pope Innocent VIII. He is most famous for his *Oration on the Dignity of Man* (1487), which proclaims the centrality, importance, and freedom of man in the universe.

Pico was a younger son in the family of the counts of Mirandola and Concordia, who ruled as feudal lords over a small territory in northern Italy. Destined by his mother for a Church career, he was named papal protonotary at the age of ten and began to study canon law at Bologna in 1477, at age thirteen. Two years later, he commenced the study of philosophy at the University of Ferrara, subsequently moving in 1482 to the University of Padua, one of the leading Aristotelian centers. Here he was the pupil of the Jewish philosopher Elia del Medigo. At this time he was in touch with humanist scholars in different places, and he visited Florence repeatedly, where he met Ficino. He spent the following years at home and on various visits, while continuing the study of Greek. In 1486, he returned to Florence, but, after becoming involved in a strange love affair, he moved to Perugia, where he studied Hebrew and Arabic under the guidance of several Jewish teachers, including the mysterious Flavius Mithridates.[25]

This period marked the beginning of his interest in the Jewish Kabbalah, a medieval mystical and speculative tradition that claimed an ancient origin but was in fact much influenced by Neoplatonism. Pico's Christian Cabala (the Latin term was usual among Renaissance Christian writers) was based on the tradition developed by Jews in Spain during the Middle Ages. Although the Jews were not finally expelled from Spain until 1492, their persecution by the Catholic authorities there had already encouraged many to flee to France and Italy. Pico learned the Kabbalah direct from the Spanish Jew Flavius Mithridates and others. This cultural transfer of Jewish wisdom from the West comparable to the earlier import of Greek learning from the East enabled Pico to immerse himself in this Jewish mystical and magical system.

This medieval Jewish Kabbalah was based on the ten *sephiroth* and the twenty-two letters of the Hebrew alphabet. The doctrine of the *sephiroth* was first laid down in the Book of Creation (*Sefer Yetzirah*), dating back to the third century A.D., when Greek Jews were also receptive to the Neoplatonist currents of late antiquity. In the twelfth and thirteenth centuries, a particular esoteric teaching emerged in Provence and northern Spain with the Book of Illumination (*Sefer Bahir*), composed by Isaac the Blind (fl. 1190–1210). This Kabbalah interpreted the *sefiroth* as powers of God arranged in a specific structure. The *Bahir* was also the first text to describe the *sefiroth* as a "tree of emanation," which from the fourteenth century onward was depicted in a detailed diagram widely familiar today as the Tree of Life. The *Bahir* also aided the development of speculative Kabbalah based on the *sefiroth* as cosmic principles arranged in a primal group of three major emanations above a lower group of seven. The doctrine was developed further in the Book of Splendor (*Sefer Zohar*), written in Spain during the thirteenth century, which represents the tradition adopted by Pico. The *sephiroth* are the ten names or expressions of God, and the created universe is seen as the external manifestation of these forces. This creative aspect of the *sephiroth* links them to cosmology, and there is a relationship between the ten *sephiroth* and the ten spheres of the cosmos, composed of the spheres of the seven planets, the sphere of fixed stars, and the higher spheres beyond these.[26]

The ten *sephiroth* are arranged in a cosmological system known as the Tree of Life, whose structure provides for twenty-two pathways between the various spheres. These pathways correspond to the letters of the Hebrew alphabet but also denote angels or divine spirits which act as intermediaries throughout the system and are themselves arranged in hierarchies. Similarly, there are also bad angels or demons, organized in hierarchies corresponding to their good opposites. Jewish Kabbalistic mysticism was also connected with the Scriptures through three kinds of exegetical techniques based on manipulations of the words and letters of the Hebrew text, known as *gematria, notarikon,* and *themurah.* These ideas derived from the *Ginnat Egoz* (*Garden of Nuts*), written in 1274 by the Castilian Joseph ben Abraham Gikatilla (ca. 1247–1305), a pupil of the famous Kabbalist Abraham ben Samuel Abulafia (1240–ca. 1292), who had introduced an ecstatic Kabbalah whereby the *sefiroth* led on to the mystical contemplation to the Divine Names of the Creator. These exercises were typically mystical, but there was also a magical side to Kabbalah. As a means of approaching the *sephiroth*, seventy-two angels could be invoked by a person who knew their names and numbers, and these were also efficient if Hebrew words, letters, or signs were suitably arranged.

Pico discerned a wonderful symmetry between the Kabbalah and Hermeticism. The Egyptian lawgiver Hermes Trismegistus had revealed mystical teachings, including an account of Creation which hinted at his knowledge of Moses' wisdom. In Pico's view, the Kabbalah offered a further body of mystical doctrine, supposedly derived from the Hebrew lawgiver, and a parallel view on cosmology. Armed with a greater knowledge of Hebrew than any other non-Jewish scholar and his burning interest in the Kabbalah, Pico set down a new synthesis of Hermetic-Cabalistic magic in twenty-six "Magical Conclusions."

Here Pico dismissed medieval magic as the work of the devil but praised "natural magic" as a legitimate establishment of links between heaven and earth by the proper use of natural substances as recommended by the principles of sympathetic magic (Magical Conclusion 1). He went on to recommend Orphic incantations for magical purposes (Magical Conclusion 2), evidently referring to Ficino's magic, whose practices he already knew well through the Academy at Florence.[27]

Flushed with confidence in the powers of Cabala, Pico then described the limitations of Ficinian practice. Pico regarded Ficino's natural magic as a weak and ineffective form of magic unless it was combined with Cabala (Magical Conclusion 15). Similarly, he held that no powerful magic could be performed without a knowledge of Hebrew (Magical Conclusion 22) and even dismissed the Orphic singing for magical operations in the absence of Cabala (Magical Conclusion 21). In his Cabalistic Conclusions and *Apology* (1487), Pico distinguishes between various forms of Cabala. "Speculative Cabala" he divides into four types: first, the mystical manipulation of letters, followed by the exploration of the three worlds—the sensible or terrestrial world, the celestial world of the stars, and the supercelestial world of the *sephiroth* and the angels.[28]

These latter categories were of prime importance to Pico's magic. Pico asserts that this kind of Cabala is a "way of capturing the powers of superior things" and is "the supreme part of natural magic." Whereas natural magic aims no higher than the terrestrial world and the stars, Cabala can be used to operate beyond in the supercelestial spheres of the angels, archangels, the *sephiroth* and God. Natural magic uses characters, but Cabala uses numbers through its use of letters (Magical Conclusion 25). Natural magic uses only intermediary causes, the stars. Cabala goes straight to the first cause, God himself (Magical Conclusion 26).[29]

Pico elaborates in his *Apology* how cabalists may use the secret Hebrew names of God and names of angels, invoking them in the powerful Hebrew language or by magical combinations of the sacred Hebrew alphabet. Just as there are superior spirits on these higher planes, higher spiritual beings, great demons also inhabit these regions. Pico solemnly warns the cabalist to work in a spirit of piety (Magical Conclusion 6). In his seventy-two Cabalistic Conclusions, Pico demonstrates his detailed knowledge of the Jewish system. He writes that the Cabalist can communicate with God through the archangels in an ecstasy that may result in the death of the body, a way of dying known as the "Death of the Kiss" (Cabalistic Conclusion 11). He sets out a table which shows the correspondences between the ten spheres of the cosmos and the ten *sephiroth* (Cabalistic Conclusion 48). He also describes the states of the soul in relation to the meanings of the ten *sephiroth* (such as unity, intellect, reason) and traditionally links the highest *sephiroth* with the lowest in a circular arrangement (Cabalistic Conclusion 66).[30]

The *Oration on the Dignity of Man*

Pico's famous *Oration on the Dignity of Man* was written as an introduction to his nine hundred theses, which he took with him to Rome in 1486 in order to engage in a great public debate. The *Oration* has rightly been regarded as a masterpiece of rhetoric, celebrating the newfound independence and confidence of Renaissance man. Pico's statement marks the sea-change between the medieval mind and the modern mind, the tremendous growth in man's sense of autonomy and dignity which had grown up with humanism. The *Oration* also rejects as inadequate the traditional grounds for Man's importance in the world: his reason, or his place as the microcosm. Pico claims that Man's true greatness lies in his freedom to become whatever he wants to be. Both animals and angels have their fixed place in the universe and are powerless to change their natures. But God gave to Man, alone of all creatures, no fixed abode, form, or function. Free of such limitations, he has the power to change and develop, to make and mould himself.[31]

What was the ultimate goal of man's existential freedom? Imagining God addressing Adam, Pico attributes to Man the power to be reborn into the higher forms. Pico opens the *Oration* with the quotation: "A great miracle, Asclepius, is man." Whereas the Fathers of the Church had placed man in a dignified position as the highest of terrestrial beings, as a spectator of the universe, Pico was citing the Hermetic text *Asclepius* with its promise of man's equality with the gods: "Man is a miracle, a living thing to be worshipped and honored: for he changes his nature into a god's, as if he were a god. . . . Conjoined to the gods by a kindred divinity, he despises inwardly that part of him in which he is earthly."[32]

Introducing the contents of his nine hundred theses, Pico ranges over all the philosophers and mysteries he has studied. A keynote of his *philosophia nova* is an attempt to establish a concordance or correlation between all ancient philosophies in support of a pristine theology (*prisca theologia*). A tribute to his precocious learning (he was only twenty-four), the names of the Latins Duns Scotus, Thomas Aquinas, Giles of Rome, Franciscus de Mayronis, Albertus Magnus, and Henry of Ghent are followed by the Arabs Avicenna, Averroes, and al-Farabi. Further back among the ancients he invokes the Greek Peripatetics and then the Neoplatonists Plotinus, Porphyry, Iamblichus, and Proclus. At the very source of the ancient wisdom stand Pythagoras, Mercurius Trismegistus,

Zoroaster, and the "Hebrew Cabalist wisemen," whose knowledge, Pico asserts, was later detected by al-Kindi, Roger Bacon, and William of Paris.[33] However, the great themes of Magia and Cabala echo through the *Oration*. The "ancient theology of Hermes Trismegistus" and "the occult mysteries of the Hebrews" offer the prime means of man's promotion to the divine realms. "As the farmer weds his elms to vines, even so does the magus wed earth to heaven." The *Oration* alludes to esoteric knowledge known only to the few. Pico speaks of occult Hebraic law, vouchsafed only to initiates, and he recalls the symbolism of the sphinxes on Egyptian temples, indicating that mystic doctrines should be kept secret from the common herd.[34]

Pico's subsequent career was turbulent. As soon as he published his nine hundred theses, several Roman theologians raised an outcry about their heretical character, and Pope Innocent VIII appointed a commission to examine them. Pico was summoned to appear several times before this commission, and several of the theses were condemned. Undaunted, in May 1487 Pico published, together with part of the *Oration*, an apologia defending the condemned theses. This challenge involved him in fresh difficulties, and bishops with inquisitorial powers were appointed to deal with his case. In July, Pico made a formal submission and retraction to the commission, and in August the pope issued a bull condemning all the theses and forbidding their publication. Lorenzo de' Medici interceded for Pico with the pope, and Pico was thereafter permitted to live in Florence under Medici protection. On 17 November 1494, the day the armies of King Charles VIII of France entered Florence, Pico died of a fever. He was thirty-one.[35]

Ficino and Pico were seminal figures in the revival of Hermeticism, Neoplatonism, magic, and Kabbalah in Renaissance Europe. Their interest in the power of sympathetic and Cabalistic magic to effect changes in nature signal a new appreciation of man's ability to operate on the mundane world through the knowledge and application of correspondences between the higher and lower worlds. As Frances Yates has suggested, this attitude anticipates the exploration and confidence of natural science. However, their emphasis on the hierarchy of spiritual intermediaries in the form of attributes, letters, numbers, and the transmutation of the soul indicate that this philosophy of nature was intimately bound up with religious experience and an approach to God. Renaissance magic is thus a form of sacred science.

FURTHER READING

Michael J. B. Allen, "Marsilio Ficino," in *Dictionary of Gnosis and Western Esotericism*,
    edited by Wouter Hanegraaff et al., 2 vols. (Leiden: Brill, 2005), Vol. 1, pp. 360–367.

———, *The Platonism of Marsilio Ficino* (Berkeley: University of California Press, 1984).

M. J. B. Allen and Valery Rees (eds.), *Marsilio Ficino: His Theology, His Philosophy, His Legacy* (Leiden: Brill, 2002).

Ernst Cassirer, Paul Oskar Kristeller, and John Herman Randall (eds.), *The Renaissance Philosophy of Man*, selections in translation (Chicago: University of Chicago Press, 1956).

Stephen Alan Farmer, *Syncretism in the West: Pico's 900 Theses (1486)*, Medieval and Renaissance Studies 167 (Tempe: Arizona State University Press, 1998).

Marsilio Ficino, *Book of Life*, translated by Charles Boer (Woodstock, Conn.: Spring, 1996).

———, *Commentary on Plato's Symposium on Love* (Woodstock, Conn.: Spring, 1985).

———, *Meditations on the Soul: Selected Letters of Marsilio Ficino* (Rochester, Vt.: Inner Traditions International, 1997).

Christian D. Ginsburg, *The Kabbalah: Its Doctrines, Development, and Literature* (London: George Routledge, 1920).

James Hankins, *Plato in the Italian Renaissance*, 2 vols. (Leiden: Brill, 1990).

Paul Oskar Kristeller, *Eight Philosophers of the Renaissance* (Stanford, Calif.: Stanford University Press, 1993), chaps. 3 and 4 on Ficino and Pico.

———, *Renaissance Thought: The Classic, Scholastic, and Humanist Strains* (New York: Harper Torchbooks, 1961).

———, *Renaissance Thought II: Papers on Humanism and the Arts* (New York: Harper Torchbooks, 1965), chaps. 4–6.

John Monfasani, *Byzantine Scholars in Renaissance Italy: Cardinal Bessarion and Other Émigrés* (Aldershot: Variorum, 1995).

Charles G. Nauert, *Humanism and the Culture of Renaissance Europe* (Cambridge: Cambridge University Press, 1995).

Jean Seznec, *The Survival of the Pagan Gods: The Mythological Tradition and Its Place in Renaissance Humanism and Art* (1940, 1953; Princeton, N.J.: Princeton University Press, 1972).

Gershom Scholem, *Kabbalah* (New York: Penguin/Meridian, 1978).

———, *Major Trends in Jewish Mysticism* (New York: Schocken, 1941).

———, *On the Kabbalah and Its Symbolism* (New York: Schocken, 1965).

———, *Origins of the Kabbalah*, ed. R. J. Werblowsky, translated by A. Arkush (Princeton, N.J.: Princeton University Press, 1990).

Angela Voss, *Marsilio Ficino*, Western Esoteric Masters series (Berkeley, Calif.: North Atlantic Books, 2006).

D. P. Walker, *Spiritual and Demonic Magic from Ficino to Campanella* (Stroud: Sutton, 2000), esp. pp. 3–59.

Frances A. Yates, *Giordano Bruno and the Hermetic Tradition* (Chicago: University of Chicago Press, 1964), chaps. 1–5.

———, *The Occult Philosophy in the Elizabethan Age* (London: Routledge & Kegan Paul, 1979), chap. 2.

3

Planetary and Angel Magic in the Renaissance

Johannes Reuchlin

Although Ficino carefully distinguished spiritual or natural magic from the demonic magic of invocations, this distinction was not generally made by the later scholar magicians of the sixteenth century. This chapter will focus on Henry Cornelius Agrippa in the Holy Roman Empire and John Dee in Elizabethan England as representative figures of the more elaborate esoteric systems which employed more syncretic forms of Hermeticism (the variant term signifying a broader range of Renaissance esoteric traditions alongside the *prisca theologia* of Alexandrine Hermetism) blended with Neoplatonism, Neopythagoreanism, magic, astrology, alchemy and Cabala.

Renaissance Hermeticism and Cabala first entered Germany through the work of the famous Hebrew scholar Johann Reuchlin (1455–1522), whose interests and travels in Italy predate Agrippa's own path of discovery by some two decades.[1] It was as a young jurist in the retinue of Duke Eberhard of Württemberg that Reuchlin first visited Florence in 1482 and met Ficino, with whom he later maintained a correspondence. Reuchlin began studying Hebrew in 1486, but it was not until he met Pico on his second visit to Italy, in 1490, that his interests turned markedly toward the study of Cabala as a powerful magical system based on the Hebrew language. In his first cabalistic study, *De verbo mirifico* (1494), Reuchlin refers to his inspiration by Pico, declaring that "in Orpheus, Pythagoras, and Plato, there were no other secrets so occult and hidden as their divine Hebraic names of virtue."[2] Through this book, Cabala was launched in the German-speaking world as a divine key to wonder-working magic. The book presents a discussion among Sidonius, an Epicurean, Baruch, a Jew, and Capnion (Reuchlin's personal Greek name), a Christian, about miracles, the power of words and figures, secret rites, and holy names. They conclude that, for a word to be magically powerful on a magical level, it must be in Hebrew as the oldest language. Like Pico, Reuchlin used Cabala as a means of vindicating Christianity as the true religion based on an esoteric interpretation of Hebrew mystical lore. He was particularly interested in showing how the Tetragrammaton, יהוה [YHVH], the unutterable name of God sacred to the Jews had, by the insertion of the letter שׁ [S], given rise to the fulfillment of Holy Scripture by producing the Christian *Pentagrammaton*, the name of Jesus, יהשׁוה [YHSVH]. In this and a number of other manipulations of Jewish letters, typical of Jewish Kabbalistic practice, Reuchlin offered a Christian Cabala as a hermeneutic device to prove that Christianity was the logical and historical fulfillment of Jewish prophecy and conviction. Reuchlin reproduced the Kabbalistic tree of life, albeit with some errors on the order and names of the *sefiroth*, and his work made a vital contribution to the Renaissance debate on the magical powers and virtues of words. Reuchlin was a towering figure in German humanist circles, and his thoughts on magic further influenced Trithemius and Agrippa, who both became important representatives of Renaissance magic in northern Europe.

Johann Trithemius and Angel Magic

Johann Trithemius (1462–1516), famous as the young abbot of the Benedictine monastery of Sponheim, was interested in alchemy and magic. He had left home early to pursue learning, and he studied at Heidelberg, where he associated with some of the foremost German humanists, including Johann von Dalberg, Conrad Celtis, and Johann Reuchlin. From the latter he received advanced instruction in Greek and Hebrew, which in turn gave him access to the mysteries of Pythagoras, Hermes Trismegistus, and the Kabbalah. In 1482, he became a novice at the abbey of St. Martin at Sponheim in the diocese of Mainz, and a year later he was named as abbot, an office he held until 1505, taking over as abbot of the monastery of St. Jacob at Würzburg from 1506 and serving there until his death in 1516. While devoting himself to studies of monastic reform, mystical theology, ecclesiastical history, and Christian humanism, he was also exploring the occult arts in terms of natural and angelic magic.[3]

FIGURE 3.1. First representation of the sefirotic tree in print, in Joseph Gikatilla, *Portae lucis,* translated by Paulus Ricius (Augsburg: Johann Miller, 1513). Courtesy of Bibliotheca Philosophica Hermetica, Amsterdam.

In 1499, Trithemius inadvertently revealed these interests by writing a letter to a Carmelite monk about a treatise he was writing on steganography, the art of writing secret messages and transmitting them. This treatise, titled *Steganographia* (ca. 1500, first published 1606), contained many numerological and astrological calculations connected with angels as well as instructions on how to summon them, to gain knowledge, and how to send messages over long distances by means of angelic agency. However, the letter arrived shortly after the monk's death and was intercepted by his unsympathetic prior, who publicly reviled Trithemius's speculations as illicit demonic magic. Trithemius's reputation as practicing black magic was reinforced when Carolus Bovillus, a French scholar visiting Sponheim, also condemned steganography and denounced his host as a demonic magician.

The three books of *Steganographia* deal with the names, sigils, prayers, and invocations of progressively more powerful spirits. Book One describes the spirits of the air, which are difficult and dangerous because of their arrogance and rebelliousness. Book Two covers the spirits of each hour of the day and night, while Book Three deals with operations with the angels and spirits of the seven planets. These spirits are invoked by prayers and incantations over an image of the spirit at the astrologically appropriate time.[4] Trithemius authored other major esoteric works, including *Polygraphia* (1508), a collection of ciphers and magical alphabets, a subject of intense interest to Renaissance intellectuals and *Veterum Sophorum Sigilla et Imagines Magicae,* a related work on sigils and magical images.

Ultimately, Trithemius's notoriety was confused with that of Doctor Faustus, as in the legend that he was summoned by Emperor Maximilian to demonstrate his necromantic powers, whereupon he conjured from the dead, together with various ancient heroes, Maximilian's late wife Mary of Burgundy to advise the emperor on his choice of a new spouse.[5] But Trithemius's work was much more than a variety of operational magic and built on the union of theology and natural magic found in the works of the great medieval scholar Albertus Magnus (1193–1280), while elaborating on the power of angels and Hebrew names derived from Pico and Reuchlin. His major magical text, *De septem secundeis* (1508), combined astrology and Cabala in a theory of occult influences based on the same system of seven planetary angels employed in his controversial steganographical treatise. *De septem secundeis* is a detailed account of the Planetary Intelligences, the "seven secondary causes" that rule the cycle of the ages, namely the Platonic Month of 2,480 terrestrial years during which the equinox precesses through each sign of the zodiac. Trithemius postulated that each Platonic Year was presided over by a succession of seven Angels of the Planetary Hierarchy, thus dividing it into equal periods of 354 years and four months. According to Trithemius, the Age of Samael would end in 1525, when the Age of Gabriel would begin, and that age would end in 1879 with the Age of Michael, our present age, which would last until 2233. Trithemius indicated how major political and religious changes corresponded

FIGURE 3.2. Portrait of Johannes Trithemius from Sigismund of Seeon, *Trithemius sui ipsius vindex sive Steganographiae* (Ingolstadt, 1616).

to each change in planetary governor. His underlying thesis is that God, the first intellect, delegated the governance of the lower world to seven secondary intelligences corresponding to the seven planets, each of which ruled for a fixed period governing the course of human history. Trithemius's writings

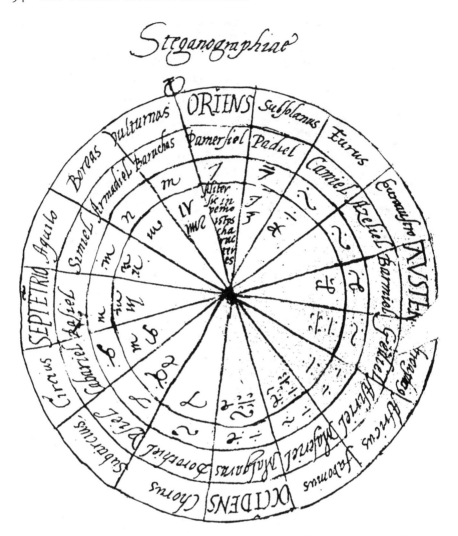

FIGURE 3.3. Folio from MS. of *Steganographiæ*. Courtesy of National Library of Scotland Adv. Ms. 18.2.12.

give a theological and religious justification of magical operations with spirits, demons, and angels.

As his intellectual biographer Noel Brann shows, Trithemius not only conceived of a cosmological context for a philosophy of history, but also suggested a rationale for predicting the future. In *De septem secundeis*, Trithemius suggests that prophecy was an extension of history into the future or that "history is consummated prophecy."[6] The idea of planetary angels and their governance of time cycles can be found in the work of Rudolf Steiner (1861–1925), who combined Theosophy and Christian esotericism in his twentieth-century movement of Anthroposophy (see chapter 12).

In the winter of 1509–1510, Henry Cornelius Agrippa studied closely with Trithemius in Würzburg. In this tapestry of influences we see how the ideas of Ficino and, especially, Pico della Mirandola entered Germany through Reuchlin, whose own works and seminal influence on Trithemius would eventually send Agrippa back to Italy in search of firsthand contact with Kabbalistic initiates.

Henry Cornelius Agrippa

Henry Cornelius Agrippa von Nettesheim (1486–1535) was born in Cologne, the son of upper bourgeoisie or lesser nobility. Little is known of his early life, save that he made rapid and impressive academic progress. In 1499, he matriculated at Cologne University, and he was admitted to the baccalaureate in 1500 and proceeded to the licentiate in 1502 (at age sixteen). At this time, Cologne University was one of the great centers of Thomism, and the arts faculty was split between the dominant Thomists and the Albertists, who preferred the authority of the great native doctor, Albertus Magnus. It is likely that Agrippa drew his interest in the natural world and the occult connections between its parts from this Albertist influence. Agrippa himself traced his magical studies back to his earliest youth, naming Albertus's *Speculum* as one of his first study texts. Since Trithemius was also influenced by Albertus's combination of theology and natural magic, we see that Agrippa's mind was prepared from his earliest studies onward for this kind of magical theology.[7]

Academic opportunities soon opened for Agrippa, once he sought the patronage of Margaret of Austria (1480–1530), governor of Franche-Comté and the Low Countries, and Antoine de Vergy, archbishop of Besançon and chancellor of the University of Dôle. The latter enabled Agrippa to give a course at Dôle on Reuchlin's *De verbo mirifico*. Here Agrippa would have been able to show how Reuchlin quoted Pico's "Cabalistic Conclusions," repeated the names of the *sefiroth* in Hebrew, and showed great interest in the Hebrew names of angels and in how to summon them. As we have already seen, Reuchlin also gave the cabalistic proof that Jesus is the name of the Messiah, being the Tetragrammaton with an S inserted, an argument already given by Pico. Agrippa was granted a paid professorship and gave his lectures gratis in honor of Margaret of Austria. Shortly afterward, and probably again to impress Margaret, he composed *De nobilitate et praecellentia foeminei sexus*, a short work that used cabalistic ideas to prove the superiority of women.[8]

De occulta philosophia

Agrippa returned to Germany at the end of 1509 or the beginning of 1510. He stayed with Trithemius at Würzburg during that winter, and on 8 April 1510 he penned the dedication of *De occulta philosophia*, his first and most famous major work on magic, to Trithemius. This treatise, which the author would add to throughout his life, shows how deeply Agrippa had immersed himself in the study of magic. His conversations with Trithemius had encouraged him to collect together his wide knowledge of magical lore, to seek to redeem magic from its ill repute by purging it of dangerous and superstitious elements, and finally to write a treatise on magic or occult philosophy. This version does not represent the more extensive form in which the book was published two decades later. Trithemius praised his young friend's efforts highly and urged him to continue his studies but, mindful of his own experience, warned Agrippa that such matters must be communicated only to trusted associates. *De occulta philosophia* circulated only in manuscript until the printing of Book One in 1531 and was not published in the full three books until 1533.[9]

In the first two chapters of the work, Agrippa lays down the outline. The universe is divided into three worlds, each of which corresponds to a different book of *De occulta philosophia:* the elemental world, the celestial world, and the intellectual or supercelestial world. Each world receives influences from the one above it: so that the virtue of the Creator descends through the angels in the intellectual or supercelestial world, to the stars in the celestial world, and thence to the elements and all things composed of them in the terrestrial world. Book One (the elemental world) is about natural magic, or magic in the elemental world: it teaches how to arrange substances in accordance with the occult sympathies between them, so as to effect operations through natural magic. Here Agrippa describes the nature and virtues of things, the planets and their sympathies and influences, the passions of the soul, humanity, human nature, and the relationship of human beings as microcosm to macrocosm.[10]

Book Two is about celestial magic, or how to attract and use the influences of the planets and stars. In this celestial world, Agrippa stresses the importance of number and calls this kind of magic mathematical magic. Accordingly, he enumerates in complex charts on a scale of one to twelve the names of thrones, powers, virtues, angels, planets, metals, precious stones, the senses, the *sephiroth* and the Hebraic Names of God.[11] Again influenced by Cabala, he expounds *notaricon*, the numerical value of the Hebrew letters and their mystical meanings as well as the related sciences of astrology, musical harmony, proportion and measure, and cosmology.

In Book Three (the supercelestial world), Agrippa discusses ceremonial magic or magic directed toward the supercelestial world of the angelic spirits, beyond which is the Creator himself. Here he presents religion in its relation to magic and the dependence of the magus on God for his knowledge. Echoing the principles of the *Hermetica*, Agrippa speaks of man's mind as a mirror of eternity and asserts that by the application of natural and celestial virtues "the soul of man ascendeth up into the divine nature, and is made a worker of miracles." Agrippa wrote here at length about angels and demons and demonstrated a clear belief in the efficacy of magical practice and theurgic invocation. His presentation of Cabala was strongly Christian for he asserted that all the magical sciences have only value as partial expressions of truth, which is alone revealed by God in Christian faith. Whatever knowledge we have is a gift of God and cannot be attained exclusively by our own efforts. Here Agrippa was also reiterating the Christian Cabala of Pico and Reuchlin, especially the idea that the name of Jesus was the final mystery providing the power to perform miracles.[12]

Agrippa was thus already versed in cabalistic, Neoplatonic, patristic, and biblical learning prior to his departure for Italy in 1511. For the next seven years he would immerse himself in political and military adventures. Agrippa was in military service to Emperor Maximilian, who at this period was allied with the French in opposition to Venice and Pope Julius II. After reaching Verona, he traveled westward and spent much of that year near Novara, at Pavia, at Casale Monferrato, at Vercelli, and at Milan.[13]

Agrippa did not spend all his time on official duties, but devoted much of his time to esoteric studies, thus offering a notable example of the influence of Italian Renaissance culture on a northern scholar. We should recall that Erasmus began his own three-year visit to Italy in 1506, following the example of his English friends John Colet (1466–1519) and the Oxford Reformers. This first golden age for such northern European contacts with the Florentine Neoplatonists had passed with Ficino's and Pico's deaths in the 1490s. By the second decade of the sixteenth century, Hermetic and cabalistic knowledge was circulating among a new generation of Italian scholars with whom Agrippa was acquainted over a considerable length of time. These were mainly in the university town of Pavia (where he lectured in philosophy and married an Italian woman), and Turin, and in other places of northern Italy, notably Milan and the court of the Marquis of Monferrato at Casale.

Agrippa and the Cabala

Returning to northern Italy in 1515, Agrippa settled in Pavia, where he lectured on the *Pimander* of Hermes Trismegistus. Agrippa was in contact with many occultists, and we know the names of at least two persons who shared his interest in ancient learning and the Cabala. Agostino Ricci, a converted Jew, had written a book titled *De motu octavae sphaerae* (1513), which dealt with "the movement of the eighth sphere in a philosophical and mathematical manner, together with the teachings of the Platonists and ancient magic (which the Hebrews call Kabbalah)." Ricci, with whom Agrippa corresponded and from whom he sought advice on the publication of his *Dialogus de homine*, was the astrologer of the Marquis of Monferrato and seems to have been Agrippa's intermediary in winning the favor of the ruler. Agostino Ricci had been a pupil of the famous Abraham Zacuto at Salamanca and continued to study under him at Carthage. Many years later he served as physician to Pope Paul III.

Agrippa may also have known Agostino's more famous putative brother, Paolo Ricci, who left Pavia for Augsburg in 1514. This Ricci, who also was a learned Jewish convert to Christianity, translated the *Sha'are Orah (Portae lucis)* (1515) of Joseph Gikatilla, a pre-Zoharic work and the chief source of Reuchlin's later detailed acquaintance with the Jewish Kabbalah. Agrippa cited this work in his own *Dialogus de homine*, written at Casale in 1516, while its dedication to the Marquis of Montferrat quotes Rabbi Moyse and Moses Gerundensis on this "secret science of marvellous operations."[14]

Just as Pico referred to the church fathers, Paolo Ricci took his authority from Dionysius the Areopagite, claiming that "if we compare ecclesiastical history with that of the Talmudists, and the works of Dionysius with that of Rabbi Simon, we discover that they were contemporaries, having lived at the time of the Lord's crucifixion and the destruction of Jerusalem." Like Pico, Ricci discovers in the Kabbalah "the mystery of the Trinity in unity, the eternal generation of the Son, the Original Sin through which death enters the world, redemption through the Passion and blood of the messiah, the holy Virgin Queen of Heaven and the limbs of Christ, the Last Judgment, the repentance and forgiveness of sins, the resurrection of the dead, the gift of prophecy, knowledge and wisdom."

Agrippa's debt to Ficino and Pico della Mirandola was also enormous. On some points, *De occulta philosophia* copies Ficino's *Liber de vita* at length, almost verbatim, a literary practice almost universal among Renaissance authors. He took over Ficino's concept of nondemonic spiritual magic but dropped the safeguards. Pico's magical view of man as master of the created world was known to Agrippa, who drew heavily on Pico's *Heptaplus* for the *Dialogus de homine* and also for *De originali peccato*. In *Dialogus de homine* Agrippa also drew on the *Crater Hermetis* (1505) of Ludovico Lazzarelli (1450–1500), a renowned Italian Hermeticist. There is a close parallel in their discussions of whether man is the image of God and whether Adam was inherently mortal before the Fall but kept from dissolution by the presence of a divine light. The increased emphasis which Agrippa gave to Hermetic writings while in Italy is evidenced in the references in his Pavia lecture on the *Pimander* (1515), probably based on the version of Ficino, and his work *De triplici ratione cognoscendi Deum* (1516). This work summarized (1) knowledge of God derived from nature; (2) knowledge of God derived from Mosaic Law (a Kabbalistic rather than literal reading); and (3) revelation in the light of esoteric writings.[15]

The governing idea in all Agrippa's Italian period treatises is the faith that the Hermetic texts, long neglected but now restored through the work of Ficino and others, and the Kabbalistic writings, the restoration of which had begun with Pico and was continuing with the work of Reuchlin and Paolo Ricci, were the gateway to true wisdom. Ancient and occult writings, forgotten by an ignorant and impious humanity, would bring men back from intellectual pride and despair to a humble acknowledgment of the goodness of God. In Agrippa's mythical history of the esoteric tradition, the writings of Hermes Trismegistus and other Egyptian sages were the link between the Pythagoreans and the Platonists in the ancient world and the original revelation to Moses in the biblical world. To bolster the ideas of a perennial philosophy and ancient theology (*prisca theologia*), Agrippa recruited a chain of initiates including Zoroaster, Orpheus, Plato and the Neoplatonists who had each preserved and developed a knowledge of transcendental magic based on a mystical link with the divine.

Agrippa believed that the enlightened soul, which had attained a true understanding of God's revelation, would not only gain mastery over its own body but also win power over all nature. Thus the study of the Cabala and the *Hermetica* led to the study of magic. Adam had lost this power over nature as a result of original sin, but with a purified soul the magus could regain this power. That prelates, clerics, and theologians were no longer able to perform miracles was proof of their corruption and lack of faith. The human mind cannot know the true nature of God by reason but only by esoteric revelation. In his *De originali peccato* (1518), Agrippa suggests that Adam represents Faith, misled by Eve, the personification of reason, who in turn has been misled by sensory experience, the Serpent. Though Agrippa regarded the rational theology of his day as vain and contentious, his emphasis on revelation anticipated his later skepticism about all knowledge.[16] An important consequence of Agrippa's discoveries among the cabalists of northern Italy is the far greater emphasis on Cabala in the published edition of *De occulta philosophia* than in the version of 1510.

Agrippa's later troubled career in northern Europe illustrates the fate of Hermeticism and Cabala in the sixteenth century. Caught in the cross-fire of the Reformation, Renaissance magic fell between the two camps of a divided Church. As the Protestant mind focused on the frailty of man, and sought salvation through piety and close attention to God's Word in the Bible, the self-confident magic of the Florentine Neoplatonists seemed sheer hubris. Once at home in the sunlit world of Renaissance Italy, the magus and voyager through higher worlds assumed a darker aspect in the northern, Germanic world. By the late sixteenth century Ficino's priest-physician and Pico's "miracle of man" had given way to the figure of Faust, a necromancer who sold his soul to the devil. Owing to the malicious legends of Agrippa's life perpetrated by hostile and credulous monks, his memory soon became entwined with the story of Faust. Writers ranging from Rabelais and Apollinaire to Goethe and Thomas Mann identified Agrippa as a prototype for the theme of Faust.[17]

Like Reuchlin before him, Agrippa played an important role in spreading Neoplatonism, Hermeticism, and Christian Cabala beyond their first modern home in Renaissance Italy. Agrippa's reputation for erudition and boldness of thought earned him the admiration of such men as Erasmus and Juan Luis Vives, and many Elizabethan and Jacobean authors in England read and quoted him, including Christopher Marlowe and Francis Bacon. Although the Reformation negated the humanistic confidence of Florentine magic and Cabala, Agrippa's reputation as a scholar magician has survived. His De occulta philosophia, has inspired students of the magical tradition from John Dee in Elizabethan England down to the occult revival of the late nineteenth and twentieth centuries. Through this legacy, the Christianized form of Kabbalah still plays a major part in ceremonial magical orders today.

John Dee

The adviser of Queen Elizabeth I, tutor and friend of the Earl of Leicester and the Sidney circle, John Dee (1527–1608) enjoyed wide renown as a philosopher, mathematician, geographer, and navigator. A scholar magician in the Renaissance tradition, he was also immersed in the occult arts and the influence of supernatural powers. He was a learned student in the fields of astrology, alchemy, and Cabala, and he later practiced theurgic rituals in order to gain direct knowledge of nature's secrets. Dee was a major intellectual force in Elizabethan England, but owing to his interest in these occult sciences and in particular his practice of angel magic, many of his contemporaries branded him a conjurer. While his fame for learning and his mathematical reputation persisted well into the seventeenth century, Meric Casaubon's 1659 edition of Dee's journal of angel magic established a negative image of Dee: a bookish and credulous fanatic deluded both by devils and by his assistant Edward Kelley.[18]

John Dee was born on 13 July 1527 in London, the son of a minor courtier to King Henry VIII. Dee was educated in London and Chelmsford and then attended St. John's College, Cambridge, at the age of 16. His academic achievements were rewarded by a fellowship in Greek at Trinity College, which had been recently founded (1546) by Henry VIII. But Dee's interests could not be satisfied in the English universities that existed at this time, and so he soon made the first of many trips abroad in search of advanced mathematical instruction. In 1547, he visited the Low Countries to study navigation with Gemma Frisius, the renowned geographer, and also became acquainted with Gerard Mercator, the famous cartographer. Dee studied at Louvain from 1548 to 1550, and in the latter year he spoke publicly on Euclid in Paris to packed lecture halls.[19]

Over the next decade, Dee made a career in England as a court intellectual by entering the service of the Earl of Pembroke and tutoring the sciences to the Dudley family. In this way he established his reputation as a leading authority on navigation, geography, mathematics, and astrology. In a time of religious upheaval and of swift succession of Tudor monarchs, such a career was not without its dangers. In 1555, Dee was briefly imprisoned under Queen Mary after he was accused of conjuring to enchant the queen by calculating the nativities of the king, the queen, and the Princess Elizabeth.[20] He remained a close friend of Robert Dudley, Earl of Leicester, and was well known to leading members of the royal court, including William Cecil, Sir Francis Walsingham, Sir Philip Sidney and his circle, and after her accession to the throne, Queen Elizabeth herself.

John Dee's Library

Toward the end of the 1560s Dee established himself at Mortlake on the Surrey shore of the River Thames. It was conveniently sited between London and Hampton Court, so that Dee was able to keep in touch with members of the court passing to and fro on the river. It was here that Dee established his famous collection of books and manuscripts which has been rightly called "Elizabethan England's Greatest Library." Over the years, Dee added rooms and buildings to house his many collections of ancient Welsh records, genealogies, his scientific instruments, and an alchemical laboratory.

Among the 2,500 or so printed books and 170 manuscripts in the library were many works concerned with the mystical thought of Ramon Lull and the medieval science of Duns Scotus, Albertus Magnus, Thomas Aquinas, and Roger Bacon. John Dee was obviously well acquainted with Florentine Neoplatonism, for he possessed the complete works of Marsilio Ficino and his translations and commentaries on Plato and Plotinus. These were joined by works by Pico della Mirandola. Dee possessed many books by Paracelsus, Agrippa, and Trithemius, as well as copies of the Hermetic *Asclepius* and *Pimander* and the Turnebus edition of the *Corpus Hermeticum* of 1554. Works by Zoroaster, Orpheus, and Iamblichus were also to be found in Dee's manuscript collection.[21]

Both Frances Yates and Peter French have concluded on the basis of this library catalogue that Dee was deeply versed in the Hermetic and cabalistic currents of Renaissance philosophy, which had become widely known in Italy, France, and Germany from the latter part of the fifteenth century onward. Indeed, they have identified Dee as the foremost proponent of these subjects at a time when the humanistic curriculum was dominant.[22]

The Development of Dee's Hermetic Thought

However, Dee did not assimilate his worldview in the form of a finished Hermetic philosophy from the ancient and Renaissance Neoplatonists. As Nicholas Clulee has shown, a close reading of Dee's major work, *Propaedeumata Aphoristica* (1558) shows how his early natural philosophy actually developed from Arabic and medieval Oxford science. Here Dee approached the subject of astrology as a kind of physics, whereby the heavens cause and order all change in the elemental or terrestrial world. Dee believed that the heavens achieved this by means of rays which are emitted by all substances and events, thus transferring the virtues of any species onto other things: "Whatever exists in actuality spherically projects into each part of the world rays, which fill up the universe to its limit." (*PA*, IIII) Light was a visible model for this process of emanation, and thus the study of geometrical optics based on lines, angles, and figures became a basis for the study of all astrological influence. Building on the work of al-Kindi (d. ca. 873), Robert Grosseteste (1175–1253) and Roger Bacon (1214/ 20–ca. 1292), Dee thus developed a concrete mechanism of astrological influence and a rationale for the mathematical study of nature. At this stage, Dee was still working within the context of an Aristotelian model of science.[23]

A powerful illustration of the emergent Hermetic cast of Dee's thought is evident from the cryptic nature of his next major work, the famous *Monas hieroglyphica* (1564). Written shortly after Dee witnessed the coronation of Emperor Maximilian at Pressburg and dedicated to the Habsburg monarch, the *Monas* represents a very different kind of thinking to the naturalistic *Propaedeumata*. Its central reference throughout the text, a short treatise of twenty-three theorems and accompanying figures, is the Monas, a complex hieroglyph which Dee promises to explain "mathematically, magically, cabbalistically, and anagogically."[24] Frances Yates has suggested that within the context of Renaissance

Hermeticism, Dee's *Monas* formulated a cabalistic mathematical alchemy in which the hieroglyph was a magical amulet whose "unified arrangement of significant signs . . . infused with astral power" would have a "unifying affect on the psyche" and allow a Gnostic ascent through the scale of being.[25] Others have argued that the hieroglyph, given the dedication to the emperor, reflects Dee's proposal for a cosmopolitan, nonsectarian, tolerant religion based on Hermeticism.[26]

Clulee, in contrast, has offered a very detailed analysis of the text involving its astrological, alchemical, and numerological aspects to demonstrate convincingly that Dee is here attempting to elaborate an "alphabet of nature." This refers to the reconstruction of the original divine language of Creation which stands behind all human languages. Dee notes that the shape of the letters in Hebrew, Greek, and Latin are generated from points, straight lines, and the circumferences of circles, and likewise the signs of the planets and the metals. Dee describes a number of complex manipulations of the Monas, involving its component parts, assembly, and dismantlement, to make deductions about the nature of the celestial and elemental worlds. However, in the final analysis, the *Monas* is less about alchemy or astrology or magic than about the mystical ascent to God as a culmination of the knowledge of the cosmos.[27]

Although Dee's studies of the mid-1550s focused on medieval science, by the 1560s Dee's worldview came to reflect a more familiar Hermetic synthesis of astrological, alchemical, and cabalistic correspondences between the mundane, celestial, and supercelestial worlds. The list of his library holdings dated 1557/59 shows that he had acquired the classics of Renaissance Neoplatonic magic: Reuchlin, Pico, Agrippa, and Ficino. He also had Trithemius's *De septem secundeis*, with its account of spiritual planetary governors, and Francesco Giorgi's *De harmonia mundi*, which offers a summa of the Neoplatonic and cabalistic ideas of Ficino's and Pico's magic.

Edward Kelley and Angel Magic

The presence of Trithemius's works in Dee's library provides the strongest clue for his later interest in angel magic. The occult nature of the *Monas* text indicates his quest for a universal science based on the unity of all knowledge and leavened with the ancient theology of Renaissance Hermeticism and Neoplatonism. But in his desire to plumb the nature of the physical and celestial worlds, he hankered for an absolute revelation of God's will whereby he might receive "true knowledge and understanding of the laws and ordinances established in the natures and properties of [God's] creatures." It was in pursuit of this direct revelation that Dee sought to communicate directly with the angels in the supercelestial world. Inspired by the examples of Enoch, Moses, and others in Scripture to whom God sent his angels to impart special wisdom, Dee regarded angelic conversation as the ultimate route to scientific certainty and a complete understanding of all creation.[28]

Dee himself lacked clairvoyant ability and employed seers or mediums to establish contact with spirits in the angelic realm by means of crystals and mirrors, while he acted as a recorder of the visions described. There is some scant evidence that Dee practiced angel magic with one Barnabas Saul in the autumn of 1581 but with no success. The unannounced arrival of Edward Talbot (alias Edward Kelley) at Dee's house on 9 March 1582 signaled the beginning of an extraordinary collaboration in angel magic that was to last until early January 1589.

Kelley was born in 1555 and possessed a sinister reputation as a forger (his ears had allegedly been cropped as a punishment) and as a necromancer who had tried to raise a corpse from the grave. However, his manifest interest in alchemy and his eagerness to collaborate with Dee in communicating with the angelic realm quickly banished any scruples the older scholar may have had about this strange partnership. On the day of his arrival, Kelley quickly proved himself a most remarkable medium, and over the next few months the two held numerous "actions" or spirit conferences that included receiving directions for manufacturing magical equipment, including a Holy Table, seals, and complex codes for the better reception and understanding of angelic communication.

The body of material resulting from Dee's actions with the spirits dwarfs, in its bulk, all his other works combined. It offers the most intimate view of Dee's personality and spiritual and intellectual life. The topics of the actions range across religion, politics, the Reformation, cosmology, theology, eschatology, and natural philosophy. There are two classes of material: (1) *Libri mysteriorum I–XVIII* (1581–1588), minutes of the séances known as the Spiritual Diaries; and (2) several books based on the angelic revelations: *De heptarchia mystica, Liber mysteriorum sextus et sanctus, 48 Claves angelicae*, and *Liber scientiae auxilii et victoriae terrestris*.

Dee believed in the spirits as good angels bearing genuine messages from God. His record of noises, voices, apparitions, and prophetic dreams in his diaries, quite independently of Kelley's involvement, indicate a personal belief in the reality of a spirit world. In the minutes, Dee noted the similarity of the angelic revelations to material in Agrippa, Reuchlin, Trithemius, and Peter of Abano. Dee did not consider these actions a type of magic but rather a variety of religious experience, sanctioned by the scriptural records of others to whom

FIGURE 3.4. John Dee's Sigillum Æmeth, wax disk in British Museum, instructions for its design obtained through spirit actions held on 19–21 March 1582. British Museum Sloane Ms. 3188, fol. 30.

God or his angels imparted special illumination. Dee thought that as "an honest Christian Philosopher," he should "have the help of God his good Angels to write his holy Mysteries."[29]

The actions took place in a simple religious atmosphere in Dee's oratory following a period of silent prayer, and ended with a short prayer of praise and thanksgiving. Dee was not invoking angels and compelling their services; rather it is a question of humbly petitioning God to send his angels, who are in no way thought to be doing Dee's or Kelley's bidding. The opening prayer Dee most often used was addressed to God and Jesus as a source of wisdom and asks that he be worthy of their aid in philosophy and understanding and that they send their spirits and angels to instruct him in the secrets of the properties and use of all God's creatures. There are no elaborate ritual preparations, quasi-sacramental ceremonies, no incantations that form part of the ceremonial magic of Agrippa's third book. Also absent are the music and Orphic hymns, fumigations, candles, talismans, or foods and substances that figured in the magic of Ficino for attracting the beneficent influences of the planets or planetary demons. What all the séances have in common is that they are catalogues of the angelic and spiritual hierarchies that govern the various regions of the earth and levels or domains of creation with descriptions of their characteristics, powers, their sigils, and the "calls" by which they may be summoned. Dee's *Libri mysteriorum* recording the spirit actions contain a wealth of evidence for the manifold correspondences and spiritual intermediaries that define esoteric cosmology.

Dee's esoteric treatise *De heptarchia mystica* (1588) presents the created world as divided into various sevenfold sequences. Seven kings, each attributed with a subordinate prince and forty-two ministers, govern geographical regions of the world and the affairs of men. These kings also have temporal correspondences to the seven days of the week. There are also forty-nine good angels and, below them, other orders of angels who preside over physical nature—groups for the cure of disease, for metals, for transformation, for the elements, for local change, for the mechanical arts, and for human knowledge of all secrets. Here the influence of Trithemius's *De septem secundeis* is apparent, yet the fact remains that this extraordinarily complex map of spiritual intermediaries, an outstanding example of Faivre's third characteristic of esoteric philosophy, was vouchsafed through Kelley's mediation in a long and laborious series of spirit actions; only later did Dee compose the text in a fair copy from the fragmentary and confusing notes scattered throughout his early Spiritual Diaries.[30]

Beginning in 1583, the angels introduced an entirely new language purporting to be the angelic language of Adam and Enoch. This was dictated in the form of numerous gridlike tables of forty-nine rows by forty-nine columns in which letters, sometimes interspersed with numbers, occur in apparently random order. These tables comprise the *Liber mysteriorum sextus and sanctus* (also called the *Liber Logaeth* and *Book of Enoch*). By some method of selection the angels chose from these tables letters to form words and sentences, which amount to another set of calls pertaining to the angels. This became the basis for the *48 Claves angelicae*, written in Cracow in 1584, which consists of a catalogue of the forty-eight angels, their characteristics, and subordinate spirits, and their calls in the Enochian language with English translations.[31]

What then is the final status of John Dee's angel magic? He regarded it as a means to a natural theology. Dee believed that communication with the spirit

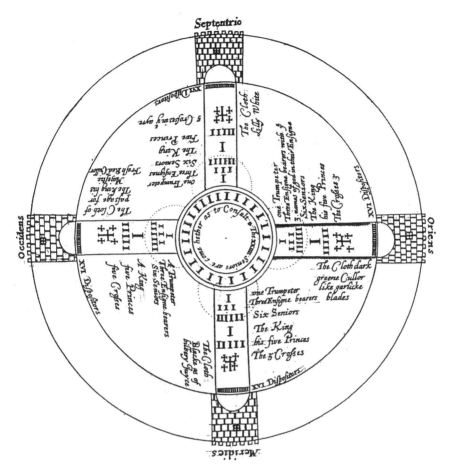

FIGURE 3.5. Edward Kelley's Vision of the Angels of the Quarters, 20 June 1584, gold disk in British Museum, illustrated in Meric Casaubon, *A True and Faithful Relation of What Passed for Many Yeers Between Dr. John Dee and Some Spirits* (London, 1659).

world was essential for an understanding of nature because the created world was organized in a complex intermediary system whereby God revealed himself through spirits and angels who vouchsafed the secrets of a quasi-mathematical order of letters and numbers underlying nature. To this extent, Dee's cosmology possessed a Kabbalistic derivation. Although Dee's and Kelley's knowledge of Cabala was limited, the emphasis on a mathematical ordering of an emanated cosmos in the angelic conversations suggests a worldview more cabalistic than Neoplatonic. The Spiritual Diaries indicate that the angels, spirits, and divine governors hold the secrets to the various realms of creation and by communicating with them, Dee will gain access to a natural theology. The recovery of the Adamic language is the key to this design because it is the language all God's creatures understand. The calls derived from the tables thus have the power to call forth and make obedient the spirits so that they will reveal the mysteries of the creation and secret knowledge.[32]

Dee sought this key to the secrets of creation through an evocatory magic, as Clulee notes, a spiritual and demonic magic of an explicit variety, albeit protected by pious Christian prayers and the request that Kelley take Holy Communion prior to actions. Dee's earlier interest in the medieval science of al-Kindi, Robert Grosseteste, and Roger Bacon, which later extended to Hermetic and Neoplatonic readings, found its conclusion in a quasi-Kabbalistic practice of spirit communications through the mediation of scryers communicating with a densely populated angelic intermediary world. In considering the progression of Western esotericism in the Renaissance, it is evident that this evocatory magic is unlike the philosophical magic and occult philosophy of Ficino and Pico and also the natural magic derived from Roger Bacon. Despite the similarity of Dee's angelology and demonology to Agrippa's, attributable to Kelley's readings, the spirit communications contain no reference to the Neoplatonic theory of the spirit as the vehicle of magical influence, or of the role of the imagination, or of the sympathetic correspondence between the divine qualities in lower things and the influence of higher things. Dee's library had formerly offered him a broad survey of medieval and Renaissance magic and Hermeticism, which led him to produce the cryptic cosmological *Monas hieroglyphica*. However, Kelley's brash promises of direct spirit communication seem to have presented an overwhelming temptation to Dee to achieve a hotline to the angelic knowledge of creation. The evident passivity of Dee's reliance on Kelley's scrying appears to have obviated Dee's own engagement with the imaginal world and the elaboration of a rich texture of correspondences. Dee's cosmos is indeed rich in intermediary spirits, but their information reflects a more encyclopedic attempt to map the external world rather than an interactive pattern of correspondences between the macrocosm and microcosm. We appear to be witnessing a scientific endeavor to capture empirical knowledge rather than a spiritual illumination. Dee's burning desire to learn the secrets of creation led rather to a mechanical reception of these secrets on the basis of a theurgic conjuration that harked back to the older practice of medieval magic.

FURTHER READING

Henry Cornelius Agrippa, *Three Books of Occult Philosophy*, edited and annotated by Donald Tyson (St. Paul, Minn.: Llewellyn, 1995).

Noel L. Brann, *The Abbot Trithemius (1462–1516): The Renaissance of Monastic Humanism* (Leiden: Brill, 1981).

———, "Johannes Trithemius," in *Dictionary of Gnosis and Western Esotericism*, edited by Wouter Hanegraaff et al., 2 vols. (Leiden: Brill, 2005), Vol. 2, pp. 1135–1139.

———, *Trithemius and Magical Theology* (Albany: State University of New York Press, 1999).

Nicholas H. Clulee, *John Dee's Natural Philosophy: Between Science and Religion* (London: Routledge, 1988).

Joseph Dan, "Johannes Reuchlin," in *Dictionary of Gnosis and Western Esotericism*, edited by Wouter Hanegraaff et al., 2 vols. (Leiden: Brill, 2005), Vol. 2, pp. 990–993.

———, "The Kabbalah of Johannes Reuchlin and Its Historical Significance," in *The Christian Kabbalah: Jewish Mystical Books and Their Christian Interpreters,* edited by Joseph Dan (Cambridge, Mass.: Harvard University Press, 1997).

The Enochian Magick of Dr. John Dee, edited and translated by Geoffrey James (St. Paul, Minn.: Llewellyn, 1994).

Peter J. French, *John Dee: The World of an Elizabethan Magus* (London: Routledge & Kegan Paul, 1972).

Deborah E. Harkness, *John Dee's Conversations with Angels: Cabala, Alchemy, and the End of Nature* (Cambridge: Cambridge University Press, 1999).

The Heptarchia Mystica of John Dee, edited by Robert Turner (Wellingborough: Aquarian, 1986).

Moshe Idel, "The Magical and Neoplatonic Interpretations of the Kabbalah in the Renaissance," in *Jewish Thought in the Sixteenth Century,* edited by Bernard Dov Cooperman (Cambridge, Mass.: Harvard University Press, 1983), pp. 188–200.

Ingrid Merkel and Allen G. Debus (ed.), *Hermeticism and the Renaissance: Intellectual History and the Occult in Early Modern Europe* (Cranbury, N.J.: Associated University Presses, 1988).

Charles G. Nauert, *Agrippa and the Crisis of Renaissance Thought* (Urbana: University of Illinois Press, 1965).

Henry Morley, *The Life of Henry Cornelius Agrippa von Nettesheim, Doctor and Knight,* 2 vols. (London: Chapman and Hall, 1854).

François Secret, *Les Kabbalistes Chrétiens de la Renaissance* (Paris: Dunod, 1964).

Lewis W. Spitz, "Pythagoras Reborn," in *The Religious Renaissance of the German Humanists* (Cambridge, Mass.: Harvard University Press, 1963), pp. 61–80.

Gerald Suster, *John Dee,* Western Esoteric Masters series (Berkeley, Calif.: North Atlantic Books, 2003).

György E. Szönyi, *John Dee's Occultism: Magical Exaltation through Powerful Signs* (Albany, NY: State University of New York Press, 2004).

———, "John Dee," in *Dictionary of Gnosis and Western Esotericism*, edited by Wouter Hanegraaff et al., 2 vols. (Leiden: Brill, 2005), Vol. 1, pp. 301–309.

Robert Turner, *Elizabethan Magic: The Art and the Magus* (Shaftesbury: Element, 1989).

Michaela Valiente, "Heinrich Cornelius Agrippa," in *Dictionary of Gnosis and Western Esotericism,* edited by Wouter Hanegraaff et al., 2 vols. (Leiden: Brill, 2005), Vol. 1, pp. 4–8.

Brian Vickers (ed.), *Occult and Scientific Mentalities in the Renaissance* (Cambridge: Cambridge University Press, 1984).

Benjamin Woolley, *The Queen's Conjuror: The Science and Magic of Dr. Dee* (London: HarperCollins, 2001).

Frances A. Yates, *Giordano Bruno and the Hermetic Tradition* (Chicago: University of Chicago Press, 1964), chap. 7.

———, *The Occult Philosophy in the Elizabethan Age* (London: Routledge & Kegan Paul, 1979), chaps. 3, 5, and 8.

Charles Zika, "Reuchlin's *De verbo mirifico* and the Magic Debate of the Late Fifteenth Century," *Journal of the Warburg and Courtauld Institutes* 30 (1976): 104–138.

4

Alchemy, Paracelsus, and German *Naturphilosophie*

Alchemy plays a large part in Renaissance esotericism. Parallel with other Hellenistic sources of Western esotericism, alchemy originated in Egypt during the first few centuries B.C. and was later transmitted to Europe through Greek and Arabic sources. The word "alchemy" is derived from the Arabic name of the art, *alkimia*, where *al* is the definite article. While many alchemical texts were available in the late Middle Ages, the period 1550–1650 witnessed a notable surge in alchemical and medico-chemical publishing in Europe. This rapid diffusion of alchemy relates directly to its combination with Neoplatonic and Hermetic approaches to nature, and especially to the controversy surrounding Paracelsus (1493–1541), the pioneer of chemical medicine, whose thought and practice were grounded in such an approach.[1]

Islamic and Medieval Alchemy

The pioneering eighth-century Arab alchemist Jabir ibn Hayyan (ca. 720–800) developed Islamic alchemy consistent with Aristotelian doctrine. The four elements of earth, water, air, and fire were the basis of Aristotelian physics, while the four related humors (blood, phlegm, yellow bile, and black bile) underpinned the medicine of Galen. By substituting the qualities (hot, cold, wet, and dry) for one another, an element could be transmuted into another. Jabir also propounded a theory of metals, whereby the metals were all composed of two elementary principles, sulphur and mercury, in different proportions and degrees of purity.[2] Again, these principles should not be identified with the modern conception of chemical elements. Sulphur was generally regarded as the principle of combustion and also of color. Its presence was ostensibly confirmed by the observation that most metals are changed into earthy substances by burning. Mercury possessed the properties of fissibility, malleability, and lustre.[3]

Jabir was influenced by the Hermetic tradition, which the Arabs had encountered upon their settlement in Egypt after 640. This Hermetic literature, in its Arab versions, portrays the discovery in Hermes' tomb of his revelations of theosophy, astrology, and alchemy. One particular text was greatly revered by the Arabs as a source of ancient wisdom. *The Emerald Tablet* is one of the oldest surviving of all alchemical documents and acted as a "founding document" of Renaissance esotericism after its existence became known in Europe in the fourteenth century.[4] Its opening statement, "As above, so below," encapsulated the correspondence between the macrocosm and the microcosm, while "adaptation" refers to the progressive unfolding of the universe, both intrinsic elements of Western esotericism.

> True, true. Without doubt. Certain. That which is below is as above, and that which is above is as below, to accomplish the miracles of the One. And as all things came from the meditation of the One, so are all things born from this One by adaptation. Its father is the Sun, its mother the Moon. The Wind carries it in its womb, its nurse is the Earth. It is the father of all the wonders of the whole world. Its power is perfect. If it be cast on Earth, it will separate the element of Earth from that of Fire, the subtle from the gross. With great wisdom it ascends from Earth to Heaven and descends again to Earth, so that it receives the power of things above and below. Thus you will possess the brightness of the whole world, and all darkness will flee you. This is the strength of all strengths, for it overcomes all that is subtle and penetrates all solid things. Thus was the world created. From this marvellous adaptations will be achieved, and the means are given here. For this reason I am called Hermes Trismegistus, because I possess the three parts of the wisdom of the whole world.[5]

Jabir's work was gathered in four groups: (1) "The Hundred and Twelve Books" derive from *The Emerald Tablet*; (2) "The Seventy Books" were translated into Latin in the twelfth century by Gerald of Cremona; (3) "The Ten Books of Rectifications" describe the alleged alchemical discoveries of ancient sages including Pythagoras, Socrates, Plato, and Aristotle; (4) "The Books of the Balances" outlined Jabir's alchemical interpretation of Aristotle's theory of the elements. One of Jabir's books refers to a conference of ancient philosophers to discuss alchemy. This is possibly a reference to a famous anonymous work, *Turba Philosophorum* (Convention of Philosophers), which appeared in Latin manuscripts during the thirteenth century. First printed in 1572, this work has both Arabic and Greek origins and was held in high esteem by medieval European alchemists.

Abu Bakr Muhammad ibn Zakariyya, known as Razi (Rhazes), the "man from Ray" (ancient Rhagae), his birthplace near Tehran, was another major Arab alchemist. Razi (825–925) pursued a medical career, achieving international renown as a practitioner, researcher and writer. Translated into Latin, some of his works were still required reading at universities in seventeenth-century Holland. Although Razi did not share Jabir's theory of balance, he did believe the transmutation of metals was feasible. For him, the object of alchemy was the transmutation of base metals into silver or gold by means of elixirs. He also thought it possible to improve common crystals such as quartz by similar means into emeralds, rubies, and sapphires. Razi also shared Jabir's sulphur-mercury theory of metals but introduced a third elementary principle of salt, which became established in later alchemical literature, especially through Paracelsus.[6]

Early medieval Europe had established crafts in dyeing, painting, glassmaking, goldsmithing and metallurgy but knew nothing of alchemy until its introduction from the Muslim world, beginning in the twelfth century. Sicily and more especially Spain became important centers for the diffusion of Arab learning to Western students, who attended the colleges and libraries of Toledo, Barcelona, and Segovia.[7] The sulphur-mercury theory of metals was held by such famous medieval alchemists as Roger Bacon (1214–1294), Arnaud of Villanova (ca. 1235–1312), and Raymond Lully (ca. 1232–1316). By the early fourteenth century, there were considerable advances in laboratory practice, including more efficient furnaces and a knowledge of distillation techniques. In England, Sir George Ripley (ca. 1415–1490), a canon of Bridlington Abbey, dedicated his book *The Compound of Alchemy* to King Edward IV in 1470, while his follower Thomas Norton (ca. 1433–1513) composed the famous *Ordinall of Alchimy* also with a royal dedication.[8]

Despite its operational emphasis, medieval alchemy possessed a twofold nature, an outward or exoteric and a hidden or esoteric. External operations were largely focused on trying to prepare the philosopher's stone, a marvelous substance capable of transmuting the base metals lead, tin, copper, iron, and mercury into the precious metals silver and gold. The stone was not only credited with the power of transmutation; also known as the elixir, it was believed to prolong human life indefinitely. As the preparation of the stone often involved notions of divine grace, alchemy developed an esoteric aspect as a spiritual discipline. In this context, the transmutation of metals became an outward symbol of the transmutation of fallen, sinful man into a pure and perfect instrument of God's will. The outward practices and processes of the laboratory were simultaneously devotional exercises involving prayer and communion with God and angels and other intermediary spirits.

Paracelsus

Paracelsus was a dominant and controversial figure in sixteenth-century medicine and alchemy. Today he is celebrated as the first modern medical theorist, the founder of iatrochemistry, homeopathy, antisepsis, and modern wound surgery. He rejected the scholasticism of ancient and medieval medicine in favor of a new medicine based on experiment, observation, and new philosophy. Nature and humankind were his sources; he believed that a pious Christian faith, the evidence of his own senses, and a system of correspondences between the macrocosm and the microcosm surpassed the book knowledge regurgitated from ancient authorities such as Hippocrates, Galen, and Avicenna. His radical approach to healing and medicine, his popular style, and his contempt for professional exclusivity and incompetence provoked the hostility of established authorities everywhere and led to his being called the "Luther of physicians." In his work we see how alchemy, when combined with Hermetic and Neoplatonic ideas, becomes a key to explain the unity and interconnectedness of nature, man, and health.[9]

Philippus Aureolus Theophrastus Bombastus von Hohenheim, later called Paracelsus, was born at Einsiedeln in Switzerland, in 1493. His mother died when he was still young, and in 1502, as a result of the Swabian wars, he and his father moved to Villach in Carinthia. Here Wilhelm von Hohenheim practiced medicine for the rest of his life and encouraged his son's interest in natural history and medicine. Paracelsus probably attended local monastery schools near Klagenfurt, and the mining school of the Fuggers and their metal ore mines near Villach likely offered both father and son a rich field for chemical and medical observation and speculation. Among his later teachers, Paracelsus identified among his tutors four bishops and the famous Cabalist Johannes Trithemius. Paracelsus probably studied for a bachelor's degree at Vienna between 1509 and 1512. He then journeyed to Italy and began studying at Ferrara in 1513, receiving his doctorate three years later.[10]

The young doctor then embarked on a series of extensive travels around Europe. Between 1517 and 1524 these wanderings led him from Italy across France to Spain and Portugal, through France again, England, Germany, Scandinavia, Poland, Russia, Hungary, Croatia, across to Italy and thence to Rhodes, Constantinople, and, possibly, Egypt. During this period he enlisted as an army surgeon and was involved in the wars waged by Venice, Holland, Denmark, and the Tartars. To his practical experience of surgery Paracelsus added the great wealth of local and traditional medical folklore among the herbalists, bath attendants, peasants, gypsies, and magicians encountered in the course of his travels.[11]

Paracelsus wanted to found a new medicine which would bring together the best of its academic knowledge and artisan practice. This unconventional ambition was his destiny. In late medieval Europe, physicians were learned scholars who seldom attended the sickbed, while barber-surgeons merely plied an artisan trade, and were uninformed by theory. Apothecaries made a good living from the herbal remedies of Galen and Avicenna, still upheld by the scholar physicians. Paracelsus's medical reforms represented a threat to all these groups, and his life became a series of clashes wherever he attempted to settle down and practice.

In December 1526, Paracelsus arrived at Strasbourg where he enjoyed the popularity and respect of the influential circle of Protestant reformers including Nicolaus Gerbelius, Kaspar Hedio, Wolfgang Capito, and Johannes Oecolampadius. Capito introduced Paracelsus to the humanist circles of Basle. The center of the humanist movement here was the publisher Froben, through whom Paracelsus became acquainted with Erasmus of Rotterdam and the Amerbach brothers. His friendship with the progressive circles of the Reformation, his medical proficiency and his opposition to medieval scholastic medicine commended Paracelsus to humanists, reformed churchmen, and the public. Oecolampadius, the Protestant theologian, was highly influential in the Basle town council and secured the appointment of Paracelsus as town physician in March 1527.[12]

Paracelsus spent only ten months at Basle, but this period marks both the climax and crisis of his life. The post of town physician gave him the right to lecture at the university, but Paracelsus provoked the university authorities by lecturing on practical and theoretical medicine as it had emerged in his own work and experience rather than on the theories of Hippocrates and Galen. Moreover, he lectured not in Latin for the academic elite but in German to large and enthusiastic audiences, which included both students and artisan barber-surgeons. In these lectures Paracelsus was forming the nucleus of his medical system during a highly fruitful phase of his life. However, his antagonism of the faculty and further disputes forced him to quit Basle in early 1528.[13]

FIGURE 4.1.   Paracelsus's "Rosicrucian" portrait in Paracelsus, *Philosophiæ Magnæ* (Cologne, 1576). Courtesy of Bibliotheca Philosophica Hermetica, Amsterdam.

Paracelsus now entered his most productive phase of medical literary activity. Firstly, he wrote the *Paragranum* (1529–1530), which argued that medicine should be based on natural philosophy, astronomy (the relationship between man and the heavens), alchemy (the science and preparation of chemical remedies), and virtue (the inherent power of the particular individual, doctor, patient, herb, or metal). At St. Gallen he completed his great *Opus Paramirum*—the "work beyond wonder"—in 1531. This book contains Paracelsus's mature medical theories, including expositions of his theory of three principles (Sulphur, Salt, and Mercury),

a chemical system of medicine that Paracelsus substituted for the ancient doctrine of four elements; the processes of digestion and nutrition; the nature of
women; the matrix (womb), sexuality, and reproduction; diseases caused by "tar-
tar" (stone); psychic phenomena and illnesses arising from the imagination.[14]

Journeying northward again, Paracelsus arrived at Augsburg where he published his great work on surgery, *Die grosse Wundarznei*, on which he had been
working for several years. From Augsburg he traveled to Mährisch Kromau,
where he had been invited to consult with Johann von der Leipnik, a dignitary
of the kingdom of Bohemia. As a patron of persecuted Protestant sects in Bohemia, Leipnik took a strong interest in the philosophical ideas of his physician
and invited Paracelsus to stay at Kromau as his guest. Here Paracelsus began
his great philosophical opus *Astronomia Magna or the whole Philosophia Sagax
of the Great and Little World* (1537–1538). This presented a systematic account of
Paracelsus's scientific worldview based on the macrocosm-microcosm correspondences of Renaissance Neoplatonism. Further travels led him to Bratislava
and Vienna, where he received two audiences with King Ferdinand. He died of
a stroke at Salzburg on 24 September 1541.[15]

Paracelsian Alchemy

Alchemy plays a major part in the thought of Paracelsus. Like the medieval alchemists, he rejected gold-making as the ultimate goal of alchemy and instead
considered alchemy to be a means of perfecting what nature had left imperfect.
Paracelsus based his alchemy on the parallels between the macrocosm and the
microcosm and the various possible transformations of the three principles of
constitution, the fluid (Mercury), the solid (Salt), and the combustible (Sulphur).
Paracelsus quoted Hermes Trismegistus, who stated that all seven metals, "the
tinctures" (generating principles) and the Philosopher's Stone all derive from
three substances, namely spirit, soul, and body. Paracelsus claimed that these
were identical to his three principles of constitution: Mercury (spirit), Sulphur
(soul), and Salt (body). Since Mercury represented the spirit, this metal was as
important as gold, the solar metal. However, Paracelsian alchemy treated Sulphur, Salt, and Mercury as principles rather than as the elements of medieval
alchemy. Also, Paracelsus used chemical reactions to explain the processes of
human physiology; medieval alchemy attempted the converse.[16]

Paracelsus was inspired by the Renaissance Neoplatonic conception that
the whole of creation—the heavens, the earth and all nature—represented a
macrocosm and that its unity was reflected in a variety of possible microcosms,
of which man was the most perfect. The analogies and correspondences

between the macrocosm and the microcosm were central to his cosmology, theology, natural philosophy, and medicine.[17] Paracelsus expressed a deep distrust of logical and rational thought as a scientific tool. Since man was the climax of creation, uniting within himself all the constituents of the world, he could have direct knowledge of nature on account of a sympathy between the inner representative of a particular object in his own constitution and its external counterpart. For Paracelsus, this union with the object is the principal means of acquiring intimate and total knowledge. Moreover, this true knowledge does not concern the brain, the seat of conscious rational thinking, but rather the whole person.

In accordance with Neoplatonic ideas, Paracelsus conceived of all creation having two sides: a visible elemental (material) part and an invisible super-elemental (astral) part. Man, the microcosm, likewise possesses a carnal elemental body and an astral body (*corpus sidereum*) which "teaches man" and is able to communicate with the astral part of the macrocosm, the uncreated virtues or direct emanations of God in the world of nature. He saw experience as a process of identification of the mind or astral body with the internal knowledge possessed by natural objects in attaining their specific ends. The researcher should try to "overhear" the knowledge of the star, herb, or stone with respect to its virtue, activity, or function and so discover the astral sympathy between himself and the object. This identification with an object penetrates more deeply into the essence of the object than mere sensory perception can accomplish. Paracelsus's science is both profound and holistic in its approach to nature.[18]

Paracelsus believed that sickness and health are controlled by astral influences, and that sickness can be eliminated and health restored by *arcana* or remedies containing virtues. The function of the remedy is to restore a celestial harmony between the inner, astral body of man and a heavenly *astrum*. The medicine is physical, but it contains the spiritual *arcanum*. Physicians thus had to be versed in astrology to know the causes of disease, and in alchemy in order to prepare the appropriate *arcana*. He wrote that "the purpose of alchemy is not . . . to make gold and silver, but in this instance to make *arcana* and direct them against diseases."

Paracelsus developed a theory of matter from these new philosophical ideas. He thought that an immanent, specific, and soul-like force determined the nature and species of an object rather than its (visible) chemical components. For him, substances were but crude envelopes which disguised an underlying pattern of spiritual forces and it was this pattern, not the corporeal cover, which dictated the composition of matter.[19] Paracelsus generally "spiritualized" matter, in claiming that such spiritual forces are the true elements and principles, while the Elements and chemical substances are only the crystallized deposits of such forces. Taking the notion of Prime Matter (*Arche* or *Ousia*) from ancient Stoicism, Paracelsus regarded the visible Elements as the results of an interaction between the qualities of heat, cold, moisture, and dryness and this Prime Matter, a kind of vital matter-spirit.

Medical Reforms

The ideas and developments of Paracelsus's theory of matter are plainly evident in his pioneering medicine. He opposed and destroyed the ancient humoral medicine and related ideas. He denied that the four humors and temperaments could explain the wide variety of diseases. He rejected the paramount importance of the constitution and its internal order in ancient pathology. Instead, Paracelsus developed a medical theory which related the macrocosm and microcosm. There were two important consequences: first, Paracelsus saw disease as something that affects the body from outside rather than as an internal imbalance; second, this wider relationship between man and the external world led to a search for specific cures and remedies relating to particular diseases and disorders. Paracelsus also used chemical remedies, based on his speculations concerning Sulphur, Salt, and Mercury, with results far more promising than those offered by Galen's herbs. For this reason, Paracelsus is often hailed as the founder of modern medicine and iatrochemistry.

Paracelsus is also often called the father of homeopathy. His chemical remedies are indeed based on the fine sympathies between the diseases and the *arcana*. This sympathy is opposed to the ancient principle of opposites in remedial action. Paracelsus denied that a "cold" remedy can cure a "hot" disease, unless this is ascribable to the other properties of the remedies concerned. He claimed that cancer corresponded to arsenic in the macrocosm and asserted that arsenic itself would cure this arsenical condition. Similarly, a stone (a hard, morbid concretion in the kidney, etc.), can be cured by other stones such as crab's claws, or lapis lazuli. A scorpion's venom can cure scorpion poisoning. Paracelsus thought that the specificity of an *arcanum* lay in its "anatomy" or structure. Because the anatomy of the remedy is identical with that of the disease agent, Paracelsus was a staunch advocate of the iso- or homeopathic principle in medicine.[20]

Many important protoscientific ideas and modern medical theories emerge in his work. His specific contributions to medicine are impressive and include a humanitarian and ethical approach toward the patient, especially the mentally ill; a recognition of the healing power of nature and the value of antiseptic principles; progressive views on syphilis and a rejection of guaiac and mercury as treatments; knowledge of the diuretic action of mercury and its curative powers in dropsy; the connection between goiter, minerals, and drinking water in certain places; studies of spa waters and observations of the beneficial digestive effects of certain acid waters (balneology); the description of "miners' disease" as an occupational illness in which he shows the greater toxic risks in metals than in salts and recounts a concrete etiology with numerous symptoms.

Hermetic Influences from Ficino

Paracelsus's philosophy of nature and alchemy initiates a specifically German variant of Renaissance Neoplatonism. His work certainly reflects Marsilio Ficino's ideas, inasmuch as his medical vocation absorbed the theory of two worlds and correspondences, the physician as magus, intervening as a transmuted soul in the spiritual hierarchy of nature. There is much textual evidence to support this interpretation of his worldview. In Ficino's *Apology* for his own attitude to astrology and medicine, we find the kernel of Paracelsian medical Neoplatonism.

Ficino recalled objections to his vocation: "'Surely Marsilius is a priest,' people will say, 'What has a priest to do with medicine?' 'What again with astrology?' 'Why should he, a Christian, interest himself in Magic and Images, and the life animating the whole of the world?'"[21] Ficino's answer is that the most ancient priests—Chaldean, Persian, Egyptian—were physicians as well as astronomers, and thereby served piety and charity. For it is the foremost act of charity to help another to maintain a sound mind in a healthy body. This, however, is best effected by combining the attitude of the priest with the physician. As, however, medicine without heavenly grace is ineffective and even harmful, the physician must embrace astronomy as an essential part leading to that priestly charity which is exercised through medicine.

Ficino spoke of the magus in the same terms as his priest-physician. Magic is not a profane cultivation of demons but captures the heavenly gifts hidden in natural objects for the promotion of health. It is "natural magic" that requires a superior mind in which celestial and earthly elements are combined and perfectly balanced. Such a mind enables the magus to adapt the inferior world to heavenly influence for the benefit of human happiness—just as the farmer prepares the field, heeding weather and air, for the benefit of growing food. Wisdom and priesthood, not sinister practices and poison, were the source of the magus's activities and achievements.

According to Walter Pagel, Paracelsus's whole life and work seem to be an attempt at implementing this ideal of Ficino's priest-physician. The contacts and parallels between the ideas of Ficino and Paracelsus are close. Together with

Hippocrates, Ficino was one of the few medical figures not reviled by Paracelsus. To him Ficino was *Italorum medicorum optimus* (the best of the Italian physicians). Ficino's work *De triplici vita* (1489) inspired Paracelsus's *De Vita Longa*, and he quoted with approval the work of the "egregius medicus Marsilius Ficinus."[22]

In Paracelsus's views on the plague and its treatment, Ficino's influence can be seen to extend from a more general Neoplatonism into specific medical theories and the application of chemical principles. While preserving some traditional Galenic material, it elaborates Ficino's chemical theories in an original Paracelsian complex of macrocosmic and microcosmic forces. In his "Antidote to Epidemics," Ficino waved scholastic qualities aside to concentrate on specific poisons: thus the pestiferous vapor is in its whole structure contrary to that of the vital spirit contained in the heart. Plague poison displays the corrosive and inflammatory nature of calcium and arsenic. Adverse astral constellations, notably a conjunction of Mars and Saturn, and eclipses, produce, strengthen, and sustain the poison. Astral influence also decides which animals are affected by the plague. The comparative resistance of the elderly will not prevail when Saturn is the master of the year, as in the Florentine plague of 1479, which took a toll of 150 dead each day.[23]

Paracelsus adapted the chemical plague-theories of Ficino in his lecture notes on the Tartaric diseases (winter 1527–1528), and introduced Mars and Sulphur as the immediate causes of plague in a process of combustion in his Nördligen tract of 1529–1530. In his *Three Books on the Plague* (mid-1530s), Mars, Venus, and the moon are called "Masters of this disease." Developing his own distinctive brand of Hermetic medicine, Paracelsus saw plague coming as a thunderbolt from heaven affecting a certain metabolism in nature at large and the corresponding process in man. But first it is man who creates the astral *semina* of the disease, giving rise to an infectious *contagium*. This is a physical entity, a body. But it is created by something noncorporeal, the sinful passion and imagination of man.[24] The Neoplatonic principle of the force of imagination is thus involved, leading to the notion of a psychic element in bodies and vice versa and thus to an abolition of strict dualism. The noncorporeal spirit begets corporeal matter, a train of thought that is recognizable in Campanella's "Sensus Rerum," and later in the philosophy of Van Helmont and Leibniz.

Paracelsian *Naturphilosophie* and German Mysticism

The full flowering of Paracelsus's Hermetic inspiration in magic and Cabala, as mediated by Ficino, Pico della Mirandola, Reuchlin, and Agrippa is customarily attributed to the suggestively titled *Astronomia Magna or the Whole Sagacious Philoso-*

phy of the Macrocosm and Microcosm (1537–1538), which forms a major summary of Paracelsus's philosophical worldview, written less than five years before his death. In this work, Paracelsus gives ample evidence of his Hermetic position. Man is made out of the macrocosm and has his nature therein. The key Paracelsian term "the light of Nature" denotes his nature philosophy, which reveals the interconnectedness of all living nature. The magus can gain that marvelous knowledge of the celestial and terrestrial worlds, enabling him to work for good in nature as a natural philosopher or physician. Likewise, the unitarian Neoplatonic position is seemingly upheld by Paracelsus's doctrine of the soul: "Man has two bodies: one from the earth, the second from the stars, and thus they are easily distinguishable. The elemental, material body goes to the grave along with its essence; the sidereal, subtle body dissolves gradually and goes back to its source, but the spirit of God in us, which is like His image, returns to Him whose image it is." Throughout the *Astronomia Magna* one sees that Paracelsus is using a threefold hierarchical view of the world: mundane, celestial, and eternal corresponding to the body, soul, and spirit. The spirit is divine and will, as in the emanationist Neoplatonic philosophy of Plotinus which was Ficino's great inspiration, return to the godhead. This was the threefold hierarchical world of Neoplatonic cosmology, which came through Ficino and Pico to Trithemius and Agrippa, still present in John Dee's rigid theurgy and Robert Fludd's wonderful engravings.

But there is a different emphasis in Paracelsus, for even here he also uses a dualist scheme to distinguish the eternal and temporal. Man, nature, and the stars comprise the macrocosmic-microcosmic worlds that are living, interconnected, and full of marvelous correspondences. Nature accordingly displays the divine seals and signatures (emanations of God), which it is the physician's business to read, understand, and act upon. These the magus or priest-physician can apprehend and apply, for he embodies this cryptic knowledge in himself as a result of the meaningful, hermetic structure of all creation. But all this is still temporal for Paracelsus. There is also an eternal wisdom which "springs directly from the light of the Holy Spirit," and, again, "man [is able] to distinguish eternal wisdom from temporal wisdom, because he is the image of God."[25]

The prior and greater emphasis given to the special relationship between God through Christ and man shows how Paracelsus's apparently Hermetic cosmology and natural philosophy was subordinated to an assertive fideistic Christianity and biblical literalism typical of the German Reformation. Even in this mature late work of philosophy on the macrocosm-microcosm one finds this deference to the Lord: "The beasts take their nature from the stars, but man draws his mortal wisdom, reason and art from the stars—and everything that comes from the light of Nature must be learned from the light of Nature, excepting only the image of God, which is subject to the spirit which the Lord has given to man. The spirit instructs man in supernatural and eternal things, and after the separation of matter from spirit it returns to the Lord."[26]

The Legacy of Paracelsus

This Paracelsian idea offers another illustration of the way in which he combines Hermetic ideas of degeneration and regeneration with the Christian idea of redemption. His belief that the whole macrocosm was the product of some "separative" process was fundamental to his philosophy. All individuation and specialization was seen as a breaking away from the original divine unity and simplicity. The whole of nature was involved in a process of splitting up, which he also saw as a kind of corruption and putrefaction. He called the sum total of all such disruptive processes the *Cagastrum*; because of it, all created things are mortal and return to nothing. But the Christian is redeemed. Redemption is wrought by Christ's atonement. As his successor and as a receiver of his sacramental body, the Christian will return to God. It is noteworthy that Paracelsus's Christology was not as radical as that of Caspar Schwenckfeld and others in doubting the true humanity of Christ, but pointed to the early modern Protestant "spiritualistic" Christology of Valentin Weigel and Jacob Boehme.

The Spanish scholar Carlos Gilly sees Paracelsus's large but only recently edited theological writings as providing the basis of a new supradenominational religious current in central Europe in the late sixteenth and seventeenth centuries. Paracelsus rejected the *Mauerkirche* (the church of stone) in *De septem puncti idolatriae christianae* (1525). He did not want to found a new sect, but strove instead for a church of the spirit, subject only to God and nature. Paracelsus's "religion of the two lights," namely the light of grace, and the light of nature, was taken up by Adam Haslmayr (ca. 1560–1630), the first commentator on the Rosicrucian manifestos, which invoked the example of Paracelsus. Haslmayr called the revelation of Paracelsus the *Theophrastia Sancta*, and this term became emblematic among followers of Valentin Weigel and others as a new gospel for a second, truly radical reformation.[27]

Paracelsus was bold and uncompromising in his views and proposed reforms. Both the man and his works possess an epic quality, so it is unsurprising that his ideas and influence should have long survived his own lifetime. Indeed, during his life only a few of his writings were published. From the early 1550s onward, more and more Paracelsian texts came to light. The publication of the numerous books, tracts, and papers during the period up to 1570 reflects the activity of the early Paracelsists, including Adam of Bodenstein, Michael Toxites,

Gerard Dorn, and Theodor and Arnold Birckmann. The collected editions were first published by Johannes Huser of Waldkirch (Baden) in 1589–1591, 1603, and 1605. At the beginning of the seventeenth century, Paracelsus gave an important impetus to the Rosicrucian movement and strongly influenced Michael Maier (1568–1622) and the famous Christian mystic Jacob Boehme (see chapters 5 and 6). Other Continental and English Paracelsists included Oswald Croll, John Dee, Francis Anthony, and Robert Fludd. This period represents the peak of his immediate influence in certain medical circles; by the second half of the century, his importance had been eclipsed by the primacy of rational empiricism in science and medicine.[28]

Paracelsus's ideas were rediscovered by Goethe, Novalis, Schelling, and other German Romantic thinkers who found in him an exponent of their own *Naturphilosophie* current from the close of the eighteenth century. His name and works were popularized as a leading figure in the revival of Neoplatonism regarded as an ancient wisdom tradition by the Theosophists H. P. Blavatsky, Franz Hartmann, and Rudolf Steiner in the modern occult revival at the end of the nineteenth century.[29] The Swiss psychoanalyst and esotericist Carl Gustav Jung regarded ancient Hellenistic religion, particularly Gnosticism, as keys to the subconscious human psyche. In the late 1920s, Jung's interests extended to alchemy as a bridge between Gnostic religion and his own unfolding ideas of psychology. Two early works were *Dream Symbols of the Process of Individuation* (1935) and *The Idea of Redemption in Alchemy* (1936). Foremost among the Western alchemists whom Jung singled out for special study were Paracelsus and his disciple Gerard Dorn. Like the seventeenth-century Paracelsians, Jung celebrated Paracelsus for his source of knowledge in the twin "lights" of nature and revelation and believed Paracelsus's work to be an early intimation of the role of the unconscious. Arguing that alchemy is "the forerunner of our modern psychology of the unconscious," he claimed Paracelsus as a pioneer of "empirical psychology and psychotherapy."[30]

Paracelsus's esoteric ideas concerning the cosmic all-life, the spiritualization of matter and the divine nature of virtue and energy are now integral elements in the new philosophies of science of vitalism and holism and in the archetypes of Jungian psychoanalysis. Today, in the new efflorescence of interest in alternative medicine, one may again detect the perennial ideas of Paracelsus. He stands as a liminal figure between Renaissance philosophy and its empirical application in nature and medicine, witness to the practical application of the key esoteric ideas of correspondences, living nature, intermediaries, and imagination, and his concept of transmutation bridged both medical alchemy and the human being's need for the grace of God.

FURTHER READING

Philip Ball, *The Devil's Doctor: Paracelsus and the World of Renaissance Magic and Science* (London: Heinemann, 2006).

Udo Benzenhöfer, *Paracelsus* (Hamburg: Rowohlt, 1997).

Udo Benzenhöfer and Urs Leo Gantenbein, "Paracelsus," in *Dictionary of Gnosis and Western Esotericism,* edited by Wouter Hanegraaff et al., 2 vols. (Leiden: Brill, 2005), Vol. 2, pp. 922–931.

Herwig Buntz, "Alchemy III: 12th/13th–15th Century," *Dictionary of Gnosis and Western Esotericism,* edited by Wouter Hanegraaff et al., 2 vols. (Leiden: Brill, 2005), Vol. 1, pp. 34–41.

Richard Caron, "Alchemy V: 19th–20th Century," in *Dictionary of Gnosis and Western Esotericism,* edited by Wouter Hanegraaff, 2 vols. (Leiden: Brill, 2005), Vol. 1, pp. 50–58.

Allison Coudert, "Alchemy IV: 16th–18th Century," in *Dictionary of Gnosis and Western Esotericism,* edited by Wouter Hanegraaff et al., 2 vols. (Leiden: Brill, 2005), Vol. 1, pp. 42–50.

———, *Alchemy: The Philosopher's Stone* (London: Wildwood House, 1980).

Allen G. Debus, *The Chemical Philosophy: Paracelsian Science and Medicine in the Sixteenth and Seventeenth Centuries* (Mineola, N.Y.: Dover Publications, 2002; first published in 2 vols. in 1977).

———, *The English Paracelsians* (New York: Franklin Watts, 1966).

———, *Man and Nature in the Renaissance* (Cambridge: Cambridge University Press, 1978).

Nicholas Goodrick-Clarke, *Paracelsus: Essential Readings* (Berkeley, Calif.: North Atlantic Books, 1999).

Bernard D. Haage, "Alchemy II: Antiquity–12th Century," in *Dictionary of Gnosis and Western Esotericism,* edited by Wouter Hanegraaff et al., 2 vols. (Leiden: Brill, 2005), Vol. 1, 16–34.

John Hargrave, *The Life and Soul of Paracelsus* (London: Victor Gollanncz, 1951).

E. J. Holmyard, *Alchemy* (London: Penguin, 1957; New York: Dover, 1990).

———, *Makers of Chemistry* (Oxford: Clarendon Press, 1931).

Jolande Jacobi, *Paracelsus: Selected Writings* (Princeton, N.J.: Princeton University Press, 1958).

Stanislas Klossowski de Rola, *Alchemy: The Secret Art* (London: Thames & Hudson, 1992). Contains a wealth of alchemical engravings and illustrations.

Walter Pagel, *Paracelsus: An Introduction to Philosophical Medicine in the Era of the Renaissance* (Basle: Karger, 1982).

John Read, *Prelude to Chemistry: An Outline of Alchemy, Its Literature and Relationships* (London: G. Bell & Sons, 1936).

F. Sherwood Taylor, *The Alchemists* (London: Heinemann, 1952).

Basilio de Telepnef, *Paracelsus: A Genius amidst a Troubled World* (St. Gallen, [1945]).

Andrew Weeks, *Paracelsus: Speculative Theory and the Crisis of the Early Reformation* (Albany: State University of New York Press, 1997).

5

Jacob Boehme and Theosophy

During the seventeenth and eighteenth centuries, esotericism found particular expression in the currents of Christian theosophy and Pietism which arose in response to the hardening orthodoxy of the Lutheran Reformation. The chief representative figure of theosophy in its first efflorescence was Jacob Boehme (1575–1624), a shoemaker in Görlitz, in Lusatia (now part of Saxony in Germany). This province had been won by the Reformation but was rich in heterodox and Hermetic traditions. Boehme early established his reputation as a leading Protestant mystic. His works present an esoteric psychology of the individual soul and its union with divinity through the mediation of Sophia (Wisdom). Esoteric notions of correspondences between a higher realm and the soul based on alchemy, astrology, and Kabbalah place his thought firmly within the Western esoteric traditions. After his death, his fame spread to Holland, England, France, Russia and the early American colonies. His writings influenced German Baroque poets, the dissenters of seventeenth-century England, and the Pietists of seventeenth- and eighteenth-century Germany. At the end of the latter century, his ideas inspired poets including William Blake, Ludwig Tieck, and Novalis, and in the nineteenth century he was admired by the German philosophers Franz von Baader, Friedrich Wilhelm Joseph von Schelling, Georg Wilhelm Friedrich Hegel, and Arthur Schopenhauer. Boehme's esoteric thought and writings are difficult, so it will first be helpful to place his life and work within the context of his locality in the century following the German Reformation.

FIGURE 5.1. Portrait of Jacob Boehme by N. van Werd in symbolic and theosophical setting (1677). In Jacob Boehme, *Mysterium Magnum, oder Erkärung über das Erste Buch Mosis* (Amsterdam & Frankfurt, 1678).

Lutheran Orthodoxy and Its Critics

By the middle of the sixteenth century, the Reformation had taken firm root in all European countries north of the Alps except France and the Netherlands. Once the opposition to Rome was complete, reformers often embraced a hard-line orthodoxy to consolidate their position. In the Holy Roman Empire, a provisional equilibrium had been reached by the Peace of Augsburg (1555), which established the principle *cuius regio, eius religio*: subjects must conform to the religion of their territorial princes. This rule allowed only for a Protestant denomination based on the doctrine of Christ's real presence in the Eucharist, which excluded Calvinists, Anabaptists, and members of other sects. The acceptable creed was further formalized by the publication of the Book of Concord (1577), which sought to codify the new articles of faith in the Lutheran churches.[1]

The anti-orthodox movements of Sebastian Franck (1499–1542), Caspar Schwenckfeld (1489–1561), and Valentin Weigel (1533–1588) opposed this growing Lutheran orthodoxy with its insistence on closely worded statements of doctrinal faith. These dissident currents led beyond the historical faith to a Protestant Spiritualism. The twentieth-century German theologian Ernst Troeltsch saw this Spiritualistic faith as typified by the spirit and *logos* of the fourth Gospel in contrast to the letter, law, and historical being of Christ. The Spiritualist rejects formal church organization, tends toward individualism, conceives a "millennium of the spirit" rather than a literal Second Coming, and emphasizes a "baptism of the spirit" rather than adult baptism. The Word is not received as an external force but as a result of the Holy Spirit acting within the believer. Troeltsch saw this sixteenth-century Spiritualism as a prototype of Quakerism; it is evident that the movement was a formative influence on the nature of Boehme's theosophy.[2]

Caspar Schwenckfeld was a Silesian nobleman and a former pupil of Luther who became an outspoken opponent of the growing Lutheran orthodoxy; he won many adherents in central Germany, who were persecuted by both Lutherans and Catholics. Many landowners and minor noblemen joined the movement, forming close-knit communities with their estate workers. Schwenckfeld stressed spiritual brotherhood and rejected the centralized church hierarchy. Like Paracelsus, he characterized the institutional church as a *Steinkirche* or *Mauerkirche* ("church of stone" or "walled church"), a product of sin and ignorance which only cut individual religious seekers off from God. He wanted a *Kirche ohne Mauer*, whose members were united in mutual tolerance. Boehme later used similar expressions in defining his ideal church. Luther had Schwenckfeld expelled from Silesia in 1540, but his followers persisted. Several groups loyal to Schwenckfeld were active around Görlitz, and one of their aristocratic members, Carl von Ender, became Boehme's leading patron among the gentry.[3]

Silesia gave refuge to many other dissident Protestant groups as well, including Anabaptists, Moravian Brethren, and Crypto-Calvinists, whose ideas carried into neighboring Lusatia. Following the publication of the Book of Concord in 1577, Lutheran orthodoxy was on the ascendant. Philipp Melanchthon, the fellow humanist reformer and successor to Luther, was blamed for having compromised the doctrine of real presence to appease the Calvinists. Toward the end of the sixteenth century, Lutherans in Saxony condemned the deviations of Philippism and Crypto-Calvinism. Around 1600, the orthodox campaign intensified to reinforce the Book of Concord. In 1600, Martin Möller was appointed chief pastor in Görlitz. Inspired by the works of St. Augustine, St. Bernard, and the medieval German mystic Johannes Tauler, Möller authored popular works in German and sympathized with the opposition to Lutheran orthodoxy. It is against this background that he organized a parochial study group called "Conventicle of God's Real Servants," which Boehme joined. By 1601, Möller himself was accused of Crypto-Calvinism, and the public controversy persisted until his death in 1606.[4]

Paracelsian Traditions

Though Lusatia had endured two centuries of religious and political upheaval, Görlitz with its large population of some ten thousand hosted a rich variety of scholars, writers, and truth seekers in the backwash of the Renaissance and Reformation. Bartolomäus Scultetus (1540–1614), mayor of the town in Boehme's time, was a renowned astronomer, cartographer, and compiler of biblical chronologies. He knew the Danish astronomer Tycho Brahe, was visited by Johannes Kepler, and conferred with Rabbi Loew, the famous Prague Kabbalist.

Alchemy was also well represented at Görlitz, whose physicians were chiefly adherents of Paracelsian medicine. The town was a center for the collection and copying of Paracelsus's writings. Johannes Huser, the editor of the first edition of his works, published at Basle in 1589–1591, corresponded with several Paracelsians in Görlitz for this purpose. Scultetus himself was also a Paracelsian and wrote a treatise on plague. Leading Paracelsians in the town included Conrad Scheer and Abraham Behem, Boehme's mentor, who corresponded with Valentin Weigel, the dissident Lutheran pastor of Zschopau, who advocated a "spiritual church" in which one could know Christ without books or scripture.[5] Dr. Balthasar Walter was another of Boehme's friends and staunch supporters. He first visited Görlitz before the turn of the century, became a close friend in 1612, and studied with him for three months in 1619–1620. Walter was also a Paracelsian and wrote a number of mystical and occult books. At the end of the sixteenth century he had traveled widely in Europe and the Middle East, pursuing studies in Kabbalah, magic, and alchemy.[6]

This Paracelsian tradition at Görlitz would have made the language of alchemy an accessible discourse if not common parlance in Boehme's time. Given
Boehme's close contacts with its representatives, especially Walter, alchemical
ideas and references form a major part of Boehme's books up until 1622. Although Boehme certainly witnessed practical alchemical work, his discussion
of alchemy focused on its meaning as a spiritual-philosophical system.

Jacob Boehme's Visionary Experience

Jacob Boehme was born, the fourth of five children, to a prosperous Lutheran
peasant couple in 1575 in Alt-Seidenberg, a village near Görlitz. Little is known
of his youth, save two mysterious incidents recorded by his disciple and first
biographer, Abraham von Franckenberg. One involved his discovery of treasure in a hidden cave; the second was a prophecy of his future greatness by
a stranger. He completed his three-year apprenticeship to a shoemaker in
Görlitz, returning from his journeyman years in 1592. In 1599, he acquired the
rights of a town burgher, married a butcher's daughter, who subsequently bore
him four sons, and bought a house. [7] In 1600, Möller was appointed pastor of
Görlitz, and later that year Boehme had his first visionary revelation. For some
time, he had suffered from melancholy. He felt oppressed by the heavens, dis-
turbed by the sun, stars, and weather and troubled by the mixture of good and
evil that he found in all living creatures as well as in stones, wood, and the elements. Sitting at home one day, Boehme caught sight of the reflection of the
sun in a tin or pewter dish and suddenly experienced himself as penetrating
the secret heart of nature. Leaving his house, he passed out through a nearby
city gate into open countryside, where he continued for some fifteen minutes
to undergo an epiphany. He saw all creation in its forms, lines, and colors anew
and felt he had been embraced by divine love, as if all life had been resurrected
from death.

   Boehme was profoundly moved by this religious experience, and he began
to study so as to formulate its significance. Over the following twelve years,
while leading a full family life, practicing his trade, buying and selling property
and involving himself in guild disputes between the shoemakers and the tan-
ners, he intermittently composed his first book *Morgenröthe im Aufgang* (*Morn-
ing Glow Ascending*), later titled *Aurora* by his followers. In the meantime, in
1610, he experienced another inner vision in which he further understood the
unity of the cosmos and that he had received a special vocation from God. He
had no intention of publishing the work. His first visionary experience formed
only a brief section of his first book (*Aurora*, Ch. 19, §5–12). However, this vision

had served to generate reflections on many themes: the inert lifelessness of elemental matter, the power of the sun and the power which holds the world together; the omnipresent life-giving spirit; the meaning of Christ's presence in the bread and wine; the occult forces of nature and the design of the macrocosm and microcosm; the freedom of the angels; the issues of war and peace, justice and tyranny, and oppression and exploitation in society.[8]

Aurora (1612)

Boehme's *Aurora* contains a wealth of esoteric speculation. Boehme presents a heliocentric view of the heavens, then novel and theologically controversial. Copernicus had laid the groundwork of his heliocentric theory between 1506 and 1512, publishing his complete theory in 1543. His theory was further developed by the refined observations of Tycho Brahe, and Johannes Kepler formulated the mathematical laws governing the planets' movements and elliptical orbits in 1609. The traditional Ptolemaic geocentric cosmology viewed the universe as a series of concentric spheres, descending from God through the angelic realms, the planets (including the sun) to the moon, below which was the earth. Though this hierarchy assigned all things to their station, Boehme experienced this order as a closed, oppressive vault that condemned human beings and the earth to a gloomy basement (*Aurora*, Ch 19, ¶11). Boehme regarded heliocentrism as a form of spiritual liberation, corresponding to the unrestrained aerial transit of all the planets in orbit around a central sun. Just as his epiphanic vision of 1600 had revealed the living forces in all nature and the unity of creation, heliocentrism offered the sun as a natural symbol for the God within and a dynamic perspective of the relationship between the natural macrocosm and the human microcosm.[9]

Geocentrism had, however, provided traditional certainties concerning salvation, nature, and human life. Boehme's purpose in *Aurora* was thus to restore the one "true ground," underlying the root or mother of philosophy, astrology, and theology. He accomplished this by envisioning the one single pattern in all creation. As God had created nature not from nothing but out of his being, the divine life of the spirit was present at every level, in macrocosm and microcosm, in every tiny organism, "in even the smallest circle of the world." To prove the presence of the divinity in everything, Boehme advanced the key ideas of *Aurora*: the divine substance *Salitter*; the qualities as reified principles; the conception of the world of seven source-spirits (*Quellgeister*); and the realm of the angels.[10]

Boehme's divine substance *Salitter* was probably based on his observation of the refined and unrefined forms of niter. Whereas unrefined niter, or saltpeter, was the nitrous earth found on farms and attributable to animal urine, refined niter (potassium nitrate) was known as a pure liquid or white, transparent crystals, much in demand as an essential ingredient in gunpowder. Niter was then a subject of great alchemical interest, giving rise to the theory of a divine niter, paralleling the material niter at a higher level of being. In *Aurora*, Boehme imagines the celestial *Salitter* as a supreme energy, rather like our notion of hydrogen in the sun and a nuclear bomb, but also as the underlying energy of life and consciousness. Andrew Weeks suggests that Boehme saw the pure *Salitter* in terms of the divine spirit-waters of Genesis, whereas our fallen world corresponds to the foul yet fertile form of nitrous earth. The refinement of impure niter was a process suggestive of the spiritual allegory of alchemy: the redemption of the soul. Boehme thus idealized the two forms of niter to represent the duality of the pure and corrupted divine substance.[11]

Boehme sought to explain the progressive manifestation of God and his creation in terms of qualities, which could also have been derived from processes associated with the transformations of niter. These qualities are similar to the oppositions of hot, cold, moist, and dry that defined the Aristotelian elements, but in *Aurora* they are transformed into the moving forces or source-spirits of the cosmos. Boehme defined quality as the "mobility, boiling, springing and driving of a thing" (*Aurora*, Ch. 1, §4). These he classified in his successive works, in varying order, as dry, sweet, bitter, hot, love, sound, and *corpus* or nature. Boehme's progression of the seven source-spirits or qualities is a dynamic perspective on the manifestation of God through the stages of his creation. The perpetual transformation of the source-spirits or qualities, one into another, is characterized as birth. Their harmonious interchange also explains how life and awareness came into being.

In chapters 8 to 11 of *Aurora*, Boehme describes the properties and action of the seven source-spirits or qualities of God in the divine *Salitter*.[12] The first, dry (*herb*), is harsh, hard, and cold. It is also the principle of contraction, obduracy, and inertia (*Aurora*, Ch. 8, §22–31). The second, sweet, is the warming, pleasant, and mild quality which allays and mitigates the harshness of the first (Ch. 8, §32–43). Their tension gives rise to the third quality, bitter, which is a force of trembling, elevating, and penetrating (Ch. 8, §44–52). Boehme identified these first three qualities as the basis of corporeal being in the universe. The fourth quality, hot, also known as fire, is the kindling of life, whereby the great mystery of the spirit enters into matter. It is this fourth quality or source-spirit that causes all the other qualities to mingle, interact, and produce growth (Ch. 8, §59–81). This warmth then produces a *Schrack* ("flash" or "fright") (Ch. 10, §12–13), which gives rise to the fifth quality of love (sometimes light), which corresponds to the reception of the Holy Ghost. Here love refers to a rational spirit, exemplified by various reciprocal phenomena such as coordination of the limbs and the attainment of consciousness through the senses (Ch. 9, §63–65). The sixth source-spirit is sound (tone or tune), whence come speech, language, and the melody and singing of angels (Ch. 10, §1). The seventh source-spirit is the *corpus* or body, which is generated from the other six. Boehme comments that both heaven and nature are formed in this composite fashion. As all heavenly things form themselves in this seventh quality, God's ultimate goal in self-manifestation is incarnation.

The sevenfold pattern of Boehme's theosophy also combines features of popular astrology with alchemical lore in its quest for the common denominator of the natural, human, and divine worlds. The seven source-spirits are not purely spontaneous ideas. Chapters twenty-five and twenty-six discuss the stars, sun, and planets in terms similar to those used for qualities. In this respect, Boehme's cosmology reflects the fundamental characteristic of esotericism in correspondences between all parts of the cosmos, animated by a living nature. Weeks has summarized the correspondences of the seven qualities, planets, and humoral-elemental associations:

1. Dry	Saturn	melancholy, power of death
2. Sweet	Jupiter	sanguine, gentle source of life
3. Bitter	Mars	choleric, destructive source of life
4. Fire	Sun/Moon	night/day; evil/good; sin/virtue; Moon, later = phlegmatic, watery
5. Love	Venus	love of life, spiritual rebirth
6. Sound	Mercury	keen spirit, illumination, expression
7. *Corpus*	Earth	totality of forces awaiting rebirth[13]

Boehme's system also followed the alchemists with their seven metals, but he did not identify his spirits with substances. Only later, when grouping his sevenfold qualities into the three worlds did he match the latter to the three philosophical principles of Paracelsian alchemy: Salt, Sulphur, and Mercury.

Boehme's source-spirits are the sources from which the qualities emanate. They mediate between the divinity and the world of elemental bodies. They cannot be regarded as personal or individual creatures. Mixing and transforming themselves, they resemble vapors or spirits rather than fixed, numinous presences. Their septenary scheme parallels the seven days of Creation, turning this "historical" record into a vision of perpetual creation, corresponding to the influences of the seven planets and the virtues at work in the seven metals or salts. At the same time, Boehme's constant references to smell and taste reflect the earthy senses of his peasant origins, while the abundance of illustrations from nature show the proximity of his metaphysics to natural philosophy.

Religious Controversy and the Thirty Years' War

Aurora was written down during the first half of 1612. Although it was claimed that Boehme wrote the work as a personal record, numerous copies of the 400-page manuscript were given to Boehme's friends, most likely by Carl von Ender, who later became Boehme's patron. A year later, a copy came to the attention of Gregor Richter, an orthodox Lutheran who was the chief pastor of Görlitz and had succeeded Martin Möller in 1606. Scenting religious enthusiasm, Richter referred the manuscript to the secular magistrates, who interrogated Boehme, confiscated his master copy, and held him prisoner for two days. Two days later, on 28 July 1613, Richter denounced Boehme as a heretic in his Sunday sermon. Boehme was then subjected to a religious cross-examination on matters of the faith and forbidden to write any more.[14]

In March of that year, Boehme had sold his shop to enter the yarn trade together with his wife. This business necessitated much travel to other towns, including Prague, so that Boehme's circle of acquaintance and influence grew. At the same time, he was exposed to the sharpening denominational conflict between the Habsburg empire and its Protestant subjects, following the succession in 1617 of Emperor Ferdinand, who put an end to a policy of religious tolerance by revoking the Letter of Majesty and suppressing the Bohemian church. In May 1618, Protestants threw Habsburg officials from a window in the royal castle of Prague, an incident that marked the beginning of the Thirty Years' War. In August 1619, the Bohemian estates invited the Protestant Elector Frederick V of the Palatinate to become king of Bohemia. Crowned in November 1619, Frederick was defeated a year later by the imperial Habsburg army in a battle near Prague and was forced to flee the country. It was against this momentous period of political and religious upheaval, affecting neighboring Lusatia and Saxony and ultimately engulfing Europe, that Boehme wrote a series of books in his final years.

Three Principles of Divine Being *(1619)*

Boehme's sympathizers and friends had increasingly encouraged him to resume his writing. In 1619, after another illumination, he began work on his second book, *De Tribus Principiis, or On the Three Principles of Divine Being.* While this work is much denser than *Aurora*, it is notable that the sevenfold pattern of the theogony is overlaid with threefold Trinitarian notions.[15] The seven qualities are here subsumed into the Trinity and three principles as follows: (1) the "dark world" of the Father (Qualities 1–2–3); (2) the "light world" of the Holy Spirit (Qualities 5–6–7); and (3) "this world" of Satan and Christ (Quality 4), which is formed in the middle, where the first and second principles overlap and human beings must negotiate their salvation.[16] This pattern of ascent again traced God's self-revelation from the *Ungrund* (abyss) through wrath in order to make himself known and the creation of humanity for the sake of revelation's fulfillment. This theogony also takes place within the individual soul, whereby God is born within the human being. Boehme extended his theosophy with the figure of the Noble Virgin of Sophia, a figure based on the allegory in the Book of Wisdom and Proverbs. She animates the second world of "eternal nature" as a serene and reflective aspect of God. Both the terms "abyss" and "Sophia" recall mythic aspects in the Gnostic aeonology of Valentinus (second century), a remarkable example of Protestant esotericism naively invoking Hellenistic heterodoxy.

In this second book, Boehme amplified and revised the interplay of the seven source-spirits in his account of God's creation out of himself. In order to explain evil, Boehme cast the first three qualities negatively: Dry is followed by Bitter and their resolution is the 'Wheel of Essences', which represents the unconscious driving force of nature ("wrath") which brings forth life. These first three qualities are the first principle or the dark world of the Father. The resulting friction produces fire and a flash of light (*Schrack*), leading to the fourth quality, water, which is turned into the sweet spirit of love. The second principle begins with the flash and the sweet water and consists of love, sound, and *corpus*. This is the light world of eternal nature and Sophia, which has transcended the dark world. The third principle is the critical juncture of fire and light and represents our world of nature, conflict, and choice. Here the human soul strives to transcend the blind wrath of the first principle through the light of Christ, thereby overcoming evil, sin, and darkness with love, harmony, and transmuted being.[17] While *Aurora* described theogony and cosmogony in macrocosmic terms, *Three Principles of Divine Being* located the microcosm of man within its scheme. The cosmogony of will with its drives, emergent spirit, and growth now read as a map of the soul's ascent.

De Signatura Rerum *(1622)*

The year 1620 marks a turning point in Boehme's accelerating literary production. During that year, he wrote *The Threefold Life of Man*, *Forty Questions on the Soul*, *The Incarnation of Jesus Christ*, the *Six Theosophical Points*, and the *Six Mystical Points*. His next major work, *De Signatura Rerum*, reworked the combination of astrology, alchemy, and Christology. While his earlier works had emphasized the self-revelation of God, this book deciphered the world as the expression of the eternal Word, both in Genesis and in nature.

In *De Signatura Rerum*, Boehme identifies the signature with his sixth source-spirit, the mercurial spirit of sound or language. "Everything has its mouth to manifestation; and this is the language of nature, whence everything speaks out of its property, and continually manifests, declares, and sets forth itself for what is good or profitable; for each thing manifests its mother, which thus gives the essence and the will to the form."[18] Signatures, as the unfolding of the concealed inner being of things, are found in natural organisms, human character, even in language. More narrowly, in the sphere of medicine, the doctrine of signatures implies that the macrocosm as a whole generates correspondences throughout all nature so as to "sign" every animal, plant, herb, or stone with a clue (usually shape or color) which indicates its therapeutic application. This aspect of Boehme's revelational theosophy matched Paracelsus's idea of the hidden seals of the divine in nature and the efficacy of the *arcana*. Like Paracelsus, Boehme was no pantheist. As an esotericist, he emphatically does not identify nature with God. Rather God has bestowed his powers upon all things: "He shines with his power through all his beings . . . and each thing receives his power according to its property" (Ch. 8, §42). Esotericism involves God's emanation of his being into creation, so that nature is signed with God's seals or virtues. Metaphors of light and reflective mirrors are frequently used to convey this idea of animation, without involving God's actual presence in things. The term "panentheism" is often used to distinguish this esoteric idea from pantheism.

Given the evident Paracelsian influence, mediated through the Görlitz milieu, the terminology of the book is densely alchemical, and Boehme also speculates on the alchemical preparation of medicinal plants (spagyrics).[19] He identifies the colors, tastes, and forms of plants and herbs in terms of their planetary correspondences. Exceptional virtue is inherent in certain signatures. For example, where "Mercury is between Venus and Jupiter, and Mars undermost, . . . then is the universal very sovereign in the thing, be it a man, or other creature, or an herb of the earth" (Ch. 8, §36). However, Boehme's spagyric medicine is more moral than physical; a wicked person cannot see these herbs, "for they are close to paradise" (Ch. 9, §35–37). The language of alchemy is also used to describe the transmutation of the soul. Boehme describes man as shut up after the Fall in a gross, dead image. Once God introduces "living Mercury" into man, Christ is born in his soul and his divine image reappears (Ch. 8, §47–48). For Boehme, the process for making the philosopher's stone is the transformation of the Word into Christ, signifying the victory of joy and light over wrath and death (Ch. 6, §24).

Final Years

After this book, Boehme turned from alchemical themes to a reformulation of his major ideas in terms of traditional Christianity. During 1623, he wrote *On Election to Grace*; *On Christ's Testaments*; his major commentary on Genesis, titled *Mysterium Magnum*; and the *Clavis* or *Key* to his major doctrines. In early 1624, he published *The Way of Christ*, a theosophical text with spiritual exercises, which prompted renewed attacks by Pastor Richter, who inflamed the local populace against Boehme. As this printing had indeed occurred without permission, Boehme was told by the town council to quit Görlitz for the time being. In May 1624, however, Boehme was invited to visit the court of Electoral Saxony at Dresden, to discuss his doctrines with friendly court officials and theologians against a background of military escalation in the war. Boehme returned to Görlitz in July, fell ill in August, and died on 17 November 1624.

As a self-educated artisan, Boehme articulated an esoteric philosophy distinct from the learned Neoplatonism of the Renaissance humanists and scholar-magicians. His more proximate sources were Paracelsus (especially in his doctrine of signatures), Valentin Weigel, and possibly the Kabbalah. He saw God not as a supreme being outside all becoming, but as an active agent, who sees in his mirror, the Divine Sophia, the world he would create. Once imagined by God, this divine image wills its temporal or earthly image into being, culminating in the human microcosm. This process of God's self-revelation through a passionate struggle of opposing qualities underlies all of Boehme's elaborate mythological themes including the sevenfold pattern of creation, the fall of Lucifer and Adam, the spiritual corporeality of the angels, the astrological and alchemical correspondences, and the idea that all exterior form is language or symbol ("signature"). Boehme's saw all reality as saturated with wondrous presences and births. His thought, with its emphasis on struggle, birth, and new beginnings, was suited to the strife of his times, and its visionary origin commended him to religious seekers throughout the seventeenth and eighteenth centuries.

Boehme's Followers

Boehme's esoteric works were grounded in individual visionary experience. The apparent complexity of his theogony and cosmology was not rooted in doctrinal reasoning and refinement but reflected his theosophy, a direct way of knowing God. Thus, Boehme's followers in Holland, Germany, England, and America did not so much accept his doctrines as use his books as guides to their own visionary experience. As a result, their works range from editions and commentaries on Boehme to visionary records of the soul's ascent, the transmutation of wrath into love, and spiritual marriages with Sophia. Their visionary experiences, documented in theosophical works, attest to a remarkable congruence in theosophical esotericism. This similarity indicates the common experience of the individual soul's responsibility for its salvation. The imaginal world of theosophy, rich in spirits and intermediaries, suggests both a Protestant spiritualist reaction to orthodoxy and a compensation for the lost imaginal world of Catholic saints, relics, and the cult of the Virgin.

In his pioneering work *Wisdom's Children*, Arthur Versluis documented the major schools of theosophy following Boehme. Johann Georg Gichtel (1638–1710) was, after Boehme, the leading Continental theosopher. Born in Germany, he was forced to leave Regensburg because of religious controversy and lived in Switzerland, where he collaborated with another theosopher, Friedrich Breckling (1629–1711). In 1668, he went to Amsterdam, where he gathered his community of the "Brethren of the Angelic Life." His four thousand pages of letters and biography, published as *Theosophia Practica* (1722), describe cycles of revelation in which Sophia appeared to Gichtel during his life. The work also contains beautiful illustrations of planetary symbolism showing the process of theosophic illumination in the human microcosm.[20]

John Pordage (1608–1681), the Anglican vicar of Bradfield, Berkshire, was the leading theosopher in England. He commenced having visions in 1649, and he attracted a circle of eminent followers who regularly communed with angels and experienced the struggle of the wrathful and beatific worlds. Pordage's *Treatise of Eternal Nature with Her Seven Essential Forms* (1681) describes the theosophical practice of the group as a visionary ascent from the natural world to the archetypal, to the seven qualities and the *Ungrund* of God. His *Theologia Mystica* (1683) presents a lucid account of Pordage's spiritual journey through the Boehmean cosmology of the three worlds of the "Dark-Fire" or wrath-world, the "Fire-Light" or severe world of common human experience, and the "Light-Fire World" or paradise. Pordage uses key images of the eye, the heart and the breath, thereby demonstrating the heightened theosophic perception of spiritual intermediaries in the imaginal world.[21]

The English Civil War and Commonwealth (1642–1653) witnessed a prolonged period of religious unrest in England, marked by the emergence of many radical, millenarian and antinomian Protestant sects. Pordage's theosophical visionary circle had no part in this movement but fell victim to official suspicion; he was twice tried for heresy and finally was ousted from his pastorate in 1654. His subsequent writings were published in German and circulated widely in that country, where his influence was considerable.[22]

Pordage's circle was succeeded in England by the Philadelphians of Jane Leade (1624–1704). She had first met Pordage in 1663 and slowly assumed leadership of the group. The name "Philadelphian" from the book of Revelation (3:7) denoted the group's belief that they had already realized a visionary spiritual reality on earth in anticipation of the imminent millennium. Francis Lee, a young fellow of St. John's College, Oxford, became a stalwart supporter of Leade's and arranged for the publication of many of her works in England, the Netherlands, and Germany. As a result of their millennial expectations and creation of a creed, the Philadelphians were regarded as a sect by Continental theosophers. They also dissented from Leade's doctrine of universal restoration (*apocatastasis*), whereby evil would cease and all creatures were destined for salvation.[23]

The Anglo-German axis of theosophy was further represented by Dionysius Andreas Freher (1649–1728), the most important British exponent of Boehmean ideas after Pordage. A native German from Nuremberg, Freher migrated to England in the late seventeenth century and gathered a faithful circle of fellow theosophers in London. He wrote numerous commentaries and illustrations that explain and amplify Boehme's teachings. However, his inspiration was his own, and his understanding of Boehme's works was rooted in his own spiritual experience. The visionary power of his complex and beautiful Boehmean illustrations must rank with those of Thomas Bromley and Gichtel's edition of Boehme's complete works.[24] William Law (1686–1761), the best-known writer among the British theosophers in the eighteenth century, was introduced in the early 1730s to Freher's circle following the latter's death. A former fellow of Emmanuel College, Cambridge, Law later devoted himself to the study of Boehme and Freher and writing his own works. Sensitive to the charges of enthusiasm leveled against Pordage and Leade, Law mentioned Boehme only in his later works, including *The Way to Divine Knowledge* (1752) and *The Spirit of Love* (1752). His work reveals how closely he had studied Boehme, but does not equal the profundity of Pordage's understanding of cosmology.

Theosophy as a Timeless Revelation within Christianity

In Arthur Versluis's view, theosophers maintain an emphasis on the "timeless revelation or gnosis within Christianity," and he sees this authentic Gnostic tradition stretching from Pseudo-Dionysius the Areopagite through Clement of Alexandria and Origen to St. Maximus the Confessor, John Scotus Eriugena, Meister Eckhart, Johannes Tauler, and thence to Jacob Boehme and his followers.[25]

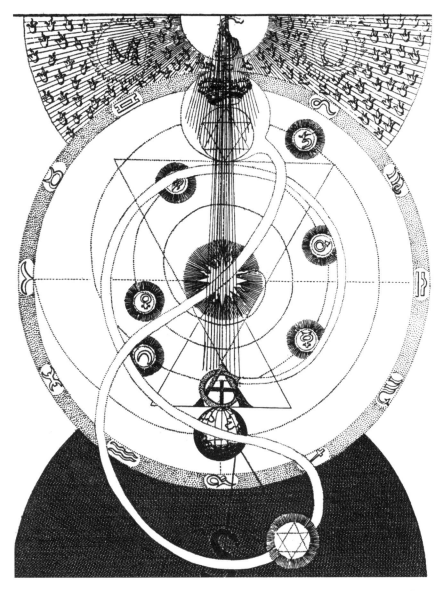

FIGURE 5.2. Figure XI, *An Illustration of the Deep Principles of Jacob Behmen . . . left by Dionysius Andrew Freher,* in William Law, *The Works of Jacob Behmen, The Teutonic Theosopher,* 4 vols. (London, 1764–1781).

Versluis sees Pseudo-Dionysius (fl. 500), the Christian monk who may have earlier studied with Proclus at the pagan school of Athens, as the seminal figure in this tradition on account of his perception of celestial hierarchies leading from the human being up to God. Dionysius's elaboration of esoteric hierarchies and intermediaries within a Christian form of Neoplatonism effected a vital synthesis that became well known in the Eastern and Western churches and the subject of repeated commentaries. Dionysius presented a mystical theology as the secret knowledge and incommunicable experience of God, nonintellectual and distinct from both natural theology and revealed theology. Through the Latin translations of his works by John Scotus Eriugena in the ninth century, Dionysius bequeathed a rich stream of mystical speculation within the traditions of the Catholic Church. His *Mystical Theology* influenced the Continental mystics Meister Eckhart (ca. 1260–1327/8), Johannes Tauler (ca. 1300–1361), and Jan van Ruysbroeck (1293–1381). But whereas the medieval commentators saw Dionysius as a mystic seeking unity with the godhead, the post-Renaissance world regarded him rather as a Neoplatonist using theosophy as a divine wisdom for ascent through the heavenly hierarchies. Thus the Protestant theosophers all drew upon this Dionysian symbolism of spiritual ascent, which included both angelic and human initiators. The celestial hierarchy is based on an emanationist cosmology descending from the One as a ray of light, and the corresponding path of ascent passes up this ray, changeless in itself, firm in its own unity, and elevating those who, according to their capacity, turn towards it.[26] Versluis regards this ladder of intermediaries as a basic characteristic of theosophy: "The function of higher beings is to illuminate those beneath them, while they in turn are illuminated by those above them."[27] Veiled in scripture and liturgy, as well as in the natural world, the ray retains its transcendent nature. It is *theophanic*, revealing God all around us.

Versluis sees Platonism and Hermeticism as intrinsic to theosophy. Platonism presents the initiatory mystery traditions in parables, myths, and poetic images, recapitulating a perennial metaphysics that can ally itself with Judaism, Christianity, or Islam. Hermeticism is likewise initiatory but also strongly cosmological. *Poimandres* speaks about the nature of the cosmos, the Logos, the "seven administrators" and the seven planets, and the spiritual constitution of human beings. These late ancient spiritual traditions combined with a medieval mystical tradition to create Christian theosophy standing for an inward transmutation of the soul effected by a "new birth" in Christ. Seventeenth-century theosophy is thus the confluence of two streams: (1) the alchemical-Hermetic stream deriving from Paracelsus, involving images, figures, and principles, where spirit informs nature; and (2) the mystical German stream deriving from Meister Eckhart, a supracosmological understanding of that which transcends nature.[28]

Regarding the historical appearance of theosophy in the early seventeenth century, it also represents a complex response to the Reformation. On the one hand, it was a response to the rigors of Lutheran orthodoxy, but on the other, it restored something that the Counter-Reformation was also providing. Although a Protestant in his quest for individual revelation, Jacob Boehme also seeks to compensate for Protestantism's loss of the universal Catholic Church and its rich liturgy. Once Protestantism had abandoned Catholic ceremonialism and iconography in favor of a simple austerity, hard pews, and a simple wooden cross, theosophy supplied a rich inward imagery of hierarchies, angelic intermediaries, planets and stars, the feminine Sophia, and celestial vistas. Theosophy also compensated for the gorgeous outer display of Catholic worship with an intensified individual piety. Thus, theosophy is not anti-ritualistic but extends liturgical awareness into everyday life with a pious celebration of community, work, service, and daily bread. While theosophy would remain an esoteric current predominantly within the Protestant fold, the example of such Catholic theosophers as Louis Claude de Saint-Martin and Franz von Baader in later centuries indicates the potential affinity of theosophy with the rich intermediary world of Catholic imagination.

Pietism

Following its "golden age" in the seventeenth century, theosophy continued to exercise a powerful influence throughout the eighteenth century, especially on the Continent. As theosophy originated as a heterodox response in a Lutheran context, German authors still predominated among its exponents in the first half of the century, but Continental high-grade Freemasonry and illuminism accompany theosophy in the second half.

Eighteenth-century theosophy is also related to Pietism, a widespread and influential reform movement from the late seventeenth century onward. This Lutheran movement traces its origins to Johann Arndt (1555–1621), whose *Vier Bücher vom wahren Christenthum* (*Four Books of True Christianity*) (1605–1610) emphasized an interior, vital Christianity as opposed to a formal, rigid, and institutional variety. Arndt's book of edification contained key esoteric references, including Hermes Trismegistus, Paracelsus, and Valentin Weigel. Philipp Jakob Spener (1635–1705) was sympathetic to the writings of Boehme and gave the Pietist movement its manifesto with his work *Pia Desideria* (1675), which emphasized rebirth, renewal, and a personal form of Christianity. Spener achieved significant influence on appointment as senior court preacher at Dresden from 1686. Spener's famous pupil August Hermann Francke (1663–1727) combined zeal with practical vision and organizational ability at Halle, where his educational foundation, orphanage, and pastoral training school were established. Radical Pietists such as Gottfried Arnold (1666–1714) often separated themselves from their original churches to found sects, and some were influenced strongly by Boehme's theosophy. A major example of separatism is the Moravian Church, deriving from the *Unitas Fratrum* associated with the name of Jan Amos Comenius (1592–1670), and refounded by Nicolaus Ludwig, Count Zinzendorf (1700–1760). However, in the duchy of Württemberg, the Protestant state of southwest Germany (Swabia), Pietism was characterized by a combination of biblical scholarship and theosophical speculation; its chief representatives being Johann Albrecht Bengel (1687–1752) and Friedrich Christoph Oetinger (1702–1782).[29]

Given its emphasis on interior spirituality, Pietism fostered an intellectual atmosphere receptive to esotericism. During the first part of the eighteenth century, Hermeticism and alchemy were widespread in Germany. In his work *Das Weltbild des jungen Goethes* (1969), Rolf Christian Zimmermann has commented on an "eclectic Enlightenment," wherein rational philosophy was accompanied by mystical, theosophical currents deriving from Boehme and carried by Pietism. Johann Konrad Dippel (1673–1734), a prominent radical Pietist converted by Gottfried Arnold, turned to Hermetic studies and alchemy as a key to nature around 1700. In 1710, Samuel Richter (alias Sincerus Renatus) launched a new wave of alchemico-Rosicrucianism with the publication of *Die wahrhaffte und volkommene Bereitung des philosophischen Steins der Brüderschaft aus dem Orden des Gülden und Rosen Kreutzes* (*The true and complete preparation of the philosophical stone of the Brotherhood, from the Order of the Golden and Rosy Cross*). Richter was a pastor from Hartmannsdorf in Silesia, who had studied Protestant theology at Halle, while his pseudonym (meaning "rebirth") indicated his Pietist inspiration. He was also steeped in Paracelsian alchemy and Boehme's theosophy as demonstrated in his longer work *Theo-Philosophica Theoretica et Practica* (1711). Alchemical works of the period evinced a theosophical background: Georg von Welling (1655–1727) published *Opus mago-theosophicum et cabbalisticum* (1719) and Anton Josef Kirchweger (d. 1746) wrote *Aurea Catena Homeri* (1723). Both works were read by Pietists and influenced the young Goethe later in the century.[30]

FURTHER READING

Dietrich Blaufuß, "Pietism," in *Dictionary of Gnosis and Western Esotericism*, edited by Wouter J. Hanegraaff et al., 2 vols. (Leiden: Brill, 2005), Vol. 2, pp. 955–960.
Jacob Boehme, *The Aurora, That Is the Day-Spring*, translated by John Sparrow (Edmonds, Wash.: Holmes, 1992; first published in 1656).
———, *The Signature of All Things* (Cambridge, England: James Clarke, 1969).
Pierre Deghaye, "Jacob Boehme and His Followers," in *Modern Esoteric Spirituality*, edited by Antoine Faivre and Jacob Needleman (London: SCM Press, 1993), pp. 210–247.

Peter C. Erb (ed.), *Pietists: Selected Writings,* Classics of Western Spirituality series (New York: Paulist Press, 1983).

Antoine Faivre, "Christian Theosophy," in *Dictionary of Gnosis and Western Esotericism,* edited by Wouter J. Hanegraaff et al., 2 vols. (Leiden: Brill, 2005), Vol. 1, pp. 258–267.

————, *Theosophy, Imagination, Tradition: Studies in Western Esotericism* (Albany: State University of New York Press, 2000).

Johann Georg Gichtel, *Awakening to Divine Wisdom: Christian Initiation into Three Worlds,* translated and edited by Arthur Versluis (St. Paul, Minn.: New Grail Publishing, 2004).

Rufus M. Jones, *Spiritual Reformers in the Sixteenth and Seventeenth Centuries* (London: Macmillan, 1914).

Adam McLean (ed.), *The "Key" of Jacob Boehme,* translated by William Law, with an illustration of the deep principles of Jacob Behmen by Dionysius Andrew Freher (Grand Rapids, Mich.: Phanes Press, 1991).

————, *The Three Tables of D. A. Freher* (Glasgow: Magnum Opus Hermetic Source-works No. 28, 2003). Black-and-white illustrations with full commentary.

————, *The Three Tables of Man: His Creation, Fall, and Regeneration Revealed in Three Elaborate Diagrams by D. A. Freher* (Glasgow: Magnum Opus Hermetic Source-works No. 31, 2005). Full-color and fold-out illustrations.

Nils Thune, *The Behmenists and Philadelphians: A Contribution to the Study of English Mysticism in the Seventeenth and Eighteenth Centuries* (Uppsala, Sweden: Almquist & Wiksells, 1948).

Arthur Versluis, "Christian Theosophic Literature of the Seventeenth and Eighteenth Centuries," in *Gnosis and Hermeticism from Antiquity to Modern Times,* edited by Roelof van den Broek and Wouter J. Hanegraaff (Albany: State University of New York Press, 1998), pp. 217–236.

————, *Theosophia: Hidden Dimensions of Christianity* (Hudson, N.Y.: Lindisfarne, 1994).

————, *Wisdom's Children: A Christian Esoteric Tradition* (Albany: State University of New York Press, 1999).

Robin Waterfield (ed.), *Jacob Boehme,* Western Esoteric Masters series (Berkeley, Calif.: North Atlantic Books, 2001).

Andrew Weeks, *Boehme: An Intellectual Biography of the Seventeenth-Century Philosopher and Mystic* (Albany: State University of New York Press, 1991).

6

Rosicrucianism

Contemporary with Jacob Boehme's writings in the first two decades of the seventeenth century, there arose another powerful and distinct current of esotericism in the German-speaking lands. This was the legend of Christian Rosenkreutz and the Fraternity of the Rosy Cross. Published as anonymous manifestos, these cryptic texts described the discovery of a new philosophy based on alchemy and related to medicine and healing but also to mathematics and mechanical arts. This discovery represented a pansophy, or universal wisdom, as well as an illumination of a religious and spiritual nature. Besides asserting the notion of perfect harmony between macrocosm and microcosm, the manifestos were millenarian in their association with a universal and general reformation. Its mythical agents throughout Europe were the Rosicrucian brothers, members of an invisible order of adepts. Against a charged background of religious and political conflict, the original Rosicrucian manifestos attracted widespread interest and a wave of applications to join the order, but these remained unanswered. However, the archetypal imagery of rose and cross, the recovery of lost knowledge, and (not least) the idea of a hidden brotherhood working for the regeneration of mankind held an enduring fascination for the esoteric imagination. From its obscure origins, the Rosicrucian myth would inspire literature, eighteenth-century Masonic adaptations, the rituals of the Golden Dawn, the leading magical order of the modern occult revival, and still exerts a powerful mystique today.

The Rosicrucian Manifestos

The first Rosicrucian manifesto, titled *Fama Fraternitatis*, was published in German at Cassel in 1614. Bound together in the same volume was a German translation of an extract from Traiano Boccalini's *Ragguagli di Parnasso* (1612) about a universal and general reformation, colored by antipapal and anti-Habsburg views in defense of Venetian independence. Also included was a reply to the *Fama*, dated 1612, by Adam Haslmayr (ca. 1560–1630), who states that he saw a manuscript of it in 1610. Haslmayr, a public notary in the Tirol, was an outspoken advocate of Paracelsus's revolutionary theological writings, which Haselmayr promoted as the *Theophrastia Sancta*, a new gospel for a supradenominational religion based on the "light of nature." The *Fama*'s publication together with these other texts is strongly suggestive concerning the Protestant and Paracelsian sympathies of the manifesto author(s).[1]

The *Fama* begins by trumpeting God's recent revelation to men of the perfect knowledge of Jesus Christ and nature so that they may renew and perfect all arts. In this way, man may "understand his own nobleness and worth, and why he is called Microcosmus, and how far his knowledge extends into Nature."[2] However, many of the learned oppose this new knowledge, preferring the obsolete authority of the pope, Aristotle, and Galen. Identifying this reformation with the aims of "our Fraternity," the manifesto then relates the imaginary story of its founder, the "highly illuminated" Christian Rosenkreutz. The life and travels of this legendary figure relate the pansophy of the *Fama* to a mythographic account of the earlier transmission of Islamic and Jewish learning to the Latin West and its subsequent penetration of Europe as a subcultural Paracelsian tradition.

The Life of Christian Rosenkreutz

Rosenkreutz's life is supposed to have spanned the fourteenth and fifteenth centuries, for we learn in the second Rosicrucian manifesto, *Confessio Fraternitatis* (1615), that he was born in 1378 and lived for 106 years, thus dying in 1484. According to the narrative of the *Fama Fraternitatis*, Brother C. R., a German, was schooled from the age of five in a cloister, and at the age of sixteen undertook a pilgrimage to the Holy Land. However, his companion died along the way, in Cyprus, and C. R. neglected Jerusalem in favor of travels through the Islamic world in pursuit of arcane knowledge. At Damcar, in Arabia, he was received by the wise men as one they had long expected. Although some translations give this name wrongly as Damascus in Syria, a town called Damar still exists in Yemen in southwest Arabia. As legends of the queen of Sheba associated this region with the Sabaeans, who in the ninth century cultivated a religion based on the *Corpus Hermeticum* and astrology, the *Fama*'s reference to Damcar (based on a cartographic misreading of Damar) may suggest a specific inspiration in biblical legend and Hermetic lore deriving from its exotic cultivation in the Muslim East.[3] At Damcar, C. R. learned medicine, mathematics, and Arabic, and he translated the Book M. (probably *Liber Mundi*) into Latin. After three years there, C. R. traveled on to Egypt, where he studied natural history, and then sailed along the Mediterranean coast of North Africa to Fez, where he spent two years studying magic and the Kabbalah. These arts enhanced his own faith, which was now based on "the harmony of the whole world." Here explicit reference is made to Johannes Kepler's recent publication on the celestial orbits and also the Hermetic idea of concord or correspondence, whereby all that is in "the whole great world" (macrocosm) is also included in "the little body of man" (microcosm), by the agreement and sympathy of the latter's religion, language, and members with God, heaven, and earth.[4] The author applauded the Arabians' and Africans' readiness to share their knowledge and stated that Germany then had many "magicians, kabbalists, physicians and philosophers" who ought similarly to collaborate.

Brother C. R. next went to Spain to communicate his new knowledge to the learned and to show how the faults of the church could be amended. But the scholars of Spain, feeling threatened, rejected this new learning. C. R. then traveled to other countries but received a similar negative reception. The manifesto author adds here that the world in these times was full of such prophecies and brought forth men who broke through the darkness. The *Fama* called Paracelsus one such man because, though not a member of the fraternity, he was deeply versed in the Book M. and well grounded in the aforementioned harmony. Paracelsus was also frustrated by reactionary scholars and unable to confer peacefully about his knowledge of nature. The reference to Paracelsus indicates an important link in Rosicrucian mythology between the medieval reception of Muslim and Jewish esoteric traditions in the Latin West and their later dissemination in Paracelsian *Naturphilosophie*, itself rooted in Renaissance Neoplatonism, alchemy, and medieval German mysticism.

Chastened by his fruitless efforts in various countries, Brother C. R. returned to Germany, where he built a house. As an adept in the transmutation of metals, he could have made a reputation, but he lived quietly, studying mathematics and making many fine instruments, an indication of the practical application of his esoteric learning in harmony. After five years, he decided to again pursue a reformation. He chose three brothers from his former cloister, and they swore to be faithful, diligent, and secretive. This was the foundation of the Fraternity of the Rosy Cross, initially by four persons, who made "the magical language and writing, with a large dictionary, which we yet daily use to God's praise and glory."[5]

The *Fama* author then continues the story of the order. Its numbers grew to eight brothers, and they established a center called the House of the Holy Spirit and composed a book of their "secret and manifest philosophy." Once they were all instructed in this wisdom, they traveled to other countries to spread their knowledge, with only two brethren remaining with the founder at its center. They had only six rules, foremost of which was they should profess only to cure the sick and accept no payment. They should wear no special habit but follow local custom in dress. On a certain day each year, they should meet in the House of the Holy Spirit or inform the other brothers, in writing, of the cause of their absence. Each brother should look for a suitable person to succeed him after his death. The word C. R. should be their sign. The fraternity should remain secret for a hundred years.

The first of the fraternity to die, simply identified as J. O., is described as someone knowledgeable in Kabbalah who had written a book on the subject. He lived his last years in England, where he cured a young earl of Norfolk of leprosy. At length, many other brothers succeeded the original brothers. This third generation of the fraternity knew no more about the original brethren than their bare names, nor even where Brother C. R. died or was buried.[6] However, the fraternity and its secret wisdom suddenly assumed new importance when the vault where C. R. was buried was miraculously discovered behind a wall in the house of one of the contemporary brothers.

The Vault of Christian Rosenkreutz

The discovery of the vault and its description are central aspects of the Rosicrucian legend and its nineteenth-century legacy. The vault had seven sides, each five feet wide and eight feet high, which were inscribed with geometrical figures and sentences. Although the sun had never shone within this closed space, it was lit by a magical, inner sun. In the center of the vault, instead of a tombstone there stood a round altar covered with a brass plate, bearing in Latin such inscriptions as "This compendium of the universe I made in my lifetime to be my tomb" and "Jesus, all things to me," together with four circular figures and mottoes. Both the ceiling and floor of the vault were divided into triangles, formed by lines running from the seven corners to the center. Along each wall of the vault stood a chest containing various things, including books by Paracelsus, a dictionary of Paracelsian terms, wonderful bells, lamps, and "artificial songs." The recurrence of Paracelsian references is strongly indicative of the Swiss-Swabian's evident inspiration to the Rosicrucian author(s).

Removing the side of the altar, the brothers found the uncorrupted body of C. R. In his hand, he held the parchment book T, the end of which describes him as a grain buried in the breast of Jesus Christ. This passage goes on to identify C. R. as a man admitted into the mysteries and secrets of heaven and earth through divine revelation, subtle thought, and tireless labor. Finding the knowledge he garnered on his travels in Arabia and Africa not suitable for his own times, he safeguarded it for posterity to discover. He constructed a microcosm corresponding in all motions to the macrocosm and drew up a compendium of all things past, present, and future. From this account we also learn that C. R. was hidden in this vault by his disciples for 120 years. (As the *Confessio* implies his death in 1484, this rediscovery of the vault thus falls in the year 1604, a decade before the printing of the manifestos.) Eight brothers subscribe themselves, followed by the statement: "We are born of God, we die in Jesus, we live again through the Holy Spirit."[7]

The Confessio Fraternitatis

Whereas the *Fama* contains the marvelous stories of Christian Rosenkreutz's life and mission, and the rediscovery of his vault, the *Confessio* is much shorter. While the *Fama* celebrated science, medicine, and philosophy under a hermetico-pansophic banner, the *Confessio*, as its title implies, offered a statement of faith. The work was published at Cassel in 1615 in Latin, suggesting a more learned audience, and it was preceded in the same volume by a work titled *A Brief Consideration of the more Secret Philosophy* by Philip à Gabella. This work consisted of quotations and commentaries on the first thirteen theorems of John Dee's *Monas hieroglyphica* (1564). Gabella (most probably a pseudonym referring to Cabala), analyses Dee's mysterious sign, which included all the planetary symbols, the sign of Aries, representing fire, and thus the alchemical processes, as well as geometrical transformations. Readers of the *Confessio* were evidently expected to relate it to the Hermetic philosophy of John Dee.

Unlike the pansophy of *Fama*, the *Confessio* accords a favored place to the Bible and insists that Rosicrucian mysteries are attainable only by means of God's grace. The address at the beginning of the *Confessio* asserts, "We do now altogether freely . . . call the Pope of Rome Antichrist." Just as saying this was formerly regarded as a mortal sin for which men were put to death, so the time shall come when the Rosicrucians' secret philosophy will be published before the whole world. The Rosicrucian author(s) claim to know the primal characters, which God has incorporated in the Bible and also imprinted in heaven and earth; this is an evident reference to the primal alphabet of nature, an idea deriving

from Christian Cabala, familiar to Agrippa and John Dee. It is from these characters that the Rosicrucians have borrowed their "magic writing," thus forging a
new language in which the nature of all things can be expressed. This is no less
than the original language of Adam and Enoch. The *Confessio*'s emphasis on the
Bible's precedence over the book of nature is a further point of agreement with
Paracelsus's Christian fideism joined to Ficinian Neoplatonism.

A strong millenarian element is also evident in the *Confessio*. Though the
pope's tyranny has been broken in Germany, his final fall is postponed until
"our times," when he shall be destroyed by "the new voice of a roaring lion."
Adam Haslmayr's response to the *Fama* had also referred to the "Lion from the
North," an apocalyptic agent of God's defeat of the Antichrist in a well-known
sixteenth-century prophecy, falsely attributed to Paracelsus.[8] References to the
Miranda sexta aetatis and God's lighting of the sixth *Candelabrium* recall the
prophecies of the twelfth-century Calabrian abbot, Joachim of Fiore (1145–1203),
who divided world history into seven cosmic days, each lasting a thousand years.
The first five corresponded to the Age of the Father, the sixth to the Age of the
Son, and the (imminent) seventh to the millennial Age of the Holy Spirit.[9] It is
likely that the Rosicrucian author(s) were influenced by the pseudo-Joachimist
pope prophecies, widespread in the sixteenth century, which testified to the imminent defeat of the Antichrist and the arrival of the millennium. The *Confessio*
also alludes to the appearance of new stars in the constellations of Serpentar-
ius and Cygnus as powerful signs of an approaching world transformation. As
these stars first appeared in 1604, this astronomical reference also underlines
the importance of the date of the opening of the vault.

The Chemical Wedding of Christian Rosenkreutz (1616)

Through these manifestos, the Brotherhood of Rosy Cross introduced itself as a
new movement using the Renaissance sciences of magic, Cabala, and alchemy
to establish an order of harmonious correspondences. The two Rosicrucian
manifestos attracted enormous interest through their announcement of a glo-
bal reformation based on a program of medical and scientific advances in the
Hermetic tradition. A year after the publication of the *Confessio*, the third anonymous Rosicrucian text, *Chymische Hochzeit Christiani Rosencreutz. Anno 1459*
(*The Chemical Wedding of Christian Rosenkreutz*), was published in German at
Strasbourg. This extraordinary romance or fantasy was an allegorical tale of a
royal marriage suffused with alchemical symbolism. Unlike the manifestos,
which addressed the transformation of society, *The Chemical Wedding* describes
the inner transformation of the soul. The wedding is dated 1459, which would

make Christian Rosenkreutz eighty-one years old on the basis of information in the earlier manifestos.[10]

The narrative is divided into seven days. The first day opens with the narrator, Christian Rosenkreutz, preparing himself on Easter eve for his Easter Communion. In this account, he is neither the founder of a secret brotherhood, nor the initiate of esoteric knowledge gleaned from exotic travels, but rather an elderly, humble hermit. Suddenly a tempest arises, and a beautiful female winged figure appears, in blue raiment spangled with golden stars. She delivers a wedding invitation which contains the following verses:

> Today—today—today
> Is the wedding of the King.
> If you are born for this,
> Chosen by God for joy,
> You may ascend the mount
> Whereon three temples stand
> And see the thing yourself.
> Take heed,
> Observe yourself!
> If you're not clean enough,
> The wedding can work ill.
> Perjure here at your peril;
> He who is light, beware!

Beside the opening line stands John Dee's *Monas* symbol, suggestive of his Hermetic philosophy, and below the verses is written *Sponsus et Sponsa* (bridegroom and bride).[11]

Christian Rosenkreutz laments his lack of esoteric knowledge, his fitness for the investigation of nature's secrets, and his preparedness for this spiritual trial. He then falls into a dream, in which he is imprisoned in a dark tower together with many others. His liberation, by means of a suspended rope, is interpreted to mean that God has granted him a light while still in this world. Waking and thus encouraged, he dresses for the wedding in his white linen coat with a blood-red belt bound crosswise over his shoulders and sticks four red roses into his hat, so that "I could be more easily recognised in the crowd by this sign."[12] These are, of course, the Rosicrucian symbols.

On the second day, Christian Rosenkreutz journeys to the wedding at a splendid castle. On arrival, he successfully passes various porters (guardian figures) and then attends a welcoming banquet. On the third day, a weighing trial is organized by a presiding figure in the tale, a virgin whose secret name is Alchimia. All the guests are weighed in scales to establish their moral worth, and a great many are found wanting and sentenced to punishments of increasing degrees of severity, according to their lies and false claims.[13] For all his humility, Rosenkreutz is given a high place. On the fourth day, an allegorical play is performed in seven acts. Its plot concerns the struggle of a princess for self-realization and freedom from the authority of her guardian, an old king; her seduction by a Moor and later liberation from this brutal captor; and eventual union with the king's son. Following the play, dinner is served, and the mood becomes increasingly somber. To Rosenkreutz's amazement, a black executioner enters and beheads three royal couples, "which seemed to me a very bloody wedding."[14]

This killing of the six royal persons is the turning point of the allegory, and Rosenkreutz now begins to assume a more active role. The sixth day is devoted to alchemical work. The virgin produces some liquids extracted the previous day from herbs and gems, and these are poured upon the corpses of the royal persons until they dissolve. Through a process of distillation, the liquid becomes more yellow and is drained into a golden sphere. Once this has cooled, it is found to contain a large, snow-white egg, from which an alchemical bird is hatched. The bird is fed on the blood of the beheaded people and undergoes three color transformations corresponding to traditional stages in the alchemical process. After the bird itself has been decapitated, its blood is collected and body burned to ashes. Two little moulds containing the moistened ashes are later opened to reveal images of a little boy and girl. These two homunculi are then fed with drops of the bird's blood, which causes them to grow in size until the resurrected young king and queen awake.[15] On the seventh day, the virgin informs Rosenkreutz and his fellow alchemists that they are now knights of the Order of the Golden Stone. In the castle, they hear the rules of their order, participate in further festivities, and then Rosenkreutz departs for home.

Authorship, Motives, and Reception

Johann Valentin Andreae and the Tübingen Circle

The authorship of the anonymous Rosicrucian texts has been hotly debated by scholars for centuries, but much of the evidence points toward a circle around Johann Valentin Andreae (1586–1654).[16] He was born at Herrenberg in Württemberg into a family of distinguished Lutheran churchmen. As chancellor of Tübingen University and professor of theology, his grandfather, Jakob Andreae (1528–1590), played a leading role in the Reformation and coauthored the Book of Concord (1577), which served as the doctrinal basis of the Lutheran Church. His father, Johannes Andreae (1554–1601), also followed a clerical career combined with a strong interest in alchemy. From 1602 to 1607, Johann Valentin Andreae studied arts and theology at Tübingen, where he befriended Christoph Besold, an older scholar who encouraged his interest in esotericism. Around 1605, he wrote the first version of *The Chemical Wedding of Christian Rosenkreutz*. In 1607, he had to break off his studies owing to a scandal, traveled through West Germany and worked as a tutor in Lauingen. He visited nearby Dillingen, a bastion of the Jesuits, whom Andreae, a staunch Protestant, regarded as the Antichrist. The anti-Jesuitical theme of Haslmayr's 1612 reply to the *Fama* would seem to confirm one of Andreae's motives in possibly coauthoring the other Rosicrucian manifestos. Returning to Tübingen in 1608, he came to know Tobias Hess, a Paracelsian physician with an interest in apocalyptic prophecy. It is in this period that Andreae is supposed to have been involved in the composition of the Rosicrucian manifestoes. After further international travels in 1610–1612, Andreae took up theological studies at the Tübinger Stift, the premier theological college of Protestant Württemberg, becoming a curate at Vaihingen in 1614, and shortly afterward marrying the daughter of a clergyman. By 1620, he had become superintendent (dean) at Calw. His subsequent ecclesiastical career brought him high office as court preacher in Stuttgart and spiritual adviser to a royal princess of Württemberg.

Christoph Besold (1577–1638) was a jurist who became a professor of law at Tübingen in 1610. More important, he was a polymath who knew nine languages, including Hebrew and Arabic, and was deeply versed in theology, medieval mysticism, and Hermetic thought. Besold hoped for a new spiritual reformation that would transcend the political and ecclesiastical limitations of the present. He was enthusiastic about Tommaso Campanella's Hermetic utopia, *The City of the Sun* (written in 1602). His own philosophy was presented in his *Signatura temporum* (1614) and *Axiomata Philosophico-Theologica* (1616), which was dedicated to Andreae. Andreae had unrestricted access to Besold's library of 4,000 volumes on theology, Kabbalah, philosophy, medicine, and history. Given Andreae's access to this library and to Besold's encyclopedic learning, it is apparent that the journey of Father C.R.C. is in one respect an allegory for the transfer of knowledge from the Muslim East to the West via Spain. Andreae could have got more background information from his friend Wilhelm Schickhardt, the Tübingen orientalist, while Dam(c)ar actually appeared on the 1569 Mercator map of Arabia, most likely available to Andreae.[17]

Tobias Hess (1568–1614), the chief inspirer of the Rosicrucian manifestos, practiced as a Paracelsian physician in Tübingen and pursued extensive scholarly interests in theology, philosophy, and science. He was engrossed in the prophecies of Simon Studion (1565–ca. 1605), another Württemberg scholar, who had written of a series of fiery trigons (conjunctions of three planets), which were

taken as signs for earthly events heralding new empires or new religious movements. Studion had made a careful study of similar ideas in the work of the Italian
heretic Giacomo Brocardo, who regarded the year 1584 as the inauguration of a
major new cycle. In 1604, Studion completed his work *Naometria*, which brought
complex number mysticism and biblical prophecy to bear on world events. Here
Studion called upon King James of England, Duke Frederick of Württemberg,
and King Henri IV of Navarre to rally behind the rose as a symbol of the new age.
Hess corresponded with Studion and agreed with him in 1597 that the Papacy
must fall in seven years, 1604. This year assumed an extraordinary importance
for Hess. Marked by the appearance of new stars, the year also fulfilled one of
Brocardo's prophecies that the last age would last 120 years from the death of
Luther in 1483. Hess's millenarian expectations had a strong influence on the
legend of Christian Rosenkreutz, the opening of whose tomb in 1604 also falls
120 years after his death and marks the beginning of a new age.[18]

Many scholars think that Andreae and a circle of his friends in Tübingen created the manifestos as a response to the contemporary crisis of European thought.
The Holy Roman Empire with its mosaic of particularist states, each following the
confession of their territorial sovereign according to the Peace of Augsburg, was
divided. The Book of Concord had not achieved the hoped-for unity among the
Lutheran states, the Counter-Reformation had been launched at the Council of
Trent (1545–1563), the Society of Jesus (est. 1540) targeted the spread of Protestantism throughout Europe, and Lutheran orthodoxy was accordingly strengthened.
Meanwhile, medical knowledge was rapidly advancing and urgently required
some reconciliation with the religious worldview of the confessions.

However, Andreae distanced himself from the manifestos and only in a
posthumously published autobiography, did he acknowledge his authorship of
The Chemical Wedding. Carlos Gilly has located four manuscript copies of the
Fama, dating from 1610 to 1614.[19] The contents of the *Fama* and *Confessio* clearly
indicate the Paracelsian, cabalistic, and "Naometrian" interests of Tobias Hess,
and references to Rosenkreutz in the two manifestos and in the earlier draft
of *The Chemical Wedding* suggest a continuity. Those considerations, together
with documentary evidence of personal association, seem to point to a collaboration. There are strong grounds for locating the authorship in a collaboration
of Hess, Andreae, and Besold over the years 1609–1611.

Nonetheless, Andreae's authorship of the manifestos is open to serious
question. Andreae acknowledged only his authorship of *The Chemical Wedding*, and as a Lutheran churchman he later gave his solemn oath that he "had
always laughed at the Rosicrucian fable and combated the little curiosity-
brothers." He followed up his publication of *The Chemical Wedding* with a series
of works—*Menippus* (1617), *Invitatio Fraternitatis Christi* (1617–1618), *Turris*

Babel (1619), and *De curiositatis pernicie syntagma* (1620)—that disparaged the esoteric nature of the Rosicrucian order and its pursuits. Although some have argued that Andreae needed to stress his Christian orthodoxy once he had embarked upon his ecclesiastical career, Montgomery has assembled strong evidence that he always distanced himself from the manifestos.[20] At Tübingen, he actually contested the millenarian and Naometrian speculations of his friend Hess, which supply so much of the Rosicrucian dating and apocalyptic in the *Fama* and *Confessio*. Since Studion had been working on these matters since before 1593 and another enthusiast, Julius Sperber, recalled material similar to the content of the manifestos as far back as 1595, the manifestos may have even been written some years before Andreae was at Tübingen.[21]

Montgomery has conducted a far-ranging study of Andreae's life and theological work. On the basis of his painstaking analysis of the manifestos' content, their prophetic context, and the religious views of Besold, Hess, and Andreae, Montgomery suggests that the myth of the Rose Cross first appeared in Germany among esoteric Protestant enthusiasts such as Aegidius Gutmann (1490–1584) and Julius Sperber (?–1615) in the last quarter of the sixteenth century, before its encounter with Studion's Naometrism in the 1590s. According to Montgomery, the manifestos were then initially composed by Hess and possibly others ca. 1593–1604 in anticipation of the opening of the vault in 1604 according to Studion's apocalyptic timetable. Montgomery explicitly excludes Andreae from the circle of authorship, offering a detailed comparison of the *Fama* and *The Chemical Wedding* as to their chronologies of Rosenkreuz's life. In their juxtaposition, Montgomery sees two distinct myth-makers: "the one officially Protestant but essentially pagan, the other deeply Christian both in 'profession and confession.'" Montgomery concludes by claiming that Andreae published his earlier "Christian-alchemical marriage" account of the Rosenkreutz story to reverse what he saw as the damage done by the manifestos' occult and pagan (i.e., Hermetic-Neoplatonic) content.[22]

Christian of Anhalt and the Palatinate

In her major work *The Rosicrucian Enlightenment* (1972), Frances Yates advances a bold thesis concerning the political inspiration of the manifestos. She has argued that they represent a Protestant propaganda offensive against the mustering forces of Catholic reaction led by the Habsburg empire. Yates identifies Prince Christian of Anhalt as the chief architect of an Anglo-German Protestant alliance against Habsburg-Catholic hegemony that culminated in the marriage in 1613 of Frederick V, the Elector Palatine with his seat at Heidelberg, to Elizabeth, the daughter of King James I of England. Anhalt also canvassed

the possibility that Frederick might become king of Bohemia, thereby extending Protestant rule into the Habsburg empire. Bohemia strongly supported
Reformed churches as a recurrent strategy in its national identity and offered
its crown to Frederick in 1619. Frederick and Elizabeth reigned only until November 1620, when Habsburg armies crushed Protestant forces in the Battle of
the White Mountain near Prague in November 1620. In Yates's thesis, the publication of the *Fama* and *Confessio* represent the hopeful expectation of a new
age of Protestant tolerance and science backed by Hermetic-cabalistic ideas.[23]

Yates's thesis has many merits as she relates the manifestos to the contemporary political and cultural landscape of Central Europe. It is possible
that Anhalt saw the political potential of the manifestos and arranged for their
publication in the period 1614–1616 as part of his campaign on Frederick's be-
half. However, the immediate religious and intellectual influences around Tobias Hess and Johann Valentin Andreae easily explain their actual contents.
The pansophic interests of Andreae and Christoph Besold interacted with the
apocalyptic expectations of Simon Studion and Tobias Hess, combined with
the latter's Paracelsian medicine, to represent a late-sixteenth-century revival
of universal Hermetic wisdom, and its hopeful deployment in a new age of
medicine, science, and genuine Christian reformation under tolerant Protestant leadership. Also, the dating of the manuscripts—*The Chemical Wedding*'s
first draft in 1605, and the *Fama* and *Confessio* most likely between 1610 and
1612—make a specifically pro-palatine inspiration less likely.

The Rosicrucian Furor in Germany

Yates implies that the *Fama* and *Confessio* were not originally intended for publication by their authors and printed without Andreae's approval—perhaps to
serve Anhalt's purposes. Once in broad circulation, repeatedly reprinting, the
manifestos looked quite different from the pious millenarian tracts once in private hands. The widespread interest in gold-making, alchemy, theosophy, mysticism, reform, and Renaissance Hermeticism in Germany and beyond brought
a massive response, both for and against the ideas of the fictitious fraternity. Between 1614 and 1620, some two hundred books and tracts flew from the presses.
Many of these overlooked the fraternity's rejection of false alchemy and sought
admission to the order to learn the secrets of transmutation. Others, such as
Theophilus Philaretus, Theophilus Schweighart, and Joachim Morsius, identified themselves with the aims of the fraternity. There was strong opposition from
the camp of Lutheran orthodoxy. Eusebius Christianus Crucigerus, Georg Ros-
tius, Johannes Hintsem, and Johannes Sivertus condemned the Rosicrucians

FIGURE 6.1. Collegium Fraternitatis C.R.C., in Theophilus Schweighart [i.e. Daniel Mögling], *Speculum Sophicum Rhodo-Stauroticum* (1618). Courtesy of Bbibliotheca Philosophica Hermetica, Amsterdam.

as Calvinists, heretics, and false prophets. Rationalist and Aristotelian criticism came from Henricus Neuhusius, Hisaias sub Cruce Atheniensis, and Andreas Libavius, who opposed the Renaissance occult sciences. Only one Catholic author, S. Mundus, entered the fray, which suggests that Rosicrucianism was seen primarily as an internal Protestant conflict.[24]

Andreae, by then established as a young pastor at Vaihingen and fearful of the implications of the furor, sought to distance himself from the published manifestos. Hans Schick has argued that Andreae's publication of *The Chemical Wedding* in the form of an allegorical tale may have been intended to weaken the manifestos' polemical impact, now an embarrassment to him. In his book *Menippus*, Andreae distances himself from pansophy and stresses his obedience to Christ. However, Andreae still attempted to found Christian sodalities. In 1617, he published an invitation to join a "Societas Christiana," which he favorably compared to "the jest of the Rosicrucians." In 1619, he published *Christianopolis*, the first German utopia in the tradition of Thomas More's and owing a certain debt to Campanella's *City of the Sun*. In 1628, he planned a "Unio Christiana." Schick has argued that these successive proposals represented Andreae's undiminished desire to found a real Rosicrucian fraternity, but with progressive emphasis on Christian piety to the exclusion of pansophy.[25]

Rosicrucianism in England

Michael Maier and Robert Fludd

The widespread response to the Rosicrucian texts represented a continuation and development of the project first launched by Hess and the Tübingen circle. Many authors of the letters, tracts, and books addressed to the invisible (and unresponsive) brotherhood identified themselves as Rosicrucians and brought to this tradition their own particular interests and emphasis. Michael Maier (1569–1622) was an outstanding Renaissance scholar, a doctor of both medicine and philosophy, deeply versed in alchemy and classical learning. He endorsed the Rosicrucian manifestos wholeheartedly, identifying himself with their goal and tracing their origins to ancient Egypt and the Eleusinian mysteries. Born at Kiel, Maier was educated at several European universities from 1587 until 1596, when he returned to practice medicine in Holstein and East Prussia. He practiced laboratory alchemy from 1602 to 1608, by which time he claimed he had produced the "Universal Medicine" (i.e., a panacea for all ills). In 1608, he traveled to Prague and was appointed personal physician to Emperor Rudolf II, who promptly made him a noble. Three years later, soon after Rudolf's abdication, Maier traveled to England, remaining there until 1616. Maier addressed a Christmas greeting to King James I with a proto-Rosy Cross emblem, and it is most likely that he was acquainted with Robert Fludd.[26]

Maier devoted two books to the defense of the Rosicrucians. The first, *Silentium post clamores* (1617), compared the Rosicrucians to the school of Pythagoras, which, in his view, rightly exacted vows of silence and secrecy. *Themis aurea* (1618) also defended the fraternity, listing arguments in favor of their rules for keeping anonymity, healing the sick, and so on. In *Symbola aureae mensae* (1617), Maier related the Rosicrucian event to the world tradition of mystery schools from that of Hermes Trismegistus in ancient Egypt, followed by the Hebrews, then the schools of Greece, Rome, and the Arabs.

According to *Arcana arcanissima* (1614), Maier's practical alchemy was concerned with the manufacture of medicine, not with gold-making. This work also interpreted the principal myths of antiquity as allegories of alchemy. His famous alchemical emblems in *Atalanta fugiens* (1618), arranged with music and poetry, also testified to his love of alchemy. Given his abiding devotion to *chymia*, Maier's defense of Rosicrucianism would tend to associate the latter with alchemy for subsequent generations.

Robert Fludd (1574–1637), the English Paracelsian physician and philosopher, was the great summarizer of the Renaissance Hermetic-Cabalistic tradition. The son of an ennobled Elizabethan military administrator, Fludd studied arts at Oxford and then traveled for six years on the Continent. Here Fludd encountered Paracelsian circles and discovered his vocation for medicine. After returning to Oxford in 1604 to study medicine, Fludd set up his practice in London and compiled his major encyclopedic work, *Utriusque Cosmi Historia* (History of the Macrocosm and the Microcosm). This massive work, replete with intricate engravings relating to cosmology and the correspondences between the celestial world, nature, man, the arts, and the sciences, was published in 1617–1626. This was, however, preceded in publication by his *Apologia Compendaria* (1616), his defense of the Rosicrucians against Andreas Libau, who had denigrated the Rosicrucians' doctrines of macro-microcosmic harmony, magic, alchemy, and Cabala, the foundations of Fludd's own worldview. Fludd also published two more works on the Rosicrucians.[27]

Rosicrucianism and Freemasonry

Schick suggested that Maier's introduction of Rosicrucianism into England was a factor in the stimulation of speculative Freemasonry, arguing that *Silentium post clamores* contained indications of the grade system and initiation which later prevailed in Masonic lodges. The origins of this idea derive from two German historians in the early nineteenth century. In 1804 Johann Gottlieb Buhle argued that speculative Freemasonry arose in England between 1629 and 1635 through the work of Robert Fludd, who had earlier been introduced to Rosicrucianism by Maier. Buhle's notion that English Freemasonry was rooted in Continental Rosicrucianism rather than in its own medieval guilds owed

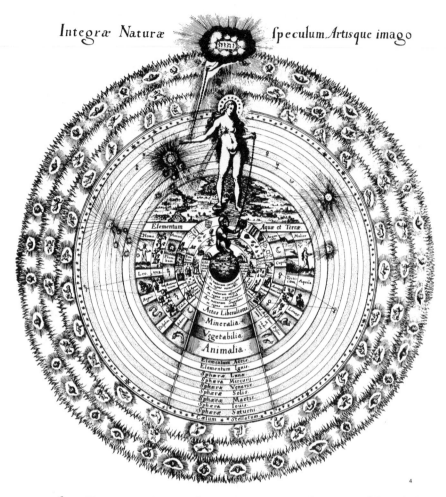

FIGURE 6.2. "Integræ naturæ speculum artisque imago" [The Mirror of the Whole of Nature and the Image of Art], in Robert Fludd, *Utriusque Cosmi Maioris ... Tomus Primus De Macrocosmi Historia* (Oppenheim, 1617), pp. 4–5.

much to Maier's identification of Rosicrucianism with Egyptian and Greek mysteries, which did form part of Freemasonry's lore. Christoph Gottlieb von Murr also found traces of Freemasonry's heritage in Maier's *Septima Philosophica* (1620).[28] However, this Maier-Fludd lineage of Freemasonry's origins has been challenged by recent scholars.

However, another link exists between English Freemasonry and Rosicrucianism. Elias Ashmole (1617–1692), the distinguished English antiquary, was admitted a Freemason in one of the earliest speculative lodges at Warrington in 1646. Ashmole was also immersed in alchemy, publishing *Fasciculus Chemicus* (1650) and his collection of medieval English alchemy, *Theatrum Chemicum Britannicum*

(1652). His interests also embraced Rosicrucianism by 1650. Among Ashmole's surviving papers is a copy of the *Fama* in his own handwriting; a fervent petition to the invisible brothers, seeking his admission to their brotherhood; and some cipher notes about their location. Also during this period, in 1652, Thomas Vaughan published the first English translation of the *Fama* and *Confessio*. The 1656 English translation of Maier's *Themis aurea* was dedicated to Elias Ashmole.[29] The possibility of an even earlier influence of Rosicrucianism upon speculative Freemasonry dating back to the 1630s in Scotland has been suggested by the historian David Stevenson.[30] The diffusion of Hermetic ideas and the art of memory in late-sixteenth-century Scotland could have accounted for gentry interest in operative lodges there, thus leading to the appearance of speculative lodges in the north of England by the 1640s, such as the one Ashmole joined.

Comenius and the Origins of the Royal Society

Several writers have noted the early introduction of Rosicrucian ideas to England through the Czech pansophist, mystic, and reformer Jan Amos Comenius (1592–1670).[31] Comenius was brought up in the Bohemian Brethren, a mystical denomination of the Hussite reformation in the Czech lands, and educated at the universities of Herborn and Heidelberg. At the former he was taught by Johann Heinrich Alsted (1588–1638), whose approach to natural science was based on pansophy or the interrelatedness of all knowledge. Comenius saw pansophy as confirmation of the creative mind or *logos* of God being present at the heart of all created things, so that they were linked in common patterns. This was a restatement of the Hermetic principle of analogy and correspondence in application to the rapidly expanding empirical study of the natural world in the seventeenth century. Comenius was a tireless student of languages, teaching methods, and natural history. He returned to Bohemia in 1614 when he began writing his first pansophic encyclopedia. After the defeat of the Elector Palatine and Protestantism in 1620, Bohemia was plunged into the ravages of the Thirty Years' War. The Bohemian Brethren was violently suppressed, and Comenius lost his family, his home, and his library. He took refuge at a Protestant nobleman's estate at Brandys, and here he wrote his mystical book *The Labyrinth of the World and the Paradise of the Heart*, which described his enthusiasm and high hopes upon reading the Rosicrucian *Fama* as early as in 1612. Comenius was strongly drawn to the ideas of Andreae, with whom he corresponded in 1628 about his Christian unions, new societies intended as practical successors to the fictitious Rosicrucian order. For his part, Andreae asked Comenius to become the executor of his reforming Rosicrucian ideas.[32]

Also interested in Andreae's Christian unions were two men whose activities had focused on the foundation and leadership of philanthropic and educational communities animated by universal reformation, the advancement of learning, and utopian ideas. Samuel Hartlib (ca. 1600–1662) had lived at Elbing in Poland, where he had taken an interest in a utopian brotherhood and communal society called Antilia to be founded along the shores of the Baltic. Here he met John Dury (1596–1680), a Scotsman with a keen interest in such projects and Palatinate connections. In 1628, after the Catholic conquest of Elbing and the failure of Antilia, Hartlib went to England and started a school at Chichester with refugees from Poland, Bohemia, and the Palatinate. Meanwhile Comenius, driven from his Czech homeland, had established an exile community of Bohemian Brethren in Poland. In 1640, Hartlib addressed the English Parliament with his utopian plans involving a new commonwealth and the advancement of learning, and he urged Comenius to come to England and join him in this work. Comenius arrived in London in 1641, the same year that Hartlib published his utopia *Macaria* and that Dury published a similar work on the advancement of learning and Protestant unity. Comenius wrote his book *The Way of Light*, in which he celebrated the Baconian ideal of the advancement of learning inspired with the evangelical and pansophic piety of the Rosicrucian manifestos. At this time the English Parliament hoped for a settlement with the king, ushering in a new age of representative government. To Continental refugees, England seemed to offer an opportunity to fulfill the promise of progressive enlightenment that had been dashed by the Thirty Years' War. However, by 1642 the strife of the English Civil War had begun, and Comenius and Dury left England to work elsewhere.[33]

It is possible to trace the earliest stirrings of the Royal Society to the influence of Comenius, Dury, and Hartlib, as expressed in their pansophic impulse toward the advancement of learning and reforming societies.[34] The Royal Society grew out of meetings held in 1645 at Gresham College in Bishopsgate, London, that were attended by John Wilkins and Theodore Haak, who both had strong Palatinate connections. Wilkins was chaplain to members of the Elector's family, author of a book based on the ideas of John Dee and Robert Fludd, and familiar with Rosicrucian literature; Haak originally welcomed Comenius to England. Robert Boyle, the famous chemist and correspondent of Hartlib, mentions an "Invisible College" in letters from 1646–1647. Subsequent meetings were transferred to Wilkins's rooms at Wadham College, Oxford, between 1648 and 1659. Thomas Vaughan (1622–1665), translator of the Rosicrucian manifestos into English, returned to Oxford in 1649. Later Vaughan devoted himself to alchemical research and experiments at London together with Sir Robert Moray (1608–1673). Moray had been initiated a Freemason in an early lodge in

1641, gained high office after the Restoration and was provided with a laboratory by the king, who shared his scientific interests. Moray was the chief intermediary between the king and the Royal Society. Such early founding members
as Ashmole, Moray, and Isaac Newton with his interest in alchemy represented
that original Rosicrucian current of inspiration and apocalyptic expectation of
reform, derived via Hartlib, Dury, and Comenius from Andreae, which would
in due course be superseded by the exoteric, empirical concerns and interests
of science committed to manufacture, navigation, and technology.[35]

The Rosicrucian Tradition from the Eighteenth Century

During the eighteenth century, Rosicrucianism was identified particularly
with alchemy and at this time it certainly interacted with the growth of Continental Freemasonry. In 1710, Sincerus Renatus linked the preparation of
the philosopher's stone and its promise of prolonged life to a secret Rosicrucian order with initiations, vows, and signs of recognition. This notion would
later materialize in the combination of Freemasonry with Rosicrucianism.
While English Freemasonry established a Grand Lodge in 1717 as its central
authority, the uncontrolled proliferation of Masonic higher grades in France,
Germany, and Austria led to the adoption of many exotic themes including
Scottish Masonry, the Knights Templar, and Rosicrucian ideas. In 1747 or 1757,
the Order of the Golden and Rosy Cross was founded, whose history, practices, and ideas can be traced to pietism and the theosophical, Kabbalistic and
alchemical subculture of eighteenth-century Germany.[36] A 1767 document of
the order described nine Rosicrucian grades according to the Kabbalistic progression on the Tree of Life. Each grade's properties and lodge ritual rehearsed
the attainment of Hermetic wisdom and the transmutation of the initiate in
an esoteric religious experience. These grades were later copied in *Der Rosenkreuzer in seiner Blösse* (1781) by Magister Pianco (i.e., Hans Heinrich von Ecker
und Eckhoffen), a polemical work that smeared the order by imputing a link
with the Jesuits. Copied by Kenneth Mackenzie in his *Royal Masonic Cyclo-
pedia* (1877), these Rosicrucian grades and themes then entered the modern
ritual magic tradition.

   The sensational and romantic genre of Gothic literature—itself a reaction
to the rationalism of eighteenth-century life and thought—also contributed to
a mysterious cult of Rosicrucianism. The novels of William Godwin, Percy and
Mary Shelley, Charles Maturin, and Sir Edward Bulwer-Lytton variously elaborated the themes of a secret invisible order, whose adepts had achieved immortality by means of the elixir of life.[37] Another legacy of the alchemical emphasis

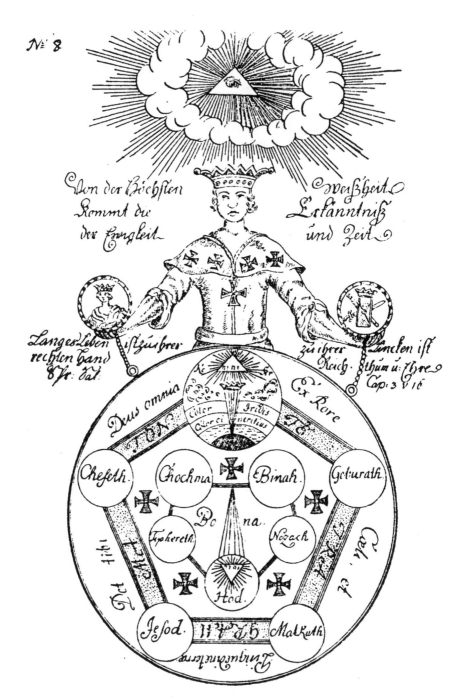

FIGURE 6.3. Allegorical image explaining the fifth grade of the *Gold- und Rosenkreuzer Order* based on the ten sephiroth or Divine Names, in Bernhard Beyer, *Das Lehrsystem des Ordens der Gold- und Rosenkreuzer* (Leipzig: Pansophie Verlag, 1925), p. 210.

of the eighteenth century, this image of secret Rosicrucian brothers would also stimulate the modern occult revival of the nineteenth century (see chapter 10).

From its seventeenth-century origins in Andreae's *Chemical Wedding* and the Tübingen circle's combination of pansophy and millenarianism, Rosicrucianism has acted as a specifically Christian symbolic current of the esoteric tradition. The implied roots of Rosicrucianism (via Michael Maier) in ancient Egypt, Eleusinian mysteries, Pythagoreanism, Gnosticism and Hermetism, Renaissance alchemy and Kabbalah have guaranteed its perennial appearance among founders of modern esoteric societies. Notable examples are the Hermetic Order of the Golden Dawn, founded in England in 1887; the extensive Rosicrucian writings of African-American Paschal Beverly Randolph (1825–1875); and the still-flourishing Ancient and Mystical Order Rosae Crucis (AMORC) at San Jose, California, founded by H. Spencer Lewis (1883–1939). The Theosophical Society, co-founded in 1875 by Helena Blavatsky (1831–1891) took some initial inspiration from the secret brotherhood, and several of its successor societies identified themselves strongly with Rosicrucianism, for example the numerous references to Christian Rosenkreutz in the writings of Rudolf Steiner (1861–1925), as he reformulated Theosophy into a Christian movement as Anthroposophy. Steiner in turn inspired the Danish-American Theosophist Max Heindel (1865–1919), who founded the Rosicrucian Fellowship in 1909 in California. Its offshoot, the Lectorium Rosicrucianum, more Gnostic than Hermetic in its doctrines, was founded in 1935 in the Netherlands and is now an international organization.[38] Rosicrucianism posits that there are invisible adepts working among the profane and uninitiated and has thus created a powerful social myth that a secret opposition is still operating within exoteric society. The hidden Rosicrucian brotherhood in more recent guises of "unknown Masonic superiors" and the "Great White Brotherhood" of New Age parlance thereby supplies a potent and perennial esoteric challenge to secularism and modernity.

FURTHER READING

Johann Valentin Andreae, *The Chemical Wedding of Christian Rosenkreutz*, translated by Joscelyn Godwin, introduction and commentary by Adam McLean, Magnum Opus Hermetic Sourceworks 18 (Grand Rapids, Mich.: Phanes Press, 1991).

[Johann Valentin Andreae et al.], *Fama Fraternitatis* and *Confessio Fraternitatis* were first published in English by Thomas Vaughan (Eugenius Philalethes) under the title *The Fame and Confession of the Fraternity of R:C:* (London, 1652). These texts are reproduced as an appendix in Frances A. Yates, *The Rosicrucian Enlightenment* (London: Routledge & Kegan Paul, 1972), pp. 238–251, 251–260.

Tobias Churton, *The Golden Builders: Alchemists, Rosicrucians, and the first Free Masons* (Lichfield, England: Signal, 2003; rev. ed. York Beach, Maine: Weiser, 2005).

———, *Magus: The Invisible Life of Elias Ashmole* (Lichfield, England: Signal, 2004); rev. ed. *The Magus of Freemasonry: The Mysterious Life of Elias Ashmole—Scientist, Alchemist and Founder of the Royal Society* (Rochester, Vt.: Inner Traditions, 2006).

J. B. Craven, *Count Michael Maier: Doctor of Philosophy and of Medicine, Alchemist, Rosicrucian, Mystic 1568–1622* (Kirkwall, Orkney: William Pearce, 1910).

———, *Dr. Robert Fludd (Robertus de Fluctibus): The English Rosicrucian* (Kirkwall, Orkney: William Pearce, 1902).

Donald R. Dickson, *The Tessera of Antilia: Utopian Brotherhood and Secret Societies in the Early Seventeenth Century* (Leiden: Brill, 1998).

Roland Edighoffer, *Les Rose-Croix*, 3rd ed. (Paris: Presses Universitaires de France, 1991), translated into German as *Die Rosenkreuzer* (Munich: C. H. Beck, 1995).

———, *Les Rose-Croix et la crise de conscience européenne au XVIIe siècle* (Paris: Dervy, 1998).

———, *Rose-Croix et société idéale selon Johann Valentin Andreae*, 2 vols. (Paris: Arma Artis, 1982/1987).

———, "Rosicrucianism: From the Seventeenth Century to the Twentieth Century," in *Modern Esoteric Spirituality*, edited by Antoine Faivre and Jacob Needleman (London: SCM Press, 1993), pp. 186–209.

Renko D. Geffarth, *Religion und arkane Hierarchie: Der Orden der Gold- und Rosenkreuzer als geheime Kirche im 18. Jahrhundert* (Leiden: Brill, 2007).

Carlos Gilly, *Cimelia Rhodostaurotica: Die Rosenkreuzer im Spiegel der zwischen 1610 und 1660 entstandenen Handschriften und Drucke* (Amsterdam: In der Pelikaan, 1995).

———, "Die 'Löwe von Mitternacht,' der 'Adler' und der 'Endchrist': Die politische, religiöse und chiliastische Publizistik in den Flugschriften, illustrierten Flugblättern und Volksliedern des Dreissigjährigen Krieges," in *Rosenkreuz als europäisches Phänomen im 17. Jahrhundert*, Bibliotheca Philosophica Hermetica (Amsterdam: Pelikaan, 2002), pp. 234–268.

Joscelyn Godwin, *Robert Fludd: Hermetic Philosopher and Surveyor of Two Worlds* (London: Thames & Hudson, 1979).

Clare Goodrick-Clarke, "The Rosicrucian Afterglow: The Life and Influence of Comenius," in *The Rosicrucian Enlightenment Revisited*, edited by Ralph White (Hudson, N.Y.: Lindisfarne, 1999), pp. 193–218.

William H. Huffman, *Robert Fludd*, Western Esoteric Masters series (Berkeley, Calif.: North Atlantic Books, 2001).

———, *Robert Fludd and the End of the Renaissance* (London: Routledge, 1988).

Harald Lamprecht, *Neue Rosenkreuzer: Ein Handbuch* (Göttingen: Vandenhoeck & Ruprecht, 2004).

Christopher McIntosh, *The Rosicrucians: The History, Mythology, and Rituals of an Occult Order*, 3rd ed. (York Beach, Maine: Samuel Weiser, 1997).

———, *The Rose Cross and the Age of Reason: Eighteenth-Century Rosicrucianism in Central Europe and Its Relationship to the Enlightenment* (Leiden: Brill, 1992).

John Warwick Montgomery, *Cross and Crucible: Johann Valentin Andreae (1586–1654), Phoenix of the Theologians*, 2 vols. (The Hague: Martinus Nijhoff, 1973).

Will-Erich Peuckert, *Die Rosenkreutzer: Zur Geschichte einer Reformation* (Jena: Diederichs, 1928).

Hans Schick, *Das ältere Rosenkreuzertum: Ein Beitrag zur Enstehungsgeschichte der Freimaurerei* (Berlin: Nordland, 1942; repr. as *Die geheime Geschichte der Rosenkreuzer* (Schwarzenburg: Ansata, 1980).

Joan Simon, "The Comenian Educational Reformers 1640–1660 and the Royal Society of London," *Acta Comeniana* 2 (26) (1970): 165–178.

Hereward Tilton, *The Quest for the Phoenix: Spiritual Alchemy and Rosicrucianism in the Work of Count Michael Maier (1569–1622)* (Berlin: Walter de Gruyter, 2003).

H. R. Trevor-Roper, "Three Foreigners: The Philosophers of the Puritan Revolution," in *Religion, the Reformation, and Social Change* (London: Macmillan, 1967; rev. ed. 1984), pp. 237–293.

George Henry Turnbull, *Hartlib, Dury, and Comenius: gleanings from Hartlib's papers* (London: Hodder and Stoughton, 1947).

Charles Webster, "Macaria: Samuel Hartlib and the Great Reformation," *Acta Comeniana* 2 (26) (1970): 149–151.

Ralph White, ed., *The Rosicrucian Enlightenment Revisited* (Hudson, N.Y.: Lindisfarne Books, 1999).

Frances A. Yates, *The Rosicrucian Enlightenment* (London: Routledge & Kegan Paul, 1972).

7

High-Grade Freemasonry and Illuminism in the Eighteenth Century

If Rosicrucianism supplied the myth of a secret society cultivating hermetic sciences, Freemasonry would later provide a vehicle for the historical transmission of theosophical and alchemical traditions. Opinion is divided as to whether Freemasonry was originally esoteric in inspiration or only later became involved with esoteric themes. The traditional accounts of Freemasonry trace its roots to the "free-stone" masons who joined a medieval guild of skilled craftsmen who built and decorated the great cathedrals of Europe. As their employment was itinerant, unusual in settled medieval society, the guild offered a supportive network of "lodges" at building sites. Modern accounts qualify this idea of Freemasonry's lineal descent from such "operative lodges" with the idea of nondenominational social clubs emerging in the early modern period. At some stage in the seventeenth century middle-class professionals and other tradesmen supposedly began joining existing "operative lodges" or founded new "speculative lodges" for the purposes of conviviality, philosophical discussion, and a special form of ritual activity based on the Bible and symbols from the masonic craft. Hence Freemasonry's cryptic designation as the Craft.[1] Some theories of Freemasonry's development, which bear closely on our topic, seek the origins of Freemasonry in Hermetic traditions and Rosicrucianism, or in Scotland, or in the crusading order of the Knights Templar. These latter legends about medieval or Renaissance origins contain certain elements of supporting evidence, but their chief impulse lies in the construction of myths about Freemasonry, which all date from the eighteenth century and reflect its esoteric alliances.

The traditional origin of speculative, nonoperative Freemasonry is typically dated to the founding in 1717 of the Grand Lodge at London by an amalgamation of four already existing lodges. James Anderson published the first *Constitutions* in 1723, outlining English Freemasonry's history and its relationship with God and religion. This version supplied a largely legendary history of the builder's craft from Adam in the Garden of Eden down to the formation of the Grand Lodge of England. As John Hamill has commented, his history was "an *apologia* constructed from legend, folklore and tradition" to give a relatively new institution an honorable descent.[2] In his second 1738 edition, Anderson supplied a much more detailed history, implying an unbroken lineage of Freemasonry through early medieval English kings and other notable figures, to claim that Freemasonry was not so much a new organization but a revival of an ancient institution recently fallen into decay through the neglect of its Grand Master, Sir Christopher Wren. According to these accounts, Freemasonry was formalized in England, initially as a two-degree system, a third degree of Master being subsequently added. The three-degree system of Entered Apprentice, Fellow Craft, and Master Mason would in due course become the hallmark of Freemasonry governed by the United Grand Lodge of England. In this form, Freemasonry was not originally esoteric, but the subsequent diffusion of Freemasonry on the Continent and the elaboration of higher grades led to its widespread involvement with esotericism.

"Scottish" and Chivalric Freemasonry

The introduction of Freemasonry to France provides the first stage in an Anglo-Scottish dispute over its origins and the preconditions for the eventual elaboration of chivalric and high-grade masonry. Following the deposition of the Stuart dynasty in 1688, King James II and many Scottish peers and knights took refuge in France. In support of their claim upon the British throne, the pretender and his successors rallied Jacobite circles on the Continent, which became hotbeds of conspiracy and political intrigue. Freemasonry was formally established as an English import in France between 1725 and 1730. It grew rapidly, partly due to a fashionable interest in English institutions among the French educated classes. Although the Parisian Grand Lodge dominated French Masonry in the 1730s, more exotic forms of Masonry began to proliferate across the nation, with courtiers developing a Masonry different from the English and using such expressions as *chevalier, chevalerie,* and *chapître.*

The recurrent theme of early French Freemasonry is that of a Jacobite connection. The claim that Freemasonry was brought to France by Scottish Jacobites gave rise to the idea that there was a senior tradition and affiliation opposed to the later introduction deriving from the London Grand Lodge.[3] While the exiled Stuart court in Paris provided a pageant of lords and knights from an ancient northern kingdom, new fashions and tastes in the Counter-Enlightenment would foster a neomedieval, chivalric, and Christian association of Freemasonry in France and Germany. The key figure in this encouragement of "Scottish," chivalric, and mystical Masonry (which actually originated in France), was Andrew Michael Ramsay (1686–1743). Born in Scotland, Ramsay attended Edinburgh University and worked in London, where he joined the Philadelphians, a sect of English devotees of Jacob Boehme's theosophy. He subsequently moved to France, studying with François Fénelon (1651–1715), the French philosopher and archbishop of Cambrai, who defended the Jansenists and the Quietist mystic Madame Guyon. By 1720, Ramsay had himself become affiliated to the Jacobite cause and briefly tutored Charles Edward Stuart the Young Pretender.

On 26 December 1736, Ramsay gave a famous oration in which he related the heritage and internationalism of Freemasonry to that of the Crusades. Ramsay's new legend suggested that the traditional Masonic access to ancient wisdom, partly biblical in origin but also reflecting Egyptian and Greek mysteries, was purified by transmission through Christian Crusaders. While alluding to the traditional ancestry of Masonry in Solomon's Temple, he identified the Crusades as a time of Masonic revival in which Masonry formed a union with the Knights of St. John of Jerusalem. To complete his historical legend, Ramsay traced a supposed history of the lodges during the Middle Ages. Kings and princes founded lodges when they returned home from the Crusades, but all these lodges died out save those in England and Scotland. Here Ramsay explained the British provenance of Freemasonry but also suggested that it was coming home to France, a Catholic and Crusader kingdom. Because Anderson's *Constitutions* had effectively de-Christianized the Craft in England, Ramsay's restored form of Christian Freemasonry was highly attractive in France. Ramsay also encouraged the tradition of "Scottish" Masonry in France by asserting the greater antiquity of the Scottish lodges and the role of Scotsmen in Masonry after the Crusades. Ramsay's influence was such that the accretion of a legendary Scottish origin became almost commonplace among Masonic innovations.[4]

While the original three craft degrees were identified as the operational legacy of the working stonemasons, Ramsay's suggestion that there had been Mason-Knights led to the introduction in French Freemasonry of "higher" degrees. These grades were reckoned superior to the mundane craft degrees; they were assigned knightly titles involving references to Scotland, chivalry, and the

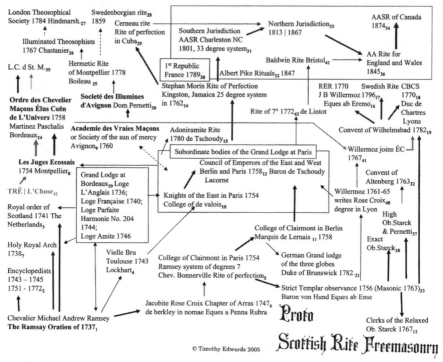

FIGURE 7.1. Chart reproduced by kind permission of Fra. Timothy Edwards, from "Proto Scottish Rite Freemasonry," paper presented at 29th Convocation of Ontario College of Societas Rosicruciana in Canada, 19 September 2005.

Crusades, and their holders were possessed of esoteric knowledge. This form of "Scottish" or *Écossais* Freemasonry spread rapidly through French chivalric lodges—called chapters, directories, lodges of perfection—with activity in Bordeaux, Arras, Toulouse, Lille, and Marseille by 1750.

It is easy to see how chivalric Masonry appealed to notions of hierarchy and social order, thereby reflecting the absolutist *ancien régime*. Although Freemasonry's brotherhood of equals enabled commoners and nobles to mix on equal terms, the introduction of higher degrees enabled the partial restoration of class consciousness within the lodge. Nobles could retain their superior status in the lodge, and some commoners could fulfill their desire for noble status by paying for the privilege.

German Templar Freemasonry

As Scottish Freemasonry spread in France in the mid-eighteenth century, it also gained a foothold in Germany and Scandinavia, and it was in Germany that Ramsay's chivalric Freemasonry first assumed Templar form. Germany's petty absolutist states and its concern with rank and hierarchy prompted a demand for a Masonic tradition compatible with conservative and neo-medieval tastes. The first rite to be practiced owed its origin to a French nobleman. Marquis Gabriel de Lernay, a French officer captured during the Seven Years' War, established a military lodge in Berlin in 1758 with the help of two Germans: the Baron de Printzen, a Mason who was master of the Three Globes Lodge at Berlin, and Philipp Samuel Rosa, a disgraced former pastor. Their system, known as the Chapter of Clermont, consisted of four higher degrees: Scottish Master, Elect Master or Knight of the Eagle, Illustrious Knight or Templar, and Sublime Knight or Knight of God. Rosa provided a legendary history of the order, together with an account of its far-flung legations across Asia and Europe. This complicated history began with God's alliance with his favorites after Adam, passed through the Order of Noachites, Nemrod, the brothers' dispersal after Babel, the reign of Solomon, decadence under Herod and revival by Christ, and later support of Emperor Constantine for the order at Jerusalem. Leaving the holy city at the time of the Saracen conquest, the brothers returned with the Crusades, at which point the brethren under the leadership of Hugo de Payen became known as the Order of the Temple.[5]

However, the most successful form of Templar Freemasonry was the Order of Strict Observance, founded by Karl Gotthelf von Hund (1722–1776), who was the hereditary lord of Lipse in Upper Lusatia and a wealthy landowner in Electoral Saxony. After attending Leipzig University and traveling extensively on the Continent, Hund became chamberlain to the elector of Cologne, attending the election of Emperor Charles VII at Frankfurt, where he first became a Freemason. From December 1742 to September 1743, he stayed in Paris, where he frequented Masonic lodges. Hund later spoke of an initiation into Jacobite Masonry at Paris in 1742 by an "Unknown Superior" whom he believed to be the Young Pretender. Six years after his return home, Hund established in 1749 the Lodge of Three Columns on his estate at Unwuerde in association with the brothers of the neighboring Lodge of Three Hammers at Naumburg. Together the two lodges formed an "Orient or Interior Order" based on the Templar-Jacobite legend.[6]

Between 1751 and 1755, Hund and his associates initially called their system "rectified masonry," basing it on the original Order of the Temple. Their "Red Book" initially provided for six grades, while the revived institution called itself the VII Province, defined by Grand Master Sylvester von Grumbach in 1301 as those Templar territories on the Elbe and the Oder. The terminology, rituals and emblems of the symbolic grades were adapted to the Templar affiliation. Its history recapitulated the Templar heritage adding a survival myth.

FREIHERR VON HUND.

FIGURE 7.2.   Portrait of Karl Gotthelf Freiherr von Hund, in Lajos Abafi, *Geschichte der Freimaurerei in Oesterreich-Ungarn*, 5 vols. (Budapest, 1890–1899), vol. 1, 192.

When the last Grand Master, Jacques de Molay, was executed on 11 March 1313, the succession was ensured by the flight of numerous Templars into northern countries, including Sweden, Norway, Ireland, and Scotland. Disguised as Masons, Pierre d'Aumont (the Provincial Master of Auvergne), Sylvester von Grumbach (Wildgraf von Salm), and seven knights escaped to Scotland together. The fugitive Templars adopted the name, costume, and customs of the Masons, and their secret history documented twenty-one successive grand masters up to the present.[7]

Hund's Rite of Strict Observance grew swiftly. By 1768, it counted some forty lodges. Firmly established in Silesia and Saxony, it was affiliated with lodges throughout northern Germany, especially in the large centers of Berlin, Hamburg, Bremen, and Stettin. It had swarmed across the Rhineland and founded colonies in Copenhagen, Vienna, Prague, Warsaw, and even in Hungary and Switzerland. The new Templars were attracted not only to the social exclusivity of noble Freemasonry but also to its promise of theosophical knowledge and alchemical secrets. The Strict Observance now faced a rival in the German pastor Johann Augustus Starck (1741–1816), who had been admitted to various Scottish degrees while in Paris. Claiming secret directors in St. Petersburg, Starck's system claimed a lineal descent not from the Knights Templar but from the clerics of that order, the true custodians of its secrets and alchemical lore. The Strict Observance continued to spread, reaching France, England, Sweden, Hungary, Italy, and Russia. In terms of its hierarchy, princes and grandees were the directors of the Strict Observance; but in terms of its culture, Starck's ideas had redirected the order toward the Hermetic and esoteric.[8] Starck and his followers seceded at the Convent of Wolfenbüttel in 1777, and the Convent of Wilhelmsbad in 1782 witnessed the abandonment of the Templar heritage in favor of the Rectified Scottish Rite and the Chevaliers Bienfaisants de la Cité Sainte, representing the Martinist influences associated with Jean-Baptiste Willermoz of Lyon.

The Counter-Enlightenment: Theosophical Sects and Illuminist Societies

The prodigious growth of secret societies operating in Germany and in France belies the image of the eighteenth century as a time of dry rationalism and secularism, an Age of Reason dominated by the *Aufklärung* (Enlightenment). Historians who have observed the proliferation of Pietism, high-grade Freemasonry, and neo-Rosicrucianism in Germany in this period have in the main tended to see the latter two movements especially as *"anti-Aufklärung,"* constituting an obscurantist Counter-Enlightenment: nostalgic, traditionalist, even repressive. Isaiah Berlin was the first to coin the term "Counter-Enlightenment" to describe currents of thought perpetrated by such thinkers as Giambattista Vico, Johann Georg Hamann, and Johann Gottfried Herder that opposed the rationalist and liberal ideals of the Enlightenment.[9]

John Roberts has described the rise of the secret societies against the background of three well-known currents of eighteenth-century thought. The first was itself the Enlightenment, characterized by a rationalizing, secularizing tendency and an advocacy of new modes of thinking and analysis above tradition and authority. The second was a new political trend, often known as "enlightened despotism," in which an absolute state challenged custom, legal privileges, and ecclesiastical immunities on utilitarian and rational grounds of efficient administration and state power. These interventions were often opposed by conservative and popular forces, which found support in those forms of Masonry that emphasized ancient nobility or the transmission of wisdom. Roberts suggests that a third trend, the growth of irrationalism, was intimately linked to this reaction against practical reforming rationalism and the Enlightenment. This found expression in a revaluation of emotional, intuitive, and spiritual experience. Its expressions were widespread, ranging from the rediscovery of medieval forms (chivalry, ballads, Gothic architecture), the pre-Romantic interest in ancient folk poetry and customs, to a Gothic literature cultivating the sublime, terror, and the supernatural. There were also continuities involving the Hermetic tradition, the spread of Jacob Boehme's theosophy, pietism, alchemy, and Rosicrucianism. Alongside the Enlightenment, there flourished an extensive counterculture of sects and secret societies devoted to these interests.[10]

These societies were overtly esoteric in their ideas and practices and developed a symbiotic relationship with Masonic lodges, whose members were themselves steeped in myths of legendary origin and Hermetic lore. Once Continental Freemasonry absorbed these esoteric ideas, its higher grades typically reflected chivalric, theosophical, Rosicrucian, and alchemical themes. High-grade Freemasonry interacted directly with these sects and secret societies devoted to mysteries, theosophy, and esoteric traditions, creating a form of Masonic theosophy. High-grade Freemasons, already impressed by initiations and secrets, were susceptible to "higher" secrets, while the sects themselves saw Freemasonry as a kindred subculture sharing similar inspiration, symbolism, and hierarchical orders. This interaction between high-grade Freemasonry and theosophical sects is well illustrated by the examples of Martinès de Pasqually, Jean-Baptiste Willermoz, Count Alessandro Cagliostro, and Swedenborgian Freemasonry.

Martinès de Pasqually and the Elect Coëns

Interacting with high-grade Freemasonry in France was a variety of esoteric movements representing theosophy, magic, and mysticism. The current known as Martinism, originally begun by Martinès de Pasqually, continued by Louis-Claude de Saint-Martin, and promoted in a high-grade Masonic context by

Jean-Baptiste Willermoz, provides an outstanding example of the growth of Masonic theosophy in the eighteenth century. Martinès de Pasqually (1709–1774) was a Spanish Jew who had converted to Roman Catholicism or been reared in a semi-Marrano Catholic family. His first experiment in high-grade Masonry was the Chapître des Juges Ecossais founded by him at Montpellier in 1754. In 1762, he settled in Bordeaux, setting up his own system, the Ordre des Chevaliers

FIGURE 7.3. Portrait of Martinès de Pasqually given in Dr. Bataille, *Le Diable au XIXe siècle* (Paris, 1896) and reproduced in A. E. Waite, *The Secret Tradition in Freemasonry* (London, 1911).

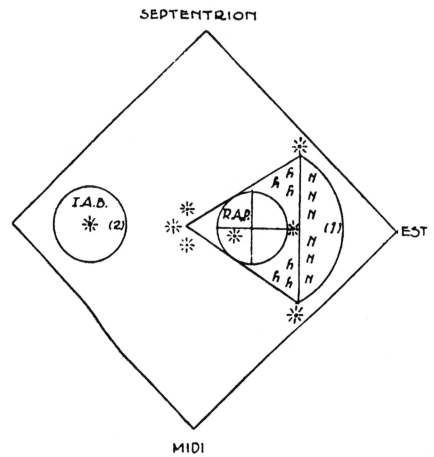

FIGURE 7.4. Diagram of Elus Coëns ritual in René Le Forestier, *La Franc-Maçonnerie occultiste au XVIIIe siècle & L'ordre des Élus Coens* (Paris, 1928), p. 83.

Maçons Elus Coëns de l'Univers around 1766. Martinès de Pasqually claimed occult powers and created a rite with a sacramental nature. His chivalric order invited "men of aspiration" to participate in the practice of a divine religion and a theurgic rite, involving invocations (called "operations") that sometimes resulted in a divine "manifestation" from the higher planes. This procedure was aimed at establishing communication with unseen intelligences by the practice of ceremonial magic. His doctrine was based on the idea that man and all animated things can be restored to their pristine state before the Fall by means of codified practices.[11]

Martinès de Pasqually elaborated his doctrine in his *Traité sur la réinté-gration des êtres dans leur première propriété, vertu et puissance spirituelle divine* (ca. 1771) as a highly complex form of Judeo-Christian theosophy and gnosis with a hint of Kabbalah based on the notion that the Eternal ceaselessly creates a hierarchy of spiritual beings into a "divine immensity" or "divine court." This divine immensity was perfect, but a fall occurred with the prevarication of rebellious spirits, which strove to become first cause like the Eternal rather than secondary causes. This created a catastrophe, inasmuch as the Eternal ordered the loyal minor ternary spirits to create the temporal material universe as a place to imprison the prevaricating spirits. While the divine denary spirits remained in the "divine immensity," other spirits were delegated to act and operate in the three divisions of the created universe, the supercelestial, celestial, and the terrestrial. This emancipation (as Martinès called it) into time and matter of the spirits led the Eternal to produce a new "minor quaternary spiritual," namely man, an emanation directly from the Eternal and not a secondary material being. Man was then the object of a double emancipation into the supercelestial, and also into the celestial, where he was known as Adam or Réau. Left to his own free will, Adam also rebelled in imitation of the perverse spirits, whereupon he found himself the prisoner of the material world.[12] Martinès de Pasqually's gnosis aimed at the redemption of mankind from this separation from God. Its cult practiced a form of theurgy that was intended to activate man's divine energies. The will is the only divine faculty that humans have retained in their fallen state, and this must be deployed to break their enslavement by the rebellious spirits in the "universal creation."

The Order of the Elect Coëns was organized in ten degrees to achieve these spiritual goals. The first three degrees comprised the three regular Masonic degrees of Apprentice, Companion, and Master. These were profane degrees "outside the temple," and only Master Masons could proceed to the higher Coën degrees, which were seven in number:

A. a transitional degree, Elect Master or Perfect Elect Master
B. the "porch" class, comprising Apprentice-Coën, Fellow-Coën, and Master-Coën
C. the "temple" class, including Grand Master of the Temple, Knight of the East
D. Réau-Croix[13]

Since the order was sacerdotal, receptions into the various degrees were "ordinations" rather than Masonic "initiations." The spirits confer on the candidate the reality of his ordination. Through them, the Coën is put in communion with one of the Chosen Ones of the Eternal, these being Adam, Abraham, Moses, Zorababel, or Jesus Christ, who presides over the particular circle in the "divine immensity" to which he is being admitted. This Chosen One is then linked through angelic mediation to the Coën in the ceremonial operations. This cooperation is the explanation of the so-called "passes" or "luminous glyphs," which sometimes appeared to Coëns during the ceremonies. A collection of some 2,400 diagrams and as many Hebrew names of angels enabled the celebrant to identify the angels who are at work from the appearance of its corresponding glyph. Members of the order were expected to say regular prayers modeled on the offices of the monastic hours, adhere to dietary rules and fasts, and practice other forms of moral and mental asceticism.[14]

Louis Claude de Saint-Martin

Martinès organized his order at Bordeaux from 1767 to 1772. His members were largely drawn from the officers serving in the army regiments garrisoned in the city and about a dozen temples, numbering a hundred members, were established during its peak activity. Louis Claude de Saint-Martin (1743–1803) was born into a pious family of minor French nobility. After studying and briefly practicing law, he embarked on a military career. Saint-Martin was introduced to the Elect Coëns around September 1768 and rose quickly through its grades. From 1768 to 1771, he worked at Bordeaux as secretary to Martinès de Pasqually, acquiring detailed knowledge of the order's practice. His duties brought him into contact with Jean-Baptiste Willermoz, the leader of the lodge of Elect Coëns at Lyon. In 1771, he resigned his army commission to devote himself to the study and spread of theosophy. Saint-Martin's first book *Des erreurs et de la vérité* (1775) set out a theosophical system in which Martinès' ideas are developed within a critique of secular Enlightenment reason. Here Saint-Martin rejects reductionistic and rationalist explanations of human institutions by arguing that the true cause of religion, social institutions, natural laws, and human nature is an active intelligent being. In his second book, *Tableau naturel des rapports qui existent entre Dieu, l'homme, et l'univers* (1782), Saint-Martin explains the physical world in relation to humans and God. As a result of the Fall, spiritual things assumed material forms. However, by reviving our will by aspiration (*désir*) and by virtue of the sacrifice of Jesus Christ, the regeneration of both man and nature to their original condition can be attained. Saint-Martin regarded himself as a "cleanser of the temple of truth," opposing both Enlightenment rationalism and orthodox Christianity.

Saint-Martin articulated a high-flown form of theosophy based on Martinès de Pasqually's concept of reintegration. Extending Martinès' notion of prevarication, Saint-Martin sees man as cut off from his divine and immortal patrimony in union with God by the thick veil of matter, which casts all nature as well as man into a state of somnambulism. Man is even imprisoned in a physical body. However, man knows that he is meant for higher things: "We are in darkness since we seek for the light, in delusion since we yearn for reality; but the fact that we desire both shows that we were made for both, and that in our present environment we are remote from the purpose of our being."[15] Like Martinès, Saint-Martin saw the origin of evil in the degeneration of the will. Will is more than a power to resist evil. It is no less than the true transcendent instrument: "Divine union is a work which can be accomplished only by the strong and constant resolution of those who desire it; that there is no other means to this end but the persevering use of a pure will."[16]

Saint-Martin was a devout Christian, and his theology was correspondingly transcendental. Saint-Martin distinguishes the First Cause, the impenetrable Deity, from an Active and Intelligent Cause, which together with two inferior principles sustains the course of nature and the order of the universe. Saint-Martin identified the Active and Intelligent Cause with the Repairer, his term for Christ, who enables the restoration of man to his original state.[17] This cause is also identical with the Word as understood by St. John. According to him, the Word once resided in man, but it was lost at the Fall. Hence the Divine Word had to intervene to sustain the universe, which is still in loss and sorrow. The recovery of the lost Word is man's first duty towards himself and nature. The way of this recovery is in the union of man with the restoring and repairing Word that has replaced him.[18]

Saint-Martin's mystical works, published pseudonymously under the name "le philosophe inconnu," found a widespread response among the French educated classes, many of whom who distrusted the rationalist tenor of the Enlightenment. Saint-Martin became interested in Mesmerism, joining its lodgelike Society of Harmony in Paris in 1784.[19] Mesmerism provided direct contact with the spiritual world, in which original man had once reigned and into which he needed to be reintegrated. He met William Law, the English theosopher on a trip to London in 1787, and resided from 1788 to 1791 at Strasbourg, where he met Baron Karl Göran Silfverhjelm, the nephew of Emanuel Swedenborg. It was also at Strasbourg that he encountered the works of Jacob Boehme through his friends Frédéric-Rodolphe Saltzmann, a Masonic theosopher, and Madame de Boecklin. Henceforth Saint-Martin regarded Boehme as a major inspiration; he learned German and translated Boehme into French (*L'aurore naissante,* 1800; *Les Trois Principes de l'Essence Divine,* 1802; *De la Triple Vie de l'Homme*, 1809; *Quarante Questions sur l'âme*, 1807). Henceforth, Saint-Martin's own works were clearly influenced by Boehme's own ideas yet still very much his own, witness *L'Homme de Désir* (1790) and *Le Ministère de l'homme-esprit* (1802). In 1792, Saint-Martin began corresponding with the Swiss theosopher, Niklaus Anton Kirchberger von Liebisdorf. Their regular correspondence introduced Saint-Martin to the writings of many other theosophers, including Karl von Eckartshausen, Heinrich Jung-Stilling, Jane Leade, John Pordage, Thomas Bromley, and Johann Georg Gichtel.

Martinesism, Martinism, and Willermozism

Although Saint-Martin had rapidly progressed within Martinès de Pasqually's Order of Elect Coëns, he gradually moved away from its theurgical practice to his inner mystical path. Such a development might have been predicted from the beginning; Saint-Martin had once asked Martinès de Pasqually, "Can all this be needed to find God?"[20] His lack of interest in ceremonial magic, ritual, and grade initiations was a certain factor in his relationship with Jean-Baptiste Willermoz (1730–1824), a wealthy textile manufacturer of Lyon, who was admitted to the Order of the Elect Coëns personally by Martinès de Pasqually in 1767. Willermoz had been initiated into Freemasonry as early as 1750, and in 1760 he helped form the Grande Loge des Maîtres Réguliers de Lyon. Holding high office there, Willermoz became an avid collector and student of Masonic rites. In 1763, he founded a chapter of a chivalric rite, Chevaliers de l'Aigle Noir et Rose-Croix, whose presidency he entrusted to his brother. Shortly after his admission to the Elect Coëns, Willermoz was nominated the leader of its Lyon lodge, and he was admitted to the Réau-Croix in May 1768. His first contact with Saint-Martin dates from the period when the latter was Martinès' secretary in Bordeaux. In 1771, Saint-Martin was living with Willermoz at Lyon, while writing his first book. In 1772, Willermoz's curiosity led him to correspond with the Strasbourg lodge of the Strict Observance. The next year he joined this order, and the year after that he set up its Lyon lodge, La Bienfaisance and became chancellor of its new province, the directory of Auvergne. The introduction of Templar Freemasonry into France aroused a certain suspicion owing to its German origins, and this was compounded by Willermoz's own imperial ambition to make the Rite of Strict Observance the dominant form of Freemasonry in France.

Willermoz continued to practice the theurgical rite of the Elect Coëns and furthermore sought to cast them in a Masonic form. At the national Convention of Lyon in 1778, Willermoz introduced the Régime Ecossais Rectifié (Rectified Scottish Rite), which combined Templar Freemasonry with the religious ceremonial of the Elect Coëns. The Rectified Scottish Rite possessed a concentric structure of four circles. The first two were the "ostensible classes" of the rite: (1) the symbolic class or Masonic Order with its four degrees of Apprentice, Companion, Master, and Scottish Master; (2) the inner order, which was chivalric, with two higher degrees, Ecuyer Novice, and Chevalier Bienfaisant de la Cité Sainte; (3) a secret class, with its two higher degrees of "Profession" and "Grande Profession." Only these three classes constitute the Rectified Scottish Rite proper. However, there was a fourth class, namely the Order of the Elect Coëns, veiled in mystery. Although the first three classes had no theurgical, Kabbalistic, or alchemical practices, they shared with the Elect Coëns the Martinesian doctrine of reintegration: the original pristine state of humanity, the Fall, and the reintegration into the primal state with the intercession of the Repairer (Christ). The Convention of Wilhelmsbad in 1782 not only confirmed this innovation but signaled the predominance of this theosophical, Martinesian Masonry over its older Templar forms for the following decade or more.[21]

Because the leading French occultist Papus (Gérard Encausse, 1865–1916) claimed to "refound" the Martinist Order in 1891, based on an alleged apostolic succession dating back from his colleagues Henri Delaage and Augustin Chaboseau to Saint-Martin himself, the idea arose that Saint-Martin had originally founded his own order in succession to the Order of the Elect Coëns. But there is no evidence that he founded a Martinist order himself, nor that he initiated persons into a cult. In contrast to Willermoz and his preference for collective activities, Masonic orders, and theurgic rituals, Saint-Martin generally inclined to an individual mystical path. He felt ambiguity about belonging to the Rectified Scottish Rite, and in July 1790 he resigned from its chivalric inner order and asked Willermoz for his name to be removed from all Masonic registers. The two remained friends, but their paths were clearly different. Willermoz possessed a genius for high-grade Freemasonry and theurgical operations—the active, extrovert aspect of French Illuminism—while Saint-Martin's theosophy, as expressed in his numerous books, brought him wide renown and a dedicated following throughout Europe. In this sense, there were many Martinists in the Illuminist subculture of France, Germany and Russia, but no actual Martinist order until Papus' own foundation ('revival') at the end of the nineteenth century.

As John Roberts has observed, Willermoz's Masonic creation "embodies in a particularly explicit and avowed form that mysticizing, antimaterialist, anti-Enlightenment trend which runs through the so much of . . . eighteenth-century culture."[22] Ultimately, the French Revolution led to the disintegration of his rite; a residual form has reportedly survived within the ranks of the Scottish Rectified Rite of France and Switzerland.

The Illuminés of Avignon

A further example of the complex interaction and mingling influences of high-grade Freemasonry and Illuminism is offered by Joseph-Antoine Pernéty (1716–1796), another theosopher and theurgist of the period. Pernéty discovered the subject of alchemy while a young Benedictine monk in France, and he later wrote two major works, *Fables égyptiennes et grecques dévoilées et réduites au même principe* and *Dictionnaire mytho-hermétique* (both 1758), in which he interpreted all mythological stories as coded descriptions of the Great Work, the preparation of the philosopher's stone. The interpretation of classical myths as a code for alchemy was a Renaissance tradition begun by Michael Maier's *Arcana arcanissima* (1614). Later, Pernety published a work on physiognomy and became enthusiastic about the works of Emanuel Swedenborg, which influenced him toward Illuminism. He translated from Latin into French Swedenborg's *Heaven and Hell* (1782) and *Divine Love and Wisdom* (1786).[23]

Appointed librarian to King Frederick the Great, Pernéty moved to Berlin in 1767, where he continued an interest in Freemasonry that had apparently originated much earlier in France. In 1779, Pernéty became one of the first members of an esoteric society at Berlin that was later described as the Illuminés of Avignon. This group included Prince Heinrich of Prussia, his librarian Guyton de Morveau (known as Brumore), who acted as a medium, Pernéty's older brother, and the Polish Count Thaddeus Grabianka. They were interested in alchemy and its practice, and in the consultation of a mysterious Kabbalistic oracle called "la Sainte Parole" that directed the members to follow Swedenborg's teachings.[24] This oracle was in fact Johann Daniel Müller, a radical Pietist, Swedenborgian, alchemist, Kabbalist, and millenarian prophet who regarded himself as the "Elias Artista" first predicted by Paracelsus. Prompted by the invisible oracle, the Illuminés evolved from an informal group into an initiatic society. The group was organized in two classes superior to the symbolic Masonic degrees: Novices or Minors, and the Illuminés, at their head the Magus, also known as Pontiff or Patriarch. The group performed consecrations over nine consecutive days on a hill near Berlin, where each candidate had to prepare an "altar of power" made of turf in the center of a circle of stones. In 1780, the oracle began to advise the group to leave Berlin to establish elsewhere the foundations of a new Sion.

In October 1784, the oracle told the group that it should move to Avignon, at that time a territory of the papal states. Two members of the original group, Brumore and Grabianka, who had been pursuing alchemy in Poland, met at Avignon. Pernéty had left Berlin at the command of the oracle in 1783, and after some wandering took up residence at a house he called Tabor not far from Avignon provided by a disciple, Marquis Vernety de Vaucroze. There Pernéty set up a temple, a laboratory, and a meeting room, where he received such leading Illuminists as Gombault, the Englishman William Bousie, and Baron de Staël-Holstein, the Swedish ambassador, and the Duchess of Württemberg, whose own regular guests at her chateau in Montbéliard included Saint-Martin and the Swiss founder of esoteric physiognomy Johann Kaspar Lavater. After Brumore's death in 1786, the Illuminés split into several parties: Pernéty continued with a society of the same name, still pursuing the original ritual and alchemical practices. Inspired by a new oracle, l'Homme-Roi (Ottavio Cappelli), discovered at Rome, Count Grabianka led his own group, the New Israel, based on his four-fold theology with a cruciform temple containing four altars for God the Father, Jesus Christ, the Holy Spirit, and the Virgin Mary; the group's confidence was damaged by Cappelli's arrest during the Inquisition and his recantation in 1790. A third group, the Filial Piety, was led by the Marquis of Montpezat. The Illuminés of Avignon finally dispersed when it was suppressed by law in 1793.[25]

Count Cagliostro and Egyptian Freemasonry

The colorful career of Count Cagliostro (1743–1795), the Italian adventurer and magus, is rich in acquaintance and incident; it also offers an outstanding example of the mystification of Freemasonry. Born in Palermo, Guiseppe Balsamo was a novice monk at a seminary, where he acquired an early interest in alchemy, the conjuring of spirits, and religious ritual. Following his expulsion from the seminary, he lived off his wits traveling to North Africa, the Levant, and around the Mediterranean. From 1765 to 1767 he was employed by the Knights Hospitallers of St. John in Malta, and there he acquired a knowledge of medical alchemy. Adopting the title of count and name Alessandro Cagliostro, Balsamo traveled throughout Europe for more than a decade performing magical wonders of clairvoyance and prediction, achieving alchemical transmutations, and healing the poor. It was, however, his encounter with Freemasonry that gave a future theme and purpose to his career. While staying in London, Cagliostro was admitted as a Freemason of the Esperance Lodge, No. 289 in Gerrard Street, Soho, on 12 April 1776. This lodge was incorporated within the Rite of Strict Observance, and it offered sumptuous ceremonial, Templar legends, and the promise of the order's revival combined with vengeance against the church establishment.[26]

As Iain McCalman has written, "Entry into the secret world of Strict Observance Freemasonry at last gave Cagliostro a framework for his remarkable

FIGURE 7.5. Count Cagliostro. Courtesy of Huntington Library, San Marino, California.

intelligence and ambition. Masonry became the crucible of his genius."[27] His experience with the theology, ritual, and organization of monastic Catholicism could find free expression in a secular church full of pageant, theater, and arcane symbolism. On leaving London in December 1777, Cagliostro and his wife proceeded to The Hague, to great acclaim in the Strict Observance Lodge of Perfect Equality. Over the next two years, Cagliostro promoted himself as the representative of the Great Cophta, an ancient Egyptian Unknown Superior at Strict Observance lodges in Nuremberg, Berlin, Leipzig, Danzig, and Königsberg. Thus recommended from lodge to lodge, he next traveled in February 1779 to Mitau, the capital of the Duchy of Courland on the Baltic coast, where he was welcomed with great expectation by the leading nobles. Count Johann von Medem and Landmarschall Otto von Medem, both high-ranking Masons, had studied in Germany, where they came into contact with alchemical and mystical groups. They had since led Masonic lodges in Mitau and presently presided over a Strict Observance lodge. Here Cagliostro fascinated the leading families with his powers of clairvoyance, promises to detect hidden treasure, and séances. After brief adventures with limited success in St. Petersburg and Warsaw, Cagliostro made his way in September 1780 to Strasbourg, then a hot-bed of high-grade Masonic lodges.

Here Cagliostro devoted himself to healing the sick with his cures and remedies, especially among the poor, from whom he took no payment. His reputation as a healer and alchemist spread fast, and Prince Cardinal Rohan lost no time in seeking his acquaintance. Soon Cagliostro and his wife were enjoying the use of the archbishop's palace at Saverne. At this time, Cagliostro began to think of his own rite of Egyptian Freemasonry, for its first definite mention dates from September 1781. He may have taken the idea from one of two contemporary works that derived Freemasonry from the Egyptian mysteries. A second edition of the first work, *Sethos* by Abbé Terrasson, had appeared in 1767, while the second work, *Crata Pepoa oder Einweihungen in der alten geheimen Gesellschaft der egyptischen Priester* by the Masons von Koeppen and von Hymnen, had appeared in successive editions in 1777, 1778, and 1782.[28] In 1783, Cagliostro left Strasbourg and traveled to Bordeaux, where he spent eleven months before going on to Lyon in October 1784. He soon sought, unsuccessfully, Willermoz's help in establishing a lodge of his rite, but still he was able to found the mother lodge La Sagesse Triomphante of his rite of Egyptian Freemasonry at Lyon on 24 December of that year.

At the end of January 1785, Cagliostro went to Paris in response to the entreaties of Cardinal Rohan, who wanted to continue their collaboration. There Cagliostro swiftly established two lodges of his Rite of Egyptian Freemasonry, and they became the height of fashion. At his grand house, provided by Rohan, Cagliostro held court in a mysterious séance room with sumptuous Oriental décor. Statuettes of Isis, Anubis, and the ox Apis stood beside a stuffed ibis, an embalmed crocodile, the traditional symbol of the alchemist, hung from the ceiling, and the walls were covered with hieroglyphics. Lackeys dressed like Egyptian slaves as seen on the monuments of Thebes stood in attendance. The Great Cophta himself appeared in a robe of black silk embroidered with red hieroglyphics, his head covered with a gold cloth turban ornamented with jewels.

Egyptian Freemasonry admitted both men and women, although their lodges and rituals were different. Candidates could profess any religion, but they had to believe in the existence of a supreme being and the immortality of the soul. Male candidates should have already achieved the degree of Master

Mason in a symbolic craft lodge. The order thus comprised the three higher grades of (Egyptian) Apprentice, Companion, and Master, similar to symbolic Masonry, and it used much of the same symbolism, including the legends of King Solomon and Hiram, king of Tyre, supplemented by Egyptian symbolism and elements of alchemy, astrology, and magic. Despite the Egyptian staging and décor, Cagliostro's ritual actually suggested Judeo-Christian theurgy; it included references to Jehovah and invocations to the seven angels Anaël, Michael, Raphael, Gabriel, Uriel, Zobiachel, and Hanachiel. The ritual for the third degree of Egyptian Master taught that man was created in the image of God, and as long as he preserved his innocence, he commanded all living beings, angels and other intermediaries. Once man abused his power, God deprived him of this superiority, made him mortal, and denied him communication with spiritual beings. This gift was then placed in the custody of a few elect beings, including Enoch, Elias, Moses, David, Solomon, and the king of Tyre. The goal of man's initiation into the Egyptian Rite was the restoration of his original purity and power by entering the world of the spirits. This degree has been described as virtually a séance of ceremonial magic in which a young boy (*pupille*) or girl (*colombe*) portraying the Dove of the Rite acted as a medium between the spiritual and physical worlds by scrying in a carafe of water. The rituals described three stages of restoration: spiritual, intellectual, and physical. Thrice restored, the initiate was capable of extraordinary acts of theurgy and healing.

The concept of the fall from grace of human beings, originally spiritual in nature, into the darkness of the material world, and the need for restoration certainly recalls the mystical doctrines of reintegration among the Elect Coëns and the Chevaliers Bienfaisants. It is possible that these notions were suggested to him already in 1781 by Barbier de Tinan, the prefect of the Chevaliers Bienfaisants at Strasbourg, and Baron de Lutzelbourg and Laurent Blessig, other knights of this rite at Strasbourg.[29] Another theory suggests that Cagliostro had encountered Martinesian ideas much earlier. According to John Yarker, Cagliostro discovered a manuscript by George Cofton on the Egyptian origins of Freemasonry on a bookstall in Leicester Square following his enthusiastic initiation as a Freemason at London in 1776. Cofton was believed to be a former Irish Catholic priest influenced by the doctrines of Martinès de Pasqually.[30]

The theurgical and alchemical aspects of Cagliostro's system are particularly evident in his prescription of two "quarantines" or magical retreats. The first of forty days involved rituals and prayers, leading to the theurgical evocation of the seven angels through talismans, seals, and pentagons. In the second retreat of forty days, directed toward physical rejuvenation and the attainment of immortality, the alchemical principle is foremost. Here the rituals prescribed involved fasting, bloodletting, and the ingestion of certain white drops, successive grains of *materia prima*. At the second grain (thirty-third day), the retreatant loses his skin, hair, and teeth, but on taking the last grain on the thirty-sixth day, the hair, skin, and teeth grow back and the subject is restored to pristine health. These wonders may be considered among the most arcane secrets encountered within esoteric Freemasonry.

The Illuminist societies and many high-grade varieties of Freemasonry were overtly esoteric in their ideas and practices. In many cases, they drew on a common pool of membership and otherwise developed a symbiotic relationship with Masonic lodges, whose members were themselves steeped in myths of legendary origin and hermetic lore. We recall that French Freemasonry early distinguished itself from the secularizing, de-Christianizing, even democratic tendency of English Grand Lodge Freemasonry (witness James Anderson's *Constitutions*) by stressing Christian, medieval, chivalric, and aristocratic forms. Once these higher grades and an implicit hierarchy were established, it was possible to associate higher grades with esoteric knowledge. The accretion of esoteric, Hermetic, theosophical, alchemical, and Rosicrucian notions is a complex process, having its roots in the survival of theosophy and pietism into the eighteenth century and their renewed assertion in the Counter-Enlightenment against the modernizing impact of rationalism and absolutist power. High-grade Freemasonry interacted directly with sects and secret societies devoted to mysteries, ancient traditions, and alchemy, creating a form of Masonic theosophy.

The Masonic career of Jean-Baptiste Willermoz illustrates how Freemasonry went "in search of its own meaning."[31] Disappointed with the banality and frivolity of his earlier Masonic affiliations, he remained convinced that Masonry veiled "rare and important truths," and he tried to reform Freemasonry in such a way that its adepts would understand these higher meanings. Like Willermoz, many high-grade Freemasons, already impressed by initiations and occult lore, were susceptible to "higher" secrets, while the sects themselves saw Freemasonry as a kindred subculture sharing similar inspiration, symbolism, and hierarchical orders. By combining high grades with esoteric themes, Continental Freemasonry was able to serve as a powerful vehicle for the transmission and dissemination of the Western esoteric traditions throughout the eighteenth century.

FURTHER READING

Isaiah Berlin, "The Counter-Enlightenment," in *The Proper Study of Mankind: An Anthology of Essays* (London: Chatto & Windus, 1997).

Robert Darnton, *Mesmerism and the End of the Enlightenment in France* (Cambridge, Mass.: Harvard University Press, 1968).

Robert Freke Gould, *The Concise History of Freemasonry* (1903, 1920; Mineola, N.Y.: Dover, 2007).

John Hamill, *The History of English Freemasonry* (Addlestone: Lewis Masonic, 1994).

Marc Haven, *Le Maître Inconnu Cagliostro: Étude historique et critique sur la haute magie* (1912; Paris: Dervy, 1995).

René Le Forestier, *La Franc-Maçonnerie occultiste au XVIIIe siècle et l'Ordre des Élus Coens* (1928; Paris: La Table d'Emeraude, 1987).

———, *La Franc-Maçonnerie templière et occultiste aux XVIIIe et XIXe siècles*, 3rd ed. (Milan: Arche, 2003).

Albert Gallatin Mackie, *The History of Freemasonry: Its Legendary Origins* (1898–1906; New York: Gramercy Books, 1996).

Edmond Mazet, "Freemasonry and Esotericism," in *Modern Esoteric Spirituality*, edited by Antoine Faivre and Jacob Needleman (London: SCM Press, 1993), pp. 248–276.

Iain McCalman, *The Last Alchemist: Count Cagliostro, Master of Magic in the Age of Reason* (New York: HarperCollins, 2003).

Micheline Meillassoux-Le Cerf, *Dom Pernety et les Illuminés d'Avignon* (Milan: Arche, 1992).

Michelle Nahon, "Élus Coëns," in *Dictionary of Gnosis and Western Esotericism*, edited by Wouter Hanegraaff, 2 vols. (Leiden: Brill, 2005), Vol. 1, pp. 332–334.

Papus, *Louis-Claude de Saint-Martin: Sa Vie—Sa Voie Théurgique—Ses Ouvrages—Son Œuvre—Ses Disciples suivi de la publication de 50 lettres inédites* (1902; Paris: Demeter, 1988).

———, *Martines de Pasqually: Sa Vie—Ses Pratiques Magiques—Son Œuvre—Ses Disciples suivis des Catéchismes des Élus Coens; Martinésisme, Willermosisme, Martinisme et Franc-Maçonnerie* (1895, 1899; Paris: Télètes, 2005).

Peter Partner, *The Murdered Magicians: The Templars and Their Myth* (Oxford: Oxford University Press, 1982).

Martinès de Pasqually, *Traité sur la réintégration des êtres dans leur première propriété, vertu et puissance spirituelle divine*, edited by Robert Amadou (1899; Le Tremblay: Diffusion rosicrucienne, 1995).

John Roberts, *The Mythology of the Secret Societies* (London: Secker & Warburg, 1972).

Louis Claude de Saint-Martin, *Theosophic Correspondence 1792–1797*, translated and with a preface by Edward Burton Penny (Exeter: William Roberts, 1863; repr. Pasadena, Calif.: Theosophical University Press, 1991).

Jan Snoek, "Dom Antoine-Joseph Pernety," in *Dictionary of Gnosis and Western Esotericism*, edited by Wouter J. Hanegraaff, 2 vols. (Leiden: Brill, 2005), Vol. 2, pp. 940–942.

———, "Illuminés d'Avignon," in *Dictionary of Gnosis and Western Esotericism*, edited by Wouter J. Hanegraaff, 2 vols. (Leiden: Brill, 2005), Vol. 2, pp. 597–600.

David Stevenson, *The Origins of Freemasonry: Scotland's Century, 1590–1710* (Cambridge: Cambridge University Press, 1988).

W. R. H. Trowbridge, *Cagliostro*, 2nd ed. (London: George Allen & Unwin, 1926).

Jean-François Var, "Martinès de Pasqually," in *Dictionary of Gnosis and Western Esotericism*, edited by Wouter Hanegraaff, 2 vols. (Leiden: Brill, 2005), Vol. 2, pp. 930–936.

———, "Willermoz," in *Dictionary of Gnosis and Western Esotericism*, edited by Wouter Hanegraaff, 2 vols. (Leiden: Brill, 2005), Vol. 2, pp. 1170–1174.

Arthur Edward Waite, *Saint-Martin, the French Mystic and the Story of Modern Martinism* (London: Rider, 1922).

———, *The Unknown Philosopher: The Life of Louis Claude de Saint-Martin and the Substance of His Transcendental Doctrine*, 3rd ed. (Blauvelt, N.Y.: Rudolf Steiner, 1970; 1st ed., 1901).

8

Emanuel Swedenborg

Emanuel Swedenborg (1688–1772) occupies a key position in the history of Western esotericism as a major representative of eighteenth-century theosophy. However, Swedenborg's theosophy little resembles the "golden age" theosophy of Jacob Boehme and his successors in the seventeenth century, and it is also distinct from the eighteenth-century theosophy of Martinès de Pasqually and Saint-Martin. Antoine Faivre has commented that while Swedenborg's theosophy involves intermediaries, correspondences, and access to the higher worlds, it lacks the mythical and dramatic elements of earlier and contemporary theosophy, such as the fall, reintegration, transmutation, and rebirth.[1] Instead, Swedenborg offers a relatively sober, matter-of-fact mesocosm full of spirits, which may be the souls of the dead, where knowledge may be gained, scripture expounded, and new theological ideas developed. In this respect, Swedenborg's esotericism was heavily influenced by Enlightenment science, rationalism, and Protestant pietism. His assimilation of these secularizing influences also identifies him as a key figure in the development of modern esotericism.

The Enlightenment Savant . . .

Swedenborg claims an exceptional place in history, both as famous scientist and as visionary. Born at the end of a troubled century, his life spanned the construction of the modern worldview based on reason, science, and material progress. Before he was yet twenty-five, the precocious genius had worked alongside Sir Isaac Newton, Edmund Halley, and other leading scientists in England, France, and Holland. Between 1680 and 1710, the date of Swedenborg's departure from Sweden for London and Paris, the new sciences of astronomy, physics, chemistry and biology were being rapidly forged in the major European centers by such figures as Christian Huygens, Robert Boyle, Robert Hooke and Hermann Boerhaave. Meanwhile, the philosophers René Descartes, Benedictus de Spinoza, and others supplied philosophies that were geometric, mechanistic, and optimistic concerning the rational and beneficial order of the universe. Between 1700 and 1740, the European sciences rapidly developed a rational understanding of nature to harness her powers for human purposes. This fast accumulation of scientific knowledge and its application in navigation, engineering, and industry unleashed an unprecedented wave of economic growth in Europe and laid the basis for her colonial expansion abroad.

Swedenborg inhabited this rapidly changing world. He worked on technical inventions, new machinery, and large engineering projects, and he held an office as assessor on the Board of Mines in Sweden from 1724 until 1747. He traveled widely through Europe and published pioneering works in such diverse fields as astronomy, physics, engineering, chemistry, geology, anatomy, physiology, and psychology. At the same time he played a prominent role in Swedish public institutions concerned with finance and politics. These worldly, rational interests totally absorbed Swedenborg. Until his fiftieth birthday he appeared uninterested in religion and hardly participated in organized church worship. Then, at the peak of his powers, a renowned figure of European science and member of the Swedish Academy of Sciences, Swedenborg's life changed forever in the spring of 1744.[2]

... and the Visionary

While traveling through Holland during Easter week, Swedenborg underwent an emotional crisis culminating in a nocturnal vision of Christ. He fell from his bed, found himself resting on Jesus' chest and felt he had been divinely commissioned to a special task. In the following months, Swedenborg sought direction and focus for his new religious feeling. He kept a revealing dream diary and wrote *Worship and Love of God*, an extraordinary blend of mythology and science. Then, in the spring of 1745, while living in London, he had his first vision of the spiritual world and its inhabitants. The Lord God appeared to Swedenborg and told him his mission was to "explain to men the spiritual meaning of Scripture."[3]

Henceforth, Swedenborg possessed the gift of vision into the spirit world and received constant inspiration for his new vocation. In 1748, he began working on *Arcana Coelestia* (*Heavenly Secrets*), a major eight-volume visionary work, which heralded a stream of books devoted to theology and Biblical exegesis, including *Earths in the Universe, The Last Judgment, New Jerusalem and Its Heavenly Doctrine*, and his most famous book, *Heaven and Hell*, all published in 1758. During the 1760s, he continued to publish substantial works, all based on an interpretation of Scripture, which the angels and the dead explained to him through spirit vision in imaginal palaces and parks, lecture halls, colleges and conferences among wonderful or ominous landscapes. Swedenborg's visionary faculty was unique. Rather than raptures, mystical union and ascent experiences, common to the famous English, German and Spanish mystics from the Middle Ages to the seventeenth century, Swedenborg's visions were always related to the meaning of Scripture, which lends his writing a remarkable matter-of-factness. We read a prosaic yet compelling record of encounters with the spirits, who offer detailed information concerning God, heaven and earth, man's purpose, the Last Judgment, and the life to come. Never before had a Christian visionary written with the intellectual training and achievements of a leading European scientist.

If Swedenborg's birth dovetailed with the rise of European rationalism, his new spiritual vocation seemed quite at odds with its climax in the Enlightenment. By midcentury, the worship of nature and reason so prominent in the thought of Voltaire, Jean-Jacques Rousseau, and Immanuel Kant accelerated the process of secularization. Swedenborg necessarily attracted controversy, and sides were quickly taken. In 1760, Friedrich Christoph Oetinger (1702–1782), the prominent German Pietist and church prelate, defended Swedenborg's work and invited him to Germany. Oetinger's highly favorable work *Swedenborgs und anderer Irrdische und himmlische Philosophie* (1765) had developed out of his own studies on Boehme and compared the Swedish seer with other contemporary thinkers. Meanwhile, Kant wrote a scathing and, by his later admission, unjust work, *Dreams of a Spirit-Seer* (1766) which damaged Swedenborg's reputation among Enlightenment thinkers. While Swedenborg's visions were the talk of England, France, and Germany, ecclesiastical controversy broke out in his native Sweden, and steps were taken to declare his work heretical. Eventually this storm blew out, and Swedenborg was rehabilitated. He died in 1772 at the age of 84 in London. By the end of the century his many followers in England had founded the New Church to promote his doctrines, which spread through missions to the United States and other countries in the nineteenth century. In 1911, Swedenborg's body was interred at Uppsala cathedral. Revered as a famous son of his country, his earthly remains lie beside those of kings and other leading figures of Sweden.

While Swedenborg has become a major figure in the history of Christian mysticism and Western esotericism, he was also representative of eighteenth-century European thought. His inspiration and towering ambition, his passionate appetite for the new mathematical sciences and prodigious capacity for research and work, his public life and political activity as a noble in the Swedish upper house and travels through Europe to Amsterdam, Leipzig, Paris, Rome and London identify him as a cosmopolitan philosopher of the Enlightenment. Swedenborg is also important in the history of European religious thought, offering new perspectives on Protestant theology, including the justification by faith, ethics, eschatology, and after-death states. It is therefore possible to place Swedenborg both in the mainstream of the Western esoteric traditions and the history of Christian visionaries.

The Age of Reason and Pietism

The readiness of thinkers and scientists to embrace a new secular, material worldview at the beginning of the eighteenth century is a key clue to Swedenborg's own appetite for the new science. The year 1710, the date of Swedenborg's first arrival in England, brings to mind images of an elegant Hanoverian London. Here stood the newly built St. Paul's Cathedral of Christopher Wren, the Greenwich Observatory under royal astronomer John Flamsteed, and the gracious mansions built by successful Whig magnates in the reign of Queen Anne. The Bank of England had opened its doors in 1694, joint stock companies were founded daily, and trade was expanding across Great Britain and Europe. But this comfortable, even complacent era was a relatively recent and hard-won phenomenon. Only a quarter century earlier, Europe had finally emerged from an age of religious wars, which had lasted practically continuously from 1559 to 1689. During that period Europe was riven by the French civil wars, the Dutch revolt, the Scottish rebellion, the Spanish Armada against England, the Thirty Years' War in Germany, and the Puritan Revolution and Civil War in England. All these conflicts had their origins in the religious controversy unleashed by the Reformation in the early sixteenth century, but their legacy had seared Europe for more than one and a half centuries. The memory of martyrs, crusaders, superstition, intolerance, denominational strife and hymn-singing armies was only too recent. Not until these ideological conflicts had finally burned out in the 1680s did European politics return to its secular pattern.[4] Henceforth, men were only too happy to embrace the mundane but comfortable worlds of business and investment, science and social improvement.

However, the Enlightenment was a nuanced phenomenon, qualified by successive generations of thinkers into early, middle, and late phases, where the first and last witnessed the concurrent blooming of mystical and pre-Romantic ideas. This early phase was linked in both Germany and Sweden to a reaction against orthodox Lutheranism that had generated the Pietist movement, into which many important German idealist philosophers were born, including Kant and Andreas Rüdiger. Swedenborg was the son of Jesper Swedberg (1653–1735), a powerful bishop in the Swedish Lutheran Church. As a young man, Swedberg had traveled widely and had encountered English Puritanism and German Pietism, a religious movement initiated by Johannes Arndt (1555–1621) and led by Philipp Jakob Spener (1635–1705) and August Hermann Francke (1633–1727). These men blended their Lutheran faith with a piety of the fiery heart in good works aimed at improving orphanages, schools, and social welfare generally.[5] Swedberg was especially influenced by Pietism's call for active Christian work, and he rejected the belief that faith alone was enough to save one's soul. As a Lutheran in his high offices as bishop, university rector, and theology professor, he sought to soften Lutheran orthodoxy through pastoral development with emphasis on personal conversion and a practical Christian life.[6] A pious believer in angels, spirits, and the efficacy of exorcism, Swedberg also saw a mortal struggle between God and Satan for every human soul, including his own in the numerous trials that plagued his life.[7] This was Emanuel Swedenborg's formative environment.

The "Geometric" Newtonian Worldview

Young Swedenborg's move toward the humanities under the tutelage of his brother-in-law, Eric Benzelius (1675–1743), in whose household he lived from 1703 to 1709, represented a major shift away from the stark religious choices and pieties of his father's house. A brilliant young professor at Uppsala, Benzelius encouraged Swedenborg in the new learning and may have been instrumental in launching him among a wide network of bright young students whom he had sent to western European cities for advanced studies unavailable in Sweden. In any case, by the time Swedenborg went to London, he was avidly consuming the scientific works of Isaac Newton, Nicolas Malebranche, John Norris, and Robert Boyle, and he seems to have forsaken church-based Christianity.

Although the bishop worried that his son had fallen among atheists and "freethinkers," Swedenborg identified rather with the contemporary idea of nature as a book of God second only to the Bible. The notion of a rational, ordered universe as a revelation of God and the visible realization of divine will suggested the idea of a science as a priestly vocation. In this respect, Swedenborg was strongly influenced by Jan Swammerdam (1637–1680), the famous Dutch natural historian, whose beautifully illustrated work on insects bore the suggestive title *Biblia naturae* (1737). Swedenborg's passion for science in his early years reflects this rational belief in an ordered realm of nature derived from God. The science that he encountered in 1710 in England was dominated by the mechanistic worldview. Mathematics, astronomy, and mechanics were subsumed within a science of number and dimension. The measurement and correlation of natural phenomena gave rise to precise laws of nature in the form of formulae, whereby unknown values could be determined by means of algebra and numerical calculation. The mathematization of physical bodies, forces, motion, weights, and measures could be applied to predict the movement of projectiles, planets, tides; to calculate the capacity of vessels, the size of dams and sluices, and the performance of machines. Swedenborg saw mathematics, geometry, and mechanics as revealing the innermost order of nature and as offering a means of subjecting it to man's rational purposes. In 1718, Swedenborg even published an article that attempted to explain spiritual and mental events in terms of minute vibrations or "tremulations," an idea that originated with the Italian scientist Giovanni Alfonso Borelli (1608–1679). In the 1720s, he continued to use mechanistic ideas to explain sense perception and human consciousness in terms of the movement of a most subtle matter.[8]

Swedenborg's scientific thought in his first major scientific work, *First Principles of Natural Things* (1734), exhibits this geometric and mechanistic worldview. However, even in this work and in his treatise *The Infinite and the Final Cause of Creation* (1734), Swedenborg explicitly exempts from this mechanistic causality the "Infinite"—a term he used to describe a "preceding cause" as a reservoir that supplies the universe with an inexplicable source of energy that streams into the human soul. Here he seems to be moving with the English Deists, a movement that began with John Toland (1670–1722) and Matthew Tindal (ca. 1655–1733) among "religion-hungry rationalists" and also, more controversially, in the wash of Arianism. This heresy, which originated in the fourth century A.D., had dispensed with the Trinity and relegated the divinity of Christ to that of the Father, the one supreme God. The emergence of a mechanistic and mathematical worldview made Arian ideas attractive to the leaders of the scientific Enlightenment in Hanoverian England, notably Sir Isaac Newton (1642–1727) and his disciples William Whiston (1667–1752) and Samuel Clarke (1675–1729), whose spectacular breaches with the church occurred during Swedenborg's first stay in London.[9]

Vitalist Ideas

Under the influence of the German Enlightenment thinkers, Swedenborg would soon abandon the geometric mechanical worldview in favor of an organic and vitalist conception that regarded nature as a living, animate whole. Gottfried Wilhelm Leibniz (1646–1716), Christian Wolff (1679–1754), and Andreas Rüdiger (1673–1731) reintroduced teleological concerns to science and rational philosophy. As a professor of philosophy at Halle and Leipzig, Rüdiger was close to Pietist thought. In his critique of the use of mathematical method in philosophy, Rüdiger initiated a new current of academic philosophy in eighteenth-century Germany. Together with his young colleague, Christian August Crusius (1715–1775), Rüdiger opposed the dominant influence of Wolff and inspired Immanuel Kant in his precritical phase. Swedenborg was especially inspired by Rüdiger's *Göttliche Physik* (*Divine Physics*) (1716), which subordinated the mechanical insights of science to an organic philosophy of nature deriving from Henry More (1614–1687), the Cambridge Platonist.

The germ of Swedenborg's vitalist thought derived from his idea of the mathematical point as created by the motion of the infinite and not yet subject to mechanical laws. To this point Swedenborg attributed an inner potential energy for movement, whose activation would lead to the first particles, which would in turn generate new arrangements of particles, thereby extending matter. Thus Swedenborg's concept of motion arising in the potential energy of the infinite becomes a concept of life which will spread throughout the physical universe. This vitalistic idea also contradicted the prevailing Cartesian distinction between mind and matter. Descartes had insisted that the soul was a purely spiritual essence and that thoughts were abstract, but this mental world lacked any tangible connection with the ostensibly "real" world of matter. Swedenborg saw an organic-vitalist science as a means of demonstrating how the mental sphere operated in the physical, how it acted as an inspirational force in forming organs, and becomes active through these organs. In this regard, Swedenborg saw the metaphysical identification of spiritual forces as transcendent and abstract as their disempowerment and effective banishment; he sought rather their combination with a physically grounded science of nature, whose animation drew on a supply of spiritual energies which then informed matter.[10]

Swedenborg's *Economy of the Animal Kingdom* (more recently translated from the Latin as *Dynamics of the Soul's Domain*) (1740–1741) and *The Animal Kingdom* (again better translated the *Soul's Domain*) (1744–1745) demonstrated the new cast of his thought. These two massive works, both of which are devoted to detailed descriptions of human anatomy, physiology, and psychology, document their author's quest for the seat of the soul. In his discussion of these books, Ernst Benz shows how Swedenborg's ideas of the *archeus* (primal energy), and *vis formatrix* or *vis plastica* (energy of formation) describe a metaphysical cosmos and an unfolding implicate order linking the macrocosm of God and heaven with the microcosm of an individual creature. Swedenborg's acknowledged debt to Henry More and Johann Baptista van Helmont (1577–1644) indicates his membership in the long tradition of the philosophy of nature (*Naturphilosophie*) ranging from Albertus Magnus and Nicholas of Cusa, through Paracelsus (1493–1541), who had coined the term *archeus*, and Jacob Boehme (1575–1624) to the Rosicrucians and Robert Fludd (1574–1637). This linkage is explored by Martin Lamm in his pioneering study, which established Swedenborg's interest in Neoplatonism and also showed that his scientific worldview was not essentially changed by his religious revelations.[11] Following Lamm's lead, Benz consolidated the scholarly recovery of Swedenborg from a contested hagiographical context and located his scientific writings in the mainstream of the Western esoteric tradition deriving from Neoplatonic and Hermetic ideas concerning the relation of the God and the soul.[12]

Correspondences

These esoteric and mystical notions relating to the theosophical triangle of God, nature, and man, macrocosm and microcosm, were evident in Swedenborg's later science. His visionary works based on the conversation of spirits and angels further explored an esoteric doctrine of correspondences. Swedenborg's own doctrine of correspondences, fully described in *Economy of the Animal Kingdom* was already summarized in a 1741 manuscript bearing the title *A Hieroglyphic Key to Natural and Spiritual Arcana by Way of Representations and Correspondences* (published posthumously in 1784). In this work, four years before his vision of vocation, Swedenborg is already teaching a fundamental law governing the realization of divine life in the various realms of the universe. There is a concordance between divine, spiritual, and natural things, and a correspondence between their signs. The relationship between the divine, spiritual, and natural realms is the relationship between archetype, likeness, and shadow.

Swedenborg's organic-vitalist worldview had already assimilated the Aristotelian idea of form and the *vis formatrix* as the creative endowment of every natural being. His notion of the creative principles acting as a seed-idea also reflected the Neoplatonic idea that the universal soul forms matter. In his work *The Worship and Love of God,* Swedenborg declares that everything in nature derives its body and form from a soul, which they reflect.[13] In Swedenborg's view, a remnant of this original form of contemplation, this insight into the essence of things, is still present in the ancient Egyptian hieroglyphs. "The Egyptians seem to have elaborated this doctrine and they identified these correspondences with various hieroglyphs, which expressed not only natural things, but also their spiritual counterparts at the same time" (*Arcana Coelestia* 6692,

7097, 7926; cf. *Spiritual Diary* 6083 [on Hermes Trismegistus]). Lamm and Benz have both commented that Swedenborg was acquainted with Neoplatonist tradition through texts describing how divine reason emanates in successive self-representations in descending hierarchies of materiality. Besides this reference to Hermetic correspondences, Swedenborg also used Marsilio Ficino's translation of Plotinus and *The Theology of Aristotle*, a pseudepigraphic Neoplatonic text, prime examples of esoteric philosophy.[14]

Initially, Swedenborg appears to have believed that original spiritual meaning resided in all words and texts, rather as Boehme understood his signatures as being universally present. However, after his vision of vocation in April 1745 Swedenborg increasingly understood the doctrine of correspondences as a doctrine of the divine Word, in which Holy Scripture appeared to him as the visible representation of divine truth, tailored to the sensory status of man, in the manner of Goethe's dictum: *Du gleichst dem Geist, den du begreifst* (*Faust, Part I*). The divine truth has descended through all the higher and lower worlds. On its first levels, it even exceeds the angels' capacity to understand. On subsequent levels, it is intelligible to the angels, and below these to other beings of the spiritual world. At its lowest level, the divine truth represents itself in a form intelligible to humans as the Word of Holy Scripture. The literal sense of the Word is the foundation, envelope, and support of its spiritual and heavenly sense. The physical word is the "container" of its spiritual and heavenly sense, just as the earthly world is the container of the higher spiritual and heavenly life. The literal form is the body of the heavenly Word, veiled in a form accessible to mankind upon earth. In *Doctrine of Holy Scripture* (1763) and *True Christian Religion* (1771), Swedenborg offered a fragmentary encyclopedia of correspondences, with specific meanings attaching to each animal, plant, and mineral, as well as to figures, colors, movements, gestures, and objects that are found in the Bible. He also applied the same symbolism to his visions and dreams.[15]

Love and the Inner Man

Once Swedenborg had received the gift of spirit vision, he abandoned his scientific work, took retirement from the Board of Mines in June 1747, and henceforth devoted himself to the study and exposition of the Bible. In his introduction to *Arcana Coelestia,* Swedenborg wrote, "Of the Lord's Divine mercy it has been granted me now for some years to be constantly and uninterruptedly in company with spirits and angels."[16] Henceforth, he would develop his theology on the basis of visions, angelic communications, and learned discussions in the spiritual world. His visionary theology included such themes as the meaning of love, the inner and outer person, the Last Judgment, and God's creative love to form a living, coherent, and implicate whole. In *Heaven and Hell,* Swedenborg viewed everyone as identical with his or her particular ruling love (*amor regnans*). A person is whatever he or she loves. Everyone determines his or her own inner form and understanding through the object of their love. During earthly life, the inner person is rooted in the outer person. The outer person forms himself or herself through outer memory, constantly receiving new impressions and stimuli, which influence attitude and determine character.[17]

After the death of the body, a person receives only inner and spiritual knowledge. The inner or spiritual person is perfected in the next life, but only insofar as this matches the preceding moral progress of the outer or natural person. The outer or natural person cannot be perfected in the next life, but retains the character it acquired in the life of the body.[18] Swedenborg's description of the relationship of body and spirit through death influenced the esoteric ideas of Johann Kaspar Lavater (1741–1801), the founder of physiognomy. These ideas relate to his notion of the archetypal man, whereby Adam and the ancients had faces characterized by the complete concordance of the inner and outer person. In the state of complete correspondence, the physiognomic expression simply becomes the archetypal language. The corporeal exterior of the ancients fully reflected the basic tendency of their being and its individual spiritual and emotional expressions. The outer form was so permeated by the inner form that the face actually signified the interior (*Arcana Coelestia* 607, 1119, 3527, 3573).

Death and the Last Judgment

After death, the inner person is liberated and can unfold in a pure fashion, whereupon it turns toward the society of his own kind. Everyone is attracted by the ruling love underlying his or her nature to those bound by the same love; the society of kindred spirits is sought. Heaven and hell are therefore not realms that await man and into which he is translated by a divine verdict after the Last Judgment. There are no angels or demons apart from men. Hell consists of societies of men, whose basic tendency is egoism and who have rebelled against God and his word here on earth (*Heaven and Hell,* §547, 548). Similarly, there is no heaven apart from that of man. Heaven consists of human societies brought together by a common love of God and one's neighbor. Every action in the community becomes its own reward, just as it becomes a punishment in hell.

Swedenborg's doctrine of heaven and hell represented a radical theology rooted in personal spiritual development. Up until his time, both Catholic and

Protestant teachings had offered the traditional dogma that the dead would be raised at the last trump in the physical resurrection of the body to face the Last Judgment and accordingly assigned to heaven or hell on account of the conduct of their earthly lives. This verdict was external and final. By contrast, Swedenborg describes heaven and hell as spiritual possibilities and enhancements of the human condition. His theology regards the development of the personality on earth and in the world beyond as a continuous process. The earthly, corporeal world is not artificially separated from the spiritual world. Instead, the inner person of the earthly life continues to evolve spiritually into the world beyond.[19]

Swedenborg as an Esotericist

By placing Swedenborg in the history of the Western esoteric tradition, the issue of the continuity of his thought before and after his vision of vocation becomes central to his evaluation as scientist and mystic. Jonsson also followed Lamm in tracing the philosophical continuity between the later scientific work and the visionary theology. However, Jonsson sought to minimize the influence of Renaissance Neoplatonism, the Cambridge Platonists, and the *Naturphilosophie* tradition of Paracelsus and Johann Baptist van Helmont on Swedenborg by emphasizing his debt to Cartesian and Enlightenment thought.[20] She argues that Swedenborg needed only to make a few changes in his psychophysical speculations in *Dynamics of the Soul's Domain* to arrive at the ideas he later received in spirit vision.[21] Inclined to the notion of unmediated revelation, Swedenborgians (members of the New Church founded by his followers) have also noted the visionary's canonical sayings that he had never read the Christian theosophers Jacob Boehme and William Law, preferring to keep his mind clear for spiritual instruction. Indeed, his visionary works eschew any references save to Scripture, the exposition of which he saw as his divine commission. This discussion would therefore counter Benz's view and tend to present Swedenborg as an essentially scientific mind whose subsequent visionary career caused him to be wrongly stigmatized as an esotericist in the wake of a rejected tradition of *Naturphilosophie*, at worst as a spirit-seer and throwback to a superstitious age.[22]

However, evidence found by Marsha Keith Schuchard emphasizes Swedenborg's deep roots in the Western esoteric tradition. She has assembled proofs of Leibniz's interest in Rosicrucianism and Christian Cabala and how he encouraged his brilliant Swedish colleague Eric Benzelius—young Swedenborg's mentor and the beloved brother-in-law in whose household he lived as a schoolboy and university student—to visit the alchemist and Kabbalist Francis Mercurius van

Helmont (1618–1698).[23] Schuchard's controversial research suggests a continuity in Swedenborg's lifelong interest in esoteric subjects, including Rosicrucianism, Freemasonry, and Christian Cabala. A particularly provocative suggestion is that Swedenborg may have had long-term involvement with an esoteric circle in London, headed by Samuel Jacob Falk, a mysterious Jewish alchemist and Kabbalist, which, at various times in its history, included William Blake and the esoteric adventurer Count Cagliostro. The picture of Swedenborg as a man not only interested in many aspects of spiritual insight but also engaged in political and social activity lends credence to this possibility.[24]

According to Faivre's definition, key characteristics of esoteric philosophy tradition consist in notions of correspondences between God, heaven, earth, and man, namely macrocosm and microcosm; the idea of a living nature; the mediation of imagination and intermediaries on hierarchies of ascent between the planes; and the transmutation of the human soul.[25] Jane Williams-Hogan, a leading authority on Swedenborg, has assessed his scientific and visionary work in the light of Faivre's categories. While the first, third, and fourth of Faivre's conditions of esotericism are fulfilled by Swedenborg's theology in his doctrine of correspondences, a rich intermediary world, and the idea of rebirth, Williams-Hogan has suggested that Swedenborg saw nature as having "no life of its own, even though it mirrors and can reveal the spiritual, and corresponds to it."[26] This reading suggests that Swedenborg saw a higher spiritual world of Life mirrored by a lower material world that is essentially dead. In this respect, the esoteric idea of a continuously animated realm uniting spirit and matter would be denied.

Through his earlier scientific endeavors in anatomy, neurology, and psychology, Swedenborg had penetrated nature to the smallest elements without finding the seat of the soul on the material plane. Attempts to find traces of the divine in nature brought him to an intellectual dead end, or in his own words, an "abyss." Swedenborg's original debt to Descartes, Spinoza, and English scientists for a geometric, mechanical worldview was indeed later qualified by the influences of Christian Wolff and especially Arnold Rüdiger, which gave Swedenborg the organic, vitalist idea of an entelechy or intelligent hierarchy underlying the divine plan of evolution in all creation. However, the fundamental dualism of the transcendent and the natural can still be discerned in Swedenborg's conception of the natural world as a Cartesian *res extensa*. It had brought Swedenborg to the limits of science. He essentially solved this impasse through a religious crisis followed by initiation into a world of spirits. Their salvific theology taught Swedenborg that a postmortem conjunction between the living Creator and his creation is possible in a place that is neither divine nor natural, but in a realm of the imagination known as heaven. Through its residual dualism (contrary to the monist pansophy of early modern *Naturphilosophie*), we see the dawn of spiritualism, scientific occultism, and a new phase in the Western esoteric tradition. Wouter Hanegraaff has observed that Swedenborg's notion of the intermediary world as one in which the human soul could work on itself after death anticipates modern psychological forms of esotericism. Moreover, his scientific and literal descriptions of the spirit world herald the rise of occultism, in which the concrete world is the point of departure.[27]

Swedenborgian Illuminism

Swedenborg undertook no steps to found a church or esoteric group, but his ideas were highly attractive to eighteenth-century Illuminists. His possible links with Dr. Samuel Jacob Falk (ca. 1710–1782) in London would have provided an important channel for such influence. Born in Podolia, Falk was a youthful convert to antinomian, millenarian Sabbatianism before migrating to Germany, where he attended various courts. In 1739–1740, Falk came to live in England, where he was known as the "Baal-Shem of London" ("master of the divine names") and acquired a controversial reputation as a Kabbalist. From the 1760s onward, he attracted mystical Freemasons, who were attracted by the Kabbalah and its promise of magical power. Marquis de Thomé, founder of a Swedenborg rite in Paris, allegedly received Kabbalistic instruction from him. It has also been claimed, on the basis of testimony from near-contemporary sources in St. Petersburg and Strasbourg, that Cagliostro worked closely with the mysterious Falk during his stay in London in 1776 to develop his Egyptian rite. Later, conspiratorial accounts of Cagliostro's career dating from his interrogation by the Holy Inquisition would also date the origins of his Egyptian rite to his alleged acquaintance with Falk in 1776.[28] The angelogical and magical aspects of Cagliostro's rite certainly have more in common with Jewish than Egyptian traditions.

Swedenborgian Illuminism was thus a potent international current throughout the 1770s and 1780s and would provide a link between a number of the esoteric Masonic societies discussed in chapter 7. The French surgeon Benedict Chastanier (1739–ca. 1816) had allegedly founded as early as 1767 in France a lodge of *Illuminés Theosophes,* based on the anonymous writings of Swedenborg. After migrating to England in 1774, Chastanier learned the identity of their author and founded a Masonic society in 1776 known as the Universal Society in London to disseminate Swedenborg's writings. Its members included the artists Richard Cosway, the artist Phillipe-Jacques de Loutherbourg, who later collaborated with Cagliostro, and General Charles Rainsford (1728–1809), the future governor of Gibraltar, an avid collector of alchemical and Rosicrucian manuscripts who had joined many high-grade Masonic lodges on the Continent in the course of his military service. In 1775 Chastanier and the Marquis de Thomé joined the *Philaléthes*, a Masonic society founded by Savalette de Langes in Paris.[29] Another Swedenborgian group in London in the 1780s was Jacob Duché's gatherings at the Lambeth Asylum for Female Orphans, where he was chaplain.[30] In 1782, Chastanier and General Rainsford reached out to kindred Illuminist groups in Berlin and Paris by publishing a brochure in French about degrees of the Universal Society. In 1783, a more public organization, the Theosophical Society, was formed to function as the publishing arm of the Universal Society.

The Swedenborgian illuminates in London demonstrate close personal links with those of esoteric societies in Paris, Avignon, and Stockholm. Chastanier maintained his links in Paris, conferred with Marquis de Thomé, who also visited the London Swedenborgians in 1784 and 1785. General Rainsford and William Bousie, an Anglo-French merchant, began corresponding with the Parisian lodge of the *Philaléthes* in the summer of 1783, preparatory to the *Philaléthes* convention at Paris in April 1785 to review the rites of many para-Masonic and esoteric societies. Rainsford provided information on Swedenborg, Falk, and the Kabbalistic symbolism of higher degrees, and Bousie, who had known Cagliostro at London in 1776 and was involved with the Universal and Theosophical Societies in 1783–1787, served as liaison between the Swedenborgians in London, Paris, and Avignon.[31] Both Bousie and Chastanier were in contact with the Illuminés of Avignon. In December 1785, Count Grabianka arrived in London with the purpose of recruiting London Swedenborgians to his millenarian cult of New Israel among the Illuminés of Avignon. He established cordial relations with Jacob Duché, regularly attended the meetings of the Theosophical Society, and promised the revelation of the key to all wisdom until his departure in 1786. In February 1787, he wrote from Avignon, recapitulating the Avignon Illuminé creed. Two English Swedenborgian artisans, William Bryan and John Wright, traveled at the end of 1788 via Paris and, through the good offices of Chastanier and Bousie, arrived in Avignon, where they stayed for seven months, copying extracts from the communications of *Sainte Parole* and worshiping with the society. In the climate of "revolutionary mysticism," with its sense of impending religious and political regeneration, many notables and aristocrats were drawn to Avignon over the next years.[32]

Legacy

Besides these Illuminist circles, Swedenborg's immediate legacy was the New Church, which began in England, since his writings had initially led to heresy trials in Sweden. Several English ministers (Anglican and Quaker), physicians, and traveling preachers took up his cause, and by 1783 the Theosophical Society (not to be confused with Boehme's contemporary followers or the creation of Helena Blavatsky a century later) existed to promote the "heavenly doctrines of the New Jerusalem." The New Church based on Swedenborg's own theology was founded in 1787 and soon spread to North America and finally throughout the world as a Protestant reformed church movement with a mystical coloration. Throughout the nineteenth century, the New Church in Great Britain grew to more than seventy congregations with more than 6,300 members. Since that time, congregations in Britain have shrunk in line with the decline in overall church attendance since the Second World War. A schism in 1890 in the United States produced two organizations, the General Convention and the General Church. While the former had declined from its peak of 7,000 members to around 2,000 by 1999, reflecting the general trend toward less institutionalized forms of worship, the General Church has emphasized education and community building in addition to worship and, by 2003, had worldwide membership just short of 5,000. The United States also boasts three tertiary New Church–inspired colleges offering a liberal arts education and training in Swedenborgian ministry.[33]

More extensive yet than denominational organizations is Swedenborg's spiritual and intellectual legacy. His rational mysticism impressed such diverse thinkers as Kant, Oetinger, Lavater, German Romantic *Naturphilosoph* Friedrich Schelling (1775–1854), and Russian theosopher Vladimir Soloviev (1853–1900). On an artistic and creative level, his ideas struck a deep chord with poets and writers such as William Blake, Johann Wolfgang Goethe, Samuel Taylor Coleridge, Robert Browning and Elizabeth Barrett Browning, Honoré de Balzac, Feodor Dostoevsky, and W. B. Yeats. Ralph Waldo Emerson (1803–1882) and Walt Whitman (1819–1892), the pioneers of American Transcendentalism, adopted Swedenborgian ideas of correspondence and the relationship of spiritual and physical reality into their own notions of symbol and "hieroglyphics." Among the James family, the elder Henry James (1811–1882) was the most prolific writer on Swedenborg in nineteenth-century America, while his son William James (1842–1910), sought coherence between science and religion, notably in his best-known work, *The Varieties of Religious Experience* (1902).[34] The Japanese philosopher D. T. Suzuki called Swedenborg the "Buddha of the North," and the French scholar of esotericism Henry Corbin compared his work to Islamic mysticism. More recently, popular culture shows the continued assimilation of Swedenborgian ideas on life and death, as evidenced by the film *What Dreams May Come* (2001), by Vincent Ward. The common theme in all these receptions of Swedenborg's ideas relates to the interplay among spirit and matter and after-death states. These topics remain his principal legacy to modern esotericism.

FURTHER READING

Ernst Benz, *Emanuel Swedenborg: Visionary Savant in the Age of Reason*, translation and introduction by Nicholas Goodrick-Clarke (West Chester, Pa.: Swedenborg Foundation, 2002). Originally published in German in 1948.

Lars Berquist, *Swedenborg's Dream Diary*, translated by A. Hallengren (West Chester, Pa.: Swedenborg Foundation, 2001).

———, *Swedenborg's Secret: A Biography* (London: Swedenborg Society, 2005).

George F. Dole and Robert H. Kirven, *A Scientist Explores Spirit: A Biography of Emanuel Swedenborg with Key Concepts of His Theology* (West Chester, Pa.: Swedenborg Foundation, 1997).

Peter C. Erb (ed.), *Pietists: Selected Writings*, Classics of Western Spirituality series (New York: Paulist Press, 1983).

Alfred J. Gabay, *The Covert Enlightenment: Eighteenth-Century Counterculture and Its Aftermath* (West Chester, Pa.: Swedenborg Foundation, 2005).

Clarke Garrett, *Respectable Folly: Millenarians and the French Revolution in France and England* (Baltimore: Johns Hopkins University Press, 1975).

Wouter J. Hanegraaff, *New Age Religion and Western Culture: Esotericism in the Mirror of Secular Thought* (Leiden: E. J. Brill, 1996), pp. 421–429.

Inge Jonsson, *Emanuel Swedenborg* (New York: Twayne, 1971).

———, "Emanuel Swedenborgs Naturphilosophie und ihr Fortwirken in seiner Theosophie," in *Epochen der Naturmystik: Hermetische Tradition in wissenschaftlichen Fortschritt*, edited by Antoine Faivre and Rolf Christian Zimmermann (Berlin: Erich Schmidt, 1979).

———, *Visionary Scientist: The Effects of Science and Philosophy on Swedenborg's Cosmology* (West Chester, Pa.: Swedenborg Foundation, 1999).

Martin Lamm, *Emanuel Swedenborg: The Development of His Thought* (West Chester, Pa.: Swedenborg Foundation, 2000).

Jonathan Rose, Stuart Shotwell, and Mary Lou Bertucci (eds.), *Scribe of Heaven: Swedenborg's Life, Work, and Impact* (West Chester, Pa.: Swedenborg Foundation, 2005).

Marsha Keith Schuchard, "Dr. Samuel Jacob Falk: A Sabbatian Adventurer in the Masonic Underground," in *Millenarianism and Messianism in Early Modern European Culture: Jewish Messianism in the Early Modern World*, edited by M. D. Goldish and R. H. Popkin (Dordrecht: Kluwer, 2001), pp. 203–226.

———, "Jacobite and Visionary: The Masonic Journey of Emanuel Swedenborg (1688–1772)," *Ars Quatuor Coronatorum* 115 (2003): 33–72.

———, "Leibniz, Benzelius, and Swedenborg: The Kabbalistic Roots of Swedish Illuminism," in *Leibniz, Mysticism, and Religion*, edited by Allison P. Coudert, Richard H. Popkin, and Gordon M. Weiner (Dordrecht: Kluwer, 1998), pp. 84–106.

———, "The Secret Masonic History of Blake's Swedenborg Society," *Blake: An Illustrated Quarterly* 26, 2 (Fall 1992): 40–51.

———, "Swedenborg, Jacobitism, and Freemasonry," in *Swedenborg and His Influence*, edited by Erland J. Brock et al. (Bryn Athyn, Pa.: Academy of the New Church, 1988), pp. 359–379.

————, "Yeats and the Unknown Superiors: Swedenborg, Falk, and Cagliostro," *Hermetic Journal* 37 (Autumn 1987): 14–20.

Cyriel Odhner Sigstedt, *The Swedenborg Epic: The Life and Works of Emanuel Swedenborg* (London: Swedenborg Society, 1981).

Michael Stanley, *Emanuel Swedenborg*, Western Esoteric Masters series (Berkeley, Calif.: North Atlantic Books, 2003).

Emanuel Swedenborg, *The Universal Human and the Soul-Body Interaction,* edited and translated by George F. Dole, Classics of Western Spirituality series (London: SPCK, 1984).

George Trobridge, *Swedenborg: Life and Teaching,* revised by R. H. Tafel Sr. and R. H. Tafel Jr. (New York: Swedenborg Foundation, 1992).

Jane Williams-Hogan, "The Place of Emanuel Swedenborg in Modern Western Esotericism," in *Western Esotericism and the Science of Religion,* edited by Antoine Faivre and Wouter J. Hanegraaff (Leuven: Peeters, 1998), pp. 201–252.

9

Mesmerism and Spiritualism

Science and Spirituality

The intellectual elite of the Enlightenment had celebrated reason as the highest authority as an instrument to control nature, depose religion, and mount a challenge to political absolutism. But reason was only a method for organizing knowledge. Reason alone, as Kant himself argued in *The Critique of Pure Reason* (1781), could not produce absolute knowledge about anything. The "thing-in-itself" (*noumenon*) remained unknown, and the finite and fallible senses could only describe the "thing-as-perceived" (*phenomenon*). These doubts about the metaphysical efficacy of empiricism combined with the limits of reason were but the internal contradictions of the Enlightenment. The devastating Lisbon earthquake (1755) made a deep impression on the European mind, checking its newfound optimism with perennial concerns about the uncertainty and injustice of life. There were both older and newer factors that qualified the Enlightenment's faith in reason and reaction to authority and religion. The Counter-Enlightenment reasserted the primacy of religion, wonders, locality, and custom over the new intellectual fashions of bourgeois elites. Already in the 1690s, the rise of Pietism led to the reassertion of spirituality in Lutheran societies, which by the early 1700s often combined with religioscientific quests in Hermeticism, alchemy, and medicine. Given their limitless hunger for money to fund their extravagant displays, absolutist princes fostered a venal interest in the possibilities of alchemy, and such occultist adventurers as Giacomo Casanova (1725–1798), Count Cagliostro (1743–1795), and the Comte de Saint-Germain (d. 1784) used astrology, Kabbalah, and alchemy to appeal to suggestible nobles and bourgeois.

Swedenborg's own career in science and his quest for the seat of the soul, the numerous illuminist and Masonic societies in France and Germany, drawing on mysticism, Renaissance Hermeticism, and ritual practice indicate the need to address the human mind and consciousness alongside a material science devoted to exact measurement and calculation of bodies and motion. Science itself during the latter half of the eighteenth century had assimilated a wide variety of organic-vitalist notions that suggested that the world was permeated by miraculous, invisible forces. Isaac Newton's gravity, Benjamin Franklin's electricity, the gases discovered by Joseph Black, Henry Cavendish, and Joseph Priestley were all intangible presences. However, their application involved extraordinary demonstrations of material power. Leyden jars, lightning conductors, hot-air balloons, and manned flight all suggested that the world was permeated by wondrous fluids. This was an old idea, traceable to Paracelsian *Naturphilosophie,* but well suited to the contemporary exploration of such new natural phenomena as electricity, magnetism, and chemistry. The combination of this notion of fluid and the powers of the mind in science would produce a powerful new current in the history of esotericism: animal magnetism.

Franz Anton Mesmer

This vitalist, pre-Romantic phase of eighteenth-century science helps to locate the thought and career of Franz Anton Mesmer (1734–1815), famous as the founder of "animal magnetism" for the therapeutic treatment of illness. Mesmer was born at Iznang near Radolfzell on Lake Constance in Swabia. First destined for the church, he studied philosophy and theology at the Jesuit universities of Dillingen and Ingolstadt in Bavaria before embarking on medical studies at the University of Vienna in 1760. Although his name became associated with occultist currents in the nineteenth century, Mesmer regarded himself as a Newtonian dedicated to discovering the mechanical laws that operate in the universe. Pondering the causes of universal gravitation, Mesmer had written his doctoral dissertation *De influxu planetarum in corpus humanum* (The influence of the planets in the human body) (1766), in which he posited the existence of an invisible, universally distributed fluid that flows continuously everywhere and serves as a vehicle for the mutual influence among heavenly bodies, the earth, and living things. Just as the oceans on earth have tides, so does the universal fluid, which passes through the earth and all creatures. Mesmer described this force as "the cause of universal gravitation and, no doubt, the basis of all bodily properties; which, in effect, in the smallest particles of fluids and solids of our bodies, contracts, distends and causes cohesion, elasticity, irritability, magnetism, and electricity; a force which can, in this context, be called *animal gravitation.*"[1]

Mesmer duly qualified as a physician and began a conventional practice in Vienna in 1767. During 1773–1774, he treated Francisca Österlin, who suffered from hysteria with a wide variety of distressing physical symptoms that ebbed and flowed during attacks. Mesmer saw a connection between her case and his cosmological theory. The symptoms of hysteria offered an outstanding example of the tidal effect of the universal fluid, or animal gravitation, coursing through the body of the patient. As a means of influencing this tide, Mesmer thought of using magnets, already in limited medical use. In 1774, he collaborated with Maximilian Hell (1720–1792), a Jesuit father and court astronomer to Empress Maria Theresia. Hell manufactured the required magnets, and Mesmer achieved a remarkable cure. When Hell claimed the discovery as his own, Mesmer insisted that the healing was attributable not to the magnet but rather to the medium through which the healing fluid was conducted. Mesmer's public reputation as a healer swiftly grew in Vienna, and he was invited to attend patients in South Germany, Switzerland, and Hungary in 1775 and 1776.[2]

In Bavaria, Prince Elector Max Joseph asked Mesmer to explain the results of Johann Josef Gassner (1727–1779), a priest who performed cures by exorcism and the laying on of hands. Mesmer regarded the faith healer's practice as fresh evidence that the cure was ascribable neither to miracles nor magnets but to a store of energy within the healer's body. His crucial concern was how to direct this energy, and Mesmer henceforth developed a therapy based on stroking, touching, hypnotic stares, and pointing with charged wands to control and remedy the ostensible imbalance of the fluid in the body of the patient. Henceforth he called his method of treatment "animal magnetism" (*animal* [Lat.] = living creature; *anima* [Lat.] = air, breath, life, soul). In Mesmer's later practice, patients sat communally around the *baquet*, a wooden tub filled with iron filings, sand, and bottles holding magnetized water. Holding iron rods immersed in the tub, the patients formed a chain through which the supposed magnetism thus generated flowed to bring relief.

Mesmerism as Rejected Science

Frustrated by the skeptical rejection of his theories by the medical authorities of Vienna, Mesmer moved to Paris in February 1778. Anxious to avoid the

FIGURE 9.1. Franz Anton Mesmer's Baquet. Courtesy of Bibliothèque Nationale, Paris.

earlier reaction to the empirical evidence of his cures, Mesmer now resolved to seek the approval of scientists for his theories of a universal fluid. In Paris, Voltaire, Diderot, and d'Alembert still presided over European thought. Laplace was working on cosmology, Buffon on biology, Lavoisier on chemistry, and Lagrange on algebra. Mesmer expected to be taken seriously in this scientific milieu. However, his reputation as a wonder-worker and the inherent difficulties in demonstrating his intangible fluid worked to prevent his recognition. His approaches to the French Academy of Sciences and the Royal Society of Medicine were fruitless. His first important convert was Charles Deslon, a member of the Paris Faculty of Medicine and personal physician to the Comte d'Artoise, later King Charles X. Meanwhile, Mesmer's healing practice was flourishing with enormous numbers of patient and widespread reports of his wonderful cures. A bitter pamphlet war between supporters and detractors of Mesmerism ensued between 1779 and 1784, triggering Deslon's expulsion from the faculty.[3]

Mesmer's *Mémoire sur la découverte du magnétisme animal*, published in 1779, outlined twenty-seven propositions concerning the universal fluid and animal magnetism. His opponents were quick to note that Mesmer's doctrine was in fact a restatement of the doctrine of cosmic fluid found in the works of Paracelsus (1493–1541), Jan Baptista van Helmont (1577–1644), Robert Fludd (1574–1637), and William Maxwell (fl. 1620–1647), the Scottish physician in ordinary to King Charles I, as documented in Michel Augustin Thouret's *Recherches et doutessur le magnétisme animal* (1784). Although it was Mesmer's own desire to found a new rational science, his theory was actually rooted in esoteric traditions. His "fluid" is a modern expression of long-standing speculations about "subtle" agents such as *pneuma*. Theories of subtle matter typify Western esotericism, especially in its view of a living, animate nature. The basic sympathy between this older tradition and Mesmerism would bring the latter many supporters among eighteenth-century illuminists and nineteenth-century occultists.

Mesmerism highlights an important issue relating to the place of esotericism in modern thought and science. Mesmer achieved astonishing results: blindness and disabilities were cured, broken lives were made whole. Ever more patients, especially the wealthy and fashionable, flocked to Mesmer's consulting rooms, where he charged the poor nothing for his services, the rich according to their pockets. Some doctors were impressed, others skeptical, many understandably envious. Although Mesmerism appeared to work, Mesmer's hypothesis for its operation was easily attacked because his intangible, invisible fluid could not be detected by any known means or instrument.

In March 1784, animal magnetism was the object of two royal commissions. The commissions consisted of Lavoisier, American diplomat Benjamin Franklin, French astronomer Jean Sylvain Bailly, and several nominees of the Academy of Sciences and the Royal Society of Medicine. The sociology of science can exert a significant influence on ideas' acceptance or rejection. According to James Webb, a historian of nineteenth- and twentieth-century occultism, one may regard such "rejected knowledge" as the heresy of irrationalism in the post-Enlightenment era.[4] This strategy of epistemological exclusion is comparable to the heresiological labels the Church used to disqualify esoteric dissent (notably Gnosticism, Hermetism, mysticism) in earlier centuries. In the age of reason, Mesmer's fluid was excluded by the professional scientists as an occult explanation. Moreover, the behavior of Mesmer's patients, who experienced trances, crises, and nervous convulsions, added to the impression of irrationality. Mesmer himself enhanced the cultic atmosphere of his sessions with an aura of mystery; the rooms were bathed in a soft light, and he wore robes embroidered with occult symbols. Already driven into a scientific subculture, Mesmer's followers sought ideological allies in the esoteric milieu.

Mesmerism and Illuminism

Although Mesmerism was officially killed off as a scientific discovery by the royal commissions' reports, it nonetheless was to flourish throughout Europe as a medical treatment and cultural phenomenon. Under the leadership of Nicolas Bergasse, a wealthy lawyer from Lyon, and Guillaume Kornmann, a banker from Strasbourg, a Society of Harmony was established at Paris in 1781 for the propagation of Mesmer's practice and ideas. From this headquarters, a network of provincial magnetic societies was established, modeled on the organization of Freemasons, notable for its own ambiguous position between rationalism and esotericism. Twenty such societies, sworn to secrecy and sectarian in their practice, existed throughout France in Strasbourg, Lyons, Bordeaux, Montpellier, Nantes, and other large towns by the mid-1780s. The societies combined medical treatment with political ideas of social emancipation, humanitarianism, and radical social reform.[5]

High-grade Masonic circles in Lyon and Strasbourg gave Mesmerism a strongly illuminist coloration in these cities. Armand Marie Jacques Chastenet, the Marquis de Puységur established a mesmerist society in Strasbourg as the Societé des Amis Réunis, which had strong associations with La Candeur, the most eminent of the twenty-nine lodges there.[6] Through his mesmerist practices, Puységur discovered induced somnambulism, which created a rich field of spiritual speculation. In 1787, the Swedenborgian Exegetical and Philanthropic Society of Stockholm corresponded with the Strasbourg society about spiritualism, indicating that its members in Sweden were communicating with spirits of the dead through a mesmerized subject.[7] Meanwhile, the Lyon society was strongly influenced by Jean-Baptiste Willermoz, whose esoteric interests were obvious from his involvement in the theurgical rituals of Pasqually's Elect Coëns. The Lyon society, La Concorde, recruited numerous theosophers, alchemists, and Rosicrucians from Willermoz's Masonic order of the Chevaliers Bienfaisants de la Cité Sainte. Louis Claude de Saint-Martin himself was directly involved in Mesmerism, having joined the Parisian society in February 1784. He would not only act as a spiritual consultant to Willermoz, but also give metaphysical advice to the Chevalier de Barberin, the leader of the Lyon society, and to the Marquis de Puységur concerning the spiritual meaning of somnambulism. Mesmer was not impressed by these developments, as he dearly wished his discovery to be granted scientific recognition, and he returned disappointed from a visit to the Lyon society in August 1784, when Willermoz made clear that he saw no distinction between visionary experiences and mesmeric trances.[8]

Animal Magnetism and Somnambulism

After successive feuds with Deslon and Bergasse, Mesmer parted company with his supporters and left Paris in 1785. However, animal magnetism was already launched on its independent career through the investigations of its phenomena by others. The Marquis de Puységur, and his brother Jacques Maxime Paul Chastenet, the viscount de Puységur, had been among Mesmer's early students in Paris. In April 1784, they began to apply these methods to cure the illnesses of their peasants on their estate at Buzancy near Soissons. They conducted their healing sessions in the open air, with their patients holding onto ropes suspended from a magnetized tree, in a bucolic version of the communal *baquet*. Whereas Mesmer's patients had typically undergone convulsions and a healing crisis, the Puységur brothers found that their subjects responded to treatment by entering a calm trance, in which they became highly suggestible to the magnetizer's instructions. In this state of somnambulism, the subject went to sleep, but was able to answer questions and report events.[9] Repeating the experiment with other patients, Armand found that this state of consciousness could be reproduced quite regularly; some somnambulists could also diagnose their own maladies, read thoughts, and perceive phenomena and events outside the normal range of perception.[10]

By the later 1780s, mesmerists tended to neglect the medical applications in favor of exploring the esoteric implications of Mesmerism. Their patients' deep trance, interpreted as a state of exaltation, frequently conferred powers of prophecy and clairvoyance. The earliest traces of modern Spiritualism can be traced back to Mesmer's legacy. Even before the end of the eighteenth century, the animists or spiritists occasionally questioned their somnambulists about the unseen or next world. Inspired by both Pasqually and Mesmer, Willermoz pursued a path of spiritualist magnetism, seeking confirmation of mankind's pristine state before the Fall. Such spiritualist phenomena involved the visions, clairaudience, and automatic writing of magnetized subjects. Willermoz investigated the trances of Jeanne Rochette, who reported contact with angelic entities and was also impressed by the divine writings received in 1785 by Marie-Louise de Monspey from the spirit of the Virgin Mary. Saint-Martin made a copy of these automatic writings which seemed to confirm the teachings of Pasqually.[11] Magnetizers were soon speculating whether, in a state of trance, the soul of the somnambulist might actually leave the body and converse with the souls of the dead. Since Mesmerism was chiefly associated with the aristocracy in France, it was swept aside by the Revolution and did not revive in that country until after the fall of Napoleon.

Puységur and his French followers, adhering to Mesmer's original thesis of a universal fluid, were known as "fluidists," whereas Chevalier de Barberin, as a Martinist, believed that all cures arising from magnetization and somnambulism were the result of will, faith, and an act of God upon the soul. Barberin did away with magnets and *baquet*, and his followers, essentially the pioneers of modern mental healing, were called "spiritists" or "animists." The animists denied the reality of animal magnetism, attributing trance states to suggestion and imagination, thus anticipating hypnosis and other aspects of psychology.

Animal Magnetism, Theosophy, and *Naturphilosophie* in Germany

Animal magnetism soon entered Germany, often combining with mystical ideas. A fertile background already existed on account of the theology of electricity developed by Prokop Divisch, Friedrich Christoph Oetinger, and Johann Ludwig Fricker during the 1760s. Active as a priest, theosopher, and natural historian, Oetinger had posited an 'electrical fire' concealed in all things, coeval with the animation of the universe, which connected the human being with all levels of life.[12] Heinrich Jung-Stilling (1740–1817), another Pietist and theosopher, and a close friend of the young Goethe, wrote about the intermediary worlds of visionary experience, incorporating animal magnetism in his *Theorie der Geisterkunde* (1808). The leading German theosopher Franz von Baader (1765–1841) also wrote an important work, *Über die Extase oder das Verzücktsein der magnetischen Schlafredner* (1817).

Animal magnetism would also be integrated into the German *Naturphilosophie* (philosophy of nature), itself closely related to theosophy. From 1790 to the 1820s, German Romanticism gave rise to *Naturphilosophie*, its own brand of natural science, which conceived of nature as a living, spiritual text to decipher by correspondences, harmonies, and analogy. By contrast with deductive science, *Naturphilosophie* dealt rather in eternities, absolutes, and "primal types," thus revealing its Hermetic conviction that the processes of the mind reflect the processes of nature. The Romantic philosopher Friedrich Joseph Wilhelm Schelling (1775–1854) had come to theosophy though Oetinger and then through reading Boehme. Schelling's early work *Die Weltseele* (1797), reasserted the Neoplatonic idea of the world-soul, while most *Naturphilosophen* were specialists in chemistry, physics, engineering, and medicine, and often associated with the University of Jena. Their contribution was most marked in areas of science concerned with dynamic processes and invisible influences, such as magnetism, galvanism, electricity, electrochemistry, and also in psychology with early concepts of the unconscious and dream interpretation.

Several *Naturphilosophen* became theorists of animal magnetism in the Romantic era. A leading German nature philosopher and theosopher, Gotthilf Heinrich Schubert (1780–1860), would contend in his books *Ansichten von der Nachtseite der Naturwissenschaft* (1808) and *Die Symbolik der Träume* (1814) that somnambulists, while in trance, were in contact with the whole of nature. In his account, animal magnetism thus restored the unity between conscious life and unconscious activity. The German nature-philosopher Adam Karl August Eschenmayer (1768–1852) coedited the academic periodical *Archiv für den thierischen Magnetismus* with Dietrich Georg Kieser, who wrote *System des Tellurismus oder thierisches Magnetismus* (1826). Eschenmayer's other works included a book about the famous somnambule known as the "Seeress of Prévorst" and a treatise on the metaphysics of nature, applied to chemical and medical objects.[13] Friedrich Hufeland wrote on the sympathy between beings, and Karl Friedrich Burdach asserted the existence of a transpersonal magnetic space to which magnetic trance provided access. By 1815, animal magnetism was a respectable academic subject in Germany with professorial chairs in the subject at Berlin and Bonn.

By contrast with the earlier French practitioners, much German speculation on animal magnetism typically involved intermediary worlds, theosophy, and esotericism. A key figure in this Romantic promotion of animal magnetism was the Swabian physician and poet Justinus Kerner (1786–1862), who had been strongly influenced by Schubert's book on dream symbolism and began studying animal magnetism during the early 1820s, subsequently publishing the first biography of Mesmer. In 1829, Kerner published his famous account of the Seeress of Prévorst, Friederike Hauffe (1801–1829), a patient to whom he had given magnetic treatment for acute hysteria.[14] Frau Hauffe was a model somnambulist under magnetic treatment, receiving some benefit for her morbid condition but also entering trance states involving acute sensitivity, clairvoyant prophecy, and visions of spirits and inner cosmic "sun circles" and "life circles." Her complex cosmological and chronological diagrams relating earthly incidents to a higher world exemplified esoteric philosophy with correspondences between the macrocosm and microcosm, imagination and intermediaries, and the transmutation of the seeress's soul. Thanks to Kerner's documentation of her case, the Seeress of Prévorst became famous throughout Europe, and knowledge of Kerner's work (translated into English in 1845) would eventually link Spiritualism with Mesmerism and esotericism.[15]

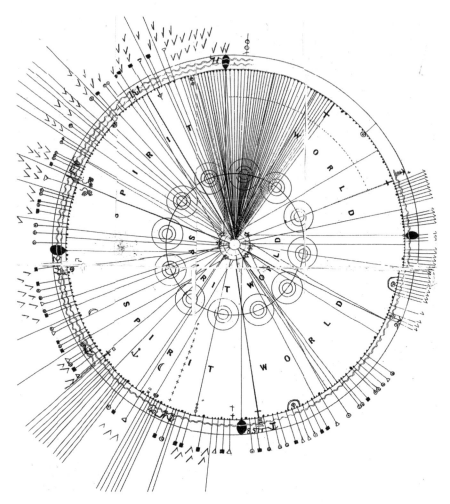

FIGURE 9.2.   Friederike Hauffe's Sun-Circles, in Justinus Kerner, *The Seeress of Prevorst, being Revelations concerning the inner-life of man and the inter-diffusion of a world of spirits in the one we inhabit. From the German by Mrs [Catherine] Crowe* (London, 1845).

Later Animal Magnetism in France and England

In post-Napoleonic France and nineteenth-century England, animal magnetism generated immense interest and controversial literature. Subsequent theorists in France were more interested in the phenomenon of will than in the mysteries of somnambulism. A pupil of Puységur's before the Revolution, Joseph Philippe François Deleuze (1753–1835) published a book, *Histoire critique de magnétisme animal* (1813), which suggested that the magnetic fluid was an emanation from ourselves guided by the will and that the magnetizer's will was the essential factor in any treatment. A Portuguese abbot, José Custodio de Faria, practicing in Paris, did not credit the existence of any fluid, but attributed the effects of treatment to the patient's susceptibility to the magnetizer's influence. His work *Le sommeil lucide* (1819) was an important influence on Alexandre Bertrand, whose *Traité du somnambulisme* (1823) anticipated the idea of suggestion as a therapeutic agency.[16] Another important French figure was Baron Jules Dupotet de Sennevoy (1798–1881), a medical student who had participated in the large public mesmerist experiments held at the Hôtel-Dieu in Paris in 1820, served on the 1831 investigative commission, and practiced as a homeopathic physician in London from 1837 to 1845. His *Introduction to the Study of Animal Magnetism* (1838) was published in London.[17]

The mesmerist demonstrations of Dupotet and Regazzoni in France and England also indicate their popular appeal as stage performances. In 1856, Regazzoni gave performances, in which blindfolded strangers were blocked by an imaginary Kabbalistic line he had drawn across the floor. In another case, a blindfolded girl was made to fall, as if struck by lightning, by the magnetic fluid emitted by Regazzoni's will. Regazzoni's feats prompted comparison with magic, and Dupotet's theoretical work, *La magie dévoilée* (1875), identified Mesmerism with the traditional practice of magic. Dupotet understood the will as the link between the power to induce trance states and the power of magic. These ideas would also influence modern occultism. Helena Blavatsky, the cofounder of modern Theosophy, also linked magic with Mesmerism, praising Dupotet as the "grand master" and "prince of French mesmerists." She quoted extensively from his work, regarding him as an adept who understood the link between trance states and the power of magic. Blavatsky was herself a staunch fluidist, not only in her copious reading and quotation of Mesmer, but also in her explanation of magic and the divine inspiration of the universe.[18]

The English physicians who took up animal magnetism were all directly influenced by Continental practitioners. Richard Chenevix had first encountered the practice in Germany around 1803 or 1804 and was convinced of its efficacy by witnessing demonstrations of the Abbé Faria at Paris in 1816. John Elliotson (1791–1868), an eminent English physician and professor of medicine at London University, was chiefly responsible for the founding of University College Hospital in 1834. Elliotson first met Chenevix in 1829, but it was not until he saw Dupotet at work in 1837 that he became an avid devotee of animal magnetism. Dupotet was a fluidist, and Elliotson followed this line of interpretation. He experimented in the wards of the hospital and performed surgeries while patients were in a somnambulistic state. He encountered strong resistance among his peers and was subsequently dismissed from the hospital. He then established a private practice and published a periodical,

The Zoist (1843–1855), that promoted phrenology together with Mesmerism, which henceforth flourished as a popular religion rather than as an acknowledged medical practice.[19]

James Braid (1795–1860), a Scottish surgeon practicing in Manchester, became interested in Mesmerism in 1841, when he observed demonstrations given by a traveling Swiss mesmerist named Charles Lafontaine (1803–1892). Braid believed that he understood the behavioral causes of this phenomenon, for which he coined the term "hypnotism" in his book *Neurypnology: or the Rationale of Nervous Sleep* (1843). He suggested that this state could be produced through visual fixation on a small bright object held eighteen inches above and in front of the eyes. His work was ignored in Britain but was rediscovered as a result of renewed work in French psychiatry in the 1860s. Divested of its fluidist explanation and esoteric interpretations, animal magnetism was ushered by Braid as hypnosis into the realm of modern psychology.[20]

Swedenborgianism and Mesmerism in the United States

Animal magnetism was introduced to the United States in 1838 by Charles de Poyen, a Frenchman, and spread rapidly among occultist and spiritualist groups from the 1840s onward, often combining with Swedenborgian ideas. Phineas Parkhurst Quimby (1802–1866), an American physician, heard Poyen speak publicly in Belfast, Maine, and began in 1840 to publicize Mesmerism himself as a traveling physician. William Levingston, an early experimenter in animal magnetism, discovered a natural trance medium in Andrew Jackson Davis (1826–1910), a cobbler known as the "Poughkeepsie seer," who was able to enter a trance state in which he mentally traveled to remote locations, lectured on topics unknown to his conscious self, read books while blindfolded, and made medical diagnoses leading to cures. Davis communicated with a spirit he later identified as Swedenborg and went on to publish *The Principles of Nature* (1847), which relayed Swedenborg's ideas of graduated spiritual worlds, spiritual marriage, and the notion that 'like attracts like' (Swedenborg's correspondences). Davis's book was notable in that it was allegedly received in a trance state, thus anticipating other channeled "scripture" of modern esoteric movements, such as Blavatsky's *Isis Unveiled*, Levi's *Aquarian Gospel of Jesus Christ*, and Jane Roberts's Seth material. *The Principles of Nature* swiftly ran through more than thirty editions, establishing itself as a founding text of modern Spiritualism.[21]

Animal magnetism had been a controversial issue in American Swedenborgian circles since 1794. American Swedenborgians were quick to make a

connection between Mesmer's magnetic state and the newer spiritualist phenomenon of communicating with spirits, and this became an urgent matter once
Andrew Jackson Davis had made his spectacular claim involving Swedenborg.
Davis's pronouncements and the Spiritualist movement caused considerable
conflict in the New Church, as Swedenborgians often divided on the issue on the
basis of Swedenborg's warning against contacting the dead, yet cooperating in
their communications. George Bush (1794–1859), a Swedenborgian and a professor of Asian languages, was convinced that Davis's mediumship was authentic,
though he was not certain that the spirit Davis had met was Swedenborg.[22]

Davis's trance lectures attracted many, including the writer Edgar Allan Poe
and the clairvoyant Thomas Lake Harris (1823–1906). Born in England, Harris
had briefly been a Universalist Church minister in America before he joined
the group around Davis. Harris was influenced by the new vogue for Spiritualism and successively organized a Swedenborgian church in New York, founded
a Spiritualist community in Virginia, then returned to Swedenborgianism to
run a new millenarian community first in New York, then at Lake Erie, and
ultimately in California from 1875. He adopted radical views on conjugal love
(distorting Swedenborg's ideas), Spiritualism, fairies, and, later, on Oriental
religion, Freemasonry, and esoteric wisdom. As Bruce Campbell has noted,
occultism was introduced to America in the mid-nineteenth century America
chiefly in the forms of Mesmerism, Swedenborgianism, and Freemasonry.[23]

New Thought and Christian Science

Phineas Parkhurst Quimby's combination of Mesmerism and faith healing
identified the health and disease of a person as products of the person's imagination. These ideas were instrumental in the proliferation of a new religious
movement in the United States concerned with healing, health, and well-being
from the 1870s onward, which took the various names of Mental Science, Mind
Cure, the Boston Craze, and New Thought. Both New Thought and the related
movement of Christian Science were based on the integration of more traditional Christian ideas with nineteenth-century metaphysical traditions. The latter were diffuse but commonly involved a secular spirituality concerned with
mystical experience and the importance of the power of the mind over the body,
particularly in enabling healing. From 1847 until his death in 1866, Quimby
devoted his life to healing the sick, and he treated more than 12,000 patients
during those years. Some of those patients helped to make Quimby famous.

Among them was Warren Felt Evans (1817–1889), who became one of the first
individuals to write seriously on Quimby's teachings, integrating his philosophy

with that of Swedenborg. Evans's works included *The Mental Cure, illustrating the influence of the Mind on the Body* (1869), *Mental Medicine* (1872), *Soul and Body* (1875), *The Divine Law of Cure* (1881), and *Esoteric Christianity and Mental Therapeutics* (1886). Former patient Mary B. Patterson, later Eddy (1821–1910) was a virtual invalid, but she instantly recovered after treatment from Quimby in 1862. Her first book, *Science and Health with Key to the Scriptures* (1875), represented a reformulation of Quimby's ideas in the context of biblical teachings, which she called the textbook of Christian Science. In 1879, Mrs. Eddy with fellow practitioners established what became the First Church of Christ, Scientist (The Mother Church).

Former Quimby patients Julius Dresser (1838–1893) and Annetta (Seabury) Dresser (1843–1935) started a Mental Science movement in Boston. In 1882, a dispute arose between Mary Eddy and a former student of hers, Edward J. Arens, and Julius Dresser, who, along with his wife and son Horatio Dresser (1866–1954) staunchly upheld the Quimby system of healing and disputed the origin of Mrs. Eddy's ideas. Julius Dresser argued for Quimby's precedence in a book, *The True History of Mental Science* (1887), and Annetta Dresser gave a similarly supportive exposition in *The Philosophy of P. P. Quimby* (1895). The Dressers launched a group to rival Mary Eddy's Christian Science; called the New Thought movement, it was made up of small independent groups that formed the Metaphysical Club in Boston in 1895 and published a magazine called *New Thought*.[24] The Dressers' movement spread quickly across the United States. By the beginning of the twentieth century, it would secure a mass audience with an extensive literature by such well-known authors as Ralph Waldo Trine, Emma Curtis Hopkins, and William Walker Atkinson (1862–1932), who published about twenty works on such subjects as Hermetic wisdom, magnetism, Hindu breathing techniques, yoga, karma, and the power of visualization. Through the New Thought movement, Mesmerism joined contemporary American attitudes regarding personal responsibility for the attainment of health, well-being, happiness, and prosperity.[25]

Modern Spiritualism

American Spiritualism, already anticipated in Europe by the pre-Revolutionary French spiritist magnetizers and the German Romantic *Naturphilosophen*, took off as a popular socioreligious phenomenon in 1848. The two sisters Catherine (Kate) (1837–1892) and Margaretta (Maggie) Fox (1833–1893) began receiving what they claimed were spirit messages in the form of rapping noises at their family home at Hydesville in Rochester, New York. When the remains of a dead peddler were discovered in the cellar, it was immediately supposed that the rappings were his communications from beyond the grave. The girls' older married sister, Ann Leah Underhill (1814–1890), took a strong hand in the subsequent promotion and management of their séances, which were soon arranged in New York City.[26] The two young girls became national celebrities. The Hydesville movement assumed social, moral, and political overtones. The manifest hunger among Protestant sects of the East Coast of the United States for supernaturalism, sensuous fulfillment in their religion, and signs of divine grace swiftly overwhelmed the critics and skeptics. The high point of enthusiasm in the United States was in the mid-1850s, with a spate of publications describing the phenomena, such as Charles Hammond's *Light from the Spirit World* (1852), Judge Edmonds and George Dexter's *Spiritualism* (1853), and Robert Hare's *Experimental Investigation of Spirit Manifestations: Demonstrating the Existence of Spirits and Their Communication with Mortals* (1855).[27]

The new movement spread swiftly with new mediums emerging throughout the Northeast, new methods of communication with the spirits, and increasingly more spectacular, theatrical demonstrations of the spirits' presence and power. The physical phenomena attending spiritualist séances included table-turning, the moving of furniture, spirit-writing on slates, phosphorescent flames, apports (telekinetic materializations) of objects, musical instruments playing unaided, the appearance of spirit hands, the levitation of the medium, spirit faces seen through an aperture in the medium's cabinet, and three-dimensional materialized bodies that walked among the séance participants. The new American movement reached England when the medium Mrs. Maria Hayden visited London in 1852 and the famous medium Daniel Dunglas Home (1833–1886) caused a sensation with his exploits, including apparent levitation in 1855.[28] The séance room offered a new kind of Holy Communion, where faith was replaced by evidence, the sacrament by manifested spirits. Spiritualism gave rise to its own denomination, with a scattering of nineteenth-century neo-Gothic churches in industrial towns. Drawn curtains, darkness, intimate circles, attractive female mediums, spirits in diaphanous apparel, strange voices, the secretion of fluid (ectoplasm) for the spirits' manifestation were so many examples of the Victorian attraction to mystery, sex, death, and the "other world," removed from the cold light of scientific reason.[29]

Spiritualism and Psychical Research

Spiritualism is significant as a new religious movement, but its relationship with esoteric philosophy is less clear. The phenomena of modern spiritualism demonstrate interesting similarities with ancient theurgy (mediums, trance states, altered voices, spirit communications). However, the frequent triviality of modern spirit messages, so often reflecting the sitters' personal concerns and hopes, and Spiritualism's lack of a coherent philosophy other than the implication of life beyond the veil of death tend to disqualify it as a variety of esoteric philosophy. The spirits of recently deceased persons typically manifested at séances; angels and other intermediaries were unknown; even the spirits of past religious leaders were surprisingly rare. Spiritualism's vision of the happy departed dwelling in "Summerland" helped promote a belief in utopian social experiments and millenarian visions of the political future (e.g., those of Thomas Lake Harris, Charles Fourier). As Patrick Deveney comments, the purpose of Spiritualism was simply the conviction of immortality, while its other goals were quite this-worldly: social progress and reform.[30]

Spiritualism is notably the product of mass society and modernity. First, its appeal to varied audiences, embracing both the industrial working classes and the leisured middle classes, indicate its religious function in the disenchanted world of secular modernity. Second, it enjoys a close dialogue with modern positivist science that increasingly triumphed as the dominant worldview by the mid-nineteenth century. The very phenomena of Spiritualism in the period after 1850 gave rise to psychical research as a variety of empirical science seeking to test their nature and validity. Outstanding British scientists and philosophers such as Sir William Crookes, Sir Oliver Lodge, Alfred Russel Wallace, Lord Rayleigh, Frederic W. H. Myers, Frank Podmore, and Edmund Gurney were all important participants in the early history of the Society for Psychical Research founded in London in 1884. As Faivre and Hanegraaff have noted, Spiritualism and much of modern occultism no longer relay the esoteric spirituality of Hermeticism, angelic intermediaries, and the primal language of nature. The spirits of the dead contacted through these means instead use trite codes to tap out messages and employ seemingly mundane practices. Their presence and their phenomena must likewise be exhibited in demonstrations and theatrical performances, recorded and tested by skeptics with technical equipment. Only a disenchanted world has need of such prosaic proofs.[31] Contemporary esotericists (e.g., Rudolf Steiner, René Guénon) have often accused Spiritualists of materialism for engaging in this lower level of discourse.

Mesmer's animal magnetism was a traditional form of pneumatology denied scientific recognition. As the covert heir of ideas stemming from Paracelsus, Robert Fludd, and William Maxwell, Mesmerism found due acclaim as an esoteric tradition among the French spiritist magnetizers and illuminists of the 1780s and again among the German Romantic theosophers and *Naturphilosophen*, with Justinus Kerner's discussion of the Seeress of Prévorst as a cardinal example. With the abandonment of the fluidist hypothesis in favor of hypnosis and suggestion, animal magnetism entered the secular currents of psychology and self-help practices. Although the ideas of Swedenborg and animal magnetism were applied to modern Spiritualism, it arose independently of these ideas, and its motives and preoccupations were relatively mundane. Besides the visionary clairvoyance and cosmological speculations of Andrew Jackson Davis, modern Spiritualism initially offered little scope for the elaboration of esoteric cosmology, intermediaries, and the transmutation of the soul. Only with the transformation of Spiritualism into modern occultism in the work of Paschal Beverly Randolph, Emma Hardinge Britten, and Helena Blavatsky would it become incorporated into the wider esoteric perspectives of magical practice, spiritual evolution, hierarchies of beings besides man on the cosmic ladder, and reincarnation.

FURTHER READING

John Beloff, *Parapsychology: A Concise History* (London: Athlone Press, 1993).

Ernst Benz, *The Theology of Electricity: On the Encounter and Explanation of Theology and Science in the Seventeenth and Eighteenth Centuries*, translated by W. Taraba (Allison Park, Pa.: Pickwick, 1989).

Charles S. Braden, *Spirits in Rebellion: The Rise and Development of New Thought* (Dallas, Tex.: Southern Methodist University Press, 1987).

Ruth Brandon, *The Spiritualists: The Passion for the Occult in the Nineteenth and Twentieth Centuries* (Buffalo, N.Y.: Prometheus, 1983).

Ann Braude, *Radical Spirits: Spiritualism and Women's Rights in Nineteenth-Century America* (Boston: Beacon Press, 1989).

Vincent Buranelli, *The Wizard from Vienna: Franz Anton Mesmer and the Origins of Hypnotism* (London: Peter Owen, 1976).

Robert Darnton, *Mesmerism and the End of the Enlightenment in France* (Cambridge, Mass.: Harvard University Press, 1968).

Henri F. Ellenberger, *The Discovery of the Unconscious: The History and Evolution of Dynamic Psychiatry* (London: Allen Lane, 1970).

Alfred J. Gabay, *The Covert Enlightenment: Eighteenth-Century Counterculture and Its Aftermath* (West Chester, Pa.: Swedenborg Foundation, 2005).

Alan Gauld, *A History of Hypnotism* (Cambridge: Cambridge University Press, 1992).

Fred Gettings, *Ghosts in Photographs: The Extraordinary Story of Spirit Photography* (New York: Harmony Books, 1978).

Alexander Gode-von Aesch, *Natural Science in German Romanticism* (New York: Columbia University Press, 1941).

Margaret Goldsmith, *Franz Anton Mesmer: The History of an Idea* (London: Arthur Baker, 1934).

Ivor Grattan Guinness (ed.), *Psychical Research: A Guide to Its History, Principles, and Practices* (Wellingborough: Aquarian Press, 1982).

Otto-Joachim Grüsser, *Justinus Kerner 1786–1862: Arzt—Poet—Geisterseher* (Berlin: Springer, 1987).

Emma Hardinge Britten, *Modern American Spiritualism: Twenty Years' Record of the Communion between Earth and the World of Spirits* (New York: author, 1870; repr. New York University books, 1970).

———, *Nineteenth Century Miracles; or, Spirits and Their Work in Every Country of the Earth* (London: William Britten, 1883).

Justinus Kerner, *The Seeress of Prévorst: being revelations concerning the inner-life of man, and the inter-diffusion of a world of spirits in the one we inhabit,* translated by Mrs. Catherine Crowe (London: J. C. Moore, 1845).

Janet Oppenheimer, *The Other World: Spiritualism and Psychical Research in England, 1850–1914* (Cambridge: Cambridge University Press, 1985).

Ronald Pearsall, *The Table-Rappers* (London: Michael Joseph, 1972).

Frank Podmore, *Modern Spiritualism,* 2 vols. (London: Methuen, 1902).

———, *The Newer Spiritualism* (London: T. Fisher Unwin, 1910).

Nancy Rubin Stuart, *The Reluctant Spiritualist: The Life of Maggie Fox* (Orlando, Fla.: Harcourt, 2005).

James Webb, *The Flight from Reason* (London: Macdonald, 1971).

Alison Winter, *Mesmerized: Powers of Mind in Victorian Britain* (Chicago: University of Chicago Press, 1998).

Nora Wydenbruck, *Doctor Mesmer: An Historical Study* (London: John Westhouse, 1947).

10

Ritual Magic from 1850 to the Present

The modern occult revival of the nineteenth century was a complex phenomenon with widespread causes. As the preceding chapter showed, Romanticism stimulated interest in the marvelous, mysterious, and unknown, which in turn created a cultural receptivity to Mesmerism, Spiritualism, and magic. Georg Konrad Horst's *Zauber-Bibliothek* (1821–1826) offered a six-part study of sorcery, theurgy, divination, and witchcraft. By midcentury, several histories of magic had been published, including Joseph Ennemoser's *Geschichte der Magie* (1844), translated into English in 1854 by William Howitt, who also wrote *History of the Supernatural* (1863). In France, Roger Gougenot des Mousseaux published his dramatic revelations as *La magie au dix-neufième siècle* (1860) and *Les hauts phénomènes de la magie* (1864). The seminal work of the French occultist Eliphas Lévi clearly falls within this milieu.

The reputation of Freemasonry as a supposed channel of Hermetic wisdom was also an important factor in the occult revival. The prevalence of high-grade Masonic theosophy, as represented by Martinès de Pasqually, Jean-Baptiste Willermoz, and Count Cagliostro, ensured that Freemasonry could easily be adopted in the construction of esoteric traditions. Ellic Howe has documented the nineteenth-century history of "fringe" Masonry in England, in which occult knowledge was propagated through a variety of minute orders and societies. These groups used a variety of legendary associations including ancient Egypt and Asia and also a Rosicrucian coloration that harked back to the Order of the Gold- und Rosenkreuz high-grade Freemasonry that flourished in eighteenth-century central Europe. By the mid-1860s, some English Masons had founded an order organized in grades called the Societas Rosicruciana in Anglia for the study of Western esoteric traditions. In 1888, some of its members founded an explicitly magical order, the Hermetic Order of the Golden Dawn, to cultivate this knowledge with grades and initiation rituals.[1]

It is possible that the growth of fringe Masonry also reflected the contemporary revival of ritualism in the Anglican Church, as represented by the Oxford Movement of John Keble, Henry Newman, and Edward Pusey that began in the 1830s. Against the plain Anglican religious service, Anglo-Catholic revivalism sought a sensuous experience of Christian worship in elaborate ritual, additional sacraments, and richly embroidered vestments. The cultural effects of this movement had achieved significant influence with sacramental worship restored to Anglican devotion and the revival of religious orders after midcentury.[2] By the end of the century, the Golden Dawn and other occult orders in France combined this rediscovered taste for ritualism with an artistic flair that also characterized fin-de-siècle culture in England and France. The ritual model of Freemasonry would also enter other occultist groups. After 1910, Annie Besant (1847–1933), Helena Blavatsky's successor, introduced fringe Masonic ideas into Theosophy with a parallel order of Co-Masonry. Her colleague, Charles Webster Leadbeater (1854–1934), a former Anglo-Catholic curate, embraced Co-Masonry, and in 1917 he founded the Liberal Catholic Church, which combined ritualism with ideas drawn from occultism.

Eliphas Lévi and the French Occult Revival

Eliphas Lévi (1810–1875) is a pioneering figure in the occult revival of the second half of the nineteenth century, influencing groups in England, France, and Germany. Born and brought up in Paris, Alphonse Louis Constant had a strong if intermittent vocation for the Catholic ministry, but also moved in literary, left-wing, and feminist circles. Besides his political radicalism, Constant was drawn to mysticism. He had studied the Kabbalah in Knorr von Rosenroth's *Kabbala Denudata* (1677–1684) and read works by Boehme, Swedenborg, Saint-Martin, and Fabre d'Olivet.[3] In 1852, Constant met Joseph Maria Hoëné-Wronski (1776–1853), an elderly Polish émigré who had had long devoted himself to esotericism and messianic prophecy and was well versed in Kabbalah, Boehme, and Gnosticism. Wronski resigned from the Russian army in 1797 to study in Germany, where he was strongly influenced by Kant, Fichte, and Schelling, and he went to France in 1800. In 1803, he experienced a mystical illumination, which he regarded as the discovery of the Absolute, and he subsequently devoted his life to the exposition of this Absolute philosophy. He also worked on a philosophy of history, which divided time into three ages, the last of which would bring human reason into accord with divine laws. Wronski acted as a powerful catalyst in focusing Constant's interest in magic and occultism. Because Wronski's thought mixed esoteric ideas with revolutionary expectations, Constant was strongly attracted by his religious and scientific utopianism.[4]

Constant published his first work on magic, *Dogme de la haute magie* (1855), followed by its companion volume, *Rituel de la haute magie* (1856), and henceforth used the name Eliphas Lévi (the Hebrew equivalents of his first names). His later works *Histoire de la magie* (1860) and *La Clef des Grands Mystères* (1861) continued his synthesis of the "occultist" tradition. Lévi's compilation of the Western magical tradition was based on medieval and Renaissance sources, as expounded in the works of Trithemius, Cornelius Agrippa, and Paracelsus. Man is a microcosm of the universe. Sympathetic correspondences link the three intelligible worlds by hierarchical analogy: the natural or physical, the spiritual or metaphysical, and the divine or religious. The magician can operate on these various levels by evoking entities and powers by means of spells, signs, Kabbalistic formulae, and talismans.[5] Lévi was inspired by the notion that all occult sciences had been veiled in symbolism and allegory as a result of their persecution and suppression in the early Christian era. Occult sciences ranging from the Tarot to alchemy and Kabbalah had therefore been transmitted in secrecy and was made available only to initiates.[6] In his construction of this syncretic magical tradition, Lévi also practiced a form of concordance, already evident among the Renaissance scholar magi and identified by Faivre as an extrinsic feature of esoteric philosophy.

Lévi's exploration of the doctrines of transcendental magic was comprehensive. In his first two books, he discussed cosmological fundamentals of dyad, triad, and tetrad in syncretic terms of the pillars of Solomon's temple, male-female sexual polarity, Gnostic, Masonic, and Taoist symbolism. He expounds on the magical virtues of the tetrad, comparing the fourfold series of magical elements and elementary spirits. The sovereignty of will over the physical soul of the four elements is represented in ritual magic by the Pentagram. The elementary spirits of earth, water, air, and fire are subservient to this sign when it is placed in a magical circle or on a table of evocations. Lévi asserted that the primary function of magic was to enable the magician to focus and direct his will. In Lévi's view, the magician used ritual magic to manipulate and transform forces within himself, which then acted on the external world of matter.[7] Lévi mixed the ideas of Mesmerism with his philosophy of magic, explaining all sympathetic magic in terms of the "Astral Light" or "Great Magical

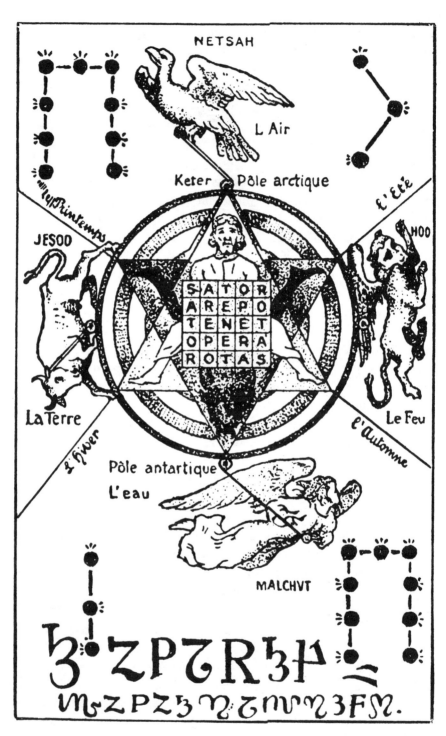

FIGURE 10.1. Tarot correspondences in the Key of William Postel, in Eliphas Levi, *The Key of the Mysteries* (London: Rider, 1950).

Agent," described as a subtle fluid that pervades the universe with four physical manifestations in heat, light, electricity, and magnetism. This agent can be affected by the human will and can act upon the human imagination. Magical operations provide access to the energies and impressions of the Astral Light, thus producing magical phenomena and clairvoyance.[8]

Successive chapters described Hellenistic mythology, the Kabbalah, alchemy, astrology, charms and philters, necromancy, black magic, and divination. Lévi's particular originality consisted in positing esoteric correspondences between the twenty-two paths on the Kabbalistic Tree of Life and the twenty-two major trumps in the Tarot pack of cards. The esoteric significance of the Tarot cards (which probably originated in fifteenth–century Italy) was first suggested by Antoine Court de Gébelin (1725–1784), a Protestant pastor, high-grade Freemason, and follower of Mesmer. He ascribed an ancient Egyptian origin to the cards in his *Le Monde primitif* (1773–1784), a nine-volume work which aimed to restore the pristine harmony of the ancient world through rediscovery of an original, universal language. This idea was picked up by Jean-Baptiste Alliette (1738–1791), an occult cartomancer who worked in Paris under the name Etteilla from the 1770s onward. Etteilla interpreted the Tarot as the Book of Thoth, revealed by priests in ancient Egypt.[9] Lévi's linkage between the Kabbalah and the Tarot as a source of magical symbolism rather than mere divination would influence the future practice of many magical orders. Almost all modern occultism admits the Tarot as a source of magical imagery and proposes its concordance with the other symbol systems of astrology, alchemy, and magic. Lévi was the first to link the Tarot to the other traditional occult sciences in this way.[10]

Lévi is thus the first of the major modern compilers of the Western esoteric tradition, whose popular illustrated works reintroduced ritual magic, Hermeticism, and the Renaissance scholar magi to educated audiences in nineteenth-century Europe and America. It has been observed that when Lévi began publishing, occultism was in a moribund condition and that his work formed "the narrow channel through which the whole Western tradition of magic flowed to the modern era."[11] In 1854, Lévi visited London, where he met English occultists, including Sir Edward Bulwer-Lytton, the author of *Zanoni* (1842), which revealed extensive esoteric knowledge. A high point of Lévi's stay was the evocation of the spirit of the ancient Greek wonder worker Apollonius of Tyana by magical rituals. Lévi revisited London in 1861, and was henceforth lionized as an adept by a younger generation of modern occultists. Kenneth Mackenzie, the Masonic historian, came to visit him in Paris, MacGregor Mathers, the cofounder of the Hermetic Order of the Golden Dawn, called him a "great qabalist." A. E. Waite published an anthology of his writings in 1886 and translated his major works into English, and Aleister Crowley believed he was a reincarnation of Lévi.

Helena Blavatsky translated his account of the evocation of Apollonius of Tyana and also quoted him repeatedly in her work *Isis Unveiled*.[12] Such recognition certainly reflects his importance to the modern Western occult revival.

Antoine Faivre has identified Lévi as the first major figure in the occultist current of the nineteenth century.[13] Whereas earlier esotericists canvassed for a Hermetic variety of science, modern occultists do not reject scientific progress or modernity. The practical triumph of positivist science and its technology invited their integration with a universal vision of the cosmos. The pansophy of the late Renaissance is still evident, but modern occultism seeks proofs and demonstrations by recourse to scientific tests or terminology. Gérard Encausse (alias Papus, 1865–1916) was a leading member of the reconstituted Hermes branch of the Theosophical Society in Paris, founded in 1887, editing his own journal *L'Initiation* from 1888. A physician, investigator, and experimenter, Papus published *Traité méthodique de science occulte* (1888), the most influential book on occultism since those of Lévi; founded other esoteric journals, including *La Voile d'Isis*; and wrote a number of medical works.[14] His many occult works on healing, Kabbalah, and palmistry included *Le Tarot des Bohémiens* (1889), which elaborated on the correlation between the Tarot and the Kabbalah. He devoted a major work *La Kabbale* (1892) to this secret tradition of the West. Papus had been strongly influenced by Joseph-Alexandre Saint-Yves d'Alveydre (1842–1910), the author of several works on occultism and political utopianism. Papus also revived the Martinist order, or rather invented it on the basis of an alleged chain of initiation deriving from Louis Claude de Saint-Martin. As head of the order, Papus founded many new lodges across Europe and America. He also joined a Kabbalistic Order of the Rosy Cross, led by Stanislas de Guaïta (1861–1897) and Joséphin Péladan (1858–1918), who represented an artistic strand of esotericism allied to the neo-romantic Symbolist movement.[15]

The Hermetic Order of the Golden Dawn

The Rosicrucian tradition of initiatory societies coupled with Freemasonry interacted with Eliphas Lévi's promotion of Western magic to generate a lively succession of English occultists involved in ceremonial magic from the end of the nineteenth century. During the latter half of the nineteenth century, Spiritualism and occultism attracted a growing following, which coincided with an expansion in Freemasonry. In 1866, a small number of master Masons interested in esoteric traditions formed a Masonic-Rosicrucian study group, the Societas Rosicruciana in Anglia (SRIA). Founded by Robert Wentworth Little (1840–1878), the SRIA adopted a hierarchy and grade names similar to those used by the eighteenth-century Gold- und Rosenkreuzer Masonic order in Germany. Little had a variety of Masonic interests and was said to be a student of Eliphas Lévi's works. He had evidently come by some old German Rosicrucian papers and consulted Kenneth Robert Mackenzie (1833–1886), a scholar of esoteric traditions and Egyptian antiquities, who claimed to have been in contact some years earlier with German Rosicrucians.[16] During the 1870s and 1880s, the SRIA worked some rituals and held lectures on esoteric subjects including Spiritualism, Masonic symbolism, and the Kabbalah. The SRIA continues to this day.

Three brothers of the SRIA founded the Hermetic Order of the Golden Dawn, which would become the prototype and leading example of para-Masonic magical orders.[17] The initiative was taken by Dr. William Wynn Westcott (1848–1925), a London coroner who had been a Freemason since 1871. He had studied medicine at University College, London, and practiced in partnership with his uncle in Somerset until 1879, when he moved to Hendon to immerse himself in the study of Kabbalah, Hermeticism, alchemy, and Rosicrucianism. These interests coincided with his joining the SRIA in 1880. His first published works were studies of the Sepher Yetzirah, the Isiac tablet of Cardinal Bembo, arithmology, and a translation of Lévi's *Magical Ritual of Sanctum Regnum,* a work based on the Tarot trumps. Westcott later edited the nine-volume series of the *Collectanea Hermetica* (1893–1902), which included new English translations of alchemical, Hermetic, and Kabbalistic texts.[18] In 1882, Westcott became acquainted with Samuel Liddell Mathers, who had that year joined the SRIA. Both men sought a more practical engagement with esotericism and were involved with Anna Kingsford's short-lived Hermetic Society, founded in 1884, for the cultivation of Western traditions in contrast to the Eastern orientation of the Theosophical Society. By 1886, Westcott had begun to conceive of a magical order based on the Western esoteric traditions in which he was then absorbed.

The origins of Golden Dawn ceremonial magic and its rituals are enveloped in mystery, since Westcott sought to create an exotic German Rosicrucian authority for the order. He claimed that in August 1887 he had acquired from Rev. A. F. A. Woodford, a parson and well-known Mason, a cipher manuscript that described five magical grades in a secret script taken from the *Polygraphiae* of Johann Trithemius (Lévi had suggested in his *Rituel* that the best texts of medieval ceremonial magic were thus encoded). It is highly probable that this cipher manuscript was originally composed by Kenneth R. H. Mackenzie, whose papers passed upon his death to Westcott. Westcott then forged or caused to be forged an imaginary correspondence with the (almost certainly fictitious) Fräulein Anna Sprengel, a German adept mentioned in the papers.[19] The purpose of this subterfuge was to establish a putative lineage from a mysterious Continental occult lodge and to obtain an authorization to found his own temple of the order in

England. The latter was of particular importance to Westcott, given the preoccupation of English Freemasonry with legitimate succession. Westcott then invited
Mathers to compose complete rituals based on the skeletal material in the cipher
manuscript. At the same time, Westcott proposed that Mathers join him as a
Chief of the order and that they spread a complete scheme of initiation. Dr. William Robert Woodman (1828–1891), a retired physician and Supreme Magus of
the SRIA was appointed the third Chief of the order. Ellic Howe's analysis of the
suspect documents involved in the Golden Dawn's origin has been extended by
Robert Gilbert's collection of statements by contemporaries.[20]

Mathers (1854–1918) was born in London, the son of a clerk, and was
brought up by his widowed mother at Bournemouth. He became a Freemason
in 1877 and began his mystical studies. He moved in 1885 to London, where he
came into contact with Anna Bonus Kingsford, president of the British Theosophical Society. Kingsford's esoteric interests were primarily occidental, and in
1884 she had founded the Hermetic Society with Edward Maitland to study the
Western Hermetic tradition and the Kabbalah. Mathers moved in these circles.
He was introduced to Blavatsky, with whom he discussed the Kabbalah, and he
lectured on the subject to the Theosophical Society in 1886. He published his
translation of Knorr von Rosenroth as *The Kabbalah Unveiled* (1887).

Mathers's prodigious research into the history, doctrines, and rituals of
magic found full expression in his composition of the grade rituals and cur-
ricula of the Golden Dawn. Mathers read extensively in the British Museum to
gather a working knowledge of Greco-Egyptian magical lore and the medieval
magical grimoires, in addition to his studies in the Kabbalah. In 1888, he published a short book on the occult Tarot, followed by a translation of the medieval
magical text *The Key of Solomon the King (Clavicula Salomonis)* (1889). Besides
magic, theories of war interested Mathers. Under the influence of the romantic
Celtic Revival, he had added MacGregor to his surname. In 1892, Mathers and
his wife, Mina, the sister of French philosopher Henri Bergson, moved to Paris,
where they founded the Ahathoor Temple No. 7 of the Golden Dawn. Here,
Mathers also used the title Comte de Glenstrae, and he translated more medieval grimoires: *The Book of the Sacred Magic of Abra-Melin the Mage* (1898); *The
Grimoire of Armadel,* which circulated in manuscript among temple members;
and an edition of the *Lemegeton (The Lesser Key of Solomon,* of which *The Goetia*
was part), which was published by Aleister Crowley in 1904. This medieval
magic of invocations, magic circles, pentagram rituals, and consecrated talismans was closely linked to the Jewish tradition and Kabbalah. Mathers's editions of the grimoires attempted to distance them from black magic. Moreover,
his Golden Dawn rituals and practices were chiefly indebted to the spiritual
magic of Alexandrian Hermetism rather than to medieval invocatory magic.[21]

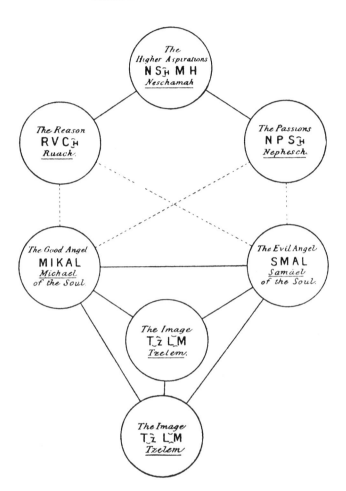

PLATE SHOWING THE FORMATION OF THE SOUL, &c
(From "Clef des Mystères" by Eliphaz Lévi Zahed.)

FIGURE 10.2. Plate showing the Formation of the Soul from Eliphas Levi,
La Clef des Grandes Mystères (1861), in S. L. MacGregor Mathers, *The Kabbalah
Unveiled* (London: George Redway, 1887).

In their considerable body of written work, including the rituals for the
Golden Dawn, Westcott and Mathers achieved a major restatement of the *prisca
theologia* tradition of Renaissance magic in its concordance of Hermetism, Neoplatonism, and Kabbalah. Both Westcott and Mathers embraced much of the
Western esoteric tradition in their writings. Following Lévi's example regarding
the rediscovery of a lost, universal tradition traceable to Zoroaster, Hermes Trismegistus, Moses, Orpheus, Pythagoras, and Plato, they consciously placed this

reconstructed tradition at the heart of their new institution for the instruction of initiates in the Western magical tradition. This tradition was more proximate in Rosicrucianism, on which Westcott published several works. The first manifesto, *Fama Fraternitatis* (1614), had stated that its philosophy was no new invention but was received by Adam and used by Moses and Solomon. Similarly, in their initiation to the second order, Golden Dawn initiates were invited to share in this *prisca theologia* passed on by Christian Rosenkreutz: "Know, O Aspirant, that the Mysteries of the Rose and the Cross have existed from time immemorial, and that the Rites were practiced, and the wisdom taught, in Egypt, Eleusis, Samothrace, Persia, Chaldea and India."[22] Wouter Hanegraaff has commented on this modern construction of *prisca theologia* in the late nineteenth century through Lévi and Blavatsky as a form of ancient wisdom based on comparative religion from an esoteric point of view.[23] In the Golden Dawn's case, this ancient wisdom was presented to initiates as a living tradition through dramatic rituals and grades.

Grade Hierarchy and Rituals

Following the Rosicrucian grade system of the *Gold- und Rosenkreuzer*, the SRIA already used a nine-grade system. As the cipher manuscript referred to the ten *sefiroth* (emanations of the deity) on the Kabbalistic Tree of Life, Mathers elaborated an almost identical grade structure arranged in three distinct orders:

First Order

Neophyte	$0°=0°$	
Zelator	$1°=10°$	Malkuth (The Kingdom)
Theoricus	$2°=9°$	Yesod (Foundation)
Practicus	$3°=8°$	Hod (Splendor)
Philosophus	$4°=7°$	Netzach (Victory)

Second Order

Adeptus Minor	$5°=6°$	Tiphareth (Beauty)
Adeptus Major	$6°=5°$	Geburah (Strength)
Adeptus Exemptus	$7°=4°$	Chesed (Mercy)

Third Order (Secret Chiefs)

Magister Templi	$8°=3°$	Binah (Intelligence)
Magus	$9°=2°$	Chokmah (Wisdom)
Ipsissimus	$10°=1°$	Kether (The Crown)

Mathers completed grade rituals and "knowledge lectures" for the first five grades.[24] Unlike the SRIA, which offered erudite lectures, the First or Outer Order of the Golden Dawn offered a fully structured curriculum in ceremonial magic. For example, the prescribed course of study for the Zelator grade included the names and alchemical symbols of the three principles of nature; the metals attributed in alchemy to the seven planets; the names of the alchemical particular principles, the sun and the moon, the Green Lion, the king and queen; the names and astrological value of the twelve houses of heaven; the names, astrological symbols and values of the aspects of the planets; the arrangement of the ten *sefiroth*, Hebrew and English, in the Tree of Life; the names of the four orders of elemental spirits; the names and descriptions of the cherubim; the names of the ten heavens of Assiah, in Hebrew and English; the names of the four Kabbalistic worlds, in Hebrew and English; the names of the twenty-two Tarot trumps and four suits.[25] Higher grades added substantially to this syllabus, and the ceremonies of advancement, based on the lodge ritual of Freemasonry, used a variety of vestments, colors, calls, signs, and grips.

The neophyte grade and ritual were designed to introduce the aspirant to a new life, take a new name or magical motto, and open his or her soul to the light. This initiation indicated the link between the macrocosm and the microcosm. The next four grades were elemental rituals of earth, air, water and fire, supplemented by Egyptian-Hermetic and Kabbalistic correspondences. In these grade rituals, the Outer Order sought to equilibrate the elemental forces in the temple (representing the macrocosm) and in the psyches of the officers and aspirants for advancement. The atmosphere of these rituals reflects cultural fashions in the late Victorian period. Whereas Freemasonry supplied the basis of temple (i.e., lodge) practice, such ceremonial also matched the ecclesiastical trend toward Anglican ritualism in the same period. The decoration of the temple, the colorful Egyptian vestments and the theatricality of the proceedings also matched the contemporary movements of neo-Romanticism and Symbolism in literature and the arts.

The Second Order (Ordo Rosae Rubeae et Aureae Crucis)

Instruction in ceremonial magic rather than its spectacle was practiced only in the second order. This had existed, on paper, from the outset as Westcott and Mathers appointed themselves to the 7°=4° grade, the highest in the Second Order. However, by 1892, Mathers had created rituals for a working Second Order of the Golden Dawn. This was a specifically Rosicrucian order, known as the Ordo Rosae Rubeae et Aureae Crucis. Aspirants who had completed the first five grade rituals were eligible for the Portal grade, which symbolized the Veil of Paroketh between the worlds of Yetzirah and Briah in the Kabbalah. This ceremony comprised an Opening, the Ritual of the Cross and Four Elements, the Rite of the Pentagram and the five paths (the twenty-first to twenty-sixth paths on the Tree of Life which cross the Veil of Paroketh and their Tarot trump correspondences), and the ceremonial Closing.[26] The grade ritual for the Adeptus Minor (5°=6°) of the Second Order was spectacularly based on the legend of Christian Rosenkreutz, involving a reenactment of the discovery of his tomb. The design of the vault and the tomb, together with their Kabbalistic, alchemical, and astrological symbols and the inscriptions, was based on the description in *Fama Fraternitatis*. The full-size replica was lavishly decorated in occult colors by Mathers and his artistic wife.[27]

The Second Order curriculum applied the correspondences of natural or sympathetic magic to primary techniques in ceremonial magic. There were precise instructions for the ritual of the pentagram and a supreme invoking ritual of the pentagram. Adepti Minores learned how to make talismans, lotus wands, Rose Cross lamens, magic swords, the four elemental weapons and the manner of their consecration. Other rituals described the consecration of planetary talismans. Mathers also studied John Dee's manuscripts and diaries in the British Museum and the Ashmolean Museum at Oxford, in order to elaborate a coherent system of Enochian magic for Second Order workings. The Second Order magical rituals and practices combining the full panoply of ceremonial vestments, invocations, and the use of magical lights, fires, candles, incense, with the richly decorated vault acted powerfully on the participants. Here magic was typically understood as an evocation, that is the activation of those elements in the psyche corresponding to macrocosmic forces of nature. The Second Order practices give important indications as to the nature and understanding of magic as a particular kind of religious experience involving will and the elevation of consciousness.[28]

Growth and Fragmentation

The original Isis-Urania Temple No. 3 in London (the first two temples were supposed to have been on the Continent according to the founding legend) was followed by Osiris Temple No. 4 in Weston-Super-Mare (1888) and Horus Temple No. 5 in Bradford (1888). Amen-Ra Temple No. 6 was founded in Edinburgh (1893), while Mathers started the Ahathoor Temple No. 7 in Paris (1893). By May 1892, the Outer Order of the Golden Dawn had achieved a membership of 150. Once Mathers had begun initiations into the Ordo Rosae Rubeae et Aureae Crucis, this growth continued. By the end of 1894, the Second Order had 50 members, and the Outer Order had 224. Many notable artistic figures were attracted to the Golden Dawn. William Butler Yeats, the Irish poet, joined in March 1890 from the rising Theosophical Society and became well acquainted with Mathers. Annie Horniman, the tea heiress, who later would build the Abbey Theatre in Dublin, joined earlier that year, and Florence Farr, a prominent actress and the mistress of George Bernard Shaw, was introduced by Yeats in July 1890. Yeats remained associated with the order and its successor, the Stella Matutina, into the 1920s. Many women were attracted from the Theosophical Society, and physicians and other professionals formed the mainstay of its (often Masonic) male membership.

Mathers's imperious style of leadership, coupled with his absence abroad, led to increased friction with other Second Order brothers and sisters. London members finally revolted in January 1900 when Mathers admitted Aleister Crowley to the Second Order. Crowley had joined the Outer Order in November 1898 and had made rapid progress to the Philosophus 4°=7° grade; however, the London members objected to him as an unsuitable person. In response to the uprising, Mathers denounced Westcott's founding myth, claiming that the Sprengel letters were forged and that only he, Mathers, had ever had any direct contact with the secret Chiefs of the Third Order. In 1902, the London rebels formed a successor order, the Stella Matutina, led by Dr. R. W. Felkin and J. W. Brodie-Innes, with its own Amoun Temple. Dr. Edward Berridge formed a loyalist order, latterly known as the Alpha et Omega (A∴O∴) with a new Isis Temple, which worked until 1913.[29]

Despite the relatively short life of the original order, the Golden Dawn has throughout the twentieth century generated numerous successor orders practicing modern ceremonial magic. Between 1936 and 1940, Israel Regardie, who had joined the Stella Matutina in 1933, published the order's complete rituals. While the original orders had become moribund, Regardie's ritual texts were reprinted in the 1970s and led a new generation of aspiring magicians to found new Golden Dawn temples in Europe and North America.[30] Meanwhile, a number of Golden Dawn initiates achieved renown as major interpreters of the Western esoteric traditions in the twentieth century.

Arthur Edward Waite

Arthur Edward Waite (1857–1942), a prolific author and editor of esoteric works, who had entered the Second Order in 1899, took over the original Isis-Urania Temple. Waite had originally joined the Outer Order in 1891, withdrawing in 1893 after advancing to the 4°=7° grade and then rejoining in 1896. Waite preferred mysticism to ritual magic. After the split of 1900, he composed Rosicrucian and Christian rituals purged of the Golden Dawn's original Egyptian, Hermetic, and pagan references. His own Independent and Rectified Order R. R. et A. C. started in 1903 and continued until 1914, when he wound it up. In July 1915, Waite founded a new mystical order, the Fellowship of the Rosy Cross, which counted Charles Williams, the author of religious allegories, among its active members for some years. Evelyn Underhill, the well-known writer on Christian mysticism, was a member of the former order, and her involvement suggests that Waite's mystical ceremonies were certainly capable of fostering religious experience. Waite's original Independent and Rectified Order also had successors. Some of its members with Rosicrucian interests arising from contact with Rudolf Steiner joined Felkin's Merlin lodge. Others, with Neoplatonic interests, had split off to form the Shrine of Wisdom, an esoteric society that publishes fine editions of the *Divine Pymander,* Plotinus, and Dionysius the Areopagite. Its Universal Order still works a ritual at their country house in Brook near Goldalming, Surrey.

Waite had come to the study of occultism long before his admission to the Golden Dawn. Following his mother's conversion to Catholicism in 1863, Waite developed a love of rituals and rites. During the 1880s, he attended séances and wrote for *Light,* one of the leading Spiritualist journals. In 1881, he discovered the writings of Eliphas Lévi and published an anthology, *The Mysteries of Magic* (1886). He later translated several of Lévi's major works. Waite's first full-length book on the occult, *The Real History of the Rosicrucians,* appeared in 1887, swiftly followed by his *Lives of the Alchemystical Philosophers* (1888) and *The Magical Writings of Thomas Vaughan* (1888). He next published *The Occult Sciences* (1891), before editing a major series of translations of alchemical works, including *The Hermetic Museum, The Triumphal Chariot of Antimony, Collectanea Chemica,* and collected works of Edward Kelley and Paracelsus. In 1894–1895, Waite published and edited his own periodical, *The Unknown World,* which was devoted to mysticism, alchemy, and Hermeticism.[31] His other works include *The Book of Black Magic and of Pacts* (1898), *The Life of Louis Claude de Saint-Martin* (1901), *The Hidden Church of the Holy Graal* (1909), *The Pictorial Key to the Tarot* (1911), *The Secret Tradition in Freemasonry* (1911), and *The Holy Kabbalah* (1929), which was praised highly by a leading scholar of Jewish mysticism, Gershom Scholem.

Aleister Crowley and Thelemic Magick

Aleister Crowley (1875–1947) joined the Golden Dawn in 1898 from Cambridge University, where he had written poetry and dabbled in occult literature.

Crowley swiftly absorbed the order's system of ritual magic. In 1900, he practiced the ceremonial magic of Abra-Melin (in Mathers's new translation) to attain the "knowledge and conversation of one's Holy Guardian Angel." After being instrumental in Mather's split of the Second Order, Crowley traveled from 1900 to 1903 in the Americas, India and China, studying yoga, Tantrism, Buddhism, and the I Ching, the ancient Chinese system of magical divination which he related to the Kabbalah. While Crowley was in Egypt in 1904, a discarnate intelligence named Aiwass apparently dictated to him *The Book of the Law*, a revelation of Thelema or the magical will. Its maxim was "Do what thou wilt shall be the whole of the Law!" Aiwass proclaimed a new dispensation, the Age of Horus, when the "slave-religions" of Christianity, Islam, and Buddhism would give way to unbridled individualism and self-fulfillment. Crowley broke with Mathers and in 1907 founded his own order, the Astrum Argentinum, using Golden Dawn rituals mixed with some yoga and other Eastern practices. The old grade structure was also retained.[32]

In 1912, Crowley was initiated into a German para-Masonic magical order, the Ordo Templi Orientis (O.T.O.) by Theodor Reuss (1855–1923), a purveyor of irregular Masonic rites. Carl Kellner (1850–1905), a wealthy German industrialist with some knowledge of yoga practices, may have given Reuss the idea of founding a magical order based on kundalini-yoga and the polar creative energies of sex. The order emerged sometime between 1906 and 1912 under Reuss's leadership, who interpreted Tantric sex-magic in terms of certain Templar-Rosicrucian-Gnostic practices. This eclectic idea was taken from the "phallic" interpretation of culture in Hargrave Jennings, *The Rosicrucians, their Rites and Mysteries* (1870), which widely circulated in occult circles, and from the writings on sex-magic of the German occultist Max Ferdinand Sebaldt (1859–1916).[33] Crowley readily embraced sex-magic as a major aspect of his magical system. Succeeding Reuss as head of the order in 1922, Crowley was subsequently lionized by sections of the German Rosicrucian subculture of the 1920s, including the Fraternitatis Saturni, which used his teachings.

Crowley elaborated his occult system of "magick" (spelled with a k to denote his own variant) from three strands: the Golden Dawn ritual magic, including astrology, Kabbalah, and oriental imports; a Western form of Tantrism derived from the Ordo Templi Orientis in Germany; and the gospel of Thelema, teaching that all should gain self-knowledge and act accordingly in defiance of moral and social restrictions. Crowley identified himself with the Great Beast 666 in the book of Revelation and gloried in all kinds of antinomian behavior. His magical rituals included sexual intercourse with male or female partners; combined with heavy drug-taking, they typically produced visions of deities, demons, and supernatural phenomena. The most concise statement of his system is contained in *Magick in Theory and Practice* (1929), and his "magick" is still practiced by several successor orders of the Ordo Templi Orientis. Gerald Gardner (1884–1964), the founder of modern witchcraft, introduced Crowleyan magick into the neopagan Wiccan movement.[34]

Dion Fortune and the Inner Light

Violet Mary Firth (1891–1946), a descendant of the Yorkshire steel-making family, is another important heir of the Golden Dawn, and she has had a significant influence on modern Western esotericism. As a student, she had a traumatic experience of psychic attack that led her to train in psychotherapy and counseling in London. Meanwhile, she was drawn to mythology and esotericism and sought contact with magical orders. She was first admitted in 1919 to Brodie-Innes's own Alpha et Omega Order (A∴O∴) (a refoundation of the Golden Dawn under Mathers's obedience in 1910), and the next year she transferred to a lodge of the A∴O∴ founded by Mina Mathers in London after being widowed in Paris. In the Golden Dawn, Firth took the magical motto "Deo Non Fortuna," which phonetically provided the pen name by which she is best known. Around this time, she also frequented a study group of the Theosophical Society in London. Although unimpressed by the lectures, she found in its library Annie Besant's *The Ancient Wisdom* (1897). Its account of the Brotherhood of the White Lodge, a hierarchy of adepts that watch over and guide the evolution of humanity, influenced her deeply. However, rather than joining the Theosophists, she became a member of a group led by Theodore Moriarty (1873–1923), a Freemason, mystic, and thaumaturge, whom she portrayed as the physician-magus in her books *The Secrets of Dr. Taverner* (1926) and *Psychic Self-Defence* (1930).[35]

Moriarty lectured on his own system of "Universal Theosophy" in a small group that also practiced symbolic rituals in a lodge admitting men and women. Dion Fortune's interest in Atlantis, esoteric healing, cosmology, and trance mediumship derive from Moriarty's influence. Glastonbury, with its ruins of a medieval abbey in Somerset, traditionally associated with Joseph of Arimathea and rich in Druidical, Christian, and Grail mythology, became an early focus. In 1921, she practiced trance mediumship here, together with the clairvoyant archaeologist Frederick Bligh Bond (1864–1945). In 1924, her group acquired land there and a London headquarters, where they practiced lodge work with three ritual grades. She used trance mediumship to establish contacts with Masters who imparted knowledge of the "inner planes" and a cosmology similar to that of Theosophy, later published as *The Cosmic Doctrine* (1925). She championed an esoteric Christianity and became president of the Christian Mystic Lodge of the Theosophical Society in 1925, but she left it in 1927 to found the Community (later Fraternity) of Inner Light. Celtic and pagan elements, the mythology of Atlantis and Avalon, and Egyptian-Hermetic magical traditions characterize the group's grade rituals in the period 1928 to 1939.

Dion Fortune's many books include *The Esoteric Orders and Their Work* (1928), *The Training and Work of an Initiate* (1930), *Spiritualism in the Light of Occult Science* (1931), and *The Mystical Qabalah* (1935), as well as a series of popular occult novels that contain many accounts of ceremonial magic. Dion Fortune's inclusion of Christian, Celtic, and pagan sources evidence a progression to nativist sources Her eclectic range of inspiration, combined with her belief in the redemptive power of the feminine, has influenced New Age expressions of magic and neopaganism. Her Fraternity of Inner Light (the Society of Inner Light since 1946) continues to practice group meditation, symbolic visualization, and ritual, and it emphasizes Egyptian sources and Kabbalah within a firmly Christian orientation. A related group, the Servants of the Light, was founded in 1965 by W. Ernest Butler (1898–1978), a student of Fortune's, and now is led by Dolores Ashcroft-Novicki. Its magical work is based on the Hermetic Kabbalah.

Modern ritual magic anticipated Jungian psychoanalytical concerns with archetypes and the collective unconscious. With their roots in Masonic symbolism and ritual, the magical orders sought to evoke powers on the inner or higher planes of reality. This evocation was practiced on the lines of traditional Renaissance magic by acting out a drama of correspondences linking the microcosm of the individual with the macrocosm of nature and the universe. The Kabbalah (with Lévi's Tarot links) played an important role in these systems, as did ancient Egyptian, Hermetic, and Rosicrucian references. The resulting syncretism is a typically modern phenomenon, as is the emphasis on the will and power of the individual.

FURTHER READING

Ithell Colquhoun, *Sword of Wisdom: MacGregor Mathers and The Golden Dawn* (London: Neville Spearman, 1975).
Ronald Decker, Thierry Depaulis, and Michael Dummett, *A Wicked Pack of Cards: The Origins of the Occult Tarot* (New York: St. Martin's Press, 1996).
Robert A. Gilbert, *A. E. Waite: A Bibliography* (Wellingborough: Aquarian Press, 1983).
———, *A. E. Waite: Magician of Many Parts* (Wellingborough: Crucible, 1987).
———, *The Golden Dawn: Twilight of the Magicians* (Wellingborough: Aquarian Press, 1983).
———, *The Golden Dawn Companion: A Guide to the History, Structure, and Workings of the Hermetic Order of the Golden Dawn* (Wellingborough: Aquarian Press, 1986).
———, *The Golden Dawn Scrapbook: The Rise and Fall of a Magical Order* (York Beach, Maine: Samuel Weiser, 1997).

————, ed., *The Magical Mason: Forgotten Hermetic Writings of William Wynn Westcott, Physician and Magus* (Wellingborough: Aquarian Press, 1983).

————, ed., *The Sorcerer and His Apprentice: Unknown Hermetic Writings of S. L. Mac-Gregor Mathers and J. W. Brodie-Innes* (Wellingborough: Aquarian Press, 1983).

Joscelyn Godwin, *The Beginnings of Theosophy in France* (London: Theosophical History Centre, 1989).

Ellic Howe, "Fringe Masonry in England, 1870–1885," *Ars Quatuor Coronatorum* 85 (1972): 242–280.

————, *The Magicians of the Golden Dawn: A Documentary History of a Magical Order 1887–1923* (London: Routledge & Kegan Paul, 1972).

Ellic Howe and Helmut Möller, "Theodor Reuss: Irregular Freemasonry in Germany, 1900–23," *Ars Quatuor Coronatorum* 91 (1978): 28–47.

Ronald Hutton, *The Triumph of the Moon: A History of Modern Pagan Witchcraft* (Oxford: Oxford University Press, 1999).

Richard Kaczynski, *Perdurabo: The Life of Aleister Crowley* (Tempe, Ariz.: New Falcon, 2003).

Francis King, *The Magical World of Aleister Crowley* (London: Weidenfeld & Nicolson, 1977).

————, *Modern Ritual Magic: The Rise of Modern Occultism* (Bridport: Prism, 1989). First published as *Ritual Magic in England 1870 to the Present* (London: Neville Spearman, 1970).

Gareth Knight, *Dion Fortune and the Inner Light* (Loughborough: Thoth, 2000).

Peter-Robert König, *Der O.T.O. Phänomen Remix* (Munich: Arbeitsgemeinschaft für Religions- und Weltanschauungsfragen, 2001).

Jean-Pierre Laurant, "Papus," in *Dictionary of Gnosis and Western Esotericism*, edited by Wouter Hanegraaff et al., 2 vols. (Leiden: Brill, 2005), Vol. 2, pp. 913–915.

Eliphas Lévi, *Transcendental Magic: Its Doctrine and Ritual*, translated by A. E. Waite (London: Rider, 1923; repr. Twickenham: Senate, 1995).

————, *The History of Magic*, translated by A. E. Waite (London: Rider, 1913; repr. York Beach, Maine: Weiser, 1999).

————, *The Book of Splendours* (1894; Wellingborough: Aquarian Press, 1981).

————, *The Key of the Mysteries*, translated by Aleister Crowley (1939; York Beach, Maine: Weiser, 2002).

S. L. MacGregor Mathers, *The Kabbalah Unveiled* (London: Routledge & Kegan Paul, 1887).

Christopher McIntosh, *Eliphas Lévi and the French Occult Revival* (London: Rider, 1972).

Helmut Möller and Ellic Howe, *Merlin Peregrinus: Vom Untergrund des Abendlandes* (Würzburg: Königshausen & Neumann, 1986).

Alex Owen, *The Place of Enchantment: British Occultism and the Culture of the Modern* (Chicago: University of Chicago Press, 2004).

Israel Regardie, *The Golden Dawn: The Original Account of the Teachings, Rites, and Ceremonies of the Hermetic Order of the Golden Dawn (Stella Matutina)*, 6th ed. (St. Paul, Minn.: Llewellyn, 1989).

Alan Richardson, *Priestess: The Life and Magic of Dion Fortune* (Wellingborough: Aquarian Press, 1987).

John Symonds, *The King of the Shadow Realm: Aleister Crowley, His Life and Magic* (London: Duckworth, 1989).

James Webb, *The Flight from Reason* (London: Macdonald, 1971).

II

Helena Blavatsky and the Theosophical Society

The Theosophical Society, founded at New York in 1875 by Helena Petrovna Blavatsky and Henry Steel Olcott, has played a vital role in propagating esotericism in the modern era. Its appearance, in common with Spiritualism and other new religious sects, reflected a widening gulf between orthodox religious belief and science in the West. The progress of science and technology was challenging traditional Christian belief in the omnipotence of God, the need for grace, and the life hereafter. This dissolution of man's place within a divine order was crystallized by the publication of *The Origin of Species* (1859) by Charles Darwin. His theory of biological evolution, based on natural selection in consequence of the struggle for material existence, violated the idea of human spiritual identity and purpose. Modern science focused on concrete, material facts, and its explanations of the physical world only deepened a lack of confidence in biblical authority. Many spiritually inclined individuals were distressed by science but could no longer find comfort in orthodox religion.

Modern Theosophy, distinct from Boehme's Christian theosophy and its heirs, addressed these concerns in a progressive way. Adapting contemporary scientific ideas to posit the idea of spiritual evolution through countless worlds and eras, Theosophy restored dignity and purpose to humankind's earthly life within a cosmic context. Whereas Spiritualism simply posited survival after death, Theosophy located human destiny in an emanationist cosmology and anthropology derived from Neoplatonism and oriental religions; it repeated the

Hellenistic embrace of exotic Eastern ideas, but now these were represented by Buddhism and Hinduism. By popularizing ideas of reincarnation and karma, secret Masters, and Tibet as the land of ageless wisdom, Blavatsky attracted many spiritual seekers in Europe, North America, and India to her new religious movement.

Theosophy was a major factor in the revival of the indigenous Western esoteric tradition. Blavatsky's writings garnered the materials of Neoplatonism, Renaissance magic, Kabbalah, and Freemasonry, together with ancient Egyptian and Greco-Roman mythology and religion, joined by Eastern doctrines taken from Buddhism and Advaita Vedanta to present the idea of an ancient wisdom handed down from prehistoric times. The notion of advanced adepts in the Himalayas, the heirs of a tradition going back to Atlantis and earlier pristine civilizations, represented the Renaissance idea of *prisca theologia* passed on by a chain of initiates combined with the Romantic fascination with the Orient. This globalization of esotericism, inspired by and preserving Western esotericism, would promote its dialogue with exotic traditions and foster its international growth in the twentieth century. Moreover, the Theosophical Society, with its emphasis on organization, publications, and instruction, became the model for many other Rosicrucian, Masonic, and occult societies committed to the spread of esoteric ideas.

Blavatsky's Early Travels and the "Masters"

Helena Petrovna Blavatsky (1831–1891) was born at Ekaterinoslav (now Dnepropetrovsk) in the Ukraine. Her parents were Colonel Peter von Hahn and Helena Andreyevna, née de Fadayev, a renowned novelist who died young. Her heritage combined Russian, French Huguenot, and German stock, and her maternal grandmother, Princess Helena Pavlovna Dolgorukov, was descended from one of Russia's oldest families. Helena's childhood was marked by numerous psychic phenomena, and she developed an early interest in esotericism, immersing herself in the large occult library of Prince Pavel Dolgorukov (d. 1838), her grandmother's father, who had been initiated into Rosicrucian Freemasonry at the end of the 1770s. An old family friend, Prince Alexander Golitsyn, a Freemason and mystic, encouraged her to travel abroad in search of ancient wisdom.[1]

She was married in 1849, at the age of seventeen, to Nikifor Blavatsky (b. 1809), vice governor of Erivan province in Armenia, but deserted her husband on their honeymoon.[2] She then began a series of extensive travels throughout the world. Described in her own accounts, which were largely uncorroborated and often conflicting in their chronology, these travels would take her around Europe, the Middle East, and North America, and possibly to India and Tibet over the next twenty-five years. These extensive journeys, extraordinary for a single woman at this time, record her tireless quest for contact with sages and occult teachers in exotic cultures.[3]

The initial focus of her travels and quest lay in the Middle East. Initially, she traveled to Turkey, Greece, and Egypt. At times she traveled with Albert Rawson (1828–1902), a young American explorer, author, and artist. In 1850, they studied with Paolos Metamon, a Copt magician, in Cairo.[4] In early 1851, the year of the Great Exhibition, Blavatsky went to London via France, and in August she first met with her "Master." He allegedly informed her that she should prepare for an important task that would require three years' preparation in Tibet.[5] Her subsequent peregrinations through the United States (allegedly again with Rawson) and Latin America led her to India in 1852, but she failed to enter Tibet on this occasion. In 1854, she was again in the United States, and she traveled throughout India, Kashmir, Burma, and parts of Tibet in 1856–1857. At Christmas 1858, she returned to her family in Russia, where she frequently displayed her involuntary ability to cause psychic phenomena (rappings, bell sounds, moving furniture, telepathy). In early 1868 at Florence, she received word from her Master that she should join him at Constantinople, and from there they traveled overland to Tibet.

Her Master, known as Morya, was said to live near the grand monastery of Tashi Lhunpo at Shigatse, the seat of the Panchen Lama. Here Morya and another Master, Koot Hoomi, Kashmiris of Punjabi extraction, ran a school for adepts adjacent to the monastery. The Masters were understood to be advanced adepts with superhuman powers who were subject neither to the monastery nor its rules but who had complete access to its library and resources. Blavatsky was taken on as a disciple (*chela*) and given the teaching for which she had always longed. She was introduced to Tibetan Buddhist sacred literature, shown the treasures of the monastery, and otherwise prepared to be the Masters' missionary to the West. She allegedly remained in this Himalayan fastness, preparing for her work, from late 1868 until the end of 1870. Blavatsky would always claim that this initiation was the cornerstone of her vocation to bring spiritual enlightenment to the West. After her return to the West, she established a short-lived society for the study of Spiritualism at Cairo in late 1871. After further travels in Europe, she briefly resided in Paris, where in 1873 she allegedly received orders from Morya to travel to the United States.[6]

It should be emphasized that Blavatsky's references to her Masters during these veiled years of travel and initiation are almost all retrospective from the later, Indian phase of her life. The very concept of the Masters can be seen to derive via high-grade Freemasonry from the Rosicrucian idea of invisible and secret adepts, working for the advancement of humanity. In this respect the idea of Masters is intrinsic to modern Western esotericism: the idea of the "Great White Brotherhood" steering mankind to higher stages of development has continued to influence twentieth-century esotericism (e.g., Annie Besant, Alice Bailey, H. Spencer Lewis, Elizabeth Clare Prophet, G. I. Gurdjieff) and also recurs in much New Age spirituality.

From Spiritualism to Ancient Wisdom

Blavatsky's public (and more documented) life began with her arrival in the United States in 1873. Blavatsky began her esoteric career in the Spiritualist movement, which then was extremely widespread in the country. In the autumn of 1874, she met her future cofounder of the Theosophical Society, Henry Steel Olcott (1832–1907), a prominent attorney with an interest in Spiritualism, at the Eddy farmhouse in Chittenden, Vermont, where he was reporting for the New York newspapers on séances producing materialized spirit forms. Blavatsky published articles on Spiritualism and became actively involved in the Spiritualist movement, conferring with a spirit called "John King" and publicly defending discredited Spiritualist mediums.[7]

Blavatsky thought American Spiritualism, however useful as an initial foil to materialism, was devoid of real occult knowledge. By February 1875, she was already describing her interest in the Western esoteric tradition, referring to Renaissance magi, the terminology of Kabbalah, and making her first use of the term "theosophy."[8] Soon she turned away from Spiritualism. In March 1875, John King was superseded as her contact by the Masters Serapis Bey and Tuitit Bey, members of a mysterious community called the Brotherhood of Luxor, which Blavatsky identified as the Egyptian group of the Universal Mystic Brotherhood. At the supposed suggestion of the Masters, Olcott and Blavatsky in May 1879 formed a society called the Miracle Club to inform the public about paranormal phenomena and their mediums.[9] In July 1875, she began writing articles for the short-lived Boston magazine *Spiritual Scientist*, referring to Gnostics, Paracelsians, alchemists, and Rosicrucians. Her sources were Eliphas Lévi, Hargrave Jennings, and other contemporary occultists. This was also her first public disclosure of the existence of occult brotherhoods of adepts.[10]

More than twenty letters from Serapis Bey were received by Olcott in the summer of 1875, many exhorting him and Blavatsky to further efforts and spiritual attainment, and even offering tactical advice. The word "Try" is continually emphasized, which implied the goals of occultism: to cultivate one's will, increase one's knowledge, master higher powers, and develop latent faculties.

FIGURE 11.1. John King painted on silk by himself, flower decorations by H. P. Blavatsky, reproduced in *H.P.B. Speaks, Volume I,* edited by C. Jinarajadasa (Adyar, Theosophical Publishing House, 1950). Original at headquarters of Theosophical Society, Adyar.

The motto "TRY" was also used by the American Rosicrucian Paschal Beverly Randolph (1825–1875). Joscelyn Godwin has commented on the wider movement in the 1870s to promote occultism as opposed to Spiritualism. While Spiritualists concentrated on séance revelations, occultists favored psychical research combined with the study of old books on magic, Hermeticism, and Kabbalah. Blavatsky's new ideas reflect this current as well as the Egyptian atmosphere of Hermeticism.[11]

Isis Unveiled and Western Esotericism

Already in September 1875, Blavatsky began writing her first book, to be published in 1877. Titled *Isis Unveiled: A Master Key to the Mysteries of Ancient and Modern Science and Theology,* this work represented an encyclopedic review of her readings in ancient religion, philosophy, mythology, and science. The Western esoteric theme is evident in its preface: "Our work, then, is a plea for the recognition of the Hermetic philosophy, the anciently universal Wisdom-Religion, as the only possible key to the Absolute in science and theology." The two-volume work accomplished a major statement of modern occultism's defiance of materialist science. The first volume, *Science*, opens with an attack on Darwin's *Origin of Species* and Thomas Huxley's *Physical Basis of Matter*, materialism being her chief target. Subsequent chapters on Spiritualism, psychic phenomena, Mesmerism, the Kabbalah, and the advanced knowledge and achievements of ancient peoples seek to expose and undermine the complacency of modern science. The second volume, *Theology*, contains polemics against Christianity, presents esoteric forms of Christianity including Gnosticism, a further discussion of Kabbalah, ancient and modern secret societies including the Jesuits and Freemasons, and a comparison of Christianity, to its general detriment, with Hinduism and Buddhism.

The underlying theme among these diverse topics is the existence of an ancient wisdom religion. The many faiths of man are said to derive from a universal religion known to both Plato and the ancient Hindu sages. The wisdom religion is also identified with Hermetic philosophy "as the only possible key to the Absolute in science and theology" (I, vii). Every religion is based on the same truth or "secret doctrine," which contains "the alpha and omega of universal science"(I, 511). This ancient wisdom religion is the religion of the future (I, 613). In a few centuries, the world religions of Buddhism, Hinduism, Christianity, and Islam will recede before the "facts" and "knowledge" of the ancient and universal doctrine. This ancient wisdom religion is a Hermetic philosophy based on an emanationist cosmology (I, 154, 285, 295f). Contrary to modern evolutionary theory, this doctrine posits the involution of man from "higher and more spiritual natures." A "divine spark" has descended into matter, and once it has reached its densest material level, it begins its ascent back to its source. Blavatsky thus assimilates modern evolutionism into her scheme, but only as the return cycle, and moreover, she rephrases its biological imperative in spiritual terms: "The human race must be finally *physically* spiritualized"(I, 296).

The terms "theosophy" and "Theosophist" also appear in the text of *Isis Unveiled*. Interestingly, Blavatsky makes only brief references to Jacob Boehme but identifies the Paracelsians or "fire-philosophers" of the sixteenth century as Theosophists (I, xxxvii, xli). Overall, the *theosophia* of the ancient Alexandrian world is her model, for example in her remark that the Neoplatonic school united the mystic theosophy of old Egypt with the refined philosophy of the Greeks (II, 41). She also frequently quoted her collaborator and editor, Professor Alexander Wilder (1823–1908), author of *New Platonism and Alchemy* (1869), who coined the term "eclectic theosophical system" to describe the thought of the Neoplatonists. Wilder is usually credited with writing the introduction to *Isis Unveiled*, titled "Before the

Veil." Blavatsky dwelled at length on the ideas of Plato, Plotinus, Porphyry, and Iamblichus in *Isis Unveiled,* and she framed their thought in terms of Wilder's eclectic theosophy. In turn, she envisaged modern Theosophy as the heir of Alexandrian Neoplatonism, effectively ignoring the Christian varieties of theosophy.

The Foundation of the Theosophical Society

Blavatsky and Olcott had considered ways and means of fostering philosophical and experimental study of spiritualist phenomena from the beginning of 1875. The Masters were again allegedly involved. Alluding to Morya, Blavatsky had (early in 1875?) written in her memorandum "Important Note" about her intervention in Philadelphia to advance occult sciences, "M∴ brings orders to form a Society—a secret Society like the Rosicrucian Lodge."[12] Blavatsky's residence at 46 Irving Place, New York, became a regular meeting place for people with occult leanings. On 7 September, a group gathered to hear George Henry Felt (1831–1906) deliver a lecture titled "The Lost Canon of Proportion of the Egyptians" or "The Cabala" (depending on the source summarizing the lecture). Others present reflected related occult interests. Dr. Seth Pancoast (1823–1889), a professor of anatomy, owned the largest library on Kabbalah in the United States and wrote books on the topic in 1877 and 1883. Emma Hardinge Britten (1823–1899) was a renowned English trance medium and occult author residing in New York. Charles Sotheran (1847–1902) was a prominent Freemason, representative of the high-grade Swedenborgian rite in the United States, and author of a book on Cagliostro. Henry J. Newton (1823–1895) was interested in spirit photography, and he was the president of the First Society of Spiritualists in New York. Charles Carleton Massey (1838–1905) was a visiting London lawyer who would later organize the British Theosophical Society (1878), help found the Society for Psychical Research (1882), and translate several German works in this field by Friedrich Zöllner, Eduard von Hartmann, and Carl du Prel.

Olcott regarded Felt's speculations about intermediary beings as potential proof of the existence of elemental spirits, which he believed could appear in many guises at séances. Blavatsky agreed with Olcott that they should form a group to investigate such matters. The next day, 17 November, a society was formed "for the study and elucidation of Occultism, the Cabala, etc."[13] At subsequent meetings, officers were elected, with Olcott becoming president, Dr. Pancoast and George Felt vice presidents, and Blavatsky corresponding secretary. The Western esoteric traditions, as evidenced in her articles and work on *Isis Unveiled,* but also involving occult science and experiment, thus provided the initial focus of the Theosophical Society in New York. Writing to the eminent

Russian psychical researcher Alexander Aksakov, Blavatsky referred to this early stage of the project:

> Olcott is now organizing the Theosophical Society in New York. It will be composed of learned occultists and Kabbalists, of Hermetic philosophers of the 19th century, and of passionate antiquarians and Egyptologists in general. We want to do experiments comparing spiritualism and the magic of the ancients by following literally the instructions of old Kabbalists, both Jewish and Egyptian. For many years I have been studying the Hermetic philosophy in theory and practice . . . coming to the conclusion that spiritualism in its physical manifestations is nothing else but the python of the ancients or the astral or sidereal light of Paracelsus.[14]

Blavatsky expressed this purpose of the Theosophical Society in *Isis Unveiled*: "The object of its founders was to experiment practically in the occult powers of Nature." The preamble to the bylaws said that the group hoped to penetrate further than science into "the esoteric philosophies of ancient times" and "to collect and diffuse a knowledge of the laws which govern the universe." Belief in universal brotherhood and the emphasis on Asian religions were added later in 1878 after the Theosophical Society became involved with Indians.

The Theosophical Society in India

Up to 1878, the Theosophical Society's promotion of the spiritual over matter focused on the phenomena of practical occultism with experiments in astral projection. Meanwhile, the attraction of the Orient beckoned as the home of spiritual mystery. Blavatsky regularly alluded to her links with Eastern adepts of the mystic brotherhood; *Isis Unveiled* (1877) and her articles made frequent reference to Hinduism and Buddhism. This romantic image of the East was the product of colonial contact with India. Following eighteenth-century British oriental studies, German Romantic scholarship had led to high regard for India as a source of wisdom. Rammohun Roy (1772–1833), the famous Hindu reformer, evangelized his idea of an Indo-European golden age, arguing all religions had a common root and linking Unitarian Christianity with Vedanta. Sir Edward Arnold's *The Light of Asia* (1879) spread a popular knowledge of Buddhism in the West. Both men are mentioned in Blavatsky's writings. Blavatsky and Olcott established relations with sympathizers in India and Ceylon, who appreciated Blavatsky's championship of their traditional religion and culture against missionary influence. These Indian contacts led to a collaboration with the Arya Samaj, a Hindu reform movement founded in 1875 in Bombay by Swami Dayanand Sarasvati, who wanted a return to the teaching of the Vedas.

In its circular of 1878, the Theosophical Society reformulated its objects to include a knowledge of natural law, especially its occult manifestations; the development of latent powers within the individual; an appreciation for oriental religious philosophies; and, chiefly, the formation of a brotherhood of humanity.[15] These were gradually formalized into the three present objectives of the society:

1. To form the nucleus of a universal brotherhood of humanity, without distinction of race, creed, sex, caste, or color.
2. The study of ancient and modern religions, philosophies, and sciences.
3. The investigation of the unexplained laws of nature and the psychical powers latent in man.

This link with the Arya Samaj provided an excuse for transferring operations to India, and in December 1878 Blavatsky and Olcott sailed for India via London, arriving in Bombay in February 1879. Initially based in Bombay, Blavatsky and Olcott tirelessly promoted Theosophy through extensive travels and relations with leading intellectual and political figures in India. In October 1879, they began publishing a journal called *The Theosophist*. Educated Indians were especially impressed by the Theosophists' championship of Indian religion and philosophy in the context of the country's growing self-assertion against the values and beliefs of the European colonial powers. In May 1880, Blavatsky and Olcott formally converted to Buddhism on a visit to Ceylon, where they were feted by enormous crowds, and new branches of the Theosophical Society were founded.[16]

Through their travels, meetings, and contributors to the magazine, Blavatsky was swiftly exposed to Indian philosophy, in particular Samkara's Advaita Vedanta, the Upanishads, and the *Bhagavad Gita*, which feature extensively in her articles and later works. Her preference for Advaita Vedanta related to its exposition of the ultimate reality as a monist, nontheistic, impersonal absolute. This nondualist view of Parabrahm as the universal divine principle would become the first fundamental proposition of *The Secret Doctrine,* which she began writing in 1883. In the same period, Blavatsky assimilated Buddhist ideas into her eclectic Theosophy, ultimately equating Buddhism and Advaita Vedanta as the common source of her esoteric doctrine.[17]

The Mahatmas and Esoteric Buddhism

Alfred Percy Sinnett (1840–1921), the Anglo-Indian editor of an influential national newspaper, *The Pioneer*, was an important convert to Theosophy in India.

Another was Allan Octavian Hume (1829–1912), the retired Secretary of the Government of India. Blavatsky was a regular visitor to the Sinnetts' summer home in Simla from September 1880 onward. During this first visit, she produced several striking paranormal phenomena. At this time, members of the secret brotherhood (soon identified as the Masters Koot Hoomi and Morya, supposedly resident in Tibet) began a voluminous correspondence chiefly with Sinnett and some initially with Hume. These so-called Mahatma ("great soul") letters to Sinnett, typically delivered by precipitation or apport, would between 1880 to 1885 number more than a hundred. Sinnett's access to the press coupled with his own books swiftly broadcast Theosophy to English-speaking readers in both India and England. His first book, *The Occult World* (1881), gave sensational publicity to Blavatsky's phenomena and the Mahatma letters, attracting the interest of the London Society for Psychical Research, and his *Esoteric Buddhism* (1883) disseminated the basic teachings of Theosophy in its new Asian cast on the basis of the philosophical and cosmological explanations contained in the Mahatma letters. In 1883, Sinnett returned to England, where he acted as vice president and secretary of the Theosophical Society's London lodge.[18]

From 1881 onward, Blavatsky and her alleged "guides" (brothers, Mahatmas) gradually disseminated an elaborate philosophical edifice involving a cosmogony, the macrocosm of the universe, spiritual hierarchies, and intermediary beings, the latter having correspondences with a hierarchical conception of the microcosm of man. A key aspect of Theosophy is the septenary (sevenfold) principle, governing both the macrocosm and the microcosm. The first formal statement of the sevenfold principle in humans was actually published in October 1881 by A. O. Hume, on the basis of teachings received from Koot Hoomi:[19]

Divisions of the Spiritualists	Subdivisions of the Occultists
1. The Body	1. The Physical body, composed wholly of matter in its grossest and most tangible form.
	2. The Vital principle—(or *Jiv-atma*)—a form of force, indestructible and when disconnected with one set of atoms, becoming attracted immediately by others.
2. The Animal Soul, or *Perisprit*	3. The Astral body (*Linga Sharira*) composed of highly etherialized matter; in its habitual passive state, the perfect but very shadowy duplicate of the body; its activity,

consolidation and form depending entirely on the *kama rupa.*

4. The Astral shape (*kama rupa*) or body of desire, a principle defining the configuration of —

5. The animal or physical intelligence or consciousness or Ego, analogous to, though proportionally higher in degree than, the reason, instinct, memory, imagination, &c., existing in the higher animals.

3. The Spiritual Soul or Spirit

6. The Higher or Spiritual intelligence or consciousness, or spiritual Ego, in which mainly resides the sense of consciousness in the *perfect* man, though the lower dimmer animal consciousness co-exists in No. 5.

7. The Spirit—an emanation from the ABSOLUTE; uncreated; eternal; a state rather than a being.

Reincarnation, Karma, and Spiritual Evolution

In *Isis Unveiled,* Blavatsky had not only asserted the triune principles of man (body, soul, and spirit), common to both Plato and St. Paul, but she denied the possibility of reincarnation on this earth.[20] By late 1882, Blavatsky had revised her view in the context of the septenary constitution of humans, which functioned as an integral part of the process of reincarnation. The three lower principles—the body, the vital principle, and its astral counterpart—are abandoned at death, and the four higher principles proceed into the next order of spirituality, the astral plane (*kama loka*), which acts as a form of purgatory. The fifth principle, *Manas,* is itself separable into higher and lower elements, and in their ensuing struggle, the best, most elevated, and spiritual portions attach themselves to the sixth principle, *Buddhi,* whereas the lower remnant associates itself with the body of desire (*Kama-rupa*) and eventually dissolves. The higher, *Manas,* the Ego of the late earthly personality, then follows the sixth and seventh principles into the spiritual condition called *Devachan.*[21] *Devachan* corresponds to the idea of heaven, a condition of subjective enjoyment, the duration and intensity of which is determined by the merit and spirituality of the life on earth prior to the reincarnation of the three higher principles into objective existence. Rebirth is said to rarely occur in less than 1,500 years, but the stay in *Devachan* may last much longer as a reward for positive karma.[22]

The development of Blavatsky's thinking from a triune view of body, mind, and spirit towards the septenary constitution of man and reincarnation was not actually linked to Hindu thought, which generally posited five principles, but indicates her inspiration in the septenary motifs of Western esotericism, prevalent in astrology, alchemy, and Kabbalah. Seven principles offered a more differentiated spiritual constitution of the human being. These principles and their function were most probably motivated by the idea of "ascendant metempsychosis" as a means of accounting for a process of spiritual evolution. As Darwinian evolution was a key Western scientific concern throughout the 1860s and 1870s, Blavatsky sought to reconcile her esoteric philosophy with modern science. If souls simply progressed through many lives, how could that process be explained in "scientific" terms and have any purposeful meaning to Western audiences? Wouter Hanegraaff suggests that she had not solved this problem while writing *Isis Unveiled,* but by 1882 karma provided the answer.[23] Karma plus reincarnation with its account of the principles in postmortem states fit the Western progressive, optimistic, Enlightenment view and also echoed the Protestant morality of self-development and self-responsibility, rather than reincarnation's traditional association with oriental fatalism.

Cosmology and Spiritual Hierarchies

Sinnett's 1882 correspondence with Koot Hoomi concerned theoretical teachings relating to the periodic cycles of manifestation (*mantavantaras*) and rest (*pralayas*) of the universe. At this point Theosophy commenced the elaboration of its characteristic vast cosmology involving the emanation of Parabrahm, according to Vedantins, or *Adibuddha,* the all-pervading supreme and absolute intelligence according to northern Buddhists. Its executive intermediaries are the periodically manifesting divinity Avalokiteshvara, supported by seven active intelligences called Dhyani Chohans which gradually form atoms, molecules, elements, then minerals, plants, animals, and human beings, on a descending involution of incarnation and materialization of spiritual substance. Sinnett's chapters on the constitution of man, the planetary chain, the world periods, postmortem states of the ego in *Devachan* and *Kama Loca,* the progress of humanity, Buddhist cosmology, and the cycles of the universe offer a clear account of the emanations and successive septenary manifestations so central to the cosmology of Theosophy. Both *The Mahatma Letters* and *Esoteric Buddhism*

demonstrate how spiritual cosmologies and hierarchies, familiar from Western traditions of Neoplatonism, Gnosticism, and Hermetism and the complex
Eastern hierarchies of Northern and Tibetan Buddhism, are here combined
quite plainly with contemporary Western scientific theories of planetary, geo-
logical, paleogeographical (the creation and disappearance of continents), and
biological and racial evolution. Both the Mahatmas Morya and Koot Hoomi and
Blavatsky make frequent references to modern science, notably the theories of
Charles Darwin, Sir Archibald Geikie, William Boyd Dawkins, and John Fiske.

Blavatsky described this cyclical manifestation and withdrawal or repose
of the universe using the cosmology of Northern Buddhism that related to progressive spiritual evolution. Thus, Adibuddha emits the First Logos (Vajrad-
hara, corresponding to Purusa), the Second Logos (Vajrasattva, corresponding
to Prakriti), and the Third Logos (Mahat). Adibuddha also emits seven Dhyani-
Buddhas (or Dhyan-Chohans), the seven Sons of Light or *Logoi* of Life. These
cosmological agents are directly responsible for the structure and government
of the universe.[24] This emanationist cosmology has been described as a "hierarchy of compassion" as each of the descending hierarchies (Adibuddha, the
three *Logoi*, Dhyani-Buddhas, Dhyani-Bodhisattvas, Super-Terrestrial Bodhisat-
tvas, Terrestrial Buddhas, and humans) relate to the increasing enlightenment
of the world. Their manifestation among the races on earth has soteriologi-
cal force. The expectation of Maitreya as the coming Buddha of the sixth root
race carried a strong salvific and millenarian charge, and became a stock idea
among later movements inspired by Theosophy.

The Secret Doctrine (1888)

Blavatsky tirelessly devoted the rest of her life to writing. She returned from
India to Europe and lived from August 1885 to May 1886 in Würzburg, where
she continued work on her major opus *The Secret Doctrine* (1888). After a period at Ostende in 1886–1887, Blavatsky settled in London, surrounded by loyal
disciples. In October 1888, the Esoteric Section of the Theosophical Society was
formed as a center for her followers in London, to whom she gave a series of
Esoteric Instructions. An Inner Group of personal pupils received her advanced
teachings from 1890 until her death in May 1891.

The Secret Doctrine is a two-volume work comprising some 1,500 pages and
purporting to be the fundamental knowledge from which all religion, philosophy and science have grown. It claims to be based on the "Stanzas of Dzyan,"
a mysterious ancient religious text written in the unknown "Senzar" language
and unknown to scholarship. This doctrinal statement of Blavatsky's mature

Theosophy was based on three principles: (1) the existence of one absolute reality, the infinite and eternal cause of all; (2) the periodicity of the universe: its appearance, growth, waning, and disappearance in cycles; and (3) the identity of "all Souls with the Universal Over-Soul: the pilgrimage of every Soul or spark through the cycle of incarnation."[25] Inspired by these principles, *The Secret Doctrine* contains four fundamental sets of ideas: evolution; man's septenary constitution; karma and reincarnation; and after-death states.

Although presented in Sanskrit, Tibetan, and Buddhist terminology, Blavatsky's cosmology retained deep roots in the Hermetic-Kabbalistic worldview of "as above, so below," so fundamental to Western esotericism. Her panorama of the cyclical creation of the universe described a differentiation of the Universal Mind into a complex hierarchy of divine powers, which gave form to all aspects of creation in the manifested universe. The microcosm of man reveals correspondences or analogies with the macrocosm of the entire universe. Everything in the higher world of divine being is mapped, by correspondences, onto the successive lower worlds of creation. Theosophy presents the universe as a living ensouled whole, replete with intermediary spirits (e.g., Dhyani Chohans, jivas, intelligences, builders, planetary spirits, lipikas). These mythological beings give form to successive layers of an ordered, hierarchical cosmos. As the eternal, spiritual component of being, the monads of Atma-Buddhi, the highest two principles of man, migrate through numerous incarnations, thereby elevating their transitory hosts and enabling spiritual evolution.[26]

The cosmic impersonality of these accounts only serves as a background for the central theme of *The Secret Doctrine*, which guarantees its abiding interest to religious seekers. Individual human destiny and moral problems of individual development are the ultimate focus of the work, which tells of the individual soul's reincarnation according to the karma, the law of cause and effect, in each preceding life, all the while seeking to evolve on higher spiritual planes. The final purpose of man is the emancipation of the soul. Both the physical body and the astral body disintegrate after death, but the higher triad of *Manas, Buddhi*, and *Atma* survives death. Many reincarnations are necessary before the whole trinity can be present in the physical body. Once that has been accomplished, the human race will be as gods.

Blavatsky's cosmology thus presents Faivre's prime characteristics of Western esotericism in (a) correspondences between all parts of the universe, the macrocosm and microcosm; (b) living nature as a complex, plural, hierarchical, and animate whole; (c) imagination and mediations in the form of intermediary spirits, symbols, and mandalas; and (d) the experience of transmutation of the soul through purification and ascent.

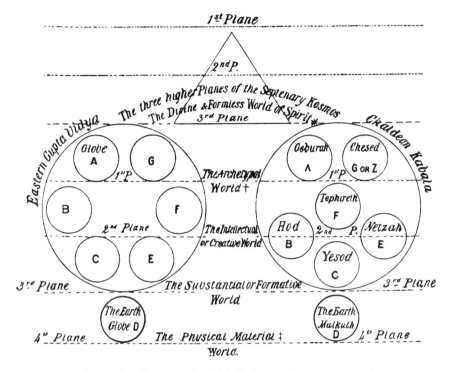

FIGURE 11.2. Comparison between the Kabbalistic and Eastern Gupta Vidya cosmological systems in Helena Petrovna Blavatsky, *The Secret Doctrine*, 2 vols. (London, 1888), vol. 1, 200.

Blavatsky's Legacy

The main contribution of Theosophy to Western esotericism consists in several important innovations: (1) its assimilation of elements of oriental religions within the perspective of comparative religion, an inspiration traceable to earlier occultist writers like Hargrave Jennings and Godfrey Higgins;[27] (2) the elaboration of the septenary principle, and its multiple relation to Gnostic, Hermetic, Kabbalist, and Buddhist cosmology and hierarchies; (3) the relation of this septenary principle to reincarnation and karma, and their application to the idea of spiritual evolution; (4) the presentation of esoteric ideas in the context of modern science, involving evolution, geology, anthropology, and racial theories. Among these innovations, Theosophy's perspective on comparative religion and its evolutionary ideas represent major developments in Western esotericism. Her spiritual guides, alternatively known as brothers, Masters, and Mahatmas may be seen as a continuation of the Rosicrucian tradition of secret adepts fostering and promoting the spiritual progress of humanity. However, by wedding the idea of adepts to spiritual evolution, Blavatsky created a powerful new idea of the highly evolved adept, whose consciousness was far advanced beyond that of ordinary human beings. The Masters and the Great White Brotherhood have continued to inspire many new religious movements in the twentieth century.

Blavatsky's influence, both on her contemporary followers and on posterity, was substantial. The ramifications of the Theosophical Society are considerable in both India and the West. The later history of the society under the presidency of Annie Besant and her presidency of the Indian National Congress underline the society's role in the growth of Indian national consciousness: both Gandhi and Nehru were drawn to Theosophy to rediscover their own religious and philosophical heritage.[28] In the West, Theosophy was perhaps the single most important factor in the modern occult revival. It redirected the fashionable interest in Spiritualism toward a coherent doctrine combining cosmology, modern anthropology, and the theory of evolution with human spiritual development. It drew on the traditional sources of Western esotericism, globalizing them through restatement in terms of the Asian religions, with which the West had come into colonial contact. Here Theosophy paved the way for the study of comparative religion, first exemplified by the World Parliament of Religions at Chicago in 1893. By emphasizing consciousness as a force in spiritual evolution, Theosophy combated materialist and mechanistic models of nature and also introduced a modern, dynamic dimension into the traditional Hermetic world picture of correspondences between the macrocosm and the microcosm.

As such, Theosophy significantly stimulated an interest in the esoteric tradition among the educated classes of America and Europe in the half-century from 1880 to 1930. Theosophical publications illuminated many aspects of the tradition back to the ancient world and the Renaissance, and cross-fertilized developments in the modern occult revival (e.g., ceremonial Masonic-magical orders such as the Hermetic Order of the Golden Dawn and its many twentieth-century derivatives). G. R. S. Mead (1863–1933) and Rudolf Steiner (1861–1925), both early major proponents of Theosophy, later emphasized the Western sources of Theosophy by elaborating the contribution of Gnosticism, Hermetism, Neoplatonism, Rosicrucianism, and Goethean science to the esoteric tradition. Mead was a seminal influence on C. G. Jung, whose theories of psychoanalysis owe much to the esoteric tradition in German Romantic natural science, while Steiner's Anthroposophy has linked the esoteric tradition to contemporary applications in education, agriculture, and medicine. Theosophy's cultural legacy has been extensive, influencing modern art, quantum physics and, more recently, New Age religion.

FURTHER READING

Geoffrey A. Barborka, *The Divine Plan: Written in the Form of a Commentary on H. P. Blavatsky's* Secret Doctrine (Adyar, India: Theosophical Publishing House, 1964).

Helena Petrovna Blavatsky, *Isis Unveiled: A Master-Key to the Mysteries of Ancient and Modern Science and Theology*, 2 vols. (1877; Pasadena, Calif.: Theosophical University Press, 1976).

———, *The Key to Theosophy* (1889; London: Theosophical Publishing House, 1987).

———, *The Secret Doctrine: The Synthesis of Science, Religion, and Philosophy*, 2 vols. (1888; Pasadena, Calif.: Theosophical University Press, 1988).

Bruce F. Campbell, *Ancient Wisdom Revived: A History of the Theosophical Movement* (Berkeley: University of California Press, 1980).

Sylvia P. Cranston, *H.P.B.: The Extraordinary Life and Influence of Helena Blavatsky, Founder of the Modern Theosophical Movement* (New York: Putnam, 1993).

Jean Overton Fuller, *Blavatsky and Her Teachers* (London: East-West Publications, 1988).

Joscelyn Godwin, *The Theosophical Enlightenment* (Albany: State University of New York Press, 1994), chapters 14–17.

Michael Gomes, *The Dawning of the Theosophical Movement* (Wheaton, Ill.: Theosophical Publishing House, 1987).

Clare Goodrick-Clarke and Nicholas Goodrick-Clarke, *G. R. S. Mead and the Gnostic Quest*, Western Esoteric Masters series (Berkeley, Calif.: North Atlantic Books, 2005).

Nicholas Goodrick-Clarke, *Helena Blavatsky*, Western Esoteric Masters series (Berkeley, Calif.: North Atlantic Books, 2004).

H. P. Blavatsky Collected Writings, edited by Boris de Zirkoff, 15 vols. (Wheaton, Ill.: Theosophical Publishing House, 1950–1991).

Paul Johnson, *In Search of the Masters: Behind the Occult Myth* (South Boston, Va.: author, 1990).

———, *The Masters Revealed: Madame Blavatsky and the Myth of the Great White Lodge* (Albany: State University of New York Press, 1994).

The Letters of H. P. Blavatsky, Vol. 1, edited by John Algeo (Wheaton, Ill.: Theosophical Publishing House, 2003).

The Mahatma Letters to A. P. Sinnett, compiled by A. T. Barker (London: Rider, 1923).

Mary K. Neff, *Personal Memoirs of H. P. Blavatsky* (London: Rider, 1937).

Henry S. Olcott, *Old Diary Leaves,* 6 vols. (Adyar, India: Theosophical Publishing House, 1895–1932).

Alfred Percy Sinnett, *Autobiography of Alfred Percy Sinnett* (London: Theosophical History Centre, 1986).

———, *Esoteric Buddhism* (London: Trübner, 1883).

———, *The Occult World* (London: Trübner, 1881).

H. J. Spierenburg, *The Buddhism of H. P. Blavatsky* (San Diego, Calif.: Point Loma Publications, 1991).

———, *H. P. Blavatsky, On the Gnostics* (San Diego, Calif.: Point Loma Publications, 1994).

———, *The Inner Group Teachings of H. P. Blavatsky to her personal pupils (1890–91),* (San Diego, Calif.: Point Loma Publications, 1995).

———, *The Vedanta Commentaries of H. P. Blavatsky* (San Diego, Calif.: Point Loma Publications, 1992).

12

Modern Esotericism and New Paradigms

Theosophical Heirs

Theosophy has played a major role in the promotion of Western esoteric traditions in the modern world. Notions of Masters, spiritual hierarchies, postmortem states, and spiritual evolution are commonplace ideas among contemporary beliefs, especially in contemporary new religious movements. The Theosophical Society itself has proved a hardy growth from whose trunk a number of important esoteric movements sprang during the early decades of the twentieth century. After Olcott's death in 1907, Annie Besant (1847–1933) and Charles Webster Leadbeater (1854–1934) led the original Adyar–based Theosophical Society, developing so-called "second-generation" Theosophy or Neo-Theosophy through to the early 1930s. Its innovative developments included an emphasis on the acquisition and practice of psychic and occult powers, notably clairvoyance, explorations of the astral plane, and past lives research based on theories of reincarnation. The Theosophical Society also embraced an Adventist claim based on a psychic reading by Leadbeater in 1909 that a young Indian boy, Jiddu Krishnamurti (1896–1986), would serve as the vehicle of the World Teacher, the Christ or Lord Maitreya (the Buddha of the sixth root race), in accordance with Blavatsky's spiritual hierarchy. Leadbeater was the chief exponent of these clairvoyant and messianic notions, and also responsible for the assimilation of Catholicism and its sacraments into the Theosophical Society (Adyar) through the ritualistic Liberal Catholic Church (est. 1917).[1] Although Krishnamurti renounced his messianic role in 1929, causing a hiatus in the fortunes of the Theosophical Society, he achieved wide renown as a spiritual leader in his own right, and his writings still attract a wide readership.

Rudolf Steiner, a scholar of Goethe's scientific works, became general secretary of the Theosophical Society in Germany in 1902, but he increasingly dissented from the Eastern cast of Theosophy under Annie Besant. While retaining most aspects of the complex cosmology and human spiritual constitution described by Theosophy, he abandoned the Tibetan Masters, reintroduced the salvific figure of Christ, and emphasized Rosicrucian traditions. In 1912, he broke away to found a society devoted to his own religious system, known as Anthroposophy. As the author of almost thirty books, Steiner also gave approximately 6,000 lectures on a wide range of esoteric subjects and pioneered their practical application, initiating Waldorf education, biodynamic farming and gardening, an approach to the care and education of the mentally handicapped, anthroposophical medical work and pharmacy, and an art of movement called eurythmy. His Anthroposophical Society, refounded in 1923, with its headquarters at the Goetheanum in Dornach near Basle, Switzerland, coordinates the national societies that disseminate Steiner's esoteric teachings, publications, and practice in the arts.[2]

The Arcane School of Alice A. Bailey (1880–1949) closely reflects Theosophy in its account of ancient wisdom, masters, and the evolution of humanity and the cosmos. Bailey made contact in 1919 with her Master, Djwal Khul (known as "the Tibetan"), whose teachings were relayed by clairvoyant dictation (channeling) in some twenty-four books she published between 1922 and the late 1940s. Djwal Khul revealed a divine plan for the universe that is being fulfilled through a succession of races and civilizations in a process of spiritual evolution. A hierarchy of spiritual leaders led by the Christ is responsible for the execution of this plan and has guided humankind throughout the centuries. According to Bailey, the Christ has been the Master of all the Masters, and the Masters of the Wisdom (or Mahatmas) were his pupils. Bailey also followed Blavatsky and the Theosophists in her ideas of karma and reincarnation.[3]

Though Bailey's doctrine recalls Christian theosophy in that it is theistic and invokes a cosmic Christ, it also assimilates many concepts from Blavatsky, notably the notion of the seven rays. With the template of the seven principles, Blavatsky related these rays to the seven great hierarchies of angels or Dhyani-Chohans, each associated with colors and sounds, and collectively forming the Manifested Logos. Each hierarchy has its characteristic color, just as the seven colors of the solar spectrum correspond to the seven rays. Each of these

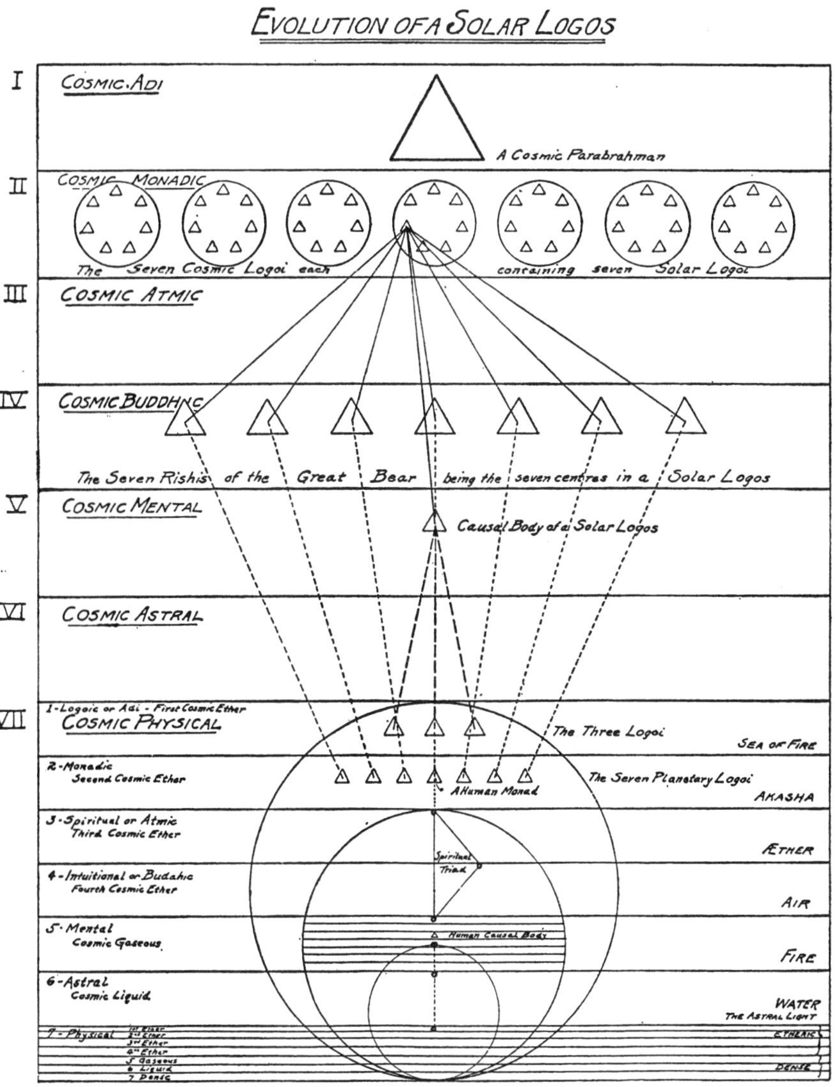

FIGURE 12.1. Evolution of Solar Logos, in Alice A. Bailey, *A Treatise on Cosmic Fire* (New York: Lucis Publishing Company, 1925), p. 344.

hierarchies acts as the builder of one of the seven kingdoms of nature and also the aura of one of the seven principles in man with its specific color. The rays play a major role as agents of correspondence in Bailey's esoteric psychology and have become a staple of New Age thinking. Bailey's idea of the spiritual hierarchy, which also derived from Blavatsky (her "hierarchy of compassion"), influenced Leadbeater in the 1920s and has subsequently entered much New Age discourse regarding the Great White Brotherhood.[4]

The influence of Theosophy extends far beyond its membership organizations and publications. As his biographer has commented, Leadbeater has had a defining influence on New Age religion: "Concepts such as Masters, reincarnation, karma, akashic records, Atlantis, Lemuria, Shamballa, astral plane, Monad, vibrations and psychic powers, so often used in modern occult literature, owe far more to Leadbeater than to anyone else."[5] Besant and Leadbeater coauthored an influential book titled *Thought-Forms* (1901), a record of clairvoyant investigation into the color and light produced by types of thought. Each thought, whether one of affection, devotion, anger, sympathy, fear, or greed, supposedly produces a corresponding vibration, which changes the coloration of the thinker's various subtle bodies corresponding to the seven principles in man according to the spiritual anatomy of Theosophy. The thoughts also produce their own floating form, as a colored geometric shape. The research extended to the thought-forms built by music, and richly colored tableaux illustrated those produced by the music of Mendelssohn, Gounod, and Wagner.[6]

Leadbeater's books on the colors and shapes of thought-forms, subtle bodies, and auras strongly influenced the early abstract painting of Wassily Kandinsky and Piet Mondrian. Kandinsky had bought a copy of *Thought-Forms* in 1908 and joined the Theosophical Society in 1909. His book *Concerning the Spiritual in Art*, published in 1911, was a turning point for modernism. His *Improvisations* series of paintings from around 1916 are considered to be directly influenced by the illustrations in *Thought-Forms*. Kandinsky also devotes a few paragraphs to Theosophy in his book, quoting from Blavatsky's *The Key to Theosophy*. Piet Mondrian also joined the Theosophical Society in 1909. He experimented with colored geometrical forms to reflect the order of the universe and kept a portrait of Madame Blavatsky hanging in his studio. Other famous modern painters influenced by Theosophy include Paul Klee, Paul Gauguin, and Nicholas Roerich.[7]

Fourth Way Groups

The Fourth Way movement associated with the Caucasian thaumaturge George Ivanovitch Gurdjieff (1866–1949) and Poitr Demianovich Ouspensky (1878–1947) offers another example of an esoteric school combining an elaborate cosmology and spiritual self-development with artistic expression. In 1907, the Russian polymath Ouspensky discovered Theosophy and embarked on an intensive study of occult literature. His first major philosophical work, *Tertium Organum* (1912), was a profoundly esoteric work addressing the cognitive power of higher states of consciousness. Strongly drawn to yoga and the promise of Eastern wisdom, Ouspensky traveled to India, visiting the Theosophists at Adyar in 1913. After his return to Russia, Ouspensky met Gurdjieff, who had surfaced in St. Petersburg after many years seeking esoteric wisdom among "masters" in Central Asia. Ouspensky believed Gurdjieff had discovered a new system of thought and all-encompassing knowledge. Meanwhile, Gurdjieff began to develop his work in ballet and sacred gymnastics (later termed "movements"). Among those attracted to his work were the Russian composer Thomas de Hartmann, artist and theatrical designer Alexandre de Salzmann, and dance instructor Jeanne de Salzmann. Gurdjieff's group migrated through revolutionary Russia, Constantinople, and Germany before settling in France, where he established his school at Fontainebleau in 1922.[8]

In *Beelzebub's Tales to His Grandson*, Gurdjieff presented his ideas in the form of a mythopoeic cosmogony involving a hierarchy of subordinate levels within a living universe and divides human history into two streams, conscious and unconscious, initiatic and profane. Gurdjieff regarded man as the prisoner of "identification," whereby the sense of self is squandered in mechanical reactions to and false identification with external stimuli. The task of enlightenment, in his view, is to "awaken" to essential being and to achieve real self-knowledge. Gurdjieff related the human condition within a cosmic context of biology, metaphysics, and cosmology. His "Ray of Creation," recalling the terminology of Theosophy, related the microcosm of the human heart and mind to an extensive hierarchy of planets and stars, up to the Absolute as the source of all creation. This entire cosmic order is discrete, its discontinuity reflected in its correspondence to the musical octave. Only once one can discover one's own essential being and latent destiny can he or she begin to draw on the universal energies which stream down through the hierarchies of the ray and play an active, conscious role. Though human beings are biologically descended as a generic species, a person's spiritual ascent or evolution must be achieved as an individual.[9]

Though Gurdjieff's system rehearses traditional ideas of Western esotericism, it is marked by innovations, such as the semitonal intervals on the diatonic scale, in contrast to the musical correspondences of Robert Fludd. Gurdjieff's Laws of Three and Seven underpin his key symbol, the "enneagram," and the Food Diagram, correlating food, air, and impressions in the microcosm. Gurdjieff offers a cosmology rich in correspondences and emphasizes the transmutation of the soul through the self-conscious "movements" and other alienating exercises to break down habitual identifications. Ouspensky sought to systematize Gurdjieff's teachings in a metaphysically coherent system, published as *In Search of the Miraculous* (1950). Subsequent British interpreters of Gurdjieff and

Ouspensky's thought carried on their work through their own groups, institutes, and writings. John Godolphin Bennett (1897–1974), a scientist, technologist, and philosopher, first met Gurdjieff in 1921 and worked with Ouspensky thereafter, establishing an institute at Coombe Springs, Kingston-on-Thames in Surrey in 1946. Bennett resumed contact with Gurdjieff in the late 1940s and became convinced that his system could be reconciled with modern science. Bennett's numerous works include the four-volume *Dramatic Universe* (1956–1966) and *The Masters of Wisdom* (1977). In late 1953, Bennett traveled through the Near East hoping to locate Gurdjieff's original sources among Sufi masters, and his account of the trip was later published as *Journeys in Islamic Countries* (1976–1977). Rodney Collin (1909–1956) also worked with Ouspensky and authored a number of works. His *Theory of Celestial Influence* (1954) represents a monumental study of humanity, civilization, and the universe according to the cosmological ideas of the Laws of Three and Seven and the enneagram. Maurice Nicoll (1884–1953), an eminent psychiatrist and Jungian analyst, studied with Gurdjieff in 1922 and continued with groups of his own in England. His monumental five-volume *Psychological Commentaries on the Teaching of G. I. Gurdjieff and P. D. Ouspensky* (1952–1954) represented his lifetime work in reconciling their esoteric philosophy with modern psychology.[10]

The Scientization of Esotericism

Since the Renaissance, esotericism has advanced a discourse that combines deductive Neoplatonic and Hermetic forms of absolute knowledge or gnosis with an empirical estimate of the natural order based on observation. Robert Fludd's magisterial surveys of the microcosm and macrocosm thus attempted to embrace all contemporary knowledge within a hierarchically ordered cosmos structured by Hermetic philosophy, Paracelsian nature philosophy, and Kabbalah. However, by the late nineteenth century, the sheer accumulation of knowledge about causal relationships in the physical world began to "flatten" traditional hierarchical worldviews toward a positivist, operational view of nature. The Western scientific emphasis on experiment, skeptical reason, and cause and effect has tended toward a fragmentary, partial view of the cosmos, in which overarching orders and vertical hierarchies are less compelling. An endless inventory of facts, formulae, and physical laws creates a world of discrete knowledge. This rational, operational knowledge can only be based on empirical sensation and thus cannot claim the status of absolute knowledge. As Kocku von Stuckrad has emphasized, one of the defining characteristics of esotericism is its claim to absolute knowledge.

In their claim to absolute knowledge, the early-twentieth-century esoteric movements have maintained the *cosmological* features of the Western esoteric traditions. Their view of the universe and the human being is intrinsically based on analogical and symbolic correspondences between the macrocosm and microcosm, in which hierarchies of spiritual intermediaries play a vital role within an animated cosmos. At the same time, the metaphors and paradigms used to illustrate these cosmologies have, to a greater or lesser extent, availed themselves of scientistic notions, that is to say ideas current in science. Blavatsky's central concern with evolution, and her panoply of globes, rounds, root races, cosmic planes, and rays were elaborated further by Leadbeater and Alice Bailey in detailed diagrams depicting esoteric cosmology.[11] A series of works on "Technical Theosophy" published in the 1920s by Lieutenant Colonel Arthur Edward Powell offers highly complex illustrations of the connections and links among force centers, chakras, vitality globules, and particles to explain macrocosmic influences in esoteric physiology. In the 1980s, the Japanese scientist Dr. Hiroshi Motoyama extended Leadbeater's speculations through electrophysiological experimental work concerning the subtle network of chakras and nadis as conductors of energy in the subtle bodies of Theosophy.[12] These systems are the modern scientized equivalents of the seventeenth-century engravings showing Fludd's cosmic hierarchies and the spiritual components of the body and brain.

This scientistic aspect of modern esotericism is much more than mere terminology; it reflects an ongoing effort to bridge the worlds of spirit and physical matter. In place of Cartesian duality, modern esoteric thought seeks to subsume the material world as the expression of a spiritual plan and forces involved in the processes of creation. Modern esoteric applications have therefore repeated traditional esoteric tropes such as Neoplatonic "pneuma," alchemical "fire," and mesmerist "fluid" under such appellations as "etheric forces," "energies," and "vibrations." Throughout the twentieth century, a broad front of practical esotericism has directly contributed to a range of alternative therapies and technologies, which emphasize these elements of will, intentionality, and subtle energy. The investigation of subtle energies in science and medicine by esoteric movements is thus directly related to the presence and effects of macrocosmic-microcosmic correspondences and intermediary hierarchies.

This kind of scientific thinking was also current between 1795 and 1830 in German Romantic *Naturphilosophie,* where nature was envisaged as a coherent, analogical, and self-revealing whole arranged in orders. Given Rudolf Steiner's inspiration in the scientific writings of Johann Wolfgang Goethe (1749–1832) on color and form in botany, there is a direct lineal descent from the latter's organic-vitalist ideas and the science practiced within the Rudolf

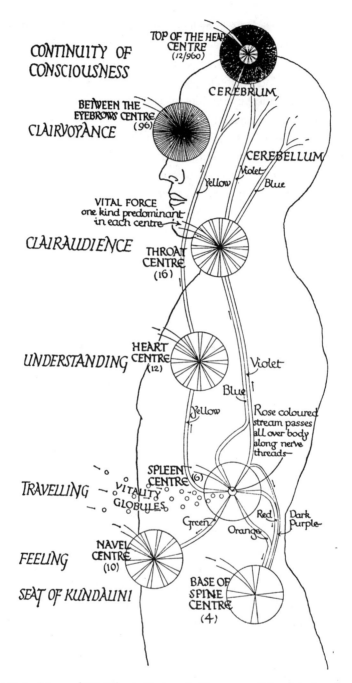

FIGURE 12.2. Man and His Etheric Centres, in Lieutenant-Colonel Arthur E. Powell, *The Etheric Double and Allied Phenomena* (London: Theosophical Publishing House, 1925), p. 56.

Steiner movement today. Steiner explicated the anthroposophical perspective on science in three lecture courses that he taught to Waldorf schoolteachers on light, heat, and astronomy between 1919 and 1921. Steiner's notion of four fundamental types of etheric influence was an intrinsic part of his complex cosmology of planetary cycles, earth rounds, and their related spiritual hierarchies.[13] Steiner himself suggested two laboratory techniques which could visibly demonstrate the formative aspects of etheric forces active in nature: capillary dynamolysis and sensitive crystallization.

Anthroposophical investigation concerning the etheric forces have been pursued in chromatography and crystallography by Ehrenfried Pfeiffer (1899–1961), a leading figure in biodynamic farming. Pfeiffer first attended Steiner's lectures in 1920 and was attracted by the idea that etheric and creative forces manifest in nature. At his laboratory in Dornach, Pfeiffer subsequently developed a technique for crystallization, where copper chloride crystallizes in a thin layer resembling "ice flowers," whose form reflect the substance added to it. The technique was used to identify subtle variations in the quality of foods and composts. Pfeiffer also made slides of crystallized blood for diagnostic purposes.[14]

Lili Kolisko (1889–1976) developed the techniques of capillary dynamolysis to illustrate etheric forces in substance. This technique involved the uptake of a solution containing the substance on filter paper and then repeating the experiment with a solution of one of the planetary metal salts. The nutritional value

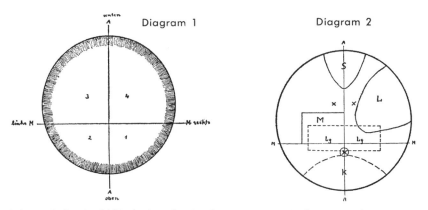

A-A = vertical axis; M-M = horizontal axis; the intersection of the A-A and M-M- axes = centre of gravity; numbers 1, 2, 3, 4 show four quadrants of the crystallization field; the hatched portion = peripheral zone; S = zone of the sexual organs; M = gastric zone; Lg = pulmonary zone; X = kidney points; ø = throat zone; K = head zone; L = liver zone.

FIGURE 12.3. Arrangement of blood crystals on slide corresponds to specific zones in patient's organism. Ehrenfried Pfeiffer, *Sensitive Crystallization Processes* (Spring Valley, N.Y.: Anthroposophic Press, 1975), p. 23.

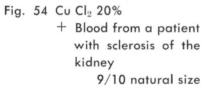

Fig. 54 Cu Cl₂ 20%
   + Blood from a patient
      with sclerosis of the
      kidney
         9/10 natural size

Fig. 56 Cu Cl₂ 20%
   + Blood from a patient
      with calcified
      tuberculosis
         9/10 natural size

FIGURE 12.4. Formative forces carried in the blood. Specimen blood slides in Ehrenfried Pfeiffer, Sensitive Crystallization Process (Spring Valley, N.Y.: Anthroposophic Press, 1975), plate XVIII.

of foods and potency of homeopathic medicines was reflected in the strength and form of the patterns (*Steigbilder*) formed by the solution on the filter paper. She later performed experiments relating astronomical events of specific planets to observable changes in the patterns formed by the corresponding planetary metal salt solutions.[15] This work has subsequently been confirmed and developed in further experimental trials by Agnes Fyfe (1898–1986), Wilhelm Pelikan, and Nick Kollerstrom to demonstrate nonlocal acausal correspondences between the planets and their corresponding metals.[16] Theodor Schwenk (1910–1986), an engineer and Anthroposophist, was interested in the notion that, in the fourth stage of planetary formation, the life ether force begins to condense out to produce the visible forms encountered in the flow of liquid or gaseous substances in nature. Schwenk pioneered the study of vortical and flow forms in water and air, relating these etheric rhythms to corporeal forms in the mineral, plant, and animal kingdoms.[17]

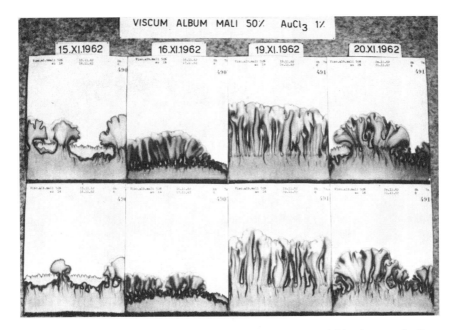

FIGURE 12.5. Lili Kolisko Capillary Dynamolysis. Typical *Steigbilder* showing dupli-
cate tests of four saps, Mistletoe with Gold Chloride, in Agnes Fyfe, *Moon and Plant:
Capillary Dynamic Studies* (Arlesheim: Society for Cancer Research, 1975), plate 6.

Theosophy has also sponsored its own scientific endeavor. In the 1890s,
Besant and Leadbeater conducted clairvoyant investigations into the atomic
nature of substances, publishing their findings as *Occult Chemistry* (1908). A
considerable number of eminent scientists were members of the Theosophical Society from the 1930s through the 1960s. Since that time Professor H. J.
Arnikar, known for his work on radiochemistry, has revived occult chemistry,
and Stephen M. Phillips, a Cambridge theoretical physicist, has published scientific work on remote viewing and the clairvoyant investigation of particles
and its confirmation of superstring theories.[18] Other, notably Indian, Theosophical scientists working in this tradition include M. Srinivasan, a former
director at the Bhabha Atomic Research Centre, Bombay; I. K. Taimni, whose
work continues the traditional synthesis of spiritual philosophy, consciousness,
and science; and Edi Bilimoria, representative of a "new wave" of trained scientists correlating conventional science with Theosophy.[19]

Field Theories and New Age Science

The scientization of esotericism described above records the empirical engagement of traditional esotericism with the natural world, involving its perception,

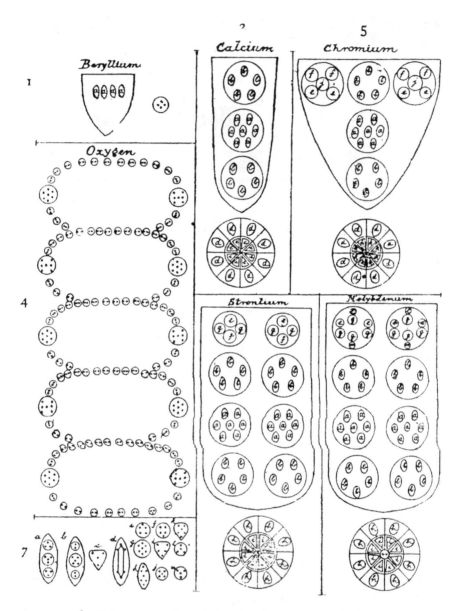

FIGURE 12.6. Clairvoyant readings of chemical elements in tetrahedral groups, Plate VIII in Annie Besant and Charles W. Leadbeater, *Occult Chemistry: Clairvoyant Observations on the Chemical Elements* (London: Theosophical Publishing House, 1919), p. 52.

imagination, and relationship to humanity in terms of correspondences, living nature, spiritual hierarchies, and the transmutation of the soul. However, there is another process at work in modern science, whereby its discourses do not merely lend themselves to esoteric colonization, but also independently suggest it. Here we see an example of Kocku von Stuckrad's analysis of discourses and how scientific hypotheses and metaphors import esoteric modes of imagination and cognition.

Since their earliest recognition by Paracelsus and Athanasius Kircher, magnetic and subsequently electric fields have offered scope for scientific speculation about agents that connect all parts of the cosmos. As agents of animation, Paracelsian sidereal influences were succeeded by mesmerist "fluid" and "astral light" in the nineteenth century. The quest to understand subtle influences has repeatedly involved experimental efforts to detect such fluids. Karl von Reichenbach (1788–1869), an accomplished German chemist known for his analysis of creosote, paraffin, and phenol, posited the existence of a new Odic force, allied to but distinct from electricity, magnetism, and heat, supposedly radiated by most substances, and to the influence of which different persons are variously sensitive. He showed that this vital force was connected with the phenomena of water divination, Mesmerism, and similar psychic phenomena. Through experiments he discovered a polarity in the human body between the left and right sides and noted that sensitives observed human auras.[20] A few years later in the United States, Edwin Babbitt (1829–1905) developed a form of color therapy based on his own clairvoyant perception of psychomagnetic lines of force surrounding the human body.[21] Leadbeater's clairvoyant auras were empirically confirmed as "magnetic radiations" by Walter J. Kilner's *The Human Atmosphere* (1911) and Oscar Bagnall's *The Origin and Properties of the Human Aura* (1937). In 1939, Semyon Kirlian discovered a form of photography revealing an electrical corona discharge around objects. He thought this offered proof of auras, and some claim that Kirlian photography can illuminate the acupuncture points of the human body.[22]

Vitalistic theories of nature and medicine played an important role in the development of the notion of a life force in nineteenth-century science. Samuel Hahnemann (1755–1843) discovered homeopathic medicine on the basis of self-experimentation. On discovering that a given remedy for a disease produced symptoms of that disease in himself, he proposed his healing principle: "That which can produce a set of symptoms in a healthy individual can treat a sick individual who is manifesting a similar set of symptoms." The basis of this medicine was rooted in a rigorous empirical procedure for testing ("proving") any prospective remedy on a healthy individual, while its use as a remedy involved the minimal dose at high levels of dilution. In the case of the normal homeopathic dilutions ("potencies"), there may remain no molecular presence of the original substance in the remedy. Hahnemann described the process whereby this absent substance caused recovery from the indicated disease in such esoteric-Romantic terms as "spirit-like (*geistartig*) substance," "potency energy," "essence" (*Wesen*), and "vital forces," although his strict empirical approach distinguished him from German *Naturphilosophie*.[23] Homeopathy has established itself throughout the United States, Europe, and India. Because homeopathy offered empirical proof of its effectiveness, if not a rational, positivist explanation for its operation, it has survived as an important form of complementary medicine. Like Mesmerism, it posited a principle for which there is no tangible evidence, yet its effects could be demonstrated.

From the 1920s through the 1950s, pioneering scientific work was carried out in the expanding and interrelated fields of bioelectricity, cell radiation, and the sensitivity of solutions and colloids to electromagnetic waves and radioactive radiation. Scientists also investigated the influence of electromagnetic fields on psychic phenomena such as water dowsing, radiesthesia (pendulum divination), hypnotism, and animals' sensitivity for direction. Many scientists were convinced that such phenomena really existed and that they were subject to recognized physical and physiological laws.[24] As this research involved the electromagnetic field in and around living organisms, new hypotheses concerning a general field of interconnection emerged. Between 1935 and the 1950s, Harold Saxton Burr (1889–1973), emeritus professor of anatomy in the Yale University School of Medicine, published numerous studies of the electrodynamic fields as the basic blueprints of all living creatures. He concluded that these fields of life (called "L-fields") demonstrated how all beings share in the purpose and destiny of the universe.[25]

The idea of a unified electromagnetic field continued to draw scientific and medical research into speculations that posit the existence of a continuous animating agency. Wilhelm Reich (1887–1957) posited a form of bioenergy he called orgone, closely related to emotional activity in the human body, and he designed machines to accumulate and utilize this energy. Other approaches to bioenergetic medicine included radionics, a controversial therapy dating from the 1920s based on the idea that all life and matter contains vibrations whose frequency can be manipulated to restore health. Radionic devices are purported to diagnose ailments and restore persons to health by applying healing frequencies to balance out the "discordant" frequencies of sickness. The therapy was first pioneered by Albert Abrams (1863–1924), and was developed from the 1940s onward by Ruth Drown, Aubrey Westlake, George de la Warr, Malcolm Rae, and David Tansley.[26] The use of a link (witness) in the form a snippet of hair from the patient as a means of both diagnosis and long-distance healing suggests a magical form of interconnection throughout nature that is both acausal and nonlocal. Radionics extends the scientific explanations of bioenergy and electromagnetic fields into a realm that is profoundly esoteric. Significantly, David Tansley (1934–1988), its leading representative and author, integrated its theory with the Theosophical cosmology and physiology of Alice A. Bailey.[27]

The idea of electromagnetic radiation in living organisms has given rise to ideas of cell communication. The orthopedist Robert O. Becker conducted extensive experiments on electromagnetic frequencies in organisms and developed new theories relating to tissue and limb regeneration. These electrochemically induced cellular regeneration technologies are based on the principle of a morphogenetic field, first advanced by the American embryologist Paul Weiss in the 1930s, which contains the blueprint for growth in the forms of electromagnetic information. Becker has outlined a theory of energy medicine based on minimal energy techniques (autosuggestion, visualization); energy-reinforcement techniques (homeopathy, acupuncture); and high-energy transfer techniques (electrotherapy).[28] Becker's conviction about the efficiency of homeopathy as an instance of electromagnetic reinforcement technique was enhanced by the research of Jacques Benveniste (1935–2004), the immunologist and director at the French National Institute for Health and Medical Research (INSERM). In 1984, Benveniste discovered that water molecules became imprinted with some electromagnetic information that reflected the chemical effect of a substance at such high levels of dilution that no molecules of the original substance were present in the solvent. His discovery offered a striking illustration of how homeopathic remedies in their high potencies can be effective. Benveniste theorized that molecules and intermolecular bonds emit electromagnetic frequencies and that these signals can be digitally recorded and replayed back to a biological organism normally sensitive to the original substance.[29]

Scientists advancing these notions of field interconnectivity do not necessarily advocate an esoteric worldview, but their findings have been linked to radically imaginative new syntheses involving the nature of consciousness and the universe. The biologist Rupert Sheldrake (b. 1942) has proposed a variety of *Naturphilosophie* involving a hypothesis of formative causation. He has applied his theory of morphic resonance, drawing on the older notion of morphogenetic fields, to such topics as animal and plant development and behavior; animal and human telepathy; perception; and metaphysics.[30] The ideas of holography have supplied another fertile soil for field speculations. The laser technique of holography is used to make three-dimensional representations of objects through the interference of two light sources deriving from the object. Holography suggests that objects can be converted into frequency patterns, which are in turn considered the fundamental order of the substance. Also, any one part of the holographic image appears to contain all the frequency information required to reconstruct the complete image. The neuroscientist Karl Pribram (b. 1919), a leading authority on the cerebral cortex of the brain, has advanced the holo-nomic brain model of cognitive function, which theorizes that the brain stores memory according to holographic principles and that perceived reality is a pro-jection of the brain's interpretation of a realm of frequencies.[31] David Bohm (1917–1992), the American-born quantum physicist, made significant contri-butions in the fields of both theoretical physics and philosophy. In 1959, he encountered the writings of Krishnamurti, whose ideas impressed him as con-gruent with his own research on quantum mechanics. Bohm also advanced a holonomic view of the brain, perception, and the underlying order of the universe, which received expression in his books *Wholeness and the Implicate Order* (1980) and *Science, Order, and Creativity* (1987).

These and other theories of consciousness and unified field theories have proved particularly attractive to individuals and groups within the broad area of the New Age. This late twentieth-century spiritual movement is opposed to the rational, positivistic, and mechanistic worldviews in modern industrial so-cieties and has accordingly embraced any number of themes involving various world religions and spirituality; altered states of consciousness; psychic phe-nomena; neopagan spirituality (Druidic, Celtic, Germanic); divination across the range of astrology, Tarot, and I Ching; and a wide variety of psychotherapies and regimes for health and healing.[32] In his pioneering study of New Age reli-gion, Wouter Hanegraaff has outlined the major contours of New Age religion under such headings as channeling, healing and personal growth, neopagan-ism, and New Age science. He has argued that New Age authors swiftly relate their own interest in holistic theories of life and nature to the varied metaphors and models arising from field theories. The quest for a unified worldview ex-pressed in terms of natural laws is typically presented by secular scientists as triumph over traditional religion and metaphysics. By contrast, New Age sci-ence suggests that these new theories can explain the workings of nature in an absolute, divine sense, and thus secure a scientific basis for religion.[33]

Popular New Age writers including Marilyn Ferguson and Lynn McTag-gart have swiftly responded to field theories by incorporating them in a world-view that reflects scientized esotericism. In *The Aquarian Conspiracy* (1980), her major manifesto for New Age spirituality, Ferguson included an extensive discussion of the theories of Ilya Prigogine, quantum theory, the holographic principle, and the work of Karl Pribram and David Bohm. Prigogine's para-digm of self-organization leads on to Erich Jantsch's theories of evolution. Ferguson highlights the esoteric implications of Pribram's work thus: "The brain's neural interference patterns, its mathematical processes, may be identi-cal to the primary state of the universe. . . . Our mental processes are, in effect, made of the same stuff as the organizing principle."[34] The monistic identity of consciousness and the natural world would become a recurrent theme among New Age science writers, indicating a secularized formulation of *Naturphiloso-phie* and the esoteric discourse of macrocosm and microcosm.

Lynn McTaggart's highly influential book *The Field* (2001) has combined such subjects as Hal Puthoff's speculations on the "zero point field," a specu-lative concept involving a limitless reservoir of energy arising from quantum particles, the work of the German physicist Fritz-Albert Popp on the emission of photons from living organisms as frequencies related to cellular DNA, and the hypotheses of Becker, Sheldrake, Benveniste, and Pribram. Consciousness, collective memory, omniscience, healing, intention, nonlocality, remote view-ing, and communication with the dead are so many possibilities supposedly indicated by the zero point field. By suggesting that the basic alphabet of na-ture is the language of waves, their phase, amplitude, frequency, interference, and coherence, McTaggart invokes a scientistic form of animation that would explain correspondence, analogy, synchronicity, and the identity of the mac-rocosm with the microcosm. "The Zero Point Field is a kind of shadow of the universe . . . a mirror image and record of everything that ever was," she writes. "Every part of the universe could be in touch with every other part instantane-ously." "Nature was not blind and mechanistic, but open-ended, intelligent and purposeful, . . . information had been encoded and transmitted everywhere at once," so that "the brain is simply the retrieval and read-out mechanism of the ultimate storage medium—the Field."[35]

The Sacralization of the Soul: Jungian Esotericism

Field theories offer theories of universal interconnectedness that reflect the es-oteric ideas of correspondence and an animated monist continuum throughout the cosmos. They also suggest a reciprocity between the mind and the perceived reality of the world. However, it is less clear that they recall the spiritual hierar-chies of traditional esotericism, nor offer ideas of the ascent or transmutation of the soul. To this extent, they still follow the secular "flattening" of the esoteric perspective on vertical orders descending from the deity through various inter-mediaries to the human soul. Instead, we find a pantheistic vision of embodied immanence represented by a continuum of electrical charge, subatomic parti-cles, or frequencies. However, once these field theories are integrated with no-tions of the human soul, the picture recalls the traditional forms of esotericism. Ever since Plato's separation of the body and the soul, Western esotericism has traced a path in which the soul has been granted some share in divinity. The *Corpus Hermeticum* recorded the source and reascent of the human mind to the divine Mind (*Nous*). In the Renaissance, Ficino related the individual soul to the world soul, while Pico della Mirandola regarded man as the nexus between the transcendent and earthly realms. The Renaissance discourse of the sovereignty and potential divinity of the human soul has ultimately led to modern post-orthodox religious ideas that the human being no longer needs a Savior or mediator with God but may now redeem himself.

The work and influence of the Swiss psychologist Carl Gustav Jung (1875–1961) has been an important factor in the development of an inner variety of esotericism through the twentieth century. As a young medical student, Jung was drawn to Spiritualism and experimented in séances, his first encounter with transpersonal entities. Jung also studied the works of Ernst Haeckel (1834–1919), professor of zoology at Jena and the leading authority on evolutionary biology in Germany. He advanced the theory that the stages of individual development (ontogeny) recapitulated the states of the development of the human race (phylogeny). This led Jung to postulate a "phylogeny of the soul" whereby the early religions and mythologies of mankind would correspond to the lower, unconscious strata of the mind. By 1909, Jung conceived of the idea of mining the unconscious by first investigating Greco-Roman mystery cults, later focusing on the Gnostics.[36] By the end of the First World War, Jung had conceived a theory of universal symbols produced by the collective unconscious, which he defined as archetypes.

This theory, continually developed between 1920 and 1940, drew Jung into new formulations of esoteric imagination. Jung suggested that dreams prefigured the evolution of the soul. Another key idea was "active imagination," a notion Jung took from Herbert Silberer (1882–1923), a Swiss Freudian analyst interested in alchemy, which involved the transmutation of the unconscious archetypes by their integration into a unified archetype of the Self. Jung termed this process "individuation." By the 1930s, these ideas, essentially esoteric, had led Jung from Gnostic mythology to alchemical texts as sources of the archetypes, and he published studies of Paracelsus and psychological interpretations of alchemy. His later work embraced studies of astrology and the *I Ching* oracle. He interpreted the process of divination as an acausal interaction of synchronicity between the subject and his situation in the world. In his last works, such as *Mysterium coniunctionis* (1955–1956), Jung posited the unity of the world, whose different levels of reality correspond with one another and are thereby able to communicate with one another and with the human psyche.[37]

Jung's initial focus on descent into the primordial realms of collective unconscious and its archetypes indicates his relationship to Romanticism and irrationalism. His proposition concerning the soul's transmutation into the potential totality of the Self indicate an inward, "psychologized" form of esotericism, that owes much to his earlier inspiration in evolutionary biology. Jung's emphasis on "depth" and primordiality contrast with Hermetic notions of "ascent" that characterize traditional esoteric forms of transmutation from Ficino to the modern Theosophists.[38] However, Jung's engagement with the esoteric materials of alchemy and astrology, his ideas on synchronicity, and the *unus mundus*, in which symbol reflects reality and reality symbol, show how his depth psychology offers another modern paradigm for esotericism.

Although Jung's earliest inspiration lay with older German psychologists such as Karl Eschenmayer, Justinus Kerner, and Carl Gustav Carus (1789– 1869), all representative of Romantic *Naturphilosophie,* his work has had a powerful influence on New Age religion in its sacralization of the Self as the divine counterpart within the human being. The earlier transpersonal paradigms of Mesmerism, mind cure, self-healing, and New Thought in the United States received a major impetus from the sacralization of the psyche implicit in Jung's work and practice when his psychotherapy became widely practiced from the 1960s onward. New forms of transpersonal psychology pointed toward ahistorical concepts of the soul, suggesting that the soul could participate in universal forms of experience. Jung's emphasis on archetypes and symbols as bridges between inner and outer worlds has also influenced interpretations of homeopathic medicine as the congruence of form or function in nature with symbol as an expression of psychic energy.[39] Jung offered a twentieth-century restatement of Paracelsus's divine seals in nature, their discovery and application. In the New Age culture, Jungian ideas of synchronicity are now widespread in divination based on astrology, Tarot, and dream interpretation. Jung's seminal influence on psychology, complementary medicine, and New Age forms of religiosity is a widespread phenomenon clearly representative of the "soulful" tendency of esotericism in the modern West, more receptive to spiritual than institutional forms of religious expression.[40] This development recalls the rise of theosophy, pietism, and Rosicrucian alchemy in seventeenth and eighteenth-century Germany, a culture in which Jung's own thought was rooted.

From their origins in the syncretic Hellenistic religious philosophies of Hermetism and Neoplatonism through to the present, the Western esoteric traditions have posited overarching orders and hierarchies linking the human being with a grand vision of the cosmos in which the individual soul has meaning, purpose, and even a share in divinity. The expression of these traditions have ranged from Neoplatonism to Kabbalah, from alchemy to astrology and magic, from Christian theosophy to Blavatsky's synthesis of Western and Eastern traditions, from Ficino's astral magic and Rosicrucianism to C. G. Jung's depth psychology. Esotericism has responded to religious and cultural change in the West, a development evident in its speculations about emanations of

God transformed into archetypes, from alchemical principles to symbols, from angels to electromagnetic frequencies. The basic family resemblance of the esoteric traditions is discernible not only in Faivre's distinctive character- istics but also in the uniquely high value that Western culture places on the individual and on the individual's relationship with the cosmos and potential for salvation and perfection. The Western esoteric traditions continue to cel- ebrate that project in an evolving variety of forms, but always seeking to claim the unique gnosis of illumination, an absolute transhistorical knowledge of higher origins that can restore the human soul to its home in the unity of being. This is the continuing heritage of Western esotericism, whose histori- cal and cultural vigor has alternated in relation to its epistemological challenge to doctrinal orthodoxies, be they religious or secular. As noted in my introduc- tion, esotericism often appears to flourish in the wake of new exotic sources of spiritual and religious speculation, which are deployed to challenge hardening or obsolescent orthodoxies and dogmas. As long as the West upholds an image of the free human being within an integrated vision of God, heaven, and earth, esotericism will undoubtedly remain a feature of its intellectual and religious landscape.

FURTHER READING

Geoffrey Ahern, *Sun at Midnight: The Rudolf Steiner Movement and the Western Esoteric Tradition* (Wellingborough: Aquarian Press, 1984).

Alice A. Bailey, *Initiation, Human and Solar* (New York: Lucis Publishing Co., 1922).

———, *A Treatise on Cosmic Fire* (New York: Lucis Trust, 1925).

Annie Besant and Charles Leadbeater, *Occult Chemistry: Clairvoyant Observations on the Chemical Elements* (1908; rev. ed., London: Theosophical Publishing House, 1919).

———, *Thought-Forms: A Record of Clairvoyant Investigation* (London: Theosophical Publishing House, 1901; 2nd Quest Book abridged ed., Wheaton, Ill.: Theosophi- cal Publishing House, 1999).

Harold Saxton Burr, *Blueprint for Immortality: The Electric Patterns of Life* (London: Neville Spearman, 1972).

Stewart C. Easton, *Rudolf Steiner: Herald of a New Epoch* (Hudson, N.Y.: Anthropo- sophic Press, 1980).

Marilyn Ferguson, *The Aquarian Conspiracy: Personal and Social Transformation in the 1980s* (London: Paladin Grafton, 1982).

Clare Goodrick-Clarke, "Rationalist, Empiricist, or *Naturphilosoph?* Samuel Hahne- mann and His Legacy," *Politica Hermetica* 18 (2004): 26–45.

Olav Hammer, "Jungism," in *Dictionary of Gnosis and Western Esotericism*, 2 vols. (Leiden: Brill, 2005), Vol. 2, pp. 653–655.

Wouter J. Hanegraaff, *New Age Religion and Western Culture: Esotericism in the Mirror of Secular Thought* (Leiden: Brill, 1996).

Paul Heelas, *The New Age Movement: The Celebration of the Self and the Sacralization of Modernity* (Oxford: Blackwell, 1996).

C. G. Jung, *Man and His Symbols* (London: Aldus, 1964).

Gary Lachman, *In Search of P. D. Ouspensky: The Genius in the Shadow of Gurdjieff* (Wheaton, Ill.: Theosophical Publishing House, 2004).

Charles Webster Leadbeater, *The Christian Creed: Its Origin and Signification*, 2nd ed. (London: Theosophical Publishing House, 1920).

———, *Man Visible and Invisible: Examples of Different Types of Men as Seen by Means of Trained Clairvoyance* (London: Theosophical Publishing Society, 1902).

Robert A. McDermott, "Rudolf Steiner and Anthroposophy," in *Modern Esoteric Spirituality*, edited by Antoine Faivre and Jacob Needleman (London: SCM Press, 1993), pp. 288–310.

Lynn McTaggart, *The Field: The Quest for the Secret Force of the Universe* (London: HarperCollins, 2003).

Dennis Milner and Edward Smart, *The Loom of Creation: A Study of the Purpose and the Forces That Weave the Pattern of Existence* (New York: Harper & Row, 1976).

James Moore, *Gurdjieff: The Anatomy of a Myth* (Shaftesbury: Element, 1981).

Peter Morrell, "British Homeopathy during Two Centuries," available at http://www.homeoint.org/morrell/british/index.htm.

Jacob Needleman, "G. I. Gurdjieff and His School," in *Modern Esoteric Spirituality*, edited by Antoine Faivre and Jacob Needleman (London: SCM Press, 1993), pp. 359–380.

———, "Ouspensky," in *Dictionary of Gnosis and Western Esotericism*, edited by Wouter Hanegraaff et al., 2 vols. (Leiden: Brill, 2005), Vol. 2, pp. 911–913.

Richard Noll, *The Jung Cult: Origins of a Charismatic Movement* (Princeton, N.J.: Princeton University Press, 1994).

Arthur E. Powell, *The Etheric Double and Allied Phenomena* (London: Theosophical Publishing House, 1925).

Karl H. Pribram, *Brain and Perception: Holonomy and Structure in Figural Processing* (Hillsdale, N.J.: Lawrence Erlbaum, 1991).

———, *Rethinking Neural Networks: Quantum Fields and Biological Data* (Hillsdale, N.J.: Lawrence Erlbaum, 1993).

Michel Schiff, *The Memory of Water: Homoeopathy and the Battle of Ideas in the New Science* (London: Thorsons, 1995).

Rupert Sheldrake, *A New Science of Life: The Hypothesis of Formative Causation* (London: Blond & Briggs, 1981).

———, *The Presence of the Past: Morphic Resonance and the Habits of Nature* (London: Collins, 1988).

Sir John Sinclair, *The Alice Bailey Inheritance* (Wellingborough: Turnstone Press, 1984).

Edward Reaugh Smith, *The Burning Bush: Rudolf Steiner, Anthroposophy, and the Holy Scriptures, Terms and Phrases*, Vol. 1, rev. ed. (Great Barrington, Mass.: Anthroposophic Press, 2001).

David V. Tansley, *Chakras—Rays and Radionics* (Saffron Walden, UK: C. W. Daniel, 1984).

————, *Dimensions of Radionics: New Techniques of Instrumented Distant-Healing* (Saffron Walden: C. W. Daniel, 1977).

————, *Radionics: Science or Magic?* (Saffron Walden, UK: C. W. Daniel, 1982).

————, *Radionics and the Subtle Anatomy of Man* (Rustington, UK: Health Science Press, 1972).

Gregory Tillett, *The Elder Brother: A Biography of Charles Webster Leadbeater* (London: Routledge & Kegan Paul, 1982).

S. W. Tromp, *Psychical Physics: A Scientific Analysis of Dowsing, Radiesthesia, and Kindred Divining Phenomena* (New York: Elsevier, 1949).

Peter Washington, *Madame Blavatsky's Baboon: Theosophy and the Emergence of the Western Guru* (London: Secker & Warburg, 1993).

Gerhard Wehr, *Jung and Steiner: The Birth of a New Psychology* (Great Barrington, Mass.: Anthroposophic Press, 2002).

Edward C. Whitmont, *Psyche and Substance: Essays on Homeopathy in the Light of Jungian Psychology* (Berkeley, Calif.: North Atlantic Books, 1991).

Notes

INTRODUCTION

1. Kocku von Stuckrad, *Western Esotericism: A Brief History of Secret Knowledge,* translated by Nicholas Goodrick-Clarke (London: Equinox, 2005), p. 3.

2. Henry Corbin, *Alone with the Alone: Creative Imagination in the Sufism of Ibn 'Arabi* (Princeton, N.J.: Princeton University Press, 1997), p. 4. First published in French as *L'Imagination créatrice dans le Soufisme d'Ibn 'Arabi* by Flammarion in 1958.

3. Ibid., pp. 209, 215.

4. Antoine Faivre, *Access to Western Esotericism* (Albany: State University of New York Press, 1994), p. 7. A translation of two works first published as *Accès de l'Esoterisme occidental* (Paris: Gallimard, 1986) and *L'Esoterisme* (Paris: Presses Universitaires de France, 1992).

5. Ibid., pp. 10–15. A similar presentation is offered in Antoine Faivre, "Introduction I," in *Modern Esoteric Spirituality*, edited by Antoine Faivre and Jacob Needleman (London: SCM Press, 1993), pp. xv–xx.

6. Wouter Hanegraaff, "On the Construction of 'Esoteric Traditions,'" in *Western Esotericism and the Science of Religion,* edited by Antoine Faivre and Wouter J. Hanegraaff (Leuven: Peeters, 1998), pp. 19–42.

7. Ibid., pp. 42–61.

8. Arthur Versluis, "What Is Esoteric? Methods in the Study of Western Esotericism," *Esoterica* 4 (2002): 1–15, available at http://www.esoteric.msu.edu/VolumeIV/Methods.htm, pp. 2–3.

9. Ibid., p. 6.

10. Hans G. Kippenberg, *Discovering Religious History in the Modern Age* (Princeton, N.J.: Princeton University Press, 2002).

11. Kocku von Stuckrad, *Western Esotericism,* pp. 9–10.

12. Ibid., p. 10.

13. Cf. Marcello Truzzi, "Definition and Dimensions of the Occult: Towards a So-ciological Perspective," *On the Margin of the Visible: Sociology, the Esoteric, and the Occult,* edited by Edward Tiryakian (New York: John Wiley, 1974), pp. 243–255.

14. James Webb, *The Flight from Reason* (London: Macdonald, 1971) and *The Occult Establishment* (La Salle, Ill.: Open Court, 1976).

15. Kocku von Stuckrad, *Western Esotericism*, p. 11.

CHAPTER 1

1. Antoine Faivre, "Ancient and Medieval Sources of Modern Esoteric Move-ments," in *Modern Esoteric Spirituality*, edited by Antoine Faivre and Jacob Needleman (London: SCM Press, 1993), pp. 3–12.

2. Brian P. Copenhaver, *Hermetica: The Greek* Corpus Hermeticum *and the Latin* Asclepius *in a New English Translation* (Cambridge: Cambridge University Press, 1992), pp. xvi–xxiii.

3. Garth Fowden, *The Egyptian Hermes: A Historical Approach to the Late Pagan Mind,* 2nd ed. (Princeton, N.J.: Princeton University Press, 1993), pp. 17–19.

4. G. R. S. Mead, *Echoes from the Gnosis,* 12 vols. (London & Benares, 1906–1908), VIII, *The Chaldean Oracles,* Vol. 1 (1908), p. 1; second edition complete in one volume (Hast-ings: Chthonios Books, 1987), p. 179. Cf. Clare Goodrick-Clarke and Nicholas Goodrick-Clarke, *G. R. S. Mead and the Gnostic Quest* (Berkeley, Calif.; North Atlantic Books, 2005), p. 12.

5. Garth Fowden, *Egyptian Hermes*, pp. 22f.

6. Ibid., pp. 25f.

7. Ibid., p. 25.

8. Ibid., pp. 27–28; Antoine Faivre, *The Eternal Hermes from Greek God to Al-chemical Magus* (Grand Rapids, Mich.: Phanes Press, 1995), pp. 15–16.

9. Brian P. Copenhaver, *Hermetica*, pp. xxxii–xxxiii.

10. The following English translations are taken from *The Way of Hermes: The Corpus Hermeticum*, translated by Clement Salaman, Dorine van Oyen, and William D. Wharton (London: Duckworth, 1999). This citation is from *CH* 11.20.

11. Faivre, "Ancient and Medieval Sources," p. 5.

12. Ibid., pp. 1, 5.

13. E. R. Dodds, *Pagan and Christian in an Age of Anxiety: Some Aspects of Reli-gious Experience from Marcus Aurelius to Constantine* (Cambridge: Cambridge University Press, 1965), p. 3; John Gregory, *The Neoplatonists* (London: Kyle Cathie, 1991), p. vii. An authoritative introduction to Neoplatonic thought is offered by Richard T. Wallis, *Neo-platonism* (London: Duckworth, 1972).

14. Standard editions of this work are Plotinus, *The Enneads,* translated by Stephen MacKenna, 4th ed., revised by B. S. Page (London: Faber & Faber, 1969), and an abridged edition with an introduction by John Dillon (London: Penguin, 1991). Representative se-lections are available in *The Essential Plotinus*, selected and translated by Elmer O'Brien, 2nd ed. (Indianapolis: Hackett, 1986).

15. Convenient summaries of Plotinus's thought may be found in John Gregory, *The Neoplatonists*, pp. 3–18; and in Pierre Hadot, "Neoplatonist Spirituality: I. Plotinus

and Porphyry," in *Classical Mediterranean Spirituality: Egyptian—Greek—Roman*, edited by A. H. Armstrong (London: Routledge & Kegan Paul, 1986), pp. 230–249.

16. Porphyry, *Life of Plotinus*, in *Plotinus*, translated by A. H. Armstrong, Loeb Classical Library (London: Heinemann, 1966), quoted in Hadot, "Neoplatonist Spirituality," pp. 230f.

17. *Porphyry's Letter to His Wife Marcella*, translated by Alice Zimmern, introduction by David Fideler (Grand Rapids, Mich.: Phanes Press, 1991). This translation was first published as *Porphyry the Philosopher to His Wife Marcella* (London: George Redway, 1896).

18. On Iamblichus, theurgy, and Proclus, see A. C. Lloyd, "The Later Neoplatonists," in *The Cambridge History of Later Greek and Early Medieval Philosophy*, edited by A. H. Armstrong (Cambridge: Cambridge University Press, 1970), pp. 272–330. A useful edition is Iamblichus, *On the Mysteries of the Egyptians, Chaldeans, and Assyrians*, translated by Thomas Taylor, with a new bio-bibliographical glossary (San Diego, Calif.: Wizards Bookshelf, 1984).

19. For a recent survey of his life and thought, see Lucas Siorvanes, *Proclus: Neo-Platonic Philosophy and Science* (New Haven, Conn.: Yale University Press, 1996).

20. A recent English-language edition is *The Chaldean Oracles*, translated and edited by Ruth Majercik (Leiden: Brill, 1989). Their text and esoteric content is commented on at length in Mead, *Echoes from the Gnosis*, VIII. *Chaldean Oracles*, Vols. 1 and 2, pp. 175–224. On the oracles and theurgy, see H. D. Saffrey, "Neoplatonist Spirituality: From Iamblichus to Proclus and Damascius," in *Classical Mediterranean Spirituality: Egyptian—Greek—Roman*, edited by A. H. Armstrong (London: Routledge & Kegan Paul, 1986), pp. 252–254.

21. Gnostic cosmology is an enormous subject and has received much scholarly attention. Earlier studies include Hans Jonas, *The Gnostic Religion: The Message of the Alien God and the Beginnings of Christianity*, 2nd ed. (Boston, Mass.: Beacon Press, 1963); Kurt Rudolph, *Gnosis: The Nature and History of an Ancient Religion* (Edinburgh: T. & T. Clark, 1983); Giovanni Filoramo, *A History of Gnosticism* (Oxford: Basil Blackwell, 1990). See also Roelof van den Broek, "Gnosticism I: Gnostic Religion," in *Dictionary of Gnosis and Western Esotericism*, edited by Wouter Hanegraaff et al., 2 vols. (Leiden: Brill, 2005), Vol. 1, pp. 403–416. Van den Broek argues that the Gnostic movement is not solely a Christian heresy but that it developed in the same spiritual context as early Christianity and was influenced by the mythical expression of Jewish ideas.

22. The important distinction between the sharp ontological dualism and world rejection of Gnosticism and the philosophical monism and relative world-affirmation of Neoplatonism and Hermetism is argued in Roelof van den Broek, "Gnosticism and Hermetism in Antiquity: Two Roads to Salvation," in *Gnosis and Hermeticism from Antiquity to Modern Times*, edited by Roelof van den Broek and Wouter J. Hanegraaff (Albany: State University of New York Press, 1998), pp. 1–20.

CHAPTER 2

1. Arnold J. Toynbee, *Hellenism: The History of a Civilization* (London: Oxford University Press, 1959).

2. A standard work remains authoritative: *Byzantium: An Introduction to East Roman Civilization*, edited by Norman H. Baynes and H. St.L. B. Moss (Oxford: Oxford

University Press, 1961); see also Cyril Mango, *Byzantium: The Empire of the New Rome* (London: Weidenfeld & Nicolson, 1980).

3. Antoine Faivre, *The Eternal Hermes: From Greek God to Alchemical Magus* (Grand Rapids, Mich.: Phanes Press, 1995), pp. 18–21.

4. For the transmission and reception of Hermetic and esoteric ideas in the Middle Ages, see Brian P. Copenhaver, *Hermetica: The Greek* Corpus Hermeticum *and the Latin* Asclepius *in a New English Translation* (Cambridge: Cambridge University Press, 1992), pp. xlv–xlvii; Antoine Faivre, "Ancient and Medieval Sources of Modern Esoteric Movements," in *Modern Esoteric Spirituality*, edited by Antoine Faivre and Jacob Needleman (London: SCM Press, 1993), pp. 26–31, 42–46; Antoine Faivre, *Access to Western Esotericism* (Albany: State University of New York Press, 1994), pp. 53–55.

5. In his study of medieval European magical traditions, Kieckhefer makes a sharp distinction between the occult sciences (astrology, alchemy, magic) mediated by Arabic and Jewish scholarship and native pagan practices, Richard Kieckhefer, *Magic in the Middle Ages* (Cambridge: Cambridge University Press, 1989).

6. Steven Runciman, *Byzantine Civilization* (London: Methuen, 1961), pp. 294–298.

7. Charles G. Nauert, *Humanism and the Culture of Renaissance Europe* (Cambridge: Cambridge University Press, 1995), pp. 26–28. For the vital role of Coluccio Salutati and other Renaissance humanists in the revival of Greek learning, see also the older work of Denys Hay, *The Italian Renaissance in Its Historical Background* (Cambridge: Cambridge University Press, 1961). The interaction between humanism, Aristotelian philosophy, and Renaissance Platonism and their preponderance in various thinkers is addressed in Paul Oskar Kristeller, *Renaissance Thought: The Classic, Scholastic, and Humanist Strains* (New York: Harper & Row, 1961), and *Renaissance Thought II: Papers on Humanism and the Arts* (New York: Harper & Row, 1965).

8. John Monfasani, *Byzantine Scholars in Renaissance Italy: Cardinal Bessarion and Other Émigres* (Aldershot: Variorum, 1995).

9. Marcel Brion, *The Medici: A Great Florentine Family* (London: Ferndale, 1980), provides a richly illustrated volume on the Medici contribution to Florentine culture and an introductory history of the dynasty. See also Maurice Rowdon, *Lorenzo the Magnificent* (London: Purnell, 1974).

10. James Hankins, *Plato in the Italian Renaissance*, 2 vols. (Leiden: Brill, 1990), offers a definitive account of the Platonic revival in Florence and elsewhere in Italy.

11. A concise account of the life and thought of Ficino, together with an anthology of his works and a research bibliography is provided by Angela Voss, *Marsilio Ficino*, Western Esoteric Masters series (Berkeley, Calif.: North Atlantic Books, 2006). See also Michael J. B. Allen, "Marsilo Ficino," in *Dictionary of Gnosis and Western Esotericism*, edited by Wouter Hanegraaff et al. (Leiden: Brill, 2005), Vol. 1, pp. 360–367; M. J. B. Allen, *The Platonism of Marsilio Ficino* (Berkeley: University of California Press, 1984); and M. J. B. Allen and Valery Rees, eds., *Marsilio Ficino: His Theology, His Philosophy, His Legacy* (Leiden: Brill, 2002).

12. Frances A. Yates, *Giordano Bruno and the Hermetic Tradition* (Chicago: University of Chicago Press, 1964), pp. 12–17.

13. Antoine Faivre, *The Eternal Hermes*, p. 40. For the continued vigor of the Hermetic tradition in the Renaissance and early modern period, see Stuckrad, *Western Esotericism*, p. 56.

14. Marsilio Ficino, *Commentary on Plato's Symposium on Love*, translated and edited by Sears Jayne (Woodstock, Conn.: Spring Publications, 1999).

15. Marsilio Ficino, *Platonic Theology*, translated and edited by Michael J. B. Allen and James Hankins, 6 vols. (Cambridge, Mass.: Harvard University Press, 2001–2006).

16. Ficino's letters are published in English as *The Letters of Marsilio Ficino*, 6 vols. (London: Shepheard-Walwyn, 1975–1990). See also *Meditations on the Soul: Selected Letters of Marsilio Ficino* (Rochester, Vt.: Inner Traditions International, 1997).

17. Nauert, *Humanism and the Culture of Renaissance Europe*, p. 60; Arthur Field, *The Origins of the Platonic Academy in Florence* (Princeton, N.J.: Princeton University Press, 1988); Paul Oskar Kristeller, *Eight Philosophers of the Renaissance* (Stanford, Calif.: Stanford University Press, 1964), pp. 41–42; cf. James Hankins, "The Myth of the Platonic Academy of Florence," *Renaissance Quarterly* 44 (1991): 429–475.

18. Ficino's Neoplatonic cosmology and philosophy of the soul and his reception of Hermetism is summarized in Angela Voss, *Marsilio Ficino*, pp. 8–21, and in Paul Oskar Kristeller, *Eight Philosophers of the Renaissance*, pp. 42–48. A detailed account of his reading of the *Corpus Hermeticum* and *Asclepius* is found in F. A. Yates, *Giordano Bruno and the Hermetic Tradition*, pp. 20–38.

19. Nauert, *Humanism and the Culture of Renaissance Europe*, pp. 62–66.

20. F. A. Yates, *Giordano Bruno and the Hermetic Tradition*, pp. 67–68.

21. The sources of Ficino's magic in medieval writers and Neoplatonic texts are extensively discussed in D. P. Walker, *Spiritual and Demonic Magic from Ficino to Campanella* (Stroud: Sutton, 2000), pp. 36–44.

22. F. A. Yates, *Giordano Bruno and the Hermetic Tradition*, pp. 62–63.

23. Francesco Cattani da Diacceto's eyewitness description of Ficino's astrological magic is discussed and quoted at length in Walker, *Spiritual and Demonic Magic*, pp. 30–35. Walker's source is Diacetto, *Opera omnia* (Basle, 1563), pp. 45–46.

24. For the ramifications of Ficico's of music-spirit theory, see Walker, *Spiritual and Demonic Magic*, pp. 3–24, and F. A. Yates, *Giordano Bruno and the Hermetic Tradition*, pp. 68–82.

25. Frances Yates offers a summary chapter on Pico's life and contribution to Kabbalistic magic in *Giordano Bruno and the Hermetic Tradition*, pp. 84–116. Cf. Paul Oskar Kristeller, *Eight Philosophers of the Renaissance*, pp. 54–71. For his Jewish teacher, see Chaim Wirszubiski's introduction to his edition of Flavius Mithridates, *Sermo de passione Dei* (Jerusalem, 1963) and his article "Giovanni Pico's Companion to Kabbalistic Symbolism," in *Studies in Mysticism and Religion*, presented to G. G. Scholem (Jerusalem, 1967), pp. 353–362.

26. For a helpful account of the historical development of Jewish Kabbalah as a current of Western esotericism, see Kocku von Stuckrad, *Western Esotericism*, pp. 31–41. Definitive studies of are offered by Gershom Scholem, *Kabbalah* (New York: Penguin/Meridian, 1978), and *Origins of the Kabbalah*, edited by R. J. Werblowsky, translated by A. Arkush (Princeton, N.J.: Princeton University Press, 1990); Moshe Idel, *Kabbalah: New Perspectives* (New Haven, Conn.: Yale University Press, 1988); *The Early Kabbalah*, edited by Joseph Dan, translated by R. C. Kiener (New York: Paulist Press, 1986).

27. Kristeller, *Eight Philosophers of the Renaissance*, pp. 61f, takes up the theme of Pico's syncretism and interest in establishing "concordance" (Faivre's fifth characteristic of esotericism) between the Kabbalah and the Bible within a *prisca theologia* identified with Hermes and Zoroaster. A substantial monograph on Pico's thought with special reference to his Roman debate and the full text of his nine hundred theses is offered by Stephen Alan Farmer, *Syncretism in the West: Pico's 900 Theses (1486)*, Medieval and Renaissance Studies 167 (Tempe: Arizona State University Press, 1998).

28. F. A. Yates, *Giordano Bruno and the Hermetic Tradition*, pp. 91, 95.

29. Ibid., pp. 96–97.

30. Ibid., pp. 98–102.

31. The *Oration on the Dignity of Man* is discussed by Kristeller, *Eight Philosophers of the Renaissance*, pp. 65–68. See also the full English translation of the text and commentary by Kristeller in *The Renaissance Philosophy of Man*, edited by Ernst Cassirer, Paul Oskar Kristeller, John Herman Randall (Chicago: University of Chicago Press, 1956), pp. 215–256.

32. Kristeller, *Renaissance Philosophy of Man*, pp. 223; the quotation refers to the sixth passage in the *Asclepius*. Cf. Copenhaver, *Hermetica*, p. 69.

33. S. A. Farmer, *Syncretism in the West*, pp. 204–205, offers an outline of Pico's first 400 theses which trace philosophy from the Latin scholastics back to the harmonious ancients and "Hebrew Cabalist wisemen." This quasihistorical survey reflects Pico's insistence on correspondences within an emanational cosmology. Cf. *Oration*, in *The Renaissance Philosophy of Man*, pp. 242–249.

34. Kristeller, *Renaissance Philosophy of Man*, p. 250.

35. Kristeller, *Eight Italian Philosophers of the Renaissance*, pp. 56–57.

CHAPTER 3

1. Frances A. Yates includes an introductory study of Johannes Reuchlin in her *The Occult Philosophy in the Elizabethan Age* (London: Routledge & Kegan Paul, 1979), pp. 23–27. See Lewis W. Spitz, "Pythagoras Reborn," *The Religious Renaissance of the German Humanists* (Cambridge, Mass.: Harvard University Press, 1963), pp. 61–80. See also Joseph Dan, "Johannes Reuchlin," *Dictionary of Gnosis and Western Esotericism*, edited by Wouter Hanegraaff et al. (Leiden: Brill, 2005), Vol. 2, pp. 990–993. A standard biography in German by L. Geiger, *Johannes Reuchlin: Sein Leben und seine Werke* (Leipzig: Duncher & Humboldt, 1871), was reprinted in 1964.

2. Reuchlin's contribution to Christian Cabala is documented in the pioneering and still definitive study of the subject by François Secret, *Les Kabbalistes Chrétiens de la Renaissance* (Paris: Dunod, 1964), pp. 44–70. A close analysis of his treatise on the "wonder-working word" is presented in Charles Zika, "Reuchlin's *De verbo mirifico* and the Magic Debate of the Late Fifteenth Century," *Journal of the Warburg and Courtauld Institutes* 30 (1976): 104–138.

3. The standard work on Trithemius is Noel L. Brann, *The Abbot Trithemius (1462–1516): The Renaissance of Monastic Humanism* (Leiden: Brill, 1981). For closer scrutiny of his thoughts on magic, see Noel L. Brann, *Trithemius and Magical Theology: A Chapter in the Controversy over Occult Studies in Early Modern Europe* (Albany: State University of New York Press, 1999).

4. *The Steganographia of Johannes Trithemius*, Book I, translated by Fiona Tait and Christopher Upton, with Book III, translated by J. W. H. Walden, edited by Adam McLean (Edinburgh: Magnum Opus Hermetic Sourceworks, 1982).

5. Frank Baron, "Trithemius und Faustus: Begegnungen in Geschichte und Sage," in *Johannes Trithemius; Humanismus und Magie im vorreformatorischen Deutschland,* edited by Richard Auernheimer and Frank Baron, Bad Kreuznacher Symposien 1 (Munich: Profil, 1991), pp. 39–60, and *Doctor Faustus from History to Legend* (Munich: Wilhelm Fink, 1978).

6. Noel L. Brann, "Johannes Trithemius," *Dictionary of Gnosis and Western Esotericism,* edited by Wouter Hanegraaff et al. (Leiden: Brill, 2005), Vol. 2, p. 1137.

7. For Agrippa's life and works, see Charles G. Nauert, *Agrippa and the Crisis of Renaissance Thought* (Urbana: University of Illinois Press, 1965). Frances A. Yates offers a nutshell account in *The Occult Philosophy in the Elizabethan Age,* pp. 37–47. See also Michaela Valente, "Heinrich Cornelius Agrippa," in *Dictionary of Gnosis and Western Esotericism,* edited by Wouter Hanegraaff et al. (Leiden: Brill, 2005), Vol. 1, 4–8. An older and somewhat imaginative biography is Henry Morley, *Cornelius Agrippa: The Life of Henry Cornelius Agrippa von Nettesheim, Doctor and Knight, Commonly known as a Magician,* 2 vols. (London: Chapman & Hall, 1856).

8. Nauert, *Agrippa and the Crisis of Renaissance Thought,* pp. 25–27.

9. Frances A. Yates offers an analysis of Agrippa's *De occulta philosophia* in *Giordano Bruno and the Hermetic Tradition* (Chicago: University of Chicago Press, 1964), pp. 130–143. See also D. P. Walker, *Spiritual and Demonic Magic from Ficino to Campanella* (Stroud: Sutton, 2000), pp. 90–96. A more recent study is Christopher I. Lehrich, *The Language of Demons and Angels: Cornelius Agrippa's Occult Philosophy* (Leiden: Brill, 2003).

10. The most accessible English-language edition of the work is Henry Cornelius Agrippa of Nettesheim, *Three Books of Occult Philosophy,* translated by James Freake, edited by Donald Tyson (St. Paul, Minn.: Llewellyn Publications, 1993).

11. Ibid., pp. 237–298.

12. Ibid., Book III, chap. 12 (pp. 484–486).

13. Agrippa's travels and studies among the Italian Kabbalists are documented in detail in Nauert, *Agrippa and the Crisis of Renaissance Thought,* pp. 35–54.

14. Ibid., pp. 41, 46–47.

15. Ibid., pp. 123–127.

16. Ibid., p. 49.

17. Ibid., pp. 330–331. Cf. Anton Reichl, "Goethes Faust und Agrippa von Nettesheim," *Euphorion* 4 (1897): 287–301; Gerhard Ritter, "Ein historisches Urbild zu Goethes Faust (Agrippa von Nettesheym)," *Preussische Jahrbücher* 141 (1910): 300–305.

18. The earliest biography of John Dee was published in Latin by Dr. Thomas Smith in 1707 and translated into English as *The Life of John Dee,* translated by William Alexander Ayton (London: Theosophical Publishing Society, 1908). Another early study was Charlotte Fell Smith, *John Dee: 1527–1608* (London: Constable, 1909). More recent studies of his career include Peter J. French, *John Dee: The World of an Elizabethan Magus* (London: Routledge & Kegan Paul, 1972); William H. Sherman, *John Dee: The Politics of Reading and Writing in the English Renaissance* (Amherst: University of Massachusetts Press, 1995); Benjamin Woolley, *The Queen's Conjuror: The Science and Magic of Dr. Dee*

(London: HarperCollins, 2001) and György E. Szönyi, *John Dee's Occultism: Magical Exaltation through Powerful Signs* (Albany: State University of New York Press, 2004).

19. French, *John Dee*, pp. 24–29.

20. Ibid., pp. 34–35.

21. Ibid., pp. 44, 50–55.

22. F. A. Yates, *The Occult Philosophy in the Elizabethan Age*, p. 80. Cf. Peter French, *John Dee*, p. 61.

23. Nicholas H. Clulee, *John Dee's Natural Philosophy: Between Science and Religion* (London: Routledge, 1988), pp. 52–57. The original text is printed in a modern edition as *John Dee on Astronomy: "Propaedeumata Aphoristica" (1558 and 1568), Latin and English*, edited by Wayne Shumaker (Berkeley: University of California Press, 1978).

24. "A Translation of John Dee's *Monas hieroglyphica*, with an Introduction and Annotations," translated and edited by C. H. Josten, *Ambix* 12 (1964): 113–114.

25. Frances A. Yates, *The Art of Memory* (Chicago: University of Chicago Press, 1966), p. 263; and Frances A. Yates, *The Rosicrucian Enlightenment* (London: Routledge & Kegan Paul, 1972), p. xii.

26. Clulee, *John Dee's Natural Philosophy*, p. 78.

27. Ibid., pp. 86–115.

28. There is an extensive analysis of Dee and Kelley's practice and records of angel magic in Clulee, *John Dee's Natural Philosophy*, pp. 203–228. The angelic communications are the special subject of Deborah E. Harkness, *John Dee's Conversations with Angels: Cabala, Alchemy, and the End of Nature* (Cambridge: Cambridge University Press, 1999). For the original text of the conversations, see John Dee, *A True and Faithful Relation of what passed for many Yeers between Dr. John Dee and Some Spirits*, edited by Meric Casaubon (London, 1659; repr. New York: Magickal Childe, 1992).

29. John Dee, *A True and Faithful Relation*, cited in Clulee, *John Dee's Natural Philosophy*, p. 206.

30. *The Heptarchia Mystica of John Dee*, 2nd enlarged ed., edited by Robert Turner (Wellingborough: Aquarian Press, 1986).

31. A English-language transcript of the *48 Angelic Keys*, together with *The Book of Knowledge, Help and Earthly Victory*, and *A Book of Supplications and Invocations*, is printed in Robert Turner, *Elizabethan Magic: The Art and the Magus* (Shaftesbury: Element, 1989). Extracts of the same are also available in John Dee, *The Enochian Evocation of Dr. John Dee*, translated and edited by Geoffrey James (Gilette, N.J.: Heptangle Books, 1984).

32. Clulee, *John Dee's Natural Philosophy*, p. 214.

CHAPTER 4

1. There are several worthwhile older introductions to the history of alchemy, including F. Sherwood Taylor, *The Alchemists* (London: Heinemann, 1952); E. J. Holmyard, *Alchemy* (London: Penguin, 1957); and John Read, *Prelude to Chemistry* (London: G. Bell & Sons, 1936). For a survey of the latest scholarship and bibliographies, see the following entries in Volume 1 of the *Dictionary of Gnosis and Western Esotericism*, edited by Wouter Hanegraaff et al. (Leiden: Brill, 2005): Bernard D. Haage, "Alchemy II:

Antiquity–12th Century," 16–34; Herwig Buntz, "Alchemy III: 12th/13th–15th Century," 34–41; Allison Coudert, "Alchemy IV: 16th–18th Century," 42–50; and Richard Caron, "Alchemy V: 19th–20th Century," 50–58.

2. Read, *Prelude to Chemistry,* pp. 17–19.

3. For an edition of Jabir, see *The Works of Geber, Englished by Richard Russell, 1678,* a new edition with introduction by E. J. Holmyard (London: J.M. Dent, 1928).

4. Holmyard, *Alchemy,* pp. 97–100; cf. Antoine Faivre, *The Eternal Hermes,* pp. 18–20, 89–92; J. Ruska, *Tabula Smaragdina* (Heidelberg, 1926).

5. Cited in Holmyard, *Alchemy,* pp. 97f.

6. G. S. A. Ranking, "The Life and Works of Rhazes," in *Proceedings of the Seventeenth International Congress of Medicine* (London, 1913), pp. 237–268.

7. Holmyard's *Alchemy,* pp. 105ff, offers a concise survey of early medieval European alchemy. See also J. Pruig, "The Transmission and Reception of Arabic Philosophy in Christian Spain (until 1200)," in *The Introduction of Arabic Philosophy into Europe,* edited by Charles E. Butterworth and Blake Andrée Kessel (Leiden: Brill, 1994), pp. 7–30, and other chapters in this volume.

8. Ripley's and Norton's works were reprinted by the English antiquary Elias Ashmole in 1652, available in a modern reprint. Elias Ashmole, *Theatrum Chemicum Britannicum, containing severall poeticall pieces of our famous English philosophers, who have written the Hermetique Mysteries in their owne Ancient Language, 1652,* with a new introduction by Allen G. Debus (New York: Johnson, 1967); Eirenaeus Philalethes, *Exposition upon Sir George Ripley's Vision* (1677), is reprinted in Stanislas Klossowski de Rola, *Alchemy: The Secret Art* (London: Thames & Hudson, 1973), pp. 23–30. Norton's work is also available in a modern edition, *The Ordinall of Alchimy,* edited by E. J. Holmyard (London, 1928). See also J. Reidy, "Thomas Norton and the *Ordinall of Alchimy,*" *Ambix* 6, 2 (December 1957): 59–85. The royal interest in Ripley and Norton's alchemy is documented in Jonathan Hughes, *Arthurian Myths and Alchemy: The Kingship of Edward IV* (Stroud, Glos: Sutton, 2002).

9. For an introductory study of Paracelsus, see my *Paracelsus: Essential Readings,* Western Esoteric Masters series (Berkeley, Calif.: North Atlantic Books, 1999), pp. 13–37. For a detailed survey of his work and thought, see Udo Benzenhöfer and Urs Leo Gantenbein, "Paracelsus," in *Dictionary of Gnosis and Western Esotericism,* edited by Wouter Hanegraaff et al. (Leiden: Brill, 2005), Vol. 2, pp. 922–931. Early studies of interest are Basilio de Telepnef, *Paracelsus: A Genius amidst a Troubled World* (St. Gallen, [1945]); and John Hargrave, *The Life and Soul of Paracelsus* (London: Victor Gollanncz, 1951). Strongly recommended as scholarly studies are Walter Pagel, *Paracelsus: An Introduction to Philosophical Medicine in the Era of the Renaissance,* 2nd rev. ed. (Basle: Karger, 1982); and Andrew Weeks, *Paracelsus: Speculative Theory and the Crisis of the Early Reformation* (Albany: State University of New York Press, 1997). A recent biography of note is Philip Ball, *The Devil's Doctor: Paracelsus and the World of Renaissance Magic and Science* (London: Heinemann, 2006).

10. Pagel, *Paracelsus,* pp. 10–13.

11. The itineraries and stations of Paracelus's early peregrinations in Europe and the Near East remain speculative, based as they are on scattered autobiographical

references in his own works. See Basilio de Telepnef, *Paracelsus*, map; Pagel, *Paracelsus: An Introduction*, pp. 13–14; Weeks, *Paracelsus: Speculative Theory*, pp. 6–7; Ball, *Devil's Doctor*, pp. 75–79 and map on endpapers.

12. Pagel, *Paracelsus: An Introduction*, pp. 18–20.

13. Ibid., pp. 21–22.

14. Ibid., pp. 24–25. For excerpts from the *Paragranum* and *Opus Paramirum*, see Nicholas Goodrick-Clarke, *Paracelsus: Essential Readings*, pp. 71–75, 76–100.

15. Pagel, *Paracelsus: An Introduction*, pp. 26–29; Ball, *Devil's Doctor*, pp. 348–353.

16. For a detailed discussion of Paracelsus's theory of matter, the elements, and the three philosophical principles, see Pagel, *Paracelsus: An Introduction*, pp. 82–95, 100–104.

17. Pagel, *Paracelsus: An Introduction*, pp. 50–55, 65–72.

18. Ibid., pp. 59–65.

19. Ibid., p. 83.

20. Ibid., pp. 146–148.

21. Marsilio Ficino, *Apologia quaedam, in qua de medicina*, appended to his edition of Iamblichus, *De mysteriis Aegyptorum* (1497) and his own *De triplici vita* (Venice, 1516), cited in Pagel, *Paracelsus: An Introduction*, p. 222.

22. Ibid., p. 223.

23. Ibid., pp. 174–176. Weeks, *Paracelsus: Speculative Theory*, pp. 57f, notes that other scholars, notably Kurt Goldammer, have also observed the differences between Ficino and Paracelsus.

24. Ibid., pp. 178–180.

25. *Astronomia Magna, in Paracelsus Sämtliche Werke*, edited by Karl Sudhoff and Wilhem Matthiessen (Munich and Berlin: O. W. Barth then R. Oldenbourg, 1922–1933), xii, 8–9, cited in Nicholas Goodrick-Clarke, *Paracelsus: Essential Readings*, p. 111.

26. *Astronomia Magna, in Paracelsus Sämtliche Werke*, xii, 20–21, cited in ibid., p. 113.

27. Carlos Gilly, "Theophrastia Sancta: Paracelsianism as a Religion in Conflict with the Established Churches," available at http://www.ritmanlibrary.nl/c/p/res/art/art_01.html.

28. See Allen G. Debus, *The English Paracelsians* (London: Oldbourne, 1965).

29. Helena Blavatsky, *Isis Unveiled: A Master-Key to the Mysteries of Ancient and Modern Science and Theology* (New York: J. W. Bouton, 1877), Vol. 1, pp. 167–171; Franz Hartmann, *The Life of Philippus Theophrastus Bombast of Hohenheim, better known by the name of Paracelsus, and the substance of his teachings* (London: G. Redway, 1887); Rudolf Steiner, *Mystics of the Renaissance* (London: Theosophical Publishing Society, 1911).

30. C. G. Jung, "Paracelsus as a Spiritual Phenomenon," in *Alchemical Studies*, Vol. 13 of *The Collected Works of C. G. Jung* (London: Routledge & Kegan Paul, 1967).

CHAPTER 5

1. B. J. Kidd, *The Counter-Reformation, 1550–1600* (London: SPCK, 1963), p. 9. The impact and regional variety of the Reformation is documented extensively in Diarmaid

MacCulloch, *Reformation: Europe's House Divided, 1490–1700* (London: Allen Lane, 2003).

2. Ernst Troeltsch, *Die Soziallehren der christlichen Kirchen,* in *Gesammelte Schriften* I (Tübingen: Mohr, 1923), pp. 863–864, 898. See a recent discussion in Karl-Fritz Daiber, "Mysticism: Troeltsch's Third Type of Religious Collectivities," *Social Compass* 49, 3 (2002): 329–341.

3. See Rufus M. Jones, *Spiritual Reformers in the Sixteenth and Seventeenth Centuries* (London: Macmillan, 1914); and R. Emmet McLaughlin, *Caspar Schwenckfeld, Reluctant Radical: His Life to 1540* (New Haven, Conn.: Yale University Press, 1896).

4. Andrew Weeks, *Boehme: An Intellectual Biography of the Seventeenth-Century Philosopher and Mystic* (Albany: State University of New York Press, 1991), pp. 23–26.

5. Details on Scultetus and the Görlitz Paracelsians may be found in Ernst Koch, "Scultetica," *Das Neue Lausitzische Magazin* 92 (1916): 20–58, which is the basis of the account in Weeks, *Boehme,* pp. 27–31.

6. Details of Balthasar Walter are recorded by Boehme's first biographer, Abraham Franckenberg, *Gründlicher und wahrhafter Bericht von dem Leben und dem Abschied des in Gott selig ruhenden Jacob Boehmes,* in Jacob Böhme, *Sämtliche Schriften,* edited by Will-Erich Peuckert and August Faust (Stuttgart: Fromanns Verlag, 1955–1961), Vol. 10.

7. A summary account of Boehme's childhood, his apprenticeship, and his mystical experiences in 1600 and 1610 are related in Hans L. Martensen, *Jacob Boehme: His Life and Teaching,* translated by T. Rhys Evans (London: Hodder & Stoughton, 1885), pp. 1–16. A new revised edition is *Jacob Boehme (1575–1624): Studies in His Life and Teaching,* edited by Stephen Hobhouse (London: Rockliff, 1949), pp. 1–14.

8. Boehme gives a firsthand account of his first mystical experience in *Aurora,* translated by John Sparrow (London, 1656; repr. Edmonds, Wash.: Holmes, 1992), chap. 19, §5–14 (pp. 486–488).

9. Boehme's acceptance of the Copernican system is discussed in Martensen, *Jacob Boehme* (1949 ed.), p. 150f; cf. Andrew Weeks, *Boehme,* pp. 57–59.

10. Boehme compares God to a divine substrate *Salitter* (or *Salnitrum*),which manifests in a succession of "qualities" in *Aurora,* chap. 4, §8–51 (pp. 89–97).

11. For a discussion of the divine substance *Salitter* and its correlation to niter, see Weeks, *Boehme,* pp. 65–68.

12. Boehme, *Aurora,* chaps. 8–11 (pp. 147–266).

13. Weeks, *Boehme,* p. 73.

14. Martensen, *Jacob Boehme* (1949 ed.), pp. 6–8; Weeks, *Boehme,* pp. 93–95.

15. Arthur Versluis, *Wisdom's Children: A Christian Esoteric Tradition* (Albany: State University of New York Press, 1999), pp. 11–14.

16. Weeks, *Boehme,* pp. 106–109.

17. Jacob Boehme, *The Three Principles of the Divine Essence* (Chicago: Yogi Publication Society, 1909), chap. 1, §11–12 (pp. 16–17); chap. 2, §7–13 (pp. 20–23); chap. 3, §12–19 (pp. 27–30); and chap. 5, §8–16 (pp. 53–56).

18. Jacob Boehme, *The Signature of All Things* (Cambridge: James Clarke, 1969), chap. 1, §15 (p. 12).

19. Versluis, *Wisdom's Children,* pp. 14–17.

20. Ibid., pp. 29–38. For a new edition of Gichtel's work, see Johann Georg Gichtel, *Awakening to Divine Wisdom: Christian Initiation into Three Worlds*, translated and edited by Arthur Versluis (St. Paul, Minn.: New Grail Publishing, 2004).

21. Versluis, *Wisdom's Children*, p. 50.

22. Ibid., p. 48.

23. Ibid., pp. 59–62, 71–77.

24. Ibid., pp. 79–81. For modern editions of Freher's rich iconographical works, see Adam McLean, ed., *The Three Tables of D. A. Freher* (Glasgow: Magnum Opus Hermetic Sourceworks No. 28, 2003); and Adam McLean, ed., *The Three Tables of Man: His Creation, Fall, and Regeneration Revealed in Three Elaborate Diagrams by D. A. Freher* (Glasgow: Magnum Opus Hermetic Sourceworks No. 31, 2005).

25. Arthur Versluis, *Theosophia: Hidden Dimensions of Christianity* (Hudson, N.Y.: Lindisfarne, 1994), p. 12.

26. Dionysius the Areopagite, *Mystical Theology and the Celestial Hierarchies* (Brook, Surrey: Shrine of Wisdom, 1965), pp. 21–22.

27. Versluis, *Theosophia*, p. 19.

28. Ibid., p. 98.

29. Peter C. Erb, *Pietists: Selected Writings* (New York: Paulist Press, 1983), pp. 1–24.

30. Rolf Christian Zimmermann, *Das Weltbild des jungen Goethe: Studien zur hermetischen Tradition des deutschen 18. Jahrhunderts. Erster Band: Elemente und Fundamente* (Munich: Wilhelm Fink, 1969), chaps. 1 and 2.

CHAPTER 6

1. A scholarly survey of the sources and inspiration of the Rosicrucian manifestos, together with their later influence is provided by Roland Edighoffer, "Rosicrucianism: From the Seventeenth Century to the Twentieth Century," in *Modern Esoteric Spirituality*, edited by Antoine Faivre and Jacob Needleman (London: SCM Press, 1993), pp. 186–209. Edighoffer has written standard works on Rosicrucianism: *Les Rose-Croix*, 3rd ed. (Paris: Presses Universitaires de France, 1991), translated as *Die Rosenkreuzer* (Munich: C. H. Beck, 1995); *Rose-Croix et société idéale selon Johann Valentin Andreae*, 2 vols. (Paris: Arma Artis, 1982/1987); and *Les Rose-Croix et la crise de conscience européenne au XVIIe siècle* (Paris: Dervy, 1998). Christopher McIntosh, *The Rosicrucians*, 3rd ed. (York Beach, Maine: Samuel Weiser, 1998), provides a concise historical introduction to the subject.

2. The texts of the *Fama Fraternitatis* and *Confessio Fraternitatis* were first published in English by Thomas Vaughan (Eugenius Philalethes) under the title *The Fame and Confession of the Fraternity of R:C:* (London, 1652). These texts are reproduced as an appendix in Frances A. Yates, *The Rosicrucian Enlightenment* (London: Routledge & Kegan Paul, 1972), pp. 238–251, 251–260. The partial quotation in the text is taken from p. 238 of the Yates book. The Spanish scholar Carlos Gilly has edited a richly illustrated exhibition catalogue bearing on the earliest manuscripts and printed texts of the manifestos, together with extensive scholarly commentary. Carlos Gilly, *Cimelia Rhodostaurotica: Die Rosenkreuzer im Spiegel der zwischen 1610 und 1660 entstandenen Handschriften und Drucke* (Amsterdam: Pelikaan, 1995).

3. On the Hermetic traditions of the Sabaeans, see Kocku von Stuckrad, *Western Esotericism*, pp. 29–30.

4. *Fama Fraternitatis*, cited in Frances A. Yates, *The Rosicrucian Enlightenment*, p. 240.

5. Ibid., p. 242.

6. Ibid., p. 244.

7. Ibid., p. 248.

8. The original source for the "Lion of the North" is IV Ezra, chaps. 11 and 12. The "Lion of the North" prophecies and their link with Paracelsus are thoroughly examined in Carlos Gilly, "Die 'Löwe von Mitternacht,' der 'Adler' und der 'Endchrist': Die politische, religiöse und chiliastische Publizistik in den Flugschriften, illustrierten Flugblättern und Volksliedern des Dreissigjährigen Krieges," in *Rosenkreuz als europäisches Phänomen im 17. Jahrhundert*, Bibliotheca Philosophica Hermetica (Amsterdam: Pelikaan, 2002), pp. 234–268.

9. Roland Edighoffer, *Die Rosenkreuzer*, pp. 32–33. Joachim's division of sacred history into three great stages and their division into seven eras of the world are set forth in his work *Liber Concordie*. Marjorie Reeves, *Joachim of Fiore and the Prophetic Future* (London: SPCK, 1976), pp. 1–28; Delno C. West and Sandra Zimdars-Swartz, *Joachim of Fiore: A Study in Spiritual Perception and History* (Bloomington: Indiana University Press, 1983), pp. 58–77.

10. The translation used here is from *The Chemical Wedding of Christian Rosenkreutz*, translated by Joscelyn Godwin, introduction and commentary by Adam McLean, Magnum Opus Hermetic Sourceworks 18 (Grand Rapids, Mich.: Phanes Press, 1991).

11. Ibid., p. 16. The link with John Dee was greatly emphasized by Frances A. Yates in *The Rosicrucian Enlightenment*. Carlos Gilly regards Dee's influence as slight compared with that of Paracelsus and late-sixteenth-century Continental alchemists, which could also account for the mercury symbol. Cf. *Cimelia Rhodostaurotica*, p. 22.

12. Ibid., p. 21.

13. Ibid., pp. 40f.

14. Ibid., pp. 70f.

15. Ibid., pp. 88–94.

16. Earlier twentieth-century German scholarship pointed definitely to Andreae's authorship of the *Fama* and *Confessio*, in some collaboration with Tobias Hess and Christian Besold. See Will-Erich Peuckert, *Die Rosenkreutzer: Zur Geschichte einer Reformation* (Jena: Diederich, 1928), pp. 400–401, 404; Hans Schick, *Das ältere Rosenkreuzertum: Ein Beitrag zur Enstehungsgeschichte der Freimaurerei* (Berlin: Nordland, 1942), pp. 70–87. However, John Warwick Montgomery makes the case that Andreae was not involved, in his *Cross and Crucible: Johann Valentin Andreae (1586–1654), Phoenix of the Theologians* (The Hague: Martinus Nijhoff, 1973), Vol. 1, pp. 160–240.

17. On Christoph Besold, see Tobias Churton, *The Golden Builders: Alchemists, Rosicrucians, and the first Free Masons* (Lichfield: Signal, 2003), pp.123–126.

18. Details of Hess's life and his interest in Simon Studion and *Naometria* can be found in ibid., pp. 90, 101–106.

19. Gilly, *Cimelia Rhodostaurotica*, pp. 25–29.

20. John Warwick Montgomery, *Cross and Crucible*, Vol. 1, pp. 178–190.

21. Ibid., 202–210.

22. Ibid., 232–237, 225–231.

23. F. A. Yates, *Rosicrucian Enlightenment*, pp. 15–29, 40.

24. The third part of Hans Schick, *Das ältere Rosenkreuzertum*, pp. 174–236, devotes three chapters to the literature produced by protagonists and opponents of the manifestos. Cf. F. A. Yates, *Roscicrucian Enlightenment*, pp. 91–102.

25. Schick, *Das ältere Rosenkreuzertum*, pp. 114–138.

26. F. A. Yates, *Rosicrucian Enlightenment*, pp. 80–88; Schick, *Das ältere Rosenkreuzertum*, pp. 246–257. See also J. B. Craven, *Count Michael Maier* (Kirkwall: William Pearce, 1910); and Hereward Tilton, *The Quest for the Phoenix: Spiritual Alchemy and Rosicrucianism in the Work of Count Michael Maier (1569–1622)* (Berlin: Walter de Gruyter, 2003).

27. On Fludd, see Joscelyn Godwin, *Robert Fludd: Hermetic Philosopher and Surveyor of Two Worlds* (London: Thames & Hudson, 1979); William H. Huffman, *Robert Fludd and the End of the Renaissance* (London: Routledge, 1988); William H. Huffman, *Robert Fludd*, Western Esoteric Masters series (Berkeley, Calif.: North Atlantic Books, 2001); J. B. Craven, *Dr. Robert Fludd (Robertus de Fluctibus): The English Rosicrucian* (Kirkwall: William Pearce, 1902).

28. Schick, *Das ältere Rosenkreuzertum*, p. 252; J. G. Buhle, *Ueber den Ursprung und die vornehmsten Schicksale der Orden der Rosenkreuzer und Freymaurer* (Göttingen, 1804), pp. 245–246; C. G. von Murr, *Über den Wahren Ursprung der Rosenkreuzer und des Freymaurerordens* (Sulzbach, 1803), pp. 75–76. This thesis is closely discussed by Tilton in *The Quest for the Phoenix*, pp. 26–29.

29. Churton, *Golden Builders*, pp. 193–197; Tobias Churton, *Magus: The Invisible Life of Elias Ashmole* (Lichfield: Signal, 2004), pp. 101–107.

30. David Stevenson, *The Origins of Freemasonry: Scotland's Century, 1590–1710* (Cambridge: Cambridge University Press, 1988), pp. 100–105.

31. Clare Goodrick-Clarke, "The Rosicrucian Afterglow: The Life and Influence of Comenius," in *The Rosicrucian Enlightenment Revisited*, edited by Ralph White (Hudson, N.Y.: Lindisfarne, 1999), pp. 193–218.

32. Ibid., p. 212. Cf. Schick, *Das ältere Rosenkreuzertum*, p. 151f.

33. G. H. Turnbull, *Hartlib, Dury, and Comenius* (London: Hodder & Stoughton, 1947); H. R. Trevor-Roper, "Three Foreigners: The Philosophers of the Puritan Revolution," in *Religion, the Reformation and Social Change* (London: Macmillan, 1967; rev. ed. 1984), pp. 237–293; Charles Webster, "Macaria: Samuel Hartlib and the Great Reformation," *Acta Comeniana* 2, 26 (1970): 149–151. For Andreae and Hartlib's communal projects, see Donald R. Dickson, *The Tessera of Antilia: Utopian Brotherhood and Secret Societies in the Early Seventeenth Century* (Leiden: Brill, 1998).

34. Joan Simon, "The Comenian Educational Reformers 1640–1660 and the Royal Society of London," *Acta Comeniana* 2, 26 (1970): 165–178.

35. Churton, *Golden Builders*, pp. 168–175.

36. Bernhard Beyer, *Das Lehrsystem des Ordens der Gold- und Rosenkreuzer* (Leipzig: Pansophie Verlag, 1925; repr. Munich: Arbeitsgemeinschaft für Religions- und Weltanschauungsfragen, 1978); Christopher McIntosh, *The Rose Cross and the Age of Reason:*

Eighteenth-Century Rosicrucianism in Central Europe and Its Relationship to the Enlighten-ment (Leiden: Brill, 1992); Renko D. Geffarth, *Religion und arkane Hierarchie: Der Orden der Gold- und Rosenkreuzer als Geheime Kirche im 18. Jahrhundert* (Leiden: Brill, 2007).

37. Marie Roberts, *Gothic Immortals: The Fiction of the Brotherhood of the Rosy Cross* (London: Routledge, 1990).

38. For modern Rosicrucian movements, see McIntosh, *The Rosicrucians*, pp. 129–144; Harald Lamprecht, *Neue Rosenkreuzer; Ein Handbuch* (Göttingen: Vandenhoeck & Ruprecht, 2004).

CHAPTER 7

1. A convenient summary of the major theories on the origins of Freemasonry is contained in Albert Gallatin Mackie, *The History of Freemasonry: Its Legendary Origins* (1898–1906; New York: Gramercy Books, 1996). A very convenient overview of Free-masonry, its history, traditions and usage, is Robert Freke Gould, *The Concise History of Freemasonry*, revised by Frederick J. W. Crowe (1903; Mineoloa, New York: Dover Publi-cations, 2007).

2. John Hamill, *The History of English Freemasonry* (Addlestone: Lewis Masonic, 1994), p. 20.

3. John M. Roberts, *The Mythology of the Secret Societies* (London: Secker & War-burg, 1972), p. 32.

4. Peter Partner, *The Murdered Magicians: The Templars and Their Myth* (Oxford: Oxford University Press, 1982), pp. 103–106.

5. René Le Forestier, *La Franc-Maçonnerie templière et occultiste aux XVIIIe et XIXe siècles*, 3rd ed. (Milan: Arche, 2003), pp. 87–91.

6. Ibid., pp. 107–111.

7. Ibid., pp. 113–117.

8. J. Roberts, *Mythology of the Secret Societies*, pp. 108–109.

9. Isaiah Berlin, "The Counter-Enlightenment," in *The Proper Study of Mankind: An Anthology of Essays* (London: Chatto & Windus, 1997).

10. J. Roberts, *Mythology of the Secret Societies*, pp. 90–94.

11. Useful background for this section can be found in two entries of *Dictionary of Gnosis and Western Esotericism*, edited by Wouter Hanegraaff (Leiden: Brill, 2005): Jean-François Var, "Martinès de Pasqually," Vol. 2, pp. 930–936; and Michelle Nahon, "Élus Coëns," Vol. 1, pp. 332–334.

12. Martinès de Pasqually, *Traité sur la réintégration des êtres dans leur première pro-priété, vertu et puissance spirituelle divine*, edited by Robert Amadou (Le Tremblay: Diffu-sion rosicrucienne, 1995), pp. 175–190.

13. Var, "Martinès de Pasqually," 934.

14. A full account of the Elect Coëns and their rituals is provided by René Le Fores-tier, *La Franc-Maçonnerie occultiste au XVIIIe siècle et l'Ordre des Élus Coens* (1928; Paris: La Table d'Emeraude, 1987).

15. Louis Claude de Saint-Martin, *Des Erreurs et de la Vérité*, Part I, pp. 38–40, cited in Arthur Edward Waite, *The Unknown Philosopher: The Life of Louis Claude de Saint-Martin*

and the Substance of His Transcendental Doctrine, 3rd ed. (Blauvelt, N.Y.: Rudolf Steiner Publications, 1970), p. 126.

16. Saint-Martin, *Theosophic Correspondence 1792–1797,* translated and with a preface by Edward Burton Penny (Exeter: William Roberts, 1863; repr. Pasadena, Calif.: Theosophical University Press, 1991), Letter 110 (19.06.1797), p. 306.

17. Ibid., Letter 19 (6.03.1793), p. 62.

18. Waite, *Unknown Philosopher,* p. 230.

19. Robert Darnton, *Mesmerism and the End of the Enlightenment in France* (Cambridge, Mass.: Harvard University Press, 1968), pp. 68–69.

20. Saint-Martin, *Theosophic Correspondence 1792–1797,* Letter 4 (12.07.1792), p. 13.

21. Jean-François Var, "Willermoz," in *Dictionary of Gnosis and Western Esotericism,* edited by Wouter Hanegraaff (Leiden: Brill, 2005), Vol. 2, pp. 1170–1174; Alice Joly, *Un mystique lyonnais et les secrets de la Franc-Maçonnerie, 1730–1824* (Mâcon: Prostat, 1938; repr. Paris: Demeter, 1986). Cf. Waite, *Unknown Philosopher,* pp. 67–70; and J. Roberts, *Mythology of the Secret Societies,* p. 115.

22. J. Roberts, *Mythology of the Secret Societies,* pp. 111f.

23. Jan Snoek, "Dom Antoine-Joseph Pernety," in *Dictionary of Gnosis and Western Esotericism,* edited by Wouter J. Hanegraaff (Leiden: Brill, 2005), Vol. 2, pp. 940–942.

24. A full account of the Illuminés of Avignon is provided by Micheline Meillassoux-Le Cerf, *Dom Pernety et les Illuminés d'Avignon* (Milan: Archè, 1992).

25. René Le Forestier, *La Franc-Maçonnerie templière et occultiste,* pp. 877–881; Jan Snoek, "Illuminés d'Avignon," in *Dictionary of Gnosis and Western Esotericism,* edited by Wouter J. Hanegraaff (Leiden: Brill, 2005), Vol. 2, pp. 597–600.

26. W. R. H. Trowbridge, *Cagliostro,* 2nd ed. (London: George Allen & Unwin, 1926), p. 111.

27. Iain McCalman, *The Last Alchemist: Count Cagliostro, Master of Magic in the Age of Reason* (New York: HarperCollins, 2003), p. 40.

28. René Le Forestier, *La Franc-Maçonnerie templière et occultiste,* pp. 768.

29. Ibid., pp. 768–769.

30. Ibid., p. 993; McCalman, *Last Alchemist,* p. 41.

31. Edmond Mazet, "Freemasonry and Esotericism," in *Modern Esoteric Spirituality,* edited by Antoine Faivre and Jacob Needleman (London: SCM Press, 1993), p. 265.

CHAPTER 8

1. Antoine Faivre, *Theosophy, Imagination, Tradition: Studies in Western Esotericism* (Albany: State University of New York Press, 2000), p. 23.

2. Standard biographical studies of Swedenborg include Cyriel Odhner Sigstedt, *The Swedenborg Epic: The Life and Works of Emanuel Swedenborg* (London: Swedenborg Society, 1981); Ernst Benz, *Emanuel Swedenborg: Visionary Savant in the Age of Reason,* translated by and introduction by Nicholas Goodrick-Clarke (West Chester, Pa.: Swedenborg Foundation, 2002; first published in German in 1948); and Lars Bergquist, *Swedenborg's Secret* (London: Swedenborg Society, 2005).

3. Cyriel Sigstedt, *The Swedenborg Epic*, pp. 198–199. Cf. Benz, *Swedenborg: Visionary Savant*, p. 194.

4. Richard S. Dunn, *The Age of Religious Wars 1559–1689* (London: Weidenfeld & Nicolson, 1971), p. ix.

5. For an excellent introduction and bibliography of Pietism, see *Pietists: Selected Writings*, edited by Peter C. Erb (New York: Paulist Press, 1983).

6. Bergquist, *Swedenborg's Secret*, pp. 194–195.

7. Benz, *Swedenborg: Visionary Savant*, pp. 12–17.

8. Ibid., pp. 118–120.

9. Maurice Wiles, *Archetypal Heresy: Arianism through the Centuries* (Oxford: Oxford University Press, 1996), pp. 77–134.

10. Benz, *Swedenborg: Visionary Savant*, pp. 122–126.

11. Martin Lamm, Swedenborg. *En studie öfver hans utveckling till mystiker och andeskadare* (Stockholm: Hugo Geber, 1915), translated by Tomas Spiers and Anders Hallengren as *Emanuel Swedenborg: The Development of His Thought* (West Chester, Pa.: Swedenborg Foundation, 2000), pp. 95–108.

12. Benz, *Swedenborg: Visionary Savant*, pp. 130–132.

13. Lamm, *Swedenborg: Development*, p. 96.

14. Ibid., p. 97; Benz, *Swedenborg: Visionary Savant*, p. 353.

15. Benz, *Swedenborg: Visionary Savant*, pp. 356–359.

16. Swedenborg, *Arcana Coelestia* §1–5, cited in Sigstedt, *Swedenborg Epic*, p. 226.

17. Swedenborg discussed the notion of ruling love in *Heaven and Hell* and in *Arcana Coelestia*. Cf. Swedenborg, *Heaven and Its Wonders and Hell*, translated by George F. Dole, edited by Jonathan S. Rose, New Century ed. (West Chester, Pa.: Swedenborg Foundation, 2000), pp. 224 n. d, 346.

18. Lamm, *Swedenborg: Development*, p. 297, cf. *Heaven and Hell* §457, 463, 477.

19. Benz, *Swedenborg: Visionary Savant*, pp. 404–405.

20. Inge Jonsson, *Emanuel Swedenborg* (New York: New York, 1971), pp. 61–62, 81–82.

21. Inge Jonsson, "Emanuel Swedenborgs Naturphilosophie und ihr Fortwirken in seiner Theosophie," in *Epochen der Naturmystik: Hermetische Tradition in wissenschaftlichen Fortschritt*, edited by Antoine Faivre and Rolf Christian Zimmermann (Berlin: Erich Schmidt, 1979), p. 251.

22. Wouter J. Hanegraaff, *New Age Religion and Western Culture: Esotericism in the Mirror of Secular Thought* (Leiden: E. J. Brill, 1996), pp. 424–425.

23. Marsha Keith Schuchard, "Leibniz, Benzelius, and Swedenborg: The Kabbalistic Roots of Swedish Illuminism," in *Leibniz, Mysticism and Religion*, edited by Allison P. Coudert, Richard H. Popkin, and Gordon M. Weiner (Dordrecht: Kluwer, 1998), pp. 84–106. However, see Jane Williams-Hogan, "The Place of Emanuel Swedenborg in Modern Western Esotericism," in *Western Esotericism and the Science of Religion*, edited by Antoine Faivre and Wouter J. Hanegraaff (Leuven: Peeters, 1998), pp. 209–211.

24. See the following works by Marsha Keith Schuchard: "Yeats and the Unknown Superiors: Swedenborg, Falk, and Cagliostro," *Hermetic Journal* 37 (Autumn 1987): 14–20; "Swedenborg, Jacobitism, and Freemasonry," in *Swedenborg and His Influence*,

edited by Erland J. Brock et al. (Bryn Athyn, Pa.: Academy of the New Church, 1988), pp. 359–379; "The Secret Masonic History of Blake's Swedenborg Society," *Blake: An Illustrated Quarterly* 26, 2 (Fall 1992): 40–51; "Jacobite and Visionary: The Masonic Journey of Emanuel Swedenborg (1688–1772)," *Ars Quatuor Coronatorum* 115 (2003): 33–72.

25. Antoine Faivre, "Introduction I," in *Modern Esoteric Spirituality*, edited by Antoine Faivre and Jacob Needleman (London: SCM Press, 1993), pp. xi–xxii; Faivre, *Access to Western Esotericism* (Albany: State University of New York Press, 1994), pp. 10–15.

26. Williams-Hogan, "Place of Emanuel Swedenborg," p. 220.

27. Wouter J. Hanegraaff, *New Age Religion and Western Culture: Esotericism in the Mirror of Secular Thought* (Leiden: Brill, 1996), pp. 427–429.

28. Marsha Keith Schuchard, "Dr. Samuel Jacob Falk: A Sabbatian Adventurer in the Masonic Underground," in *Millenarianism and Messianism in Early Modern European Culture: Jewish Messianism in the Early Modern World*, edited by M. D. Goldish and R. H. Popkin (Dordrecht: Kluwer, 2001), pp. 203–226. Cf. Hermann Adler, "The Baal-Shem of London," *Transactions of the Jewish Historical Society of England* 5 (1902–1905): 148–173; Gordon Hills, "Notes on Some Contemporary References to Dr. Falk, the Baal-Shem of London, in the Rainsford MSS. at the British Museum," *Transactions of the Jewish Historical Society of England* 8 (1915–1917): 122–128.

29. James Hyde, "Benedict Chastanier and the Illuminati of Avignon," *New Church Review* 14 (1907): 181–205; J. E. S. Tuckett, "Savalette de Langes, Les Philaletes, and the Convent of Wilhelmsbad, 1782," *Ars Quatuor Coronatorum* 30 (1917): 131–171; Schuchard, "Secret Masonic History," 40–51.

30. Clarke Garrett, "The Spiritual Odyssey of Jacob Duché," *Proceedings of the American Philosophical Society* 119, 2 (1975): 143–155.

31. Schuchard, "Secret Masonic History," p. 43 and n. 44.

32. M. L. Danilewicz, "'The King of the New Israel': Thaddeus Grabianka (1740–1807)," *Oxford Slavonic Papers*, n.s., 1 (1968): 49–73; Clarke Garrett, *Respectable Folly: Millenarians and the French Revolution in France and England* (Baltimore: Johns Hopkins University Press, 1975), pp. 104, 109–113; Alfred J. Gabay, *The Covert Enlightenment: Eighteenth-Century Counterculture and Its Aftermath* (West Chester, Pa.: Swedenborg Foundation, 2005), pp. 67–70.

33. Jane Williams-Hogan and David B. Eller, "Swedenborgian Churches and Related Institutions in Great Britain, the United States, and Canada," in *Scribe of Heaven: Swedenborg's Life, Work, and Impact*, edited by Jonathan S. Rose, Stuart Shotwell, and Mary Lou Bertucci (West Chester, Pa.: Swedenborg Foundation, 2005), pp. 245–310.

34. Robert H. Kirven and David B. Eller, "Selected Examples of Swedenborg's Influence in Great Britain and the United States," in *Scribe of Heaven*, ibid., pp. 195–242.

CHAPTER 9

1. Vincent Buranelli, *The Wizard from Vienna* (London: Peter Owen, 1976), pp. 34–37 (p. 36).

2. Ibid., pp. 59–63.

3. Robert Darnton, *Mesmerism and the End of the Enlightenment in France* (Cambridge, Mass.: Harvard University Press, 1968), pp. 48–50.

4. James Webb, *The Occult Establishment* (Glasgow: Richard Drew, 1981), pp. 9–10.

5. Robert Darnton, *Mesmerism and the End of the Enlightenment in France*, pp. 51–52.

6. Alfred J. Gabay, *The Covert Enlightenment: Eighteenth-Century Counterculture and Its Aftermath* (West Chester, Pa.: Swedenborg Foundation, 2005), pp. 45–47.

7. Ibid. p. 86.

8. Darnton, *Mesmerism*, pp. 67–70; Buranelli, *Wizard from Vienna*, pp. 170–172.

9. Margaret Goldsmith, *Franz Anton Mesmer: The History of an Idea* (London: Arthur Baker, 1934), pp. 150–159; Buranelli, *Wizard from Vienna*, pp. 117–119.

10. Armand Marie Jacques de Chastenet, marquis de Puységur, *Mémoires pour servir à l'histoire et à l'établissement du magnétisme animal* (Paris: Dentu, 1784–1785), cited in Goldsmith, *Franz Anton Mesmer*, p. 159.

11. Christine Bergé, "Illuminism," in *Dictionary of Gnosis and Western Esotericism*, edited by Wouter Hanegraaff et al. (Leiden: Brill, 2005), Vol. 1, pp. 600–606 (p. 602).

12. Ernst Benz, *The Theology of Electricity*, translated by Wolfgang Taraba (Allison Park, Pa.: Pickwick, 1989), pp. 45–53, 55.

13. Alexander Gode-von Aesch, *Natural Science in German Romanticism* (New York: Columbia University Press, 1941), pp. 70f, 158–166.

14. Otto-Joachim Grüsser, *Justinus Kerner 1786–1862: Arzt—Poet—Geisterseher* (Berlin: Springer, 1987), pp. 189–194, 201ff, 209–216.

15. Justinus Kerner, *The Seeress of Prévorst: being revelations concerning the inner-life of man, and the inter-diffusion of a world of spirits in the one we inhabit*, translated by Mrs. Catherine Crowe (London: J. C. Moore, 1845).

16. Goldsmith, *Franz Anton Mesmer*, pp. 180–183.

17. Joscelyn Godwin, *The Theosophical Enlightenment* (Albany: State University of New York Press, 1994), pp. 156–157.

18. Nicholas Goodrick-Clarke, *Helena Blavatsky*, Western Esoteric Masters series (Berkeley, Calif.: North Atlantic Books, 2004), pp. 89–93, 100–102.

19. Alan Gauld, *A History of Hypnotism* (Cambridge: Cambridge University Press, 1992), pp. 199–208; Alison Winter, *Mesmerized: Powers of Mind in Victorian Britain* (Chicago: University of Chicago Press, 1998), pp. 46–50, 154–155.

20. Gauld, *History of Hypnotism*, pp. 279–288.

21. James Webb, *The Flight from Reason* (London: Macdonald, 1971), pp. 10–14.

22. Marguerite Beck Block, *The New Church in the New World: A Study of Swedenborgianism in America* (New York: Swedenborg Publishing Association, 1984), pp. 133–137. Cf. Robert H. Kirven and David B. Eller, "Selected Examples of Swedenborg's Influence in Great Britain and the United States," in *Scribe of Heaven*, pp. 195–242 (pp. 218–223).

23. Bruce F. Campbell, *Ancient Wisdom Revived: A History of the Theosophical Movement* (Berkeley: University of California Press, 1980), pp. 14, 20.

24. Horatio W. Dresser, *A History of the New Thought Movement* (New York: Thomas Y. Crowell Co., 1919).

25. For recent scholarly discussion of the New Thought movement in America, see Charles S. Braden, *Spirits in Rebellion: The Rise and Development of New Thought* (Dallas:

Southern Methodist University Press, 1987); and J. Gordon Melton, *New Thought: A Reader* (Santa Barbara, Calif.: Institute for the Study of American Religion, 1990).

26. The Fox sisters' saga is documented by Nancy Rubin Stuart, *The Reluctant Spiritualist: The Life of Maggie Fox* (Orlando, Fla.: Harcourt, 2005).

27. Frank Podmore, *Modern Spiritualism* (London: Methuen, 1902), Vol. 1, pp. 202–250. See also the two massive histories of the early years of Spiritualism by Emma Hardinge Britten: *Modern American Spiritualism: Twenty Years' Record of the Communion between Earth and the World of Spirits* (New York: author, 1870; repr. New York University books, 1970); and *Nineteenth Century Miracles; or, Spirits and Their Work in Every Country of the Earth* (London: William Britten, 1883).

28. Peter Lamont, *The First Psychic: The Peculiar Mystery of a Notorious Victorian Wizard* (London: Little, Brown, 2005), pp. 109–110, 183–187.

29. For historical surveys of the movement, see James Webb, *The Occult Underground* (La Salle, Ill.: Open Court, 1974), chap. 1; Ruth Brandon, *The Spiritualists: The Passion for the Occult in the Nineteenth and Twentieth Centuries* (Buffalo, N.Y.: Prometheus, 1983); Ann Braude, *Radical Spirits: Spiritualism and Women's Rights in Nineteenth-Century America* (Boston: Beacon Press, 1989); Godwin, *The Theosophical Enlightenment*, chap. 10; Janet Oppenheim, *The Other World: Spiritualism and Psychical Research in England, 1850–1914* (Cambridge: Cambridge University Press, 1985).

30. John Patrick Deveney, "Spiritualism," in *Dictionary of Gnosis and Western Esotericism*, edited by Wouter Hanegraaff et al. (Leiden: Brill, 2005), Vol. 2, pp. 1074–1082 (p. 1078).

31. Antoine Faivre, *Access to Western Esotericism*, p. 88; Wouter J. Hanegraaff, *New Age Religion and Western Culture: Esotericism in the Mirror of Secular Thought* (Leiden: Brill, 1996), pp. 439–442.

CHAPTER 10

1. Ellic Howe, "Fringe Masonry in England, 1870–1885," *Ars Quatuor Coronatorum* 85 (1972): 242–280.

2. Geoffrey Rowell, *The Vision Glorious: Themes and Personalities of the Catholic Revival in Anglicanism* (Oxford: Oxford University Press, 1983); Nigel Yates, *Anglican Ritualism in Victorian Britain, 1830–1910* (Oxford: Clarendon Press, 2000).

3. For a comprehensive study of Lévi's life and works, see Christopher McIntosh, *Eliphas Lévi and the French Occult Revival* (London: Rider, 1972). Cf. Ronald Decker, Thierry Depaulis, and Michael Dummett, *A Wicked Pack of Cards: The Origins of the Occult Tarot* (New York: St. Martin's Press, 1996), pp. 166–193.

4. For a biography of Höené-Wronski, see Philippe d'Arcy, *Hoene-Wronski: Une philosophie de la création* (Paris: Seghers, 1970). See also the account of his life, work and influence on Constant in James Webb, *The Flight from Reason* (London: Macdonald, 1971), pp. 164–168.

5. McIntosh, *Eliphas Lévi and the French Occult Revival*, p. 147.

6. Eliphas Lévi, *Transcendental Magic: Its Doctrine and Ritual*, translated by A. E. Waite (London: Rider, 1923; repr. Twickenham: Senate, 1995), pp. 1–4, 10–12.

7. Ibid., pp. 250–256.

8. Ibid., pp. 67, 74, 78f, 83, 130, 150.

9. Ronald Decker, Thierry Depaulis, and Michael Dummett, *A Wicked Pack of Cards*, pp. 52–64, 74–87.

10. Ibid., pp. 185–191.

11. Ibid. p. 168.

12. S. L. Macgregor Mathers, *The Kabbalah Unveiled* (London: Routledge & Kegan Paul, 1887), p. 17; "The Magical Evocation of Apollonius of Tyana," in *The Spiritual Scientist* (4 November 1875), repr. *H. P. Blavatsky: Collected Writings*, edited by Boris de Zirkoff (Wheaton, Ill.: Theosophical Publishing House, 1950–1991), Vol. 1, pp. 144–150.

13. Antoine Faivre, *Access to Western Esotericism* (Albany: State University of New York Press, 1994), p. 88.

14. Joscelyn Godwin, *The Beginnings of Theosophy in France* (London: Theosophical History Centre, 1989), pp. 12–20.

15. Jean-Pierre Laurant, "Papus," in *Dictionary of Gnosis and Western Esotericism*, edited by Wouter Hanegraaff et al. (Leiden: Brill, 2005), Vol. 2, pp. 913–915. Cf. James Webb, *Flight from Reason*, chap. 5.

16. Ellic Howe, *The Magicians of the Golden Dawn: A Documentary History of a Magical Order 1887–1923* (London: Routledge & Kegan Paul, 1972), p. 27.

17. A recent scholarly assessment of the Golden Dawn is offered by Alex Owen, *The Place of Enchantment: British Occultism and the Culture of the Modern* (Chicago: University of Chicago Press, 2004), chap. 2.

18. For a collection of Westcott's many articles on Rosicrucianism, Kabbalah, divination, and Freemasonry, see Robert A. Gilbert, ed., *The Magical Mason: Forgotten Hermetic Writings of William Wynn Westcott, Physician and Magus* (Wellingborough: Aquarian Press, 1983).

19. Ibid., pp. 1–25; Robert A. Gilbert, *The Golden Dawn Scrapbook: The Rise and Fall of a Magical Order* (York Beach, Maine: Samuel Weiser, 1997), pp. 25–30.

20. Robert A. Gilbert, *The Golden Dawn Companion: A Guide to the History, Structure, and Workings of the Hermetic Order of the Golden Dawn* (Wellingborough: Aquarian Press, 1986), pp. 1–29.

21. Biographical details of Mathers may be found in Ithell Colquhoun, *Sword of Wisdom: MacGregor Mathers and "The Golden Dawn"* (London: Neville Spearman, 1975), pp. 49–107; Gilbert, *Golden Dawn Scrapbook*, pp. 93–113; for a collection of his many articles on occult subjects, see Robert A. Gilbert, ed., *The Sorcerer and His Apprentice: Unknown Hermetic Writings of S. L. MacGregor Mathers and J. W. Brodie-Innes* (Wellingborough: Aquarian Press, 1983).

22. Israel Regardie, *The Golden Dawn: The Original Account of the Teachings, Rites, and Ceremonies of the Hermetic Order of the Golden Dawn (Stella Matutina)*, 6th ed. (St. Paul, Minn.: Llewellyn, 2000), p. 231.

23. Wouter Hanegraaff, "Tradition," in *Dictionary of Gnosis and Western Esotericism*, edited by Wouter Hanegraaff et al. (Leiden: Brill, 2005), Vol. 2, pp. 1125–1135 (p. 1132).

24. Gilbert, *Golden Dawn Companion*, pp. 85–94.

25. Regardie, *Golden Dawn: Original Account*, pp. 50–59.

26. Ibid., pp. 198–220.

27. Ibid., pp. 221–247.

28. Howe, *The Magicians of the Golden Dawn*, pp. 75–109. Alex Owen has written at some length on these magical practices as an example of late Victorian preoccupation with human consciousness and a psychology of the self. See Owen, *The Place of Enchantment*, pp. 116–123.

29. The crises precipitating the split in the second order are described in Howe, *Magicians of the Golden Dawn*, chap. 14. The complex history of the Golden Dawn's fragmentation and its successor orders and personnel are documented in Colquhoun, *Sword of Wisdom*, chaps. 13 to 16.

30. Regardie, *The Golden Dawn: An Account of the Teachings, Rites and Ceremonies of the Order of the Golden Dawn*, 4 vols. (Chicago: Aries Press, 1937–1940). Many magical groups today claim descent from the original Golden Dawn. A leading contender is the Hermetic Order of the Golden Dawn, based in Florida and led by Chic and Sandra Tabatha Cicero.

31. The standard biography of A. E. Waite is Robert A. Gilbert, *A. E. Waite: Magician of Many Parts* (Wellingborough: Crucible, 1987). See also Robert A. Gilbert, *A. E. Waite: A Bibliography* (Wellingborough: Aquarian Press, 1983), for a complete record of his literary work and order rituals.

32. The literature on Crowley is legion. The most standard biography is written by his literary executor, John Symonds, *The King of the Shadow Realm: Aleister Crowley, His Life and Magic* (London: Duckworth, 1989). A recent authoritative biography is Richard Kaczynski, *Perdurabo: The Life of Aleister Crowley* (Tempe, Ariz.: New Falcon, 2003). See also *The Confessions of Aleister Crowley: An Autohagiography*, edited by John Symonds and Kenneth Grant (London: Jonathan Cape, 1969).

33. For Theodor Reuss, Carl Kellner, and the Ordo Templi Orientis, see Ellic Howe and Helmut Möller, "Theodor Reuss: Irregular Freemasonry in Germany, 1900–1923," *Ars Quatuor Coronatorum* 91 (1978): 28–47; and Helmut Möller and Ellic Howe, *Merlin Peregrinus: Vom Untergrund des Abendlandes* (Würzburg: Königshausen & Neumann, 1986).

34. On the growth and proliferation of the Ordo Templi Orientis, see Peter-Robert König, *Der O.T.O. Phänomen Remix* (Munich: Arbeitsgemeinschaft für Religions- und Weltanschauungsfragen, 2001). The influence of Crowley on the Wicca movement via Gardner is examined in Ronald Hutton, *The Triumph of the Moon: A History of Modern Pagan Witchcraft* (Oxford: Oxford University Press, 1999), pp. 206–232.

35. For Dion Fortune's life and work, see Alan Richardson, *Priestess: The Life and Magic of Dion Fortune* (Wellingborough: Aquarian Press, 1987); Janine Chapman, *Quest for Dion Fortune* (York Beach, Maine: Samuel Weiser, 1993); Gareth Knight, *Dion Fortune and the Inner Light* (Loughborough: Thoth Publications, 2000); and Hutton, *Triumph of the Moon*, pp. 180–188.

CHAPTER 11

1. Sylvia L. Cranston, *HPB: The Extraordinary Life and Influence of Helena Blavatsky, Founder of the Modern Theosophical Movement* (New York: Putnam, 1993), pp. 3–38.

2. Jean Overton Fuller, *Blavatsky and Her Teachers* (London: East-West Publications, 1988), p. 4; Cranston, *HPB*, pp. 35–38.

3. Numerous sources for these travels and a speculative chronology are collected in Mary K. Neff, *Personal Reminiscences of H. P. Blavatsky* (London: Rider, 1937).

4. Overton Fuller, *Blavatsky and Her Teachers*, pp. 5–6; Albert Rawson, "Mme. Blavatsky: A Theosophical Occult Apology," *Theosophical History* 2, 6 (April 1988): 209–220 (first published 1895); Rawson's account has been queried by John Patrick Deveney, "The Travels of H. P. Blavatsky and the Chronology of Albert Leigh Rawson: An Unsatisfying Investigation into H.P.B.'s Whereabouts in the Early 1850s," *Theosophical History* 10, 4 (October 2004): 8–31. Cf. Joscelyn Godwin, *The Theosophical Enlightenment* (Albany: State University of New York Press, 1994), p. 279.

5. Overton Fuller, *Blavatsky and Her Teachers*, pp. 7–10; Cranston, *HPB*, pp. 45–47.

6. Overton Fuller, *Blavatsky and Her Teachers*, pp. 28–31.

7. *H. P. Blavatsky Collected Writings*, edited by Boris de Zirkoff (Wheaton, Ill.: Theosophical Publishing House, 1950–1991), Vol. 1, p. 73; Nicholas Goodrick-Clarke, *Helena Blavatsky* (Berkeley, Calif.: North Atlantic Books, 2004), pp. 31–33.

8. Letter 21 (HPB to Prof. Hiram Corson, 16 February 1875), *The Letters of H. P. Blavatsky*, Vol. 1, edited by John Algeo (Wheaton, Ill.: Theosophical Publishing House, 2003), pp. 85–87.

9. Neff, *Personal Memoirs*, pp. 248f.

10. Helena Petrovna Blavatsky, "A Few Questions to 'Hiraf***,'" *Spiritual Scientist* (15 and 22 July 1875), in *H. P. Blavatsky Collected Writings*, Vol. 1, pp. 101–119.

11. Godwin, *Theosophical Enlightenment*, pp. 291–303.

12. *H. P. Blavatsky Collected Writings*, Vol. 1, p. 94.

13. Michael Gomes, *The Dawning of the Theosophical Movement* (Wheaton, Ill.: Theosophical Publishing House, 1987), p. 86.

14. Letter 55 (HPB to A.N. Aksakov, 20 September 1875), *Letters of H. P. Blavatsky*, pp. 195–96.

15. "The Theosophical Society: Its Origins, Plan, and Aims," in *H. P. Blavatsky Collected Writings*, Vol. 1, pp. 375–378; Neff, *Personal Memoirs*, pp. 241f.

16. Henry S. Olcott, *Old Diary Leaves* (Adyar, India: Theosophical Publishing House, 1895–1932), Vol. 2, pp. 167–187.

17. H. P. Blavatsky, "Mistaken Notions," *Theosophist* 4, 5 (February 1883): 103–104, in *H. P. Blavatsky Collected Writings*, Vol. 4, pp. 304–306. Cf. H. P. Blavatsky, "Parabrahm, defined by Vedantins," *Theosophist* 4, 8 (May 1883): 204–205, in *H. P. Blavatsky Collected Writings*, Vol. 4, pp. 450–451. For extensive analysis of Blavatsky's reference to Vedanta and Buddhism, see H. J. Spierenburg, *The Buddhism of H. P. Blavatsky* (San Diego, Calif.: Point Loma Publications, 1991); and H. J. Spierenburg, *The Vedanta Commentaries of H. P. Blavatsky* (San Diego, Calif.: Point Loma Publications, 1992).

18. *Autobiography of Alfred Percy Sinnett* (London: Theosophical History Centre, 1986).

19. Allan O. Hume, "Fragments of Occult Truth, No. 1," *Theosophist* 3, 1 (October 1881): 17–22.

20. Blavatsky, *Isis Unveiled*, Vol. 1, pp. 289, 351–352, and Vol. 2, pp. 279–287.

21. Alfred Percy Sinnett, *Esoteric Buddhism*, 8th ed. (London: Theosophical Publishing Society, 1903), pp. 80–81.

22. Ibid., pp. 84–102.

23. As Hanegraaff observes, the *Isis Unveiled* index shows many references to reincarnation, metempsychosis, and transmigration but only three to karma, whereas the index to *The Secret Doctrine* shows many more references to karma. See Wouter Hanegraaff, *New Age Religion and Western Culture*, p. 482 n. 305.

24. Helena Petrovna Blavatsky, *The Secret Doctrine* (London: Theosophical Publishing Co., 1888), Vol. 1, pp. 571–572. An extensive analysis of Blavastky's cosmology is provided in Geoffrey A. Barborka, *The Divine Plan: Written in the Form of a Commentary on H. P. Blavatsky's Secret Doctrine* (Adyar, India: Theosophical Publishing House, 1964).

25. Blavatsky, *Secret Doctrine*, Vol. 1, pp. 14–17.

26. For an analysis of Blavatsky's complex cosmology and spiritual hierarchies and their relation to Western esotericism, see Nicholas Goodrick-Clarke, *Helena Blavatsky*, pp. 131–174.

27. Godwin, *Theosophical Enlightenment*, pp. 76–90, 261–275.

28. Cranston, *HPB*, pp. 191–198.

CHAPTER 12

1. Gregory Tillett, *The Elder Brother: A Biography of Charles Webster Leadbeater* (London: Routledge & Kegan Paul, 1982), describes Leadbeater's life and work and gives the best account of the Theosophical Society before the First World War and during the 1920s.

2. For an introductory view of Steiner and his writings, see Cees Leijenhorst, "Rudolf Steiner," in *Dictionary of Gnosis and Western Esotericism*, edited by Wouter Hanegraaff et al. (Leiden: Brill, 2005), Vol. 2, pp. 1084–1091; Robert A. McDermott, "Rudolf Steiner and Anthroposophy," in *Modern Esoteric Spirituality*, edited by Antoine Faivre and Jacob Needleman (London: SCM Press, 1993), pp. 288–310; Stewart C. Easton, *Rudolf Steiner: Herald of a New Epoch* (Hudson, N.Y.: Anthroposophic Press, 1980); Geoffrey Ahern, *Sun at Midnight: The Rudolf Steiner Movement and the Western Esoteric Tradition* (Wellingborough: Aquarian Press, 1984).

3. Alice A. Bailey, *The Unfinished Autobiography* (New York: Lucis Publishing Co., 1951), pp. 139–141.

4. Helena Blavatsky, *E. S. Instruction No. II* (March/April 1889), in *H. P. Blavatsky Collected Writings*, edited by Boris de Zirkoff (Wheaton, Ill.: Theosophical Publishing House, 1950–1991), Vol. 12, pp. 561, 567–69; Helena Blavatsky, *The Secret Doctrine* (London: Theosophical Publishing Co., 1888), Vol. 1, p. 572. Cf. Geoffrey A. Barborka, *The Divine Plan*, pp. 66–73; Alice A. Bailey, *Initiation, Human and Solar* (New York: Lucis Publishing Co., 1922), pp. 48–49; C. W. Leadbeater, *The Masters and the Path* (Adyar, India: Theosophical Publishing House, 1925; 3rd ed. 1969), diagram 5, facing p. 248.

5. Tillett, *Elder Brother*, p. 261.

6. Annie Besant and C. W. Leadbeater, *Thought-Forms: A Record of Clairvoyant Investigation* (London: Theosophical Publishing House, 1901; 2nd Quest Book abridged ed., Wheaton, Ill.: Theosophical Publishing House, 1999).

7. Wassily Kandinsky, *Über das Geistige in der Kunst* (1912), translated into English by Michael T. H. Sadler as *Concerning the Spiritual in Art* (London: Tate, 2006). The influence of Theosophy on Mondrian's and Kandinsky's art is extensively analyzed in Fred Gettings, *The Hidden Art: A Study of Occult Symbolism in Art* (London: Cassell, 1978), pp. 127–145. Cf. Sixten Ringbom, *The Sounding Cosmos. A Study in the Spiritualism of Kandinsky and the Genesis of Abstract Painting* (Åbo, Finland: Åbo Akademi, 1970).

8. See J. H. Reyner, *Ouspensky: The Unsung Genius* (London: Allen & Unwin, 1981); Gary Lachman, *In Search of P. D. Ouspensky: The Genius in the Shadow of Gurdjieff* (Wheaton, Ill.: Theosophical Publishing House, 2004); Jacob Needleman, "Ouspensky," in *Dictionary of Gnosis and Western Esotericism,* edited by Wouter Hanegraaff et al. (Leiden: Brill, 2005), Vol. 2, pp. 911–913.

9. James Moore, *Gurdjieff: The Anatomy of a Myth* (Shaftesbury: Element, 1981). Cf. Jacob Needleman, "G. I. Gurdjieff and His School," in *Modern Esoteric Spirituality,* edited by Antoine Faivre and Jacob Needleman (London: SCM Press, 1993), pp. 359–380 (pp. 362–366).

10. For accounts of Bennett, Collin, and Nicoll, see Peter Washington, *Madame Blavatsky's Baboon: Theosophy and the Emergence of the Western Guru* (London: Secker & Warburg, 1993); and Gary Lachman, *In Search of P. D. Ouspensky.* See also the biography of Nicoll by Beryl Pogson, *Maurice Nicoll: A Portrait* (London: Vincent Stuart, 1961).

11. Charles Webster Leadbeater, *The Christian Creed: Its Origin and Signification,* 2nd ed. (London: Theosophical Publishing House, 1920), plates facing pages 37 and 43. Also published in Leadbeater's *Man Visible and Invisible: Examples of Different Types of Men as Seen by Means of Trained Clairvoyance* (London: Theosophical Publishing Society, 1902; Adyar: Theosophical Publishing House, 1999), plates II, III after p. 22. See Alice A. Bailey, *A Treatise on Cosmic Fire* (New York: Lucis Trust, 1925), pp. 56, 117, 344, 817, 823, 1238–1239.

12. Arthur E. Powell, *The Etheric Double and Allied Phenomena* (London: Theosophical Publishing House, 1925). Powell's later titles expand on the analysis of the principles of man and correspondences, viz. *The Astral Body* (1926), *The Mental Body* (1927), *The Causal Body and the Ego* (1928), and *The Solar System* (1930), same publisher; Hiroshi Motoyama, *Theories of the Chakras: Bridge to Higher Consciousness* (Wheaton, Ill.: Theosophical Publishing House, 1981).

13. For a diagrammatic overview of the many components of Steiner's cosmology, see Edward Reaugh Smith, *The Burning Bush* [Rudolf Steiner, Anthroposophy and the Holy Scriptures, Terms and Phrases, Vol. 1], rev. ed. (Great Barrington, Mass.: Anthroposophic Press, 2001), Charts and Tabulations, pp. 550–590. Cf. Ahern, *Sun at Midnight,* pp. 106–132, 229–233. The etheric forces were further elaborated by Steiner's follower Günther Wachsmuth, *The Etheric Forces in Cosmos, Earth, and Man* (London: Anthroposophical Publishing Co, 1932). For a survey of anthroposophic scientific thought and practice, see Dennis Milner and Edward Smart, *The Loom of Creation: A Study of the Purpose and the Forces That Weave the Pattern of Existence* (New York: Harper & Row, 1976).

14. Ehrenfried Pfeiffer, *Formative Forces in Crystallisation* (New York: Rudolf Steiner Publishing Co., 1936), and *Sensitive Crystallisation Processes: A Demonstration of Formative Processes in the Blood* (Dresden, 1936; 2nd ed., Spring Valley, N.Y.: Anthroposophic Press, 1975).

15. Lily Kolisko published *Workings of the Stars in Earthly Substances* (Stuttgart: Orient-Occident Verlag, 1928) and a series of privately published studies of her capillary dynamolysis experiments on planet-metal correspondences. Cf. her works *The Moon and the Growth of Plants* (Bray: Anthroposophical Agricultural Foundation, 1936) and *Spirit in Matter* (Edge, Glos: Kolisko Archive, 1948).

16. David J. Heaf, "Capillary Dynamolysis," available at http://www.anth.org.uk/Science/capillary_dynamolysis.htm; Agnes Fyfe, *Moon and Plant: Capillary Dynamic Studies* (Arlesheim: Society for Cancer Research, 1975); Nick Kollerstrom, *Astrochemistry: A Study of Metal-Planet Affinities* (London: Emergence Press, 1984).

17. Theodor Schwenk, *Sensitive Chaos: The Creation of Flowing Forms in Water and Air* (London: Rudolf Steiner Press, 1965).

18. Annie Besant and Charles Leadbeater, *Occult Chemistry: Clairvoyant Observations on the Chemical Elements* (1908; London: Theosophical Publishing House, 2000); Hari Jeevan Arnikar, *Essentials of Occult Chemistry and Modern Science* (Adyar, India: Theosophical Publishing House, 2000); Stephen M. Phillips, *Anima: Remote Viewing of Subatomic Particles* (Adyar, India: Theosophical Publishing House, 1996); Stephen M. Phillips, *ESP of Quarks and Superstrings* (New Delhi: New Age International, 1999).

19. M. Srinivasan, *Introduction to Occult Chemistry: The Amazing Phenomenon of Extra-Sensory Perception of Nuclear Structure and Subatomic Particles* (Adyar, India: Theosophical Publishing House, 2002); I. K. Taimni, *Man, God, and the Universe* (Adyar, India: Theosophical Publishing House, 2005); Edi D. Bilimoria, *The Snake and the Rope: Problems in Western Science Resolved by Occult Science* (Adyar, India: Theosophical Publishing House, 2006).

20. Reichenbach's early work was published as *Researches on magnetism, electricity, heat, light, crystallization, and chemical attraction in their relations to the Vital Force* (London: Taylor, Walton, and Maberly, 1850; repr. Seacaucus, N.J.: University Books, 1974). His later titles include *Odisch-Magnetische Briefe* (1852); *Der sensitive Mensch und sein Verhalten zum Ode* (1854); *Wer is sensitive, wer nicht?* (1856).

21. Edwin Babbitt, *The Principles of Light and Colour* (New York: author, 1878; 2nd ed., Seacaucus, N.J.: Citadel Press, 1980).

22. Brian Snellgrove, *The Unseen Self*, rev. ed. (Saffron Walden: C. W. Daniel, 1996), pp. 17–20, 41–54.

23. Peter Morrell, "British Homeopathy during Two Centuries," article available at http://www.homeoint.org/morrell/british/index.htm; Clare Goodrick-Clarke, "Rationalist, Empiricist, or *Naturphilosoph?* Samuel Hahnemann and His Legacy," *Politica Hermetica* 18 (2004): 26–45.

24. S. W. Tromp, *Psychical Physics: A Scientific Analysis of Dowsing, Radiesthesia, and Kindred Divining Phenomena* (New York: Elsevier, 1949), contains a bibliography of some 1,500 scientific publications relating to this field during the period up to the 1940s.

25. Harold Saxton Burr, *Blueprint for Immortality: The Electric Patterns of Life* (London: Neville Spearman, 1972).

26. Peter Morrell, "Radionic Homeopaths," article available at http://www.homeoint.org/morrell/british/radionic.htm.

27. Four works by David V. Tansley are relevant: *Radionics and the Subtle Anatomy of Man* (Rustington: Health Science Press, 1972); *Dimensions of Radionics: New Techniques*

of Instrumented Distant-Healing (Saffron Walden: C. W. Daniel, 1977); *Radionics: Science or Magic?* (Saffron Walden: C. W. Daniel, 1982); *Chakras—Rays and Radionics* (Saffron Walden: C. W. Daniel, 1984).

28. Robert O. Becker and Gary Selden, *The Body Electric: Electromagnetism and the Foundation of Life* (New York: William Morrow, 1985), pp. 50–54. Robert O. Becker, *Cross Currents: The Promise of Electromedicine, the Perils of Electropollution* (New York: Tarcher Putnam, 1990), pp. 56–65, 92ff.

29. Benveniste's work is described at length in Michel Schiff, *The Memory of Water: Homoeopathy and the Battle of Ideas in the New Science* (London: Thorsons, 1995).

30. Rupert Sheldrake, *A New Science of Life: The Hypothesis of Formative Causation* (London: Blond & Briggs, 1981), and *The Presence of the Past: Morphic Resonance and the Habits of Nature* (London: Collins, 1988).

31. Karl H. Pribram, *Brain and Perception: Holonomy and Structure in Figural Processing* (Hillsdale, N.J.: Lawrence Erlbaum, 1991), and *Rethinking Neural Networks: Quantum Fields and Biological Data* (Hillsdale, N.J.: Lawrence Erlbaum, 1993).

32. The history of New Age religion, extending back to the modern occult revival of the late nineteenth century, draws on Theosophy, the archetypal psychology of Carl Gustav Jung, and the esoteric movements of Rudolf Steiner, Alice Bailey, and G. I. Gurdjieff. See the comprehensive study of Paul Heelas, *The New Age Movement: The Celebration of the Self and the Sacralization of Modernity* (Oxford: Blackwell, 1996), which includes a valuable bibliography.

33. Wouter J. Hanegraaff, *New Age Religion and Western Culture: Esotericism in the Mirror of Secular Thought* (Leiden: Brill, 1996), p. 63.

34. Marilyn Ferguson, *The Aquarian Conspiracy: Personal and Social Transformation in the 1980s* (London: Paladin Grafton, 1982), p. 198.

35. Lynn McTaggart, *The Field: The Quest for the Secret Force of the Universe* (London: HarperCollins, 2003), pp. 32, 34, 124.

36. Richard Noll, *The Jung Cult: Origins of a Charismatic Movement* (Princeton, N.J.: Princeton University Press, 1994), pp. 51–54.

37. C. G. Jung, *Man and His Symbols* (London: Aldus, 1964), pp. 67–69; C. G. Jung, *Die Psychologie der unbewussten Prozesse* (Zurich: Rascher & Cie, 1917), p. 117. In the latter work, Jung used the term "dominants"; he redefined them as "archetypes" in "Instinct and the Unconscious," *British Journal of Psychology* 10 (1919): 15–26. For an overview of Jung's work and its relationship to esotericism, see Christine Maillard, "Carl Gustav Jung," in *Dictionary of Gnosis and Western Esotericism*, edited by Wouter Hanegraaff et al. (Leiden: Brill, 2005), Vol. 2, pp. 648–653.

38. Gerhard Wehr, *Jung and Steiner: The Birth of a New Psychology* (Great Barrington, Mass.: Anthroposophic Press, 2002).

39. Edward C. Whitmont, *Psyche and Substance: Essays on Homeopathy in the Light of Jungian Psychology* (Berkeley, Calif.: North Atlantic Books, 1991), pp. 22–26.

40. Hanegraaff, *New Age Religion and Western Culture*, pp. 482–513. Cf. Olav Hammer, "Jungism," in *Dictionary of Gnosis and Western Esotericism* (Leiden: Brill, 2005), Vol. 2, pp. 653–655.

Index